ISBN 978-1-332-51813-5
PIBN 10251180

1 MONTH OF
FREE
READING

at

www.ForgottenBooks.com

By purchasing this book you are eligible for one month membership to ForgottenBooks.com, giving you unlimited access to our entire collection of over 700,000 titles via our web site and mobile apps.

To claim your free month visit:

www.forgottenbooks.com/free251180

Similar Books Are Available from
www.forgottenbooks.com

CORRESPONDENCE

OF

THE FAMILY OF HATTON

BEING CHIEFLY LETTERS ADDRESSED TO

CHRISTOPHER FIRST VISCOUNT HATTON

A.D. 1601—1704.

EDITED BY

EDWARD MAUNDE THOMPSON.

VOLUME I.

PRINTED FOR THE CAMDEN SOCIETY.

M.DCCC.LXXVIII.

WESTMINSTER :

PRINTED BY NICHOLS AND SONS,

25, PARLIAMENT STREET.

[NEW SERIES XXII.]

COUNCIL OF THE CAMDEN SOCIETY

FOR THE YEAR 1878-79.

CORRIGENDA.

Vol. i. page 27, note ^a, *for* Doctorum *read* Ductor Dubitantium, the title of a work by Jeremy Taylor.

„ i. „ 50, note ^b, line 1, *for* after *read* often.

„ i. „ 73, note ^e, line 3, *for* Charles *read* John.

„ i. „ 74, line 17, *delete* is *after* sworne.

„ i. „ 106, *delete the foot-note.*

„ i. „ 173, line 12, *for* B[ishop] *read* D[uke].

„ i. „ 241, note ^b, *for* hwn *read* own.

„ ii. „ 145, line 20, *insert a comma after* Shales.

PREFACE.

THE letters which are printed in these volumes have been selected from the correspondence of the family of Hatton which forms part of the Hatton-Finch papers preserved in the British Museum. These papers, contained in forty-nine volumes, comprise—as their title indicates—the general correspondence and papers of the connected families of Hatton, Viscounts Hatton, and Finch, Earls of Nottingham and Winchilsea. They extend over the years 1514-1779; but the larger portion concerns the Hattons, and of those which relate to the Finches the greater number are political papers of the second Earl of Nottingham. The collection was purchased by the Trustees of the British Museum in 1874, and now bears the numbers, Additional MSS. 29,548-29,596.

That branch of the family of Hatton with which we have to do was descended from John Hatton, a younger brother of William, the father of Sir Christopher Hatton, Queen Elizabeth's Lord Chancellor. John Hatton had a son of the same name, of Long Stanton, co. Cambridge, who became the father of Sir Christopher Hatton of Kirby, the writer of the first of our letters. Sir Christopher, who was a Knight of the Bath, became heir to the estate of his namesake, the Lord Chancellor, on the death of his cousin, Sir William Newport-Hatton, and, dying in 1619, was succeeded

by his son Christopher. This second Christopher was likewise
made a K.B. at the coronation of Charles the First, and was raised
to the peerage in 1643, with the title of Baron Hatton of Kirby,
co. Northampton. After the restoration he was appointed Governor
of the island of Guernsey. He married Elizabeth, daughter and
coheir of Sir Charles Montagu of Boughton, by whom he had two
sons and three daughters, and died in 1670. He was succeeded in
the title and also in the government of Guernsey by his eldest son,
a third Christopher, who, in 1682, was further advanced to be Viscount Hatton of Gretton, co. Northampton.

It is to this Viscount Hatton that the bulk of the Hatton papers
belonged; and the greater number of the letters here printed were
addressed to him.[a] He was born in 1632, and in 1667 married his
first wife, Cecilia, daughter of John Tufton, second Earl of Thanet.
By her he had three daughters, two of whom died in infancy; the
third, Anne, married Daniel Finch, second Earl of Nottingham.
Lady Hatton was killed in the explosion of the powder magazine
at Cornet Castle, in Guernsey, which was struck by lightning on
the night of 29-30 December, 1672. Lord Hatton himself had a
remarkable escape, having been blown in his bed on to the battle-
ments without suffering injury. His mother also perished, together
with some of the servants; while two of his children who were in
the castle were uninjured.[b]

In 1676 Lord Hatton married again. His second wife was
Frances, daughter of Sir Henry Yelverton, of Easton Mauduit, co.
Northampton, Bart., who bore him several children, all of whom
however died in infancy, except one daughter. After the death of

---

[a] Of the letters here printed, those addressed to Lord Hatton are titled with the
names of the writers; those addressed to other persons bear the names of the writers
and of the recipients.

[b] See Colonel Chester's *Westminster Abbey Registers*, p. 178.

this wife, in 1684, Lord Hatton remained a widower for little more than a year, and, in August 1685, married his third wife, Elizabeth, daughter of Sir William Hazlewood, of Maidwell, co. Northampton. By this lady he also had a large family. He died in 1706.

The letters before us may be taken as a fair sample of the correspondence of a family of the higher classes in the seventeenth century. The selection has been made chiefly with the view of giving such letters as contained matter of historical or social interest. It is true that many of them may be called simply news-letters; but, as such, they are of value as showing the impression that passing events made upon the mind of the writers, as well as the style of news and town gossip that was acceptable to those who were living in the country. Perhaps there is nothing very new of historical matter to be found in these pages, but it is interesting to watch the daily records of events and the way in which the different writers tell their story. Of the two principal news-men, Charles Hatton writes with some humour, and, after William's accession, with a certain Jacobite zest for fault-finding; Lyttelton, in a blunt straightforward way of his own. It should not however be un-noticed that Charles Hatton's connection with Scroggs put it in his power to hand down to us a few facts of political interest. Nor are Nottingham's letters, written at the crisis of the Revolution by one who had so large a share in the settlement, without a special value.

At the risk of here and there printing a dull page, I have not thought it improper to include letters which contained perhaps only a single peculiar phrase or word, or even an ingenious mis-spelling; for of such small things is the history of social manners made.

Of some writers I could wish that we had more. Scroggs, it is true, writes of nothing but wine, but then he writes so well on that theme that it is a pity his letters are so few. Perhaps Lord Hatton thought them too wicked to keep. Again, it must be attributed to the low standard of women's education after the Restoration that we cannot give a greater variety of ladies' letters. Nothing can be greater than the difference between their diction and their spelling, and the fearful atrocities committed in the latter respect prove what a painful operation letter-writing must have been to the greater number of women of that time. To quote Lord Macaulay's words: "During the latter part of the seventeenth century, the culture of the female mind seems to have been almost entirely neglected. If a damsel had the least smattering of literature she was regarded as a prodigy. Ladies highly born, highly bred, and naturally quickwitted, were unable to write a line in their mother tongue without solecisms and faults of spelling such as a charity girl would now be ashamed to commit."[a] Excluding the letter of Lady Hatton, printed in vol. i. p. 3,—a letter which one reads with another kind of feeling – as being of an earlier time than that to which these remarks apply, and beginning with the lady who, among other curiosities of spelling, writes: "mythinks the reats are resnabell enufe," we shall find not a single letter of a female writer in which Lord Macaulay's charity-girl might not have corrected some blunder. But there her powers would probably cease; she could not, at least in most instances, have expressed herself so well.

Even Lady Nottingham, whose education appears to have been far above the average, uses phrases which, if not provincialisms, must be attributed to ignorance, and invents a few spellings which are entirely her own. Thus she writes " wait of" for " wait on," and repeatedly spells " queen " and " town " as qeueen " and "twone." Her confusion of the sounds of b and p, in " blundering " for " plundering " (ii. 115), which is repeated by her half-sister,

[a] *History of England*, chap. iii.

who writes " bay " for " pay " (ii. 242), was perhaps a failing common to the family.

But while the women's education was so far below that of the men—though the latter could not boast much of purity of spelling and grammar—they fortunately condescended to trifles, and hence we often learn more of the manners and ways of our forefathers from a single letter of a female writer than from ten written by the other sex; and we therefore regret that they are not more numerous.

The following illustrations of the every-day life of those times are worth noting.

Lady Hatton, in 1620, undertakes to make her son Christopher, then a student at Cambridge, a suit of summer clothes (i. 3). In 1654, a muff and mantle of fur were valued at as much as 40l., tippets being then not so much the mode (i. 11). Lord Windsor, in 1658, is willing to venture 5l. for a little riding-sword and belt, now that all gentlemen wear swords, and he does not wish, as he rather ambiguously expresses it, to look more like a bumpkin than the rest (i. 15). In 1680, Anne Montague is very suddenly to appear " extreame fine " in a cherry-coloured satin " manto," embroidered heavily with silver and a little black, and lined with black velvet, her petticoat to match being of rich gold and silver stuff, with a broad lace at the bottom; but the young lady cannot " brage of the good husfrey " displayed by Lady Hatton, who makes her own fine mantle (i. 241). The generation of 1699 developes certain new-fashioned wigs, which have so much hair in them that a good one cannot cost less than 60l.; and it is no wonder that Lord Antrim's little face looks not so well in that monstrous setting (ii. 241).

In an age when the nation was divided on the merits of the Popish Plot and the Exclusion Bill it was only natural that the

Pope should be burnt with due honours; but when we are told
that on one occasion the belly of the effigy was filled with live cats,
"who squawled most hideously as soon as they felt the fire," it
seems that kindness to the lower animals was not a weakness of
that time (i. 157). Harry Savile's drunken absurdities (i. 129)
Rochester and Etherege's pranks (i. 133), and Lady Mary Gerard's
escapades (ii. 39), are just what one might expect. It is also worth
noting that, in 1676, it was the custom for the servants of the
accused to hand round wine and biscuits for the refreshment of the
court and company in general in an interval of the trial of a peer
(i. 136); and that the President of the Council could divert himself
at Tunbridge Wells, in 1684, with such innocent amusements as
nine-pins and "the other usual courses whereby this place is
entertaining" (ii. 49). Then, as now, fogs were not unknown in
London (i. 140) ; but a thaw was a serious matter, for it might
break up the roads and delay the passage of the Northampton coach
for a week or more (i. 141).

Perhaps nothing is more striking than the change which the
advance in medical science has wrought in men's ideas. In 1678,
Mary Hatton writes to her brother: "I am not afraid of your
getting the small-pox, but for God's sake have a care of coming
near those that have the fever" (i. 169); and still later, in 1695,
Lady Nottingham, with great complacency, tells her father how
she has done her best to make one of her children take infection of
small-pox from another, no doubt with the feeling that as the
illness was inevitable the sooner it was over the better, with the
chance of the little patient escaping unmarked (ii. 211).

A few other domestic matters are recorded. In 1668, the wages
of a housekeeper who could preserve and still well were 8l. (i. 54).
In 1695, a German dancing-master's charge was 3l. a month for
each pupil; but, by way of a bargain, he would also teach a tiny

member of the family to walk and "make a leg" (ii. 214). In 1692, a loaf of bread cost twelve-pence, mutton cost five-pence, and beef three-pence a pound (ii. 174). And human nature was then the same as now: nurses could be "mighty proud and passionate" (i. 153), and hackney-coachmen sometimes demanded more than their legal fare (i. 231).

In conclusion, I would draw attention to a few words and phrases which were either used in different senses from those of the present day, or which were then making their way in the language:—

"Resentment" in its twofold sense—
  i. Resentment of wrong, A.D. 1659 (i. 19).
  ii. "Tenderest resentments," A.D. 1673 (i. 104); "resentments of friendship," A.D. 1683 (ii. 26).
"Personell"—private person, A.D. 1678 (i. 163).
"Representation"—apparently a new term as a political word A.D. 1679 (i. 182).
"Distasted against"—dissatisfied with, A.D. 1679 (i. 184).
"To greatten"—to increase, A.D. 1680 (i. 218).
"To hope"—to expect; used in a passage where its sense would now be considered ambiguous, A.D. 1680 (i. 237).
"Ugly"—cross or disagreeable, A.D. 1687 (ii. 65).
"Good my Lord," A.D. 1688 (ii. 99).
"Gutted"—apparently a new term as applied to the sack of a house, A.D. 1695 (ii. 216).
"Disgrrubl'd"—dissatisfied, A.D. 1689 (ii. 131). It is to be hoped that this word is a solecism of the writer.

Lord Macaulay, when enlarging upon the stormy period of agitation which preceded the Exclusion Bill, marks the traces which that eventful year has left upon our manners and language. "In that year," he writes, "our language was enriched with two words, Mob and Sham, remarkable memorials of a season of tumult and imposture."[a]   "Sham" occurs in a letter of 1690 (ii. 151), and a kindred word, "flam," is found as early as the beginning of 1679 (i. 184). Of "mob" we have something more to say. It is never used by any of the writers in these volumes except in its full form, "mobile" (ii. 40, 99, 124, 156); and, whatever may have been its colloquial use, it did not make its way in the written language till a much later time. Addison, writing in the "Spectator,"[b] in 1711, in the course of his remarks on the facility which the English have for shortening words, instances "mob" as one of the abbreviations which have come into use in familiar writing and conversation, and he will not venture to say that such terms will not in time be looked upon as part of our tongue. And Swift, a little later, sneers at Burnet for employing such a word in his History.

As every reader of seventeenth-century papers knows, the word "than" was always, or nearly always, written "then." The change in the form of spelling took place apparently about the end of the century. Charles Hatton invariably writes "then" until the year 1698, when we find him at last using "than" (ii. 234). It is true that Dr. King writes "than" as early as 1684 (ii. 49), but his spelling was so eccentric that I can only suppose that he adopted this form by accident. It may also be noticed that "whether" is nearly always written "whither."

October 1878.

---

[a] *History of England*, chap. ii.

[b] No. cxxxv. Aug. 4, 1711. He has also something to say on the phonetic spellers of that time: "Nay, this humour of shortening our language had once run so far that some of our celebrated authors, among whom we may reckon Sir Roger L'Estrange in particular, began to prune their words of all superfluous letters, as they termed them, in order to adjust the spelling to the pronunciation; which would have confounded all our etymologies, and have quite destroyed our tongue."

CORRESPONDENCE

OF

THE FAMILY OF HATTON.

SIR CHRISTOPHER HATTON[a] TO ALICE FANSHAW.

SWEETE M^{RES} ALES,   [About A.D. 1601.]

As I never liked ye amorous gallants of our tyme y^t make a traffique of lovinge and a trade of dissemblinge, lovinge whom ere they see, and ownlie lovinge whilst they see; soe am I not composed of soe hard a mettle but y^t fine beautie can pearce, and compleate perfections ravish, my admiringe soule. Hithertoe have I beene good tutor to my owne youthfull fancies, makinge keepe whom (*home*) in a plain whomly breast; but, since of late y^r beauty procured them a litle liberty, they are flowne abroad and have burnte theire winges in affections flame, soe y^t I feare they will never flye whome againe. I have ofte observed it to bee ye effect of base and a dull discerninge eie to dote upon every obiect without distinction, and have markt it out as true property of ye fierie soule to honour chast

---

[a] Sir Christopher Hatton, K.B., cousin of the Chancellor, and successor to his estate on the death of his cousin Sir William Newport-Hatton in 1597. He married the lady to whom he addresses this letter, Alice, daughter of Thomas Fanshaw, of Ware Park, co. Herts., who died in 1623. Sir Christopher died 10 September, 1619.

CAMD. SOC.   B

beauty where ever it harbers, and to love ye verie windowes of y^t house where soe faire a guest as vertue soiourneth. In which sole regarde my iudgment and affection, of olde enimyes, provinge true friends, are resolved for ever to dwell together, my affection commendinge my iudgment for soe faire a choice, my iudgment applaudinge my affection for her eager persute of soe woorthy a game. Both which ioyntlie dedicate unto yow, upon this paper altar, love answearable to y^r owne vertuous desertes, and farr more then these fewe lines, the stammeringe servantes of a speackinge mynde, can utter.

Onely thus y^r vertue made mee to wounder; from admiration sprunge my love; from unspotted love this letter, the atturnie of cause which must often plead for mee in the court of beautie, since ye disadvantage of ye tymes, my many iealious observers prevent my presence. Maye it therfore plaese yow to answeare my love with likinge, and my letters hereafter with a line or twoo; y^t both of us, disaccustomed to this newe theame of love, maye write y^t freely which our tongues, devided with modestie and reverence, could hardly utter.

Meane tyme receave from him y^t loves yow woorthylie his harte (beecause hee hath nothinge deerer then his harte), vowed to bee an æternall bed for y^r love to rest on. Receave the wish of y^r full content from him who must live discontented, tyll expiringe, and extracted favour set a period to his chast longinge desires.

Y^{rs}, in all harty affection,

CHR. HATTON.

Thus have I rudely rigde this paper saile,
Soone maye hee waufted bee with happie gaile;
Nor needs it piratts feare, for, though it die,
Loves endles trafique in this breast doth lie.

LADY HATTON TO CHRISTOPHER HATTON.[a]

[About A.D. 1620?]

SONNE, I have received both your letters, and am glad to see your hand mende. I have not heard from your tutor scince I saw you, which maketh me thinke his desier is to leave you behind him. He did likewise tell me soe when he was heere, and gave me resons which seemed to me verie good, as, his spedie returne, your loss of time, my house groeth mow unholsom, and your iorneys are verie chargable. Theese considernations hath made me so resoulfe of meeting you at Ware park, as soune as my busines will give me leave. I am now going to Jankins for a weeke; at my returne I will make you a sommer sute. I have written more of this matter then needeth, for I make noe doubt but you knowe your duetie to me so well that my will had been a sufficient reason to you for your not comming at this time. You must knowe frome me that, if I did not strive som times against the fond affections of a mother, I should send oftner for you then you whould be willing to com, if you love your one good, as I hope you doe. I am now in hast, and yeat I must put you in minde of your cheefe dutie, which is to God, which I charge you not to neclect, but to dedicate your first thoughts to Him constantly; read His worde reverently; heare sermonns; strive to take notes that you may meditate on them, without which you can never practise, which is the onely end for which you were created, to knowe God's will and to indever to doe it. What panes soever you take hearin, it will vannish, and the proffit will remaine with you. It is contrarie in fruitles pleasures, the sweetnes whereof is quicly gon, the sorrow lonely stayes. Idlenes is much like or wours, which I wish you to avoyde, even for your health sake, but especially because it is a sinn, and that not a lickle

[a] Chistopher Hatton, son of the writer of the preceding letter, made a knight of the Bath at the coronation of Charles I., and raised to the peerage as Baron Hatton, of Kirby, co. Northampton, 29 July, 1643. He died 4 July, 1670. This letter is addressed to him at Jesus College, Cambridge. He did not take a degree.

one, it being the cause of many others. Thus, desiering God of His greate goodnes to bless you and all your studies and indevers, I rest   Your verie loving mother,

ALES HATTON.

SIR WILLIAM LE NEVE, CLARENCEUX,[a] TO SIR CHRISTOPHER HATTON, K.B.

NOBLE SIR,   London, Thursday, 24th Sept., 1640.

Sir Henry St. George's[b] letters to me from Yorke, dated the 18th of this instant, intimate that it was then there fresh news that the Scots had taken Yarum, a town situated upon the river of Teyes, an inlett into Cliveland; where it is thought that they will fortifye, as they have done at Durham, for a place of retreat, there being adjoyning a hill apt for that purpose. By their manner of proceeding it's thought they will make a winter warre, and that the armies are not like to meete to put a period that way this winter.

That afternoone the Lord Conway,[c] with 2,000 horse and three regiments of foote, 1,000 firelockes, and 15 feild peices, marched towards the borders of Yorkeshire, to secure them from the Scots incursions.

The gentry of that countie promised his Matie, on Saturday was a seavennight, to maineteyne their trayned bandes one month longer. They were very urgent with a petition of their grievances, and therein to crave of the King a parliament. The first part my

---

[a] William Le Neve became Mowbray Herald in 1624, knighted in 1634, and Clarenceux in 1635. He was present with Charles at the battle of Edgehill, previous to which he officially summoned the Parliamentary army to surrender, but "did it with great marks of fear, having a feeling sense of danger." In 1658 he lost his reason, which he never recovered. He died in 1661.—Noble, *History of the College of Arms*, p. 279.

[b] Norroy King of Arms, became Garter in 1644.

[c] Edward, second Viscount Conway, died in 1655.

Lord Lieutenant[a] proferred to his Matie; but prevayled with them to leave out the last, upon his Lops assurance that he knewe the King was resolved to call a parliament very suddenly.

The poore citty of Yorke hath lent the King 5,000li; and this weeke three score thousand pounds of the paper money is from hence sent thither. And soe have the citizens of London sent their peticions, to be delivered this day, 4 aldermen, as sayd, having signed with them. The like hath divers parsons sent theirs against the canons by one Sedgewicke.[b]

As Lesly writt to the citty, soe we now heare he hath done to the Lowe Countries and France, to invite them to a free trade of coale.

The Scots refused to render their prisoners, our souldiours, saying they would keepe them to see what we would doe by theirs, if perchance we take any of them. Their wives multiply unto New castle.

My Lord Lieutenant was certeynely elected Knt of the Garter about ten dayes since.

The Scots demands of Durham and Northumberland are now turned into money: a Scotche tricke to involve all at last.

Sir Thomas Glemham,[c] by his faire comportment hath soe wrought with the people of Hull and made them soe sensible of theise tymes, that they dayly send him 4 or 5 hundred men, woemen, and children to assist his regiment in making fortificacions, which were very defective before his comming, though otherwise before informed.

Alderman Cranmore is likely to dye, and Sir Abraham Dawes,[d] past hope of recovery. Our neighbour Mr. Riplingham[e] of the Wardrobe dyed this last weeke.

[a] Thomas Wentworth, Earl of Strafford.

[b] Obadiah Sedgwick, one of the Westminster Assembly of Divines.

[c] The Royalist officer who commanded at York when taken by the Parliament in 1644, and subsequently at Oxford.

[d] Sir Abraham Dawes, Knt., of Putney, one of the farmers of the Customs.

[e] This is apparently Thomas Ripplingham, an officer of the Wardrobe, who had the reversion of the clerkship of the Wardrobe, and whose death is conjectured, in the Calendar of State Papers (Domest. 1637-8, p. 49), to have occurred in 1637.

It's thought the citizens will not choose Sir William Acton[a] lord maiour, although he be next in course.

Here is a report that some of our horse are cutt of, yet hoped not true, but, as thought, proceeding from the badd spiritts of ill-affected humours. At this instant I heare it is not soe, but by lettres from Yorke, dated on Sonday last, is thus:

On Friday last, 3 troopes lying at Richmond under the command of Captain Digby,[b] sonne to the Earl of Bristow, had notice that, at a place called Stapleton, a mile from Croft-Brigge, divers of the Scottish horse lay; whereupon hee sent two of the troopes to Croft-Brigge, and Sir John Digbyes troope went to Stapleton, where they found them at breakfast in a papists house which they had rifled, where they slewe about 30 (and 2 were drowned in the river of Teyes), tooke their captain, Sir Alexander (or Archiball) Dowglas, his lieutenant and cornett prisoners. Those w[ch] thought to escape by Croft-Brigge were eyther taken or slayne (which I beleive was part of the nomber), and all their horse and armes taken.

It is now rumoured that Edenburgh Castle is rendred, and that the souldiours are come only with 2 peeces of ordinances to Bar-wicke, where they die miserably of the scurvy.

By lettres from Sir Henry St. George I understood you were to goe to Yorke (upon Mr. Gascoynes relacion), which I am glad to see you doe not.

Freeman and Cooper I will presently remember, &c. I desire your favour in sending Vincentt Marshall bookes, and to putt Sir Thomas Shirley in mind of his promise to me.

My service to yourselfe and noble Lady, my kinde love to Mr. Dugdale, &c. In hast I rest,

Your most affectionate servant

WM. LE NEVE, Clarencieux.

[a] Sir William Acton, Bart. was Lord Mayor of London in 1641.
[b] John, second son of John Digby, Earl of Bristol.

S. Mewce^a to Lady Hatton.^b

MADAME,   21th of Aprill, 1653.

*   *   *   *

The long sitting parlament was dissolved in a trice, without
noyse.^c The Generall and Harison came into the House, where,
when hee was sett down and putt on his hatt, he made a sharp
speech, and in perticuler reproched the Speaker, the Comissioner
Whitlock, Sir Henry Vane, Coll. Alger. Sidney, and some other
members, and then comanded that bable the mace to bee taken
awaye; wch done, hee comanded those pryme men whome hee
had formentioned to goe forth; which not redyly obaying, hee
comanded Harison to call up the soldiers, whoe sone putt out those
that seemed unwilling; and the rest easily obeyed and all departed,
and the dores are locked up after them. It is said that the Speaker
is committed, and your La^p acquaintance, Ald[erman] Allon,^d
and divers others secured. Wee must nowe every day looke for
newe things. God knowes what will followe; but generally this
change is not unwelcome to the people. Your La^{ps} freinds heere
present there respects to you. I am,

Madame,

Your La^{ps} humble servaunt,

S. Mewce.

^a A lawyer, and London agent to the family.

^b Elizabeth, wife of Christopher, first Lord Hatton, and daughter of Sir Charles
Montagu, brother of Henry, first Earl of Manchester. This lady was killed by the
explosion at Cornet Castle, Guernsey, 29-30 December 1672.

^c On the previous day, 20th April.

^d Francis Allen, member for Cockermouth. He had the courage to speak out, as
appears from Ludlow's narrative, printed in Cobbett's *Parliamentary History*,
vol. iii. p. 1385, in which is the following: " Then Cromwell applied himself to
the members of the House, who were in number between eighty and a hundred,
and said to them, 'It is you that have forced me to this, for I have sought the
Lord night and day, that He would rather slay me than put me upon the doing
of this work.' Hereupon Alderman Allen told him, 'That it was not yet gone

THE SAME TO THE SAME.

MADAME,   28th Aprill, 1653.

Your great packuitt is come to my hand wch I am yet some
thing unresolved to send awaie by this post, because the last weeke
letters were stopt heere, and what is become of them I know not.
This is a change that people looke on with some astonishment,
as unresolved which waye it is like to settle; but all is quiett, and
the hall at Westminster full, as it usually is in the begining of a
terme.   Comittee sit and little or noe change yet appears.   But the
army flocketh to this towne and neere to it, and a more full
declaration then is yet made is expected and promised.   That w^{ch}
is I heere enclosed, if perchance you have not seene it.   Heere is a
short declaration from part of the fleete, expressing there resolution
to bee faithfull to there country and to fight against the enemyes of
it, whether Dutch or others; but it takes noe notice of this change,
and indeed is a verie empty thing, as I conceave.   It is a report
that the nation shalbe devided into seven provinces, over each of
which one cheife man shalbe set.   Sir Gilbert Pickering[a] is said to
bee one, and that every county shall chouse 4 or 5 whom they

so far but all things might be restored again, and that, if the soldiers were commanded out of the House and the mace returned, the public affairs might go on in
their former course.' But Cromwell, having now passed the Rubicon, not only
rejected his advice, but charged him with an account of some hundred thousand
pounds for which he threatened to question him, having been long Treasurer for
the Army; and in a rage committed him to the custody of one of the musketeers.
Alderman Allen told him, ' That it was well known that it had not been his fault
that his account was not made up long since, that he had often tendered it to the
House, and that he asked no favour from any man in that matter.' " At the end of
the same volume of the *Parliamentary History* is reprinted a tract entitled " The
Mystery of the Good Old Cause," wherein the Alderman is thus described: " Francis
Allen, a goldsmith at St. Dunstan's in Fleet Street, was made Customer of London,
besides other offices and gifts, and hath purchased at low rate the Bishop of Chester's
house at Winchester and Waltham, was one of his Sovereign's Judges, and a constant Rumper."

   [a] Sir Gilbert Pickering, of Tichmersh, co. Northampton, a Nova Scotia baronet.

thinke fitt, out wch one for every county shalbe elected by the **7**, and those together shalbe the newe representive and over all the army; but perchance this is a fancy which may give your La^p a little devertisement   *   *   *

Madame,

Your La^{ps} humble servaunt

S. MEWCE.

THE SAME TO THE SAME.

MADAME,   11th August, 1653.

*   *   *   *   *

That the Dutch are soe conquered as you heare I yet beleive not.^a The first day they had the better of us, but afterwards Penn gott betwixt them and home with 16 or 17 frigotts; and then they were worsted, but fought stoutly. Wee say ours have destroyed about 30 of there ships, but I heare of none they have brought awaie. Wee say wee have lost 250 men and have 700 wounded. Lynnen to dresse the wounded men was required in the churches last Sonday. The English fleete is come home, wch will give the Dutch opportunity to get home there merchaunts. The 25th of this monith is appoynted for a day of thanksgiving, and it is said the Dutch wilbe as thankfull as wee. However wee speed heere, 4 of our Est India shipps are taken by the Dutch in the Persian Gulf, of which newes is come to the discomfort of the Est India Company. Lilburne is again uppon his triall. The Court of Chancery is voted downe. And nowe I have troubled your La^p long enough. Your friends heere salute you, and I rest,

Madame,

Your La^{ps} most humble servaunt,

S. MEWCE.

---

^a Monk and Penn's victory, on the last days of July, over Van Tromp, who was killed in the action.

CAMD. SOC.   C

THE SAME TO THE SAME.

MADAME,   5th of January, 1653[4].

Your newes there was such as had past heere, but is vanished into
nothing, as perchance anything I may write may doe ere these
come to your hands; yet I beleive them that tell mee that Whitehall is making verie fyne to interteyne the newe Protector, and that
hee and his lady tooke the places, I meane the clossetts looking
into the chaple at Whitehall, wch formerly were used by the King
and lately by the Queenes retinewe. Wee say 12 chaplains are
nowe chosen, 6 Presbiterian, 6 Independents. I doubt not but hee
may fynd sects enough to make up 48 and not exceed six of a sort,
and yet not troble himself with popish or prelaticall people. Great
meanes are make for places in this new houshold. I am told the
Dutch agents went away on Tuesday night at midnight, the tide it
seemes then serving for that purpose; but the busyness is not done,
some say, but suspended.^a Others say they have beene courted and
great offers made to them. Perchance they have outwitted us;
but wee say that, out of a noble disposion, the Protector hath let
them goe, when hee might have taken there heads whoe had layne
soe long heere as spies. Much such stuff I might trouble your
Ladyship withall, but I thinke better to spare you and myself, and
with all humble respects from my wife and myself rest,
                         Madame,
                              Your La^{ps} most humble serv^t,
                                        S. MEWCE.

    ^a The peace was concluded in April.

THE SAME TO THE SAME.

MADAME, 12 January, 1653[4].

*   *   *   ..   *

Nowe the daies begin to lengthen, men are generally full of expectation of variety of action. The Scotts are numerous and busy; the Irish sectaries disagreeing among themselves; the Leivetennent [a] sent for; and the Lord Henry Cromwell designed for that place; supplies hastned towards Scotland and pressing of seamen and hast made that waie; the active people heere still but not well content; great preparations for fitting the house for our new Protector, of whome prophett Arise Evans [b] hath greater hope then I believe any wise man in England can have. But hee will have the K[ing] heere by our Lady day and thother the meanes of it   *   *
I rest,

Madame,

Your La[ps] obedient servaunt,

S. MEWCE.

CHARLES LYTTELTON.[c]

DEEREST KYTT, Sep. 28, [16]54.

I doe most humbly beg Mrs. B. pardon for not remembring the last time I writt to give her an account of her command concerning the sables. They tell me for 40[li] she may have muffe and mantle

a Lieut. General Charles Fleetwood, Lord Deputy, succeeded by Henry Cromwell in 1655.

b Arise, or Rice, Evans, or, according to Anthony Wood, John Evans, a Welsh astrologer. His personal appearance is worthy of remembrance: " He was the most perfect saturnine person that ever was beheld. He was of a middle stature, broad forehead, beetle-brow'd, thick-shouldered, flat-nos'd, full lips, down-look'd, of black curling stiff hair, and splay-footed."—Wood, *Athen. Oxon.* ii. 552.

c Charles Lyttelton, a lineal descendant of the famous Judge Lyttelton, was a younger son of Sir Thomas Lyttelton, of Hagley, co. Worcester, Bart., who fought (for tippets is not ye mode soe much) of such as will be thought of ye best sort. For triall, if you send to my cousine Kytty Newport to see her muff, wch cost but 15^{li} and for wch she was offred 30^{li} as soone as she had it brought over, I doubt not she will lend it you; and then, if she please I should find her a chapman, let me but know it, and I will doe what I can to find out such a one, that

and suffered as a Royalist. He was born about 1630; and, while still a boy, took arms and was in Colchester during the siege. After its surrender he escaped to France; but returned in 1659, and took part in Sir George Booth's rising, when he was made prisoner. Being set at liberty, he joined Charles in Holland, and was employed in the secret negotiations with the King's friends in England. After the Restoration he was appointed, in 1661, Lieutenant-Governor of Jamaica, under Lord Windsor, whom he accompanied to that island, and was about the same time knighted. Lord Windsor retiring almost immediately, Lyttelton succeeded him as Governor, and during his tenure of office was engaged in settling the island. The town of Port Royal was built in his time. He did not improve his fortunes in Jamaica; his wife and child died; and he returned to England in 1664. He soon afterwards obtained a commission in the Duke of York's (or Admiral's) regiment, which was employed, when occasion required, on board the fleet; and appears to have been appointed colonel almost immediately. He was also governor of Harwich and Landguard Fort, and afterwards of Sheerness; and held the office of cupbearer in the royal household. He finally rose to the rank of a brigadier-general under James II.; and sat in the parliament of 1685 for Bewdley.

After the Revolution he refused the oaths, and, resigning his appointments, retired to a country life at Hagley. In 1693, on the death of his brother Henry, he succeeded to the baronetcy, and died at an advanced age in 1716.

He was twice married. His first wife was Catherine, daughter of Sir William Fairfax, of Steeton, co. York, who had previously been married to Sir Martin Lister, son of Sir William Lister, of Thornton, co. York. She and her child died in Jamaica. Lyttelton chose for his second wife Anne, daughter of Thomas Temple, of Frankton, co. Warwick, and maid of honour to the Duchess of York. By her he had a large family. She is one of the characters in Grammont's Memoirs, wherein she figures as a dupe in a silly intrigue with Rochester. Lyttelton also appears in the same pages with the epithet of "sérieux." Seriousness was not exactly a weakness of those times, least of all in Charles's court; and Lyttelton, in spite of the sneer, does not sink in our estimation under the charge. Those who read his many letters in these volumes will probably be of Evelyn's mind, who calls him "an honest gentleman and souldier." His friendship with Hatton, begun in youth, was only ended by death. He was a most diligent correspondent; his letters fill three thick volumes.

may lay out her mony to yᵉ best advantage. But the truth is, the person whom I relyed upon as most skilld in that affayre, I beleeve (if he be not allready) is leavmg that countrey to come into this.

The lady you tell me of is not soe well furnishd as you imagine, and you may remember there never growes good haye upon a bogge; but no more of that.

It was no newes to me the stabbing of my Lord Newbury;ᵃ for I had a letter from Niccols, which told me he spoke with an officer at Calais that sayd he was forced to leave yᵉ Spaniards quarters for killing him who had beaten him with a cudgell first.

I have bine all day abroad with the rest of our company at Westwood, and I have nothing that I can thinke of more to say but that I can be never enough

Yours.

RICHARD LANE.ᵇ

My deare Kitt, Summerset House, Sept. the 10th [1656].

You should not have had the first blow if I had thought you had him within my reach ; but truly I did immagin you might have bin gone to my Lord Windsor. I am sorry you founde such cold entertainment at Kirby, it beinge much contrary to what you use to find at Berk[eley] House. Kitt, there is more worke for you now at St. Jameses, and that would bee the worde to the coachman if you were now here, for there is (though not the Lady Betty) yet Queene Betty, who is safely arrived, and for the present lyes att Sir Hary's quarters. She came on Munday, and yet I

ᵃ Sir James Livingston, of Kinnaird, Bart. created Viscount of Newburgh in 1647, and Earl of Newburgh and Viscount of Kinnaird in 1660. He died in 1670.

ᵇ Afterwards Groom of the Bedchamber to Charles II. I believe him to have been the son of Sir Richard Lane, Lord Keeper in 1645.

have not seene her; what do you thinke of that? But you know
affayres and buisnesse take place of all women. This day I intende
to see her and stande the batteries of her eyes. I wish you could
doe as much; but, Kitt, here is such doinges that I have noe humor
left for foolinge. It is reported Charles Stuart hath got a great
army, which puts us in such a fright that we rest not night nor
day. Great preparations are a makinge; the army is drawinge all
to towne and recrutinge ; the poore cavilers are by proclamation
banishd the towne for six mouthes; the ports are strictly guarded,
and noe passes granted to goe out of the kingdome. Sir Hary
Vane ᵃ is sent prisoner to the Ile of Weight; many persons have
bin taken up; that night Jacke Russell,ᵇ the Lord Tufftin,ᶜ and
severall others of quallity were taken out of their beds and carried
to the Tower; soe that I have noe reason to expect to escape, yet I
will, if hidinge out of the way will doe it; for a winter's imprisonment and the payment of fifty poundes will be noe pleasant thinges'
I had once thought of comminge into the country, but thes thinges
have diverted mee; for a London jayle with frinds and drinke, &c.,ᵉ
I am for that much before your country shackle. Deare Kitt, I am
att present a little straitned in time, therefore you must excuse mee
if I say noe more now. If my heeles and hands bee att liberty, my
next shall be longer; soe, deare rogue, adeiu and love

Thyne owne

R[ICHARD] L[ANE.]

ᵃ The elder Sir Harry Vane. He was sent to Carisbrook.
ᵇ Third son of Francis, fourth Earl of Bedford, a royalist officer, and, after the
Restoration, colonel of the 1st Foot Guards.
ᶜ Nicholas Tufton, Earl of Thanet in 1664, He was kept in prison for two
years.

LORD WINDSOR.[a]

DEAR KITT, [October, 1658.]

I thought you would have been in the country before this time, and therefore did not wright untell Charles Lytleton assured mee you were in London, which puts mee in fear you will not have time to see us here, synce you wilbe invited to see the manifficent funerall of his late Highnes [b] and the instolling of the present Protector ; which, with your owne building, will deprive us of seeing you here before the tearme. I observe all gentlemen were swords; and that I may not looke more lyke a bumking then the rest, I desire you will bwy mee a lytle wryding sword and belt. I would not exced five pound price. I did see Andrew Newport's, which hee baught over against the Temple. At the same time Nor: Phill: Howard baught such a one in the same place. If there be another of the same to be had, I desire it, and that you will send it downe by the Sturbridge horse carrier who lyes at the Castle in Wood streete and comes oute of the towne on Saterday. This will give you trouble enough, therefore I aught to begg your pardon, and conclude with the assurance of ever being,

Dear Kitt,

Your most affectionate and obliged servant,

THO: WINDSOR.

RICHARD LANE.

DEARE KITT, Hardwicke, Dec. 10th [1658 ?].

I have received your letter of prevention, which serves mee to make this discovery, that though you have not got a wife yet you

---

[a] Thomas Windsor-Hickman, seventh Lord Windsor. He distinguished himself in the Royalist cause, especially at the battle of Naseby, and was created Earl of Plymouth in 1682. He was appointed Governor of Jamaica soon after the Restoration. Died 1687.

[b] Cromwell died on the 3rd Sept. and was buried on the 22nd October, 1658.

have a mistresse, which your courtshipp and frequent visits to
seemes for the smoake to betray your fyer. Well, Kitt, doe any
thinge but marry her, and that too if shee have money enough; but
without it you shall neer have my consent, since that is to reduce you
to filthy dowlas and breade and cheese, which, whilst the love lasts,
is fancyed partridge and pheasant, but when that is gone (and wee
know it will goe), then it turnes to cheese againe; and what will
you doe then? Though I say this, I doe not feare you, for that
were to question your discretion; however, I thinke it my part to
cry, Take heede. Uppon my worde and creditt, I have writt twice
to my Lady Cholmely[a] in Sir John Bales behafe; but, if you
thinke that not sufficient to satisfie him, I will sende you a letter
to her, which you may shew him, though I beleive shee will thinke
mee madde to wright soe often for one shee knowes I know not.
Thou canst not bee more desierus of my company then I am of
thine, but I know not yet how to come to thee; my nage is sicke
and consequently weake and (sic) pace, and the weather ill too, soc
that I know not how to move for the present. Wee expect Colonell
Cooke here shortly, and my designe is to returne with him if it bee
possible, for I never was so heartily weary of any place in my life.
Fine Phill hath bin with us this weeke, and I beleive stayes as
much longer at least. It goes on sweetly, but not a word from me.
I am sorry for the Count Warwicke.[b] I hope Charles lookes bigg.
My service to them and Lady Mary. Now and then present mee
at Monmouth House; another while carry mee to our frends at St.
Johnses, and devide mee amongst them, but keepe thy owne share,
which, beleive me, is the best and shall bee soe whilst I am

R[ICHARD] L[ANE].

[a] Perhaps Elizabeth, daughter of Sir John Saville, of Methley, Bart., who married:
first, Sir William Cholmley, of Whitby, Bart., ob. 1663; and secondly, Sir Nicholas
Strode, Bart.

[b] Perhaps he refers to Robert Rich, third Earl of Warwick, who died in the following year.

ELIZABETH BODVILE.[a]

London, March 9th, 1658[9].

I am glad you like the country aire so well. I wish it may prove so to you in all respects; but you need not bee so much consarned for my goeing to the mountins, for I thinke it is a very good plase to live in. But I will not give you the troubel of hearing of it, senes you doe not love it; and as for our goeing hard by London I know not of any cuch thing, nether doe I belive it. I am glad you have so much good pastime, for this plase is very dull, and therfore you will but make your selfe wors in changing your habbitacion; and I doe not belive but that your one inclinashons is as much to the towne, if I ware not in it, as if I ware. You need not make any of your compliments to mee, for I doe not except them. I have delivered your letters to the coll.,[b] and he intends to writ to you and to my Lord Spencer, hoes buisnes and yours may both bee done at a time. Hee tells mee of a mach which your mother has implied a frind of his about for you. I beclive hee would gladly goe halfes with him in it. I sopose 3 hundord pounds will doe much with him; therefore, if you pleas, I will bee your frind to him in it. Both hee and shee often tells mee of this, and profesis a great dell of love to you. My thinks the reats are resnabell ennfe. Your cosen Montagu[c] is this day gone with the fleete, which dos extremly troubell my Lord Chisterfild,[d] hoe is agoeing into Francs himselfe. My Lord Middillcexs[e] is like to diy of the small pox;

[a] The letters which I have assigned to this lady are without signature; but I have no doubt that she was the writer. She was, in all probability, one of the Bodviles of Carnarvonshire, perhaps a sister or near relative of Sarah, daughter of John Bodvile, who married Robert Robartes, Viscount Bodmin, son of the Earl of Radnor.

[b] A Colonel Hawley is mentioned in other letters.

[c] One of the Manchester family.

[d] Philip Stanhope, second Earl of Chesterfield, was brought up in Holland and rendered much service in forwarding the Restoration.

Lionel Cranfield, third Earl of Middlesex. Died 1674.

CAMD SOC.　　　　　D

and Mrs. Crue is like to rune quit mad, for shee was but 3 quarters mad before.   I am to bee marrid to my Lord Lichfield,[a] and Mrs. Shruly is to have my Lord of Worwike,[b] hoe might bee a widdo within a very short time, for hee had like to have made a sivilel retreat the other night, but that God spares him still for a better intent, which is, to have mee, for all I am to be marrid. But I shall saive the parson a labor and have nobody, which is best; without I can have him, that I may not bee troubeled long with him.   Mistress Francis Murry [c] is to have Dick Savigh,[d] my Lady Mary Savigh is brother; but you must not take any notis of it.

CHARLES LYTTELTON.

DEEREST KYTT,   May 25, [16]59.

I cannot possibly describe to you the humour I am in at the writing of this letter.   You may easily guesse it when I shall but begin to tell you my m[rs] was married yesterday in y[e] afternoone to Sir Thomas Rouse,[e] I knowing nothing of it and as little suspecting it when I came into her chamber this morning and found him with her; and I am confident he that could have guessed it from what I knew of her intentions but the night before at eleven a clock must pretend to have bine better skilld in her thoughts and

---

[a] Charles Stuart, Earl of Lichfield, became Duke of Richmond and Lenox in 1660; died 1672. His third wife was La Belle Stuart.

[b] Robert Rich became Earl of Warwick in 1658. He made his " civil retreat " very soon, in 1659.

[c] Frances, daughter of David Murray, Esq., Charles Lyttelton's flame, who jilted him for Sir Thomas Rouse, as appears below.

[d] Richard, son of Thomas Savage, Earl of Rivers, married Alice Trafford. His sister Mary married Henry Killigrew.

[e] Sir Thomas Rouse, of Rouse Lench, co. Worcester, Bart. His second wife was the lady above referred to, Frances, daughter of David Murray. He died in 1676.

designes then she was herself. How it was discovered first to mee and my resentments is not for a letter discourse, when they are soe apt to miscarry; but, in short, when shee had told it mee after her sister (for I could not beleeve her), I swore and stormed, &e. But, in fine, I chose another way, and, instead of quarrelling at that any farther wch could not be helped, I bore it like a man and put her againe into his armes with all ye expressions of joy that a friend could have done, and that with such an evenesse that I thinke I was no longer suspected for a rivall. I will not now tell you neither what crying there has bine both before and since the wedding, but I verily thinke there never was any like it. How unworthily her sisters have dealt with mee I am not able to tell you, and I have no mind they should for the present perceive what my opinion is. I saw my friend to night, who is gone to see them bedded, wch they were not last night. To morrow (it may be) I shall heare more, wch you may have an account of in time. I would goe there myself but that I have yet no cloathes that I can weare, those I had being sent out of towne last weeke, when I intended to have followed them sooner after then I am now like to doe. And yet, as the ease stands, I have not, to say truth, much to doe heere. Deerest Kytt, a dieu! I doe not thinke upon what has happened. I ought [not] to count myself the more unhappy, but strangely unfortunate; and soe, as nothing but an uncontroulable fate could have brought [it] upon mee, I cannot thinke I am ye lesse obliged to you.

" Tam teneor dono, quam si dimittar onustus." [a]

---

[a] Horace, Epist. I. vii. 18.

THE SAME.

DEERE KYTT,   Breda, May 6, 1660.

*   *   *   *   *

The news of Lambert's being at the head of a party cannot be more unwelcome to any body with you then it pleased some with us who love to be fishing in troubled waters. There are some who feare that, unlesse they regaine theyr creditt and interest by a warr, they shall not be able to maintaine those greate thinges they pretend to; but wee hope the valiant generall Monke and the wisdome of the parliament will take such care as to settle thinges, without theyr help, more to the King's sattisfaction and the good of the nation, and let all such interested mutineeres be — &c. I need not tell you who I meane by these; they are too well knowne; but least you mistake—130 and his blousistering troope. There is not soe perfidious a false coxcombe as he is and of soe turbulent a temper in the world, I thinke. Sam Tuke [a] came heere yesterday. What are his pretences and buisnesse I know nothing. I heare he writt the King's charrectker. I heare to day father Talbot is expected every hower with y[e] Spanish mony soe long upon the way, w[ch] will be very welcome, I assure you, notwithstanding all our greate newes from England; for, with all that, wee are as poore as ever, though I confesse it be a wonder to me how it comes to bee. Wee hope wee shall be with you very soone, but upon what meanes I cannot tell more then that allmost all you doe seemes to intend it. I writt to you the last weeke and thanked you for the remembrance of mee about the 800[li] buisnesse, w[ch], if I could get done for my self any way, would be very seasonable. Adieu.

[a] Samuel Tuke, of Cressing-Temple, co. Essex, made a baronet after the Restoration. The "King's Character," which is here ascribed to him, is probably the pamphlet entitled, "The Faithful yet Imperfect Character of a Glorious King, King Charles I., His Country's and Religion's Martyr. Written by a Person of Quality." London, 1660, 12mo.

I desired you to send for Bay, if you could, and to put him in to the Isle of Dogs, to be in order against I come.

Since I writt, Morris Bartly is come, who tells us the Generall and Councill of State have declared for the King; which makes hope to see you very soone.

ELIZABETH BODVILE.

[July ? 1661.]

*　　　*　　　～　　　*　　　*

One Munday I was at the new aprer,[a] and I chancd to sett next to Mr. Lane, hoe told mee a black cap and a staf was a better sight then that was, and many other things which would but troubell you to reed. I went with Mr. Hindrad Robbarts,[b] and I had the best sport with my govenner, hoe is resould to tell all things. I was this day thare agane, where I mett one of the godly partty, my Lady Canly by name. Sir Charles Sidly is like to diy;[c] and my Lady Killdare[d] has a daughter and has bin like to diy. Heare is nuwes that a yong lady in Chambridg shier has drounded her selfe for love, they say; but more fool shee, for that is but cold love, my thinks. Shee thru her selfe into a well and the water was not deepe enufe, and they say shee was starvd to death. And now to break your hart, my Lady Barkle[e] is like to diy of a fright, being with child. Pray doe not you be desparat and dround your selfe in a well to, for you know as long as there is life thers hopes.

---

[a] Sir William's Davenant's Opera at the Duke's Theatre in Lincoln's Inn Fields. Pepys, on the 2nd July, 1661, "went to Sir William Davenant's Opera; this being the fourth day that it hath begun."

[b] Hender Robartes, M.P. for Bodmin, second son of Lord Robartes.

[c] He lived to 1701.

[d] Elizabeth, daughter of John Holles, Earl of Clare, married to Wentworth Fitz-Gerald, Earl of Kildare.

[e] George, first Earl of Berkeley, married Elizabeth, daughter of John Massingberd, of co. Lincoln.

THE SAME.

[A.D. 1661.]

I doe not love to tell things which will not bee wellcome, but I sopose you have allreddy hard it; but I hope you have more witt then to bee troubelld att it. I was att Court, whare the Duck of York came and told mee that this day the King had giveing my Lord Robarts the privi seall.[a] I was to aqnant you that to morrow att ten you are expected; likewis, I would have you belive to that you will not bee worst lookt one by y[r] friends for y[r] father's not being Lord Privi Seall. Good night, and pray sleep never the les. I hope y[r] good fortune is still to come; and pray bee well to morrow, or I shall bee Mrs. Otter.[b]

CHARLES LYTTELTON.

DEERE KYTT,   Hagley, Aug. 31, [1661].

If you take but such revenges as those, you are never like to be ridde of such troubles as these, because you cannot more oblige mee then when you expresse most kindnesse to your friend. Wee have beene mightily alarumd heere with reports of plotts from London, and heere is very strict eys over all the fanatique party, orders being given out to disarme divers, at least to search for armes in theyr houses; and the 9 of Septembr there is a generall rendevouze of all the militia appointed to meete at Worcester, when I and all my brothers, except George,[c] who is at Windesore, are to

[a] John, second Lord Robartes, Lord Privy Seal 1661; Lord Lieutenant of Ireland 17 June, 1669; created Earl of Radnor 1679.

[b] One of the principal characters in Ben Jonson's play, "Epicœne or the Silent Woman." See Pepys's *Diary*, 30 July, 1667, for another application of the play.

[c] George Lyttelton, married Elizabeth, daughter of Sir Thomas Browne, of Norwich. He afterwards had a company in his brother's regiment. Died in 1717.

troope it in Sir Harryes[a] troope. This is all the newes I can tell you, unlesse that corne is like to be excessive deere, w[ch] I thinke you are as little concerned in [as] I that am goinge to Jamaica, to w[ch] place though I am affraid I shall make lesse hast then I have a will to, for I perceive by others, for I have not seene him my self since his coming downe, that my Lord,[b] having got his pension settled, will delay his going as long as he can, and that, he says, he hopes will be till spring, vainely imagininge, as I conceive, that he shall receive it though he tarry heere. If it be to any purposse, I beleeve I shall get more servants to take with mee then I am able to provide for. I am sorry my friend continues soe ill with all my heart, and I am of the minde it were much better her father would pay the doctor's fees for himself then for her.

My Lady Windsore,[c] I heare, is returned from Oxford farr from a recovery.

My humble service to all y[r] good company.

THE SAME.

DEEREST KYTT,   Sep. 3rd [1661].

I thanke you for y[e] trouble you have of my letters. I dined yesterday with my Lord Windsore at Sir Ralph Clares,[d] who came thither to visit his new bought house in Kydermaster, with w[ch]

---

[a] Sir Henry Lyttelton.   [b] Lord Windsor.

[c] Anne Savile, sister of George Savile, Marquess of Halifax, the Trimmer, and wife of Lord Windsor. His second wife was Ursula, daughter of Sir Thomas Widdrington, of Sherburne Grange, co. Northumberland.

[d] Sir Ralph Clare, of Caldwell, co. Worcester, a most active Royalist, was taken prisoner at the battle of Worcester. He is best known as a determined opponent of Richard Baxter at Kidderminster. Nash in his *History of Worcestershire*, ii. 45, engraves their portraits together. Sir Ralph died in 1670, aged 83.

I am not much taken, and besides I beleeve it will cost him some hundred pounds before it be convenient to dwell, though his wive's gentlewoman came thither purposse to visitt it and to designe the lodginges and offices for her dwelling in it this winter. My Lady, I heard too by her woman, is as bad as she was before her going to Oxford, not likely to undertake the voyage he says he intends about Christmasse; for before then he says he does not thinke of it. He pleases himself with the expectation of his pension's going on now that it is settled, and that he shall get that payd him before he goes, which at Michlemas will be 500^{li}, and at Christmasse as much more, though I doe not thinke he will find it in his accounts; for, though I beleeve he may get what is due or more when they are readie to send him away, I am not of opinion they will part with any thing before hand. There met him a greate many countrey men who were concerned in his water worke,[a] who cry out mightily at ye prejudice they thinke they shall sustaine by it ; but he is resolvd to proceede, it being a publike act, to get an act passe for it.

Sir Harry has beene more troubled with his fitts of ye spleene since his coming downe then he has beene a greate while, of which it is a strange thing to consider how often he wants his naturall rest, sleepe, and as often a disposition to his diet, and yet that he lookes as well as ever and grows fatt.

I received a mighty obliging letter from my sister Lyttelton [b] this post upon the account I gave her, with an excuse why I told her no sooner, of my marriage. My humblest services, pray, to all y^r company. I should be glad you could enquire out a chapman for my place, for I doe not find my brother of the mind he seemed at first to be of to buy it.

---

[a] A scheme to render the Salwarp navigable, for the benefit of the salt trade of Droitwich, by means of locks. Lord Windsor persevered some time, but finally had to abandon the undertaking.—Nash's *Worcestershire*, ii. 306.

[b] Philadelphia, daughter of Thomas Carey, second son of Robert, Earl of Monmouth, and wife of Sir Henry Lyttelton. Died in 1663.

THE SAME.

DEEREST KYTT, Arely, 15 October [1661].

You must acknowledge wherever I am you will be persecuted with such troubles as these, and therefore you will have reason to be sattisfied wth the thoughts I am likely to be shortly where they can come to you but seldome.[a] I received a letter just now from my Lord Win[dsor], wch tells mee that Mr. Coventry[b] acquaints him the King has given him 2000^li advance for his journey, and that the Councell is now readie to consider of his preparations and instructions, as soone as he please. But he says he shall not be at London till the parliament sitt, unlesse Mr. Coventry tell him it is necessarie; by wch time I intend to wayte on you too, and would be sooner, were not my mother soe desirous to see my wife[c] before our going, that I cannot but desire her comming hither to wayte on her, and that then it is necessarie I stay for her. This enclosed is to that purposse, for wch reason I pray let it be carefully sent the next post. I cannot tell how to mention my dear friend, because I know not how she does. Dr Kyt, I am in hast. Pray tell Dick Lane from mee, if you see him, I am married; and tell mee what they all say of it truly.

---

[a] He sailed early in 1662 for Jamaica.

[b] William, a younger son of Lord Keeper Coventry, secretary to the Duke York. He became a Privy Councillor, and was knighted in 1665, and was a commissioner of the Treasury in 1667.

[c] Catherine, daughter of Sir William Fairfax, of Steeton, co. York, and widow of Sir Martin Lister, son of Sir William Lister, of Thornton, co. York. She died, with her little son, in Jamaica, 26 Jan. 1663.

JEREMY TAYLOR, BISHOP OF DOWN AND CONNOR,[a] TO LORD HATTON.

MY DEAREST LORD,   Dublin, Novemb. 23, 1661.

I perceive my letters to y^r Lor^p have some way or other mis-carried, for else I flatter my selfe I should have had ye honour to have received a line under ye hand of my dearest Lord Hatton. My Lord, I inquire concerning y^r Lor^p of every honourable person that I meet, that I suppose may have conversed with your Lor^p. I assure y^r Lor^p I am pleasd in all my discourses concerning y^r Lor^p, especially because God hath bless'd y^r Lor^p with a cleare and honour-able fame, and every one speakes kindly or honourably of you. But say, my best Lord, why is your Lor^p so retir'd as to deny a litle communication with an old freind, whom naturally you ought to love because you have so greatly oblig'd? My Lord, I should be greatly pleas'd, but I could not love or honour you more, though you had as many great imployments and increase of dignity as you doe deserve. It is better that it should be as God please then as we please. But your Lor^{ps} present case puts me in mind of an excellent saying of Cato Major: "malle se ab hominibus cur statuam non haberet quam cur haberet exquiri." My Lord, that's your case. All good men that know you confesse you to deserve the greatest things. But I say to y^r Lor^p as S. Austin of Cato: "honores quos expetunt multi Cato petere non debuit, sed eos civitas ob ejus virtutem non petenti dare." My Lord, I doe frequently remember your Lor^p in my devotions, and I pray passionately in relation to y^r whole case. My Lord, if I might have leave, and knew how, whether and in what circumstances to addresse my letters to your

---

[a] Born in 1613. Bishop of Down and Connor in 1660, and appointed to administer the see of Dromore in 1662. He died in 1667. Let not the reader smile at the obsequiousness of the letter. In the seventeenth century a peer was a personage to be approached only in one way; and even the author of "Holy Living" and "Holy Dying" was not in advance of his time.

Lor^p, so that they might come readily to your hand, I would write often, for though I be an uselesse person, yet no body loves and honours my deare Lord Hatton so much as I doe. My Lord, if my letters be unwelcome, then doe not write to me back. Truly, my Lord, I doe not remember to have receiv'd one letter from y^r Lor^p since my last leaving London, and to him that so loves and honours y^r Lor^p that is a great trouble. I pray, my Lord, renew y^r kindnesse to me, and let me heare but of your health, for I am and must be concern'd in it. When the spring comes, I intend to send over your Tractatus DD. and Salmedron,[a] if y^r Lor^p will tell me whether to direct them. The King hath beene pleas'd to forgive all the clergy of Ireland their first fruits and 20th parts, and sends us over a lieuetenant[b] who (we thinke) will excel ye Earle of Strafford in his kindnesse to ye Church. Farewel, my dearest Lord. My wife will needes present her humble service to y^r Lor^p, and I mine to sweet Mr. Hatton. My Lord, I must, as long as I live, be

Your Lor^{ps} most endeared, as most obliged,
freind and servant,

JEREM: DUNENSIS.[c]

LADY LYTTELTON.[d]

DEAR FREIND,   [Jamaica,] Sep. 3rd, 1662.

I thought I should not bee able to write a word to you, wch was a great troble to mee, for I am very weak, and accidentally I begunn other letters before yours, and, by that time they weer done,

---

[a] That is, I presume, Tractatus Doctorum and Salmeron.

[b] James Butler, Duke of Ormond.

[c] The Bishop's affectionate regard even extends to the address of the letter, which is " To the Right Honble and my Dearest Lord," &c.

[d] Catherine, wife of Sir Charles Lyttelton.. See above, p. 12, note.

I was soe ill I was not able to write another; but, now the ships are
staid longer then I thought, I have recovered a little strenth to tell
you I am alive, though not well at all, being trobled wth all the
simtomes and pains of a consumtion, wch I feard before I went
from England.   Yett I have a pritty little boy, and if you saw him
make faces you would swear hee weer ligitimate, besides blew eyes.
I know not whether Charles bee able to write to you, for hee is
very ill; but I hope the worst is past wth him; but the desease of
the country, wch is a gripeing of the guts, has made him very
weak.   Hee told you all bee could from Barbadoes, and I have
little more to say but that wee are heer, and that the towne of St.
Jago[a] is very pleasantly situated, but the country is much in disorder and looks wild, but in time may bee made a good place.   Our
greatest want is good company; but I am soe dull wth beeing
continually sick, that I think I could hardly divert my self wth any
thing.   You cannot expect therfore any account from mee of any
thing of any description, for I have seene little since I came hither;
yett, for as much as I have seene, I cannot wish you should bee at
the troble of such a jorney to come hither, though it would bee the
greatest joy to mee that can come to see a freind I love soe well
before I dye; but I cannot bee so much for my self, when I consider
the inconvenience it will bee to you; but I will not plead against my
self.   The truth is, I can say noe more of any thing, for I am
allready soe weary I know not what to doe.   Therefor adieu, dear
freind.   I am,

Y^r most affectionat

freind and servant,

K. LYTTELTON.

[a] Spanish Town.

SIR CHARLES LYTTELTON.[a]

DEEREST KYTT,   Jameico, Jan. 13, 1662[3].

I have writt to you soe often from this mellancholy place, and
having noe returns I can scarce tell how to entertaine you w[th]
enough to fill up a letter, unlesse it be of the sadd storyes of my
owne family, w[ch] indeed I have had a deepe share of, it pleasing
God to bring sickness upon every one in it but myself since I writt
last to you. My poore wife has bine, as it were by miracle, raised to
life twice with Sir W. Rawleigh's cordiall, when given over by her
phizitians and all her friends, and is now, I thanke God, in a probable way to recover, though yet so weake she can scarce stand.
Her disease has bine a feaver together with a violent cough w[ch]
yet has not left her. She desires exceedingly to returne for
England, w[ch] I am desirous of too, and, if it please God to give
her strength to get a shippboard, I am willing she should venture
the voyage; for in this place she cannot live, there being nothing
in this countrey like to cure the spleene, w[ch] is indeed the ground
of all her illnesse. My brother Con[stantine] enjoyed a very good
health a long time, but at length the feavor seized him wth the
yellow jawndies, whereof he died; w[ch] has bine a greate affliction
to mee, and a losse otherwise ; for I was deeply engaged wth him
upon a planting interest, whereby I had greate hope to have settled
a good fortune, w[ch] now is quite lost, I being not at leizure, by
reason of my other employment, to attend that, nor, if I were not,
could I hope to doe what was expected by all from him, then
whom indeed no man that ever came hither there was a better
opinion of, for that matter, and was in this respect esteemed a greate
losse to the place, and soe lamented by them. My man Matt died a
few days before him, leaving a dolefull widdow, w[ch] was my wife's
mayd Besse. This has been a terrible sick place and a greate many
have died that came wth us.

a Lyttelton was knighted before leaving England.

I have written to you formerly of severall thinges concerning my stay heere, wch I hope will not miscarry; and truly, I have soe much to write of the publique now, that I cannot attend my owne concerne soe much as I have need of, to repeate them. Besides that, I am soe buisy wth all in the dispatch of a fleete I am sending upon the Spanish coasts, wch I have hopes will doe his ^Matie and our nation some honour and service.^a I have writt thereof to Sir Edward Nicolas ᵇ and Mr. Coventry and my Lord Windsore. I pray informe me what opinion they have of my adventure therein, as of the rest I endeavor to serve the King in heere. I have, I hope, deserved well from his ^Matie by my care in the building the fort heere, wch I would have you, as you have ocasion, enquire if the King be made to understand. My Lord, your father, I conceive, may by enquiry of Mr. Secretary Nicolas doe mee greate favour therein. Wee have bine hugely slighted heere, having never had one shipp sent us since wee came away, wch would have broke my Lord's heart, though nothing else had contributed, if he had stayd. If this find thee at Guernsey or England, or in any part of the world, I could be glad to be with thee for some time. Soe, d^r Kytt, farewell, and contrive y^t kindnesse to your servant

C. LYTTELTON.

I get very little mony heere and spend a greate deale, my wife's illnesse obliging mee to keepe two familyes apart, by reason that [they] will not give her leave to live heere at the sea side, and my employment will engage mee to be muche there. If I considered my owne interest alltogether, I am, I doubt, some hundreds worse then when I came out. The Seale office is worth nothing to mee.^a

---

ᵃ In the latter part of 1662, Lord Windsor equipped an expedition against Cuba, which effected a landing and destroyed the town of St. Jago. It appears by this letter that Lord Windsor had already left Jamaica, leaving Lyttelton in command. There appears to be no record of the despatch of the fleet above referred to; at all events, it did nothing.

ᵇ Sir Edward Nicholas, Secretery of State.

ᶜ Lyttelton was Chancellor of the Island under Lord Windsor's government.

I cast up my accounts to day, and I have made of it in all but 45^{li}, wch is worse then I hope to doe againe this halfe yeare. They are all very poore and thinke theyr title good enough allready, since they are not disturbed in it. I have received yet but 150 groates for soe many acres of all the land of Jameico. The rest has bine for houses built upon the point Cague.[b]

THE SAME.

DEEREST KYTT,   Jamaica, Feb. 26, 1662[3].

There is nobody in the world I can soe justly complaine to of the losse of your deare friend,[c] because you were best acquainted how well I loved her and how much she deserved it; nor is there any one, I am sure, will pertake with mee soe much of my trouble in kindnesse to your self and mee, having both lost a friend. I can hardly tell (though of a different relation) to wch of us she was the most valuable; and as the returnes she made us both were just, though very greate, I had ever the better esteeme of the share I challendged for that wch she would ever acknowledge was due to you; and yet how unkind am I now to you, that I cannot help from saying, what would I not give to be with you to tell the many sadd storyes w^{ch}, whenever you heare, I am sure you will be troubled enough for! And there are some concerning that poor

[a] Point Cagua or Cagway, the end of the long spit of land, part of which forms the ill-omened Palisades, at the entrance to Port Royal Harbour. On this point stood the first town of Port Royal, begun in 1657 and in course of construction at the period of this letter. It was destroyed by the terrible earthquake of 7 June, 1692. The name of Cagua is said to be a corruption of caragua or coratoe, the Indian name of the great aloe, which flourished in the neighbourhood. In the early maps Port Royal is called Cagway Harbour.—See *History of Jamaica*, 1774, vol. ii. 139.

[b] Lady Lyttelton died on the 26th January.

girle w^{ch}, by the appearance of other transactions you cannot suspect, I have soe much reason as I have to hate and will make you doe soe too (but for the present I must be silent) somebody that I have bine necessitated (I confesse basely enough) to acknowledge to the world my self most obliged; and yet I have something to palliate the matter in theyr behalf, if unheard of pride and inhumane discourtesy to a lady of her meritt may be allowed of, because it wanted the mallice to be purpossely acted to her prejudice. You cannot guesse what this meanes, nor is it fitt for mee to tell you yet, not knowing into what hands this may fall; nor, it may bee, doe they that did it remember it, for, to say truth, I could never make them understand how sensible I was of it, but by makeinge her condition, as my owne, soe much the worse another way, there being no medium to complaine of such a thinge and not to quarrell about it, wch was not to be done with one I was forced to depend on, and besides that, it could not be mended afterwards. But, least this may give you any suspition there was any thinge of the common rudenesses to women in this, I have allready expressed it, as well as I can, to be of a quite different nature. I did not intend ever to have told you so much till wee mett, and, it may be, I shall never more mention it to theyr prejudice, because I know it was soe absolutely forgiven by her, if not forgotten, and soe I know desired it should be by mee; though it had this in it to be remembered, that I verily perswade myself (if there be any exception to what the will of God has determined), had this mischiefe and inconvenience bine prevented, she might at this day have bine a healthfull and truly a happy woman, there being nothing I know wch made either of us, while we could enjoy one another's company, lesse soe then the most envyed, had wee bine freed from those wants and penury in our fortune, wch I thank God truly I, nor would she, have had but small reason now to compleine of; a consideration wch makes my happinesse therein the lesse, and my losse of her the greater, who knew not how to covett for any thinge soe much as for her sake, as will appeare enough by my slighting soe much as I doe the being continued in this employment. And truly I am wholly indifferent to whatever my master thinkes mee most capable to serve him in ; but, if he recall my comission as Governor, I shall stay heere I thinke but a little while after, any other employ in this place being not worth the owninge, nor, as my Lord has ordred that I have, is that much better; but, if I am continued, I doubt not I shall have a commission from a better hand. You must not wonder at blotts in writinges from hence, for you cannot imagine how infinitely this place does indispose every one to writing or any kind of study. I am now soe weary I can scarce tell what I write, and therefore desire you will sattisfie yourself in other matters concerning mee out of my brother's letters. Deerest Kytt, continue to love thyne owne

C. L.

THE SAME.

DEEREST KYTT,   [London,] Aug. 16, 1664.
****

* * *   *

My buisnesse has not given mee leave yet to goe into the countrey, where my friends are desirous to see mee; but I have another reason w^{ch}, between us two, makes mee not care much for that journey. Sir H. is, I beleeve, too farr gone to retreate in his address to a lady [a] there, with whom I have such cause to doubt he is foold both in opinion of her and her fortune, that I thinke it my best to keepe as farr of as I can, least I consent to what I doe not like for his sake, or seeme forward at a thing I may possibly give some suspicion is for an interest of my owne.

I can tell you but little newes from hence. Most are of opinion wee shall yet have warr with the Dutch, though neither side seems

---

[a] This appears to be Elizabeth, daughter of Francis Newport, Viscount Newport, who became the second wife of Sir Henry Lyttelton.

much to desire it.[a]   The King of Spaine has consernd us once more, being recovered againe after it was confidently reported he was dead.   The King of France they say had an army ready to seize Flanders, if he had died.   The victory over the Turkes holds yet, but I doubt there is not such good confirmations of it yet as to build ower faith upon.   The affaires at court are, I beleeve, just as they were when you left them.   The King is, in my opinion, in much better health then he seemed when I first saw him.   He has had a cough w[ch] much troubled him and for w[ch], I thinke, he yet is advised to take asses milk; but he hunts frequently and rides hard chases, w[ch] shewes him strong and vigorous; but not long since it was much feared he was in a consumption.   I doe not observe he comes at all to y[e] Chancellor's now, nor that there are so many clients at his doores besides.   Yet undoubtedly he still retaines the primier ministre's place and has the greatest manage of affaires in his hands; and I cannot tell well how it should bee otherwise, for they that seeme to rivall him in it are, in my opinion, too much the companions of his pleasure to be at leizure to drudge in y[e] matters of state.[b]   The King, Queene, Duke, &c. dine though to day with the Chancellor at Twittnam, and I beleeve will be as gloriously treated as the place can admitt, for I saw a vast deale of the richest plate that ever I saw put up to be sent thither for this end.   The King, I am informed, will quitt his claime to all the Irish forfeitures, w[ch] is a sadd defeate to many that looked to make up theyr fortunes upon that score ; but this with a salvo to severall of y[e] grandees who had theyr pretences that way, as the Lord Fits-Hardin,[c] Mr. Secretary Ben[nett].[d]   I cannot tell you just how it lyes, but upon the account of this settlement 'tis thought tha

---

[a] War was formally declared in March 1665.

[b] Reasoning justified by the event, for Clarendon retained the great seal and kept his enemies at bay till August, 1667.

[c] Charles Berkeley, Viscount Fitzhardinge, afterwards Earl of Falmouth.   He was killed in the sea-fight with the Dutch, 3 June, 1665.

[d] Sir Henry Bennett, Secretary of State, afterwards Earl of Arlington.

Duke of Ormond will get 100,000 ^{li} a yeare. I wish that all that were concerned deserved it half as well, though that be a greate deale for one man's reward.

This morning came Hugh May to mee and told mee that there is one Baker. since my wife's death, has sued the Duke of Buckingham for an annuity wch her husband, Mr. Lyster, purchassed of Hugh May, wch was to be paid him by the Duke during his life; and that his pretence is, that he bought Martin Lyster's title to the sayd annuity of him. I have not yet had time to examine those papers wch I have concerning that businesse; but I beleeve I shall find that Baker has forged this pretence, and that the 500 ^{li} which he has recovered of the Duke did belong to my wife, Martin having never parted with his interest therein to him. But, if you will doe mee the favour to enquire of this businesse of Coll. Lambert,[a] who I heare is with you, I doubt not he can fully sattisfie us in all that, because he was concerned therein. But if you please, without telling him that any thing is recovered, aske if he knows whither Mr. Lyster did ever make away his title to that annuity to this Baker or any other, and if he have any papers or other way of dis covering the cheate, if there be any. For my part, truly I am not much concerned for my owne interest, because I doe not thinke it were honest, though I might recover it, to take it to myself, since the advantage ought to redound rather to Mr. Lyster's creditors, wch I doubt such a somme will not neere sattisfie; and among these I know that Coll. Lambert is one, and whom I would take a greate deale of paines to serve that or any other way, being the person in the world my wife has frequently owned to mee she and her husband has received the greatest obligation and support from. And this leades mee to say to you something I have heard since I came hither, wch is, that some of his friends have complained to mee that my Lord your father has treated him very severely under

---

[a] The parliamentary general John Lambert, kept prisoner in Guernsey, where he died.

his government at Guernesey; though it be that I cannot possibly creditt, and that it is rather soe given out to hide his kinder usage.

They say the King goes next weeke to my Lord Treasurer's;[a] but, if wee have a Dutch warr, I don't thinke heele be at leizure to be from hence.

Will Coventry gives mee some hopes of getting mee a company through the Duke's favour; and I am in some treaty of buying a place in the Custom House, but that must not be spoke of, though I feare there is a worse reason to conceale it, because I ha'nt mony enough for the purchasse. I writt to Sir Harry to joyne wth mee, and he answers mee soe warily, that I thinke I would rather be without it then have such a dry illiberall partner. Dick Lane is at Lees in Essex. I am glad you like Guernsey soe well, since you must be there, but am sorry I have no hope to see you heere but in parliament time, since theyr meeting is but to adjourne. When I have settled all my buisnesse heere, 'tis a thousand to one but I make a tripp to you, for I desire to see you, without complement, more then any thing in the world. My most humble service to my Lord. I heare Charles is not wth you, nor none of your family but y[r] uncle, to whom I pray remember my services.

Yours.

The Same.

London, October 19, 1664.

DEEREST KYTT,

I writt to you the last weeke soe largely that I have little more to say now, save what wee heare by Sir John Lawson[b] and Captain Bartly (now Sir William Bartly)[c] that De Ruyter is gone out of

---

[a] Thomas Wriothesley, Earl of Southampton.

[b] Admiral Sir John Lawson, distinguished himself in the service of the Parliament. Joined Monk in aiding in the Restoration. Died of a wound received in the action of 3 June, 1665.

[c] Sir William Berkeley, Vice-Admiral of the White; killed in action 1 June, 1666.

the Straights wth that fleete for Guinnee and soe cousened us who only provided against the fleete they seemed to prepare for that designe out of Holland, and wch wee doubt will unhinge all that trade we thought soe well settled there by the accessions made by Captain Holmes,[a] in ye castles he tooke upon the coast and the beating of and taking theyr shipps there wch endeavoured to disturbe it, because wee feare, before the Prince can gett thither, De Ruiter will have done his worke. Yet wee are not without hope he is gone soe ill provided both of provision and his shipps being sheathed that he can only seoure the cost, but not tarry to doe any feates ashore. This morning I am told that the goods on board Prince Rupert's shipp for Guinnee are unlading at Portsmouth, wch makes mee beleeve hee is resolved to stay to pull the crow with them at home; though that matter be otherwise soe secrettly carryed, that this morning there was not the least intimation given what to depend on, even to them who are commonly knowing enough in the affaires of that kind. All possible preparation is undoubtedly making to sett forth another fleete, and ye Duke still declares to goe out wth it in person; yet some are of opinion an accomodation is yet endeavoured. Lord Chanc[ellor] and Lord Treasu[rer] are of that side. The Dukes of Buck[ingham], Rich-[mond], Monmouth, Earle of Oxford, Lord Bartly,[b] Fitzharden, Harry Howard of Suffolk,[c] wth many more, have declared theyr wayting on the Duke; amongst whom I think I told you I was one, to as little purposse as some others, but to shew our selves brave men and servants to his Royall Highnesse. The Lord Sandwich[d] is heere. I suppose you have heard the Emperour has concluded of a peace for 7 or 10 yeares wth the Turke.

I am very glad to find such an account as you give mee from

[a] Afterwards Admiral Sir Robert Holmes.

[b] George, Lord Berkeley, made an Earl in 1679.

[c] Henry Howard, brother of George, fourth Earl of Suffolk, whom he succeeded.

[d] Edward Montagu, Earl of Sandwich, killed at the battle of Southwold Bay, 28 May, 1672.

Coll: Lamb[ert] of that businesse concerning Baker. But it will be necessary, before wee goe about to recover any thing from him, to be able to prove the cheate; for he has undoubtedly some pretended writinges to shew his title, and has gott some knights of ye post to sweare to them. But I cannot be certain what proofes he had till that one comes to towne who my Lord of Buck. imployed in the suite, wch when he does, I shall endeavor to informe my self fully, and, if I find any meanes to recover it, I will use all my interest for Coll. Lamb., if it prove his, as if it were my owne. I am very glad you keepe such good correspondency that he has no more reason to complayne.

*

Sir H. and mother come to towne on Saturday. Sir Harry's match is not concluded, nor I heare like to bee. More of that by the next. I am glad you are growne soe good a fellow, and, when-ever wee meete, feare not you will find mee as complizant as when you may remember wee chirpt it sometimes in Duke streete. At present I am soe troubled wth obstructions, the disease allmost of all that come soe long a voyage for a time, that I cannot eate or drinke any thinge but with inconveniency; but I hope to get over that quickly. My brother Thomas Fairfax[a] is made captain of the King's company in Ireland. I expect him every hower in towne to receive his comission and to thanke his generall for the favor, my Lord Duke Ormond, who lodges now in Sir John Denham's house in Scotland Yard. His lady goes w^{th}in a day or two to More Parke, wch they have bought.

This afternoone the Lord Mayor and Aldermen have beene wth the King to stopp the designe of the bridge at Lambeth, wch some venture to say is ill-timed, when the King has soe much

---

[a] Second son of Sir William Fairfax of Steeton, and so Lyttelton's brother-in-law. He served in Jamaica, and afterwards became Colonel of the 4th Foot, Brigadier-General, and Governor of Limerick in 1696. He died in 1712.

ocasion to make use of the citty purse, and that the doing that will be soe much to theyr damage. Dick Lane lyes at Thomas Windham's in the Mewes. I tòld you all I can more of him in my last.

Lord Ch[ancellor] had ocasion for to make use of some stone for his building which was prepared for Paul's, and, being not to be soe soone used for that end, he borrows it and undertooke to deliver the like quantity at the time it could be employed. But this has given such a checque to the benefactors that one told mee last night he heard a complaint by some churchmen who have to doe therein, as if it had put a stopp to all the contributions, and that they thought they had lost a 100,000 pound by it. There has bine writt upon the walls of that house (as I heard) " Dunkirke," and since, " Templum Pacis," w[ch] is by some supposed to referre to the peace with the Dutch.[a] It will be a noble structure, as I heard one say yesterday that I thinke is a pritty good judge, and they say too is intended for the Duke of Cambridge.[b] But who can penetrate soe farr into the breast of soe wise a man, w[th]out he please to reveale himself, w[ch] I dare say he has not yet done to that matter?

The Duke is often troubled with rheumes and defluxions, and lately kept his chamber for it, but is well againe. There was greate festivity at his birth-day, and at night a ball, where really, Kytt, I saw but a few such beautyes as, w[th]out flattery to our selves or them, you and I have had the happinesse to doe more then wayte upon and serve in our time. I thinke the race of fine women mightily decayed, or else it is that, being growne older, I am not soe apt to spy them out, or soe concerned for them when I doe.

---

[a] So Pepys, 14 June, 1667: "Mr. Hater tells me at noon that some rude people have been, as he hears, at my Lord Chancellor's, where they have cut down the trees before his house and broke his windows; and a gibbet either set up before or painted upon his gate, and these three words writ: 'Three sights to be seen, Dunkirke, Tangier, and a barren Queene.'" Clarendon House was in St. James's Street.

[b] James, son of the Duke of York, created Duke of Cambridge, 23 Aug. 1664; died 1667.

Last night one Morgan, who married my old Lady Newbourg,[a] and one of the King's hors guard fell upon Hatton Rich,[b] and in the fray broke his arme and has stobd him soe deepe in the head that I thinke the surgeons make some question of his life, wch was more then he did before of being Lord Warwick, though wth some doubt what would become of the estate, for he has soe much dis-obliged his brother, my Lord,[c] that he threatens him hard to dispose of it better. Poore Lord! he lyes continually tormented with the goute, and never stirrs but on crutches when he is at the best ease, the malady leaves such a weakenesse in his limbes. Farewell, d^r Kytt, I am eturnally thine,

C. L.

THE SAME.

DEEREST KYTT,   Southampton, Nov. 26, 1664.

His R[oyal] High[ness] went aboard the Swiftsure on Thursday last; the Charles wth ye rest of ye fleet being not then come to Portsmouth out of ye Downes, as they did yesterday morning; soe that now the Duke is aboard his owne shippe, and has under his flagg most certainely the best fleete that ever the sea boare, if what account wee had of the ancients be not a mistake and that they were short of the present times; for none in our age, in ye opinion of all our seamen, was ever soe good as this. And, as Sir John Lawson says, according to an eye of reason and if God says amen to it, the Dutch are not able to deale with our master the King of England. When the Duke went aboard, the wind was at E.S.E., fayre for the

---

[a] Catherine, second wife and widow of Edward Barrett, Lord Barrett of Newburgh, commonly styled Lord Newburgh. She was daughter of Hugh Fenn, of Walton-under-Edge, co. Gloucester.

[b] Younger son of Robert, second Earl of Warwick. His two elder brothers suc-ceeded to the title.

[c] Charles Rich, fourth Earl of Warwick; died 24 Aug. 1673.

Dutch to come out. Yesterday and the night before, it blew soe hard that, if they did, I beleeve they wisht themselves at home againe, having none of our ports to friend. At present it is calme, and soe our fleete cannot stirr; but, if the Dutch be out and the wind come fayre, you will heare of an engagement in a day [or] 2 or 3; and if it be soe soone, I shall not have the pleasure nor the danger in being in it, for the Duke has commanded mee hither wth the remaining part of his regim^t, wch are allmost 1,000 men, there being but 250 gone to sea, to settle them in theyr quarter at this place; and, after, has given mee leave to wayte on him in the fleete, wch I shall make w^{ht} hast I can to doe. The Duke's traine is not soe greate neere as it had beene, by reason of a command from the King that all the Parliam[ent] men should returne to sitt in the house, wch mett on Thursday, for it mightily concerned him that the house fayle not of theyr assistance to ye carrying on of the warr, wch has beene prepared for hitherto contrary to the expectation of the Dutch, and surely of the whole world; and sure you are much to blame, if you can help it, not to be heere at such a time as this.

My Lord Fitzharden came to ye Duke, the day he went aboard, from France, where he has beene, I presume, to feele the French how they will concerne themselves between us and ye Dutch; and I beleeve he has brought back a favourable account, because he seemes well pleased wth his journey, and was mightily carressed by rich presents and other honours done him there.

The French have bine lately mightily humbled at Gigery[a] by the losse of at least 4 or 5,000 men, theyr fort, and 36 brasse gunnes; and, since that, have lost a shipp going thither wth recruites of 800 men, wch was half the regim^t of Picardie, the best they had in France. The peace to in Germany went hugely ags^t the haire wth him; and the greatest mischiefe of the Turkes army,

---

[a] The Duc de Beaufort's expedition to Gigeri, or Djidjelli, in Algeria, to chastise the Algerine corsairs.

in the last fight, fell cheifely on the French, who were allmost all cutt of.

I thinke I told you in my last by Mr. Morhead that Ld Fitz-Arden had declared his mariage wth Mrs Bagott^a that was the Duchesses mayd. I beleeve I told you too Mr Oneale^b was dead, and Mr Hamilton^c had his place in the bedchamber, and Sr William Blakestone^d his troope of horse. I mistake: Ld Hawley^e had his troope, and Sr William Ld Hawley's. I know nothing more now to tell you, for I have beene out of towne this weeke. O yes! I had forgott a mighty thing. Northern Tom Howard is married to ye Duchesse of Richmond,^f and they say [they] are the fondest couple that can be. I heare she will have a considerable joynture, above 4,000^{li}.^g Duke of Buck., they say, was mightily troubled at ye match; and I heare the Duke of Ormond upon it desired the Duke of Buck. to settle his estate on his daughter in law, Lady Arran;^h but hee refused it, saying, that if his sister have a sonne (and by the way she is wth child), he thought it more reasonable that [it] should inherritt his estate, as well as it will doe his honours; soe that Ld Arran's expectations are mightily defeated in this match, but 20,000^{li} he has certaine and a high borne pritty lady. I heard one say it was the only thing had gone crosse to ye Duke of Ormond's grandeur since his returne from abroade, and I thinke it be pritty true. Oneale died not soe rich as the

---

^a Elizabeth, daughter of Colonel Hervey Bagot.

^b Daniel O'Neil, husband of Catherine, Countess of Chesterfield.

^c James Hamilton, eldest son of Sir George Hamilton, of the Abercorn family. He lost a leg in action against the Dutch, and died in 1673.

^d Sir William Blakiston, of Gibside, Bart.

^e Francis, Lord Hawley, died in 1684.

^f Mary, daughter of George Villiers, first Duke of Buckingham, married 1, Charles, Lord Herbert, son of Philip, Earl of Pembroke; 2, James Stuart, Duke of Richmond and Lenox; and 3, Thomas Howard, brother of the Earl of Carlisle. She had no issue by this last marriage.   ^g ? £40,000.

^h Mary, daughter of the Duke of Richmond and the above Mary Villiers, and thus niece of George, second Duke of Buckingham, married to Richard, Earl of Arran, son of the Duke of Ormond.

world thought him. His new house had mightily drained him. I verily hoped, when I saw y^t groome heere, he had bine come from you; but found he has bine heere ever since I saw him at London, and y^r horses. Hee says hee sent my letters, but y^r tobacco and chocolato I thinke he says are in the shipp still wth the horses. I long to heare from you, wch I have not done a greate while.

Y^{rs} eturnally.

THE SAME.

DEEREST KYTT,   Southampton, Dec. 10, 1664.

By the last post from London I received y^{rs} of the 24 of No^{br} 1664, and before this I hope you have had severall of mine wch lay here windbound wth y^r servant, and hors, and one I writt by him since I came hither. I have bine heere ever since to looke after the regim^t, wch is a duller thinge then Guernesey by half; and I cannot tell when I am like to be released, but expect by my Coll. or some other of ye officers coming downe very speedily, wch will be too late I feare though to doe you any service in w^{ht} you desire of mee. For most certainely (I beleeve) Capt. Sheldon,[a] as I told you, has his comission to be Deputy Govr of Garnsey, and his company was raised before I came out of towne; but why not marcht this way, as they were designed, and soe to be transported to you, I never enquired before now and cannot yet be resolved. If they are gone any other way, you have heard on them, I presume, ere this. Because you desire it, I must acquaint you that the common whispers and open talke has beene that you have received the pay of ye souldier at Garnesey for above a 12 month and payd the souldier never a penny; and, if this be not true, you will doe very well to say something in justification of

a Captain William Sheldon, of Broadway, co. Worcester; died in Guernsey in 1680.

y^r selves. Of y^r other transactions I heare never a word. When I speake next wth Capt. Dorvill, who is now at London, it may be I shall heare more.

The Dutch came out as farr as Goree and suddenly tooke a resolution to returne into théyr ports. Upon which, his R. H., after being 6 or 7 days at sea, returned wth most of the fleete, and last Sunday morning hee and Prince Rup[ert] went for London, there being nothing for our shipps to doe, but to ply too and againe to pick up theyr merchant shipps, wch they have done to a considerable number. But wee feare that the last Saturday, in the greate mist, most of theyr Bordeaux fleete stole by. Wee tooke about 16 of them. Yet the last post I saw a letter to Mr Risball of this towne that the Dutch were making all the preparation they could to put out againe to sea; but I can't give credit to it. The 2,500,000^{li} the pariiam^t has given the King no doubt has mightily apaled theyr courage and given us soe great a reputation that the course they intended, by protracting the warr and soe wearying of us out, will in theyr owne judgm^{ts} little avayle them. And they must needes see, or they will in reason feele to theyr cost, that theyr force is not able to contend wth us.

How the K^g of Franee will appeare further in this affaire is hard to guesse; but the reception of ye Ld Fitz-Arden was very courtly, and they have sent another, I know not who, since, in ye quallity he went of envoye extraordinary, by way of returne to his complem^t; wch I should tell you, by the by, was pretended only for to visit the Queene of France, who was upon the matter a dying and was brought to bed of a child, some say all black, others mulatto only; but it is very odde most certainely. I have heard, half black and half white.

My company is quartered at Winchester. We are mighty well paid. Prince Rupert by a chance has bruised his head and cannot gett cured. He is gone up to London, to endeavor it there; and, if effected, they say he comes downe this winter to Tichfield, my Ld Treasorer's house, and will live there. He is mightily worne away, and, in theyr opinions that are much about him, is not long lived.[a] He would faine goe yet to Guinnee, and, I heare, is endeavoring to be dispatcht thither. He believes the warmth of that clyme would doe him good; besides, there will be more to be gott, w[ch] I thinke he has no reason or very little though to consider.

Adieu. I am y[rs],
C. L.

Dec. 11. I heare againe by the post that the Dutch have given order to new victuall theyr fleete and will out this winter. They have taken too, I heare, some of our colliers from Newcastle; and yet they say there came an ambassador extraordinary from them who had audience a Thursday last.

Lord Windsor.

Dear Kitt, Mar. 4, 1664[5].

Your letter gives mee greate satisfaction by telling mee of the King's kindness to you, which you have alwayes so well deserved from him; and though hee would have loaded you with business, which from an other person might have been insuportable, yett the favour of a king does much inable one to dispatch business, for it gives a fresh life to wearied spirritts; and if you will give mee leave to bee so free with you as to tell you my judgment of y[r] selfe, it is (and so you will finde it) that you are fitter for business and can make quicker dispatch of it then your lazy humour will suffer you to beleeve. But business of reputation [is] an advantage will soone cure you of that disease, and, if you have but good success in the transeactions (which you have no reason to doute of), you will take more pleasure in that sort of toiling then ever you did in other

<hr style="width:30%">

[a] He lived till 1682.

entertainements. If your short stay will give you leasure, I desire you will first ingage to keepe my councell and then make this discovery for mee without letting Sir Charles Lytleton know I am att all concearned for it. I thinck 'tis not in some degree unknowne to you that in our voiage to Jamaica, and whilest I was there and when I came away, that I did advantage him and oblige him all that was possible for mee to doe, if hee had been my owne brother tenn thousand times, and, synec my returne, by your letter to him, I did release him of his promis of giving mee one halfe of his gaines (which I am hartely glad are so much as it appeers to be), in returne of which I thought his freindship to mee would rather have been increased and confirmed then declined and estrainged, so much that I have never (as formerly) been of his councell in anything or receaved the civillity of one letter synce I left London, being 9 months att least, although Sir Ralph Clare and others in these parts have, whome I am sure hath not deserved so well of him (or are likely to doe so); and I have had but two commands of proffitt given mee synec the King's returne, one was the troope of horse, and I gave him of my owne accord the next command to myselfe and the whole proffitt of the troope, which he did acknowlidge came to as much as the whole pay, and the like at Jamaica; and I doe protest I came home poorer by near 2000[1] then I was when I sett to sea (and that he can not say). I have no want of his freindship, neither doe I beleeve I ever shall, and therefore I will not seek the restoration oft; but I desire you will discover what is the ground of his declining mee, for I never tooke delight in losing a freind.

Your most affectionate freind and very humble servant,

WINDSOR.

SIR CHARLES LYTTELTON.

DEERE KITT, Yorke, August 7, 1665.

Last night wee gott hither,[a] having bine mightily feasted and welcomed by the appearance of the nobillity and gentlemen of the contrys with the volunteer troopes as wee passd; but more especially at S[r] George Saville's, whose entertainment was indeed very splendid. Hard by his house mett us on the way my L[d] of Newcastle and my Lady,[b] whose behavior was very pleasant, but rather to be seene then told. She was dressd in a vest, and, insteed of courtesies, made leggs and bows to the ground with her hand and head. The Duke made his entry heere very gloriously, being attended by a greate many nobillity and gentry of theese parts, wth guards of severall regim[ts] and troopes; the Lord Mayor (who presented him, after a very long and courtly speech, to acknowledge his Royal High[ss] his merrit from the nation for the late victory and other his heroick acts, wth a purse of a 100[li] in gold, and another to the Duchesse) and all the aldermen and chiefe cittisens going bare before us

Our stay heere, I see, does absolutely depend on the healthinesse of the south; unlesse some other mischeife blow northward, w[ch] I doe not find is apprehended.

Wee have no news of the fleete. I beleeve I shall stay heere as long as the Court, and, it may be, have businesse of my owne, you may guesse w[ht], to ingage mee. The Duke and Duchesse have bine both very obliging to mee therein, and, though I cannot tell you it has bine with such success as I have yet reaped any greate advantage by, I beleeve it more possible then I did to gaine greater in time.

[a] The Duke and Duchess of York went down to York in this, the year of the plague, on the 5th August, and stayed till the 23rd Sept. See Reresby's *Memoirs*.

[b] Margaret Lucas, sister of Lord Lucas, second wife of William Cavendish, first Duke of Newcastle.

I lay a Friday night at Steeton, where you were much enquired of. Bell[a] is growne very tall, and, to my thinking, much handsomer. I shall be very glad to heare how you doe. Pray let mee doe it, as soone and as often as you can.

I am
Yrs.

My humble services to all wth you.

THE SAME.

Dr KYTT,   From my house in ye Mues, Jan. 30, [1666.]

Y^{rs} of the 27 I have, and find you a kind of prophett, for wee are really in greate apprehension of ye French landing upon us, they having drawn downe a greate force to Dunkirke, and broughte thither boates and preparations for to make some such attempt; and besides have another army in Normandie, wth wch they seeme to designe an attaque some other way. The K^g has satt very hard at a councell of warr, since his being at Hampton, w^{ht} opposition shall be made; the effects of which I presume wee shall quickly know. In the meane time, we have better news at home, for the sicknesse is like to abate quite, and the King will be heere on Thursday, and, I beleeve, hardly returne againe. The Queene too we have greate hope heere is wth child. Last night my Ld Arlington writt to Doctor Hinton[b] to hasten his attendance upon her Matie; and I saw a letter from a lady at Oxford of our acquaintance that does hugely confirm it. I am in hast, soe farewell.

I am y^{rs},
C. L.

---

[a] This should be a daughter of William Fairfax, of Steeton, Lyttelton's brother-in-law. According to Foster's *Yorkshire Pedigrees*, however, his daughter Isabella was born later.

[b] Perhaps a mistake for William Denton, the physician.

THE SAME.

[March, 1666.]

The Queene Mother of Portugall is dead,[a] for w[ch] we are like to goe into mourning againe the other 6 months. The Queene has bine ill lately and let blood twice. Robin Holmes was knighted lately in his new shippe, the Defiance. L[d] St. Albans[b] went away to day for France. The Queene Mother its sayd not like to returne till the fall of the leafe. The French have a greate army drawne to the sea coaste, and in it the soldiers talk of little but sharing the English lands amongst them, w[ch] yet does not allarum us to the raising of our landmen, w[ch] they say the French take ill of us for soe slighting him. Wee relye wth muche confidence upon our traind band of forces.

Mr. Grattrix,[c] the stroaker, grows in that esteeme among us that I heard the B[p] of Hereford[d] yesterday say he had done thinges, to his owne certaine knowledge, beyond all the power of nature, though, if you will reade my friend Mr. Stubbs[e] upon him, you may thinke he may be mistaken, and yet enough to make it wonderfull w[ht] he does.

I am eturnally y[rs].

[a] Queen Louisa, widow of John IV., died 28 Feb. 1666. The news seems to have reached England only at the end of March.—See Pepys's *Diary*, 28 Mar. 1666.

[b] Henry Jermyn, Earl of St. Alban's.

[c] Valentine Greatrakes, an Irishman. He entered the service of the Parliament; but, on the Restoration, being thrown on his own resources, he found himself ·inspired from Heaven to effect cures. He first began with the king's evil, which he pretended to cure by prayer and touching; but soon advanced to all other infirmities, and seems really to have done something by "stroaking" or rubbing. At all events many trustworthy persons attested his success.

[d] Dr. Herbert Croft.

[e] "The Miraculous Conformist, or An Account of severall Marvailous Cures performed by the stroaking of the Hands of Mr. Valentine Greatarick; with a Physicall Discourse thereupon, in a letter to the Honourable Robert Boyle, Esq. By Henry Stubbe, Physician at Stratford-upon-Avon, in the county of Warwick." Oxford, 1666, sm. 4to.

CAMD. SOC.   H

LADY HATTON.

MY DEARST DEAR,   Sept. 22 [1666].

Since y^r father tells me y^t your stay att London is by my
L^{ad} Thenit[a] and Sicelea command to wait one y^m into ye contry,
I must not chid you, though I cannot but tell you, and y^t truly,
that I am very much troubled y^t I doe not see you, and the
more because I fear y^r father will not give me leave to goe up
wth him w^n he goes. I presume you were shewed ye fine things
y^r father brought me: farrender for a gowne, and 6 pair of gloves,
and a paire of stockens, wch is more y^n I hoped for; and so
sensible I am of ye kindnes y^t I desir you to help me to thank
him for it. He is pleased to speak kindly to me, and is more
cheerfull y^n he was when he was last in the contry; and I shall
be as carfull not to say any thing y^t may displease him, w^{ch}
puts me to a great stand in respect of other necessarys, both for
myself and y^r poor sister Mary, who he has not given ye worth
of one penny to, nor till to day has not spoak one word to her,
wch is a very great trouble both to her and me. I thank you for
y^r letter by ye carrier last week. I did not writ again by him,
because I had writ so lately by ye boy y^t carried up y^r father's
horses. My humble service to ye Lady Thanet and my Lady
Cicelea. Y^r sister desir ye same to you and to the L^a Cicelea.
She is so troubled att y^r fathers not looking one her as upon
others, that really you must excuse her not writting to you. My
dear, though I doe not see you, I hope you think often of me. I
assure you I do of you wth as great kindnes as any mother can doe
for a childe, and trust God will hear the prayers y^t are made day
and night for you by

Y^r most truly affectionat mother, ye afflicted

E[LIZABETH] HATTON.[b]

---

[a] Margaret, daughter of Richard Sackville, third Earl of Dorset, married John
Tufton, seeond Earl of Thanet, who died in 1664. Her daughter Cecilia married
Christopher Hatton in 1667.

[b] This lady after signs herself "the afflicted." One might imagine that her
affliction was a morose husband; it seems, however, to have been loss of children.

Sir Charles Lyttelton.

DEEREST KYTT, Harwich, Ap. 11, 1667.

If I did not beleeve you the best friend I have in the world, and that you beleeve I thinke you soe, I should make you an apollogie for coming out of towne w^th^out seeing you, but know you will consider it was soe sudden, and my buisnesse needs must be soe much, I had not a minnite to spare; nor indeed have I had soe since I came hither, at least have had my thoughts soe full of it, it has diverted mee from enjoying myself allmost any other way; for you must know that I have it all upon mee that is to be done heere, I meane ye oversight. and direction of it, wch you may judge is enough for one soe unexperienced. As yet, I thanke God, it goes bravely on, as far as concernes my part; the fault is the want of our materialls to employ us and of carpenters for ye pallisadoes, gates, bridges, &c.[a] I hear Dick Lane is come over, and that it is an avowed matter his being to marry Mrs Jones. Pray say, and let mee heare from thee as often and as much as you can spare time.

My humblest services to Lady Cicilly.

The same.

DEEREST KYTT, Harwich, May 21, 1667.

I have kept my chamber ever since last Tuesday, falling very ill again then of a feavor and ague; but I thanke God am now gott downe staires againe, yet dare not venture abroade, the wind blows soe hard, and colder I thinke too then anywhere in the world else, at this time of ye year, wch not only I that am sick but allmost every one els complaines on. I have not heard from you a greate while,

[a] Referring to the works at Harwich and Landguard Fort.

wch makes mee feare you are not well neither. My ensigne went to London wth my leave, about a weeke after I came hither, for 8 days, and is not yet returned. The last post I had a letter to excuse it, because he was sick; but since, I am well informed, hee has married a dirty tapstresse, and, this being knowne, have an opinion hee is ashamed to returne among us. For other reasons I am not much in love wth his companie, and would be glad to bee ridde of him; yet am not resolved to adde to his misfortune by turning him out agst his will. But, if it soe happen that wee agree to part, I give you this account, to put you in mind of w^{ht} Commissary Baynes spoke to mee concerning another young gentleman allmost as unlucky as himself, my namesake, though I know the service I would doe him in this matter would help him but a little out of it, and is indeed alltogether unworthy of him who deserves soe much better; yet, if hee be resolved that way, I doubt his relations he has lately contracted may obstruct his pretences to any thing that way much more considerable, and that the being entred once into employment, though soe meanely, will give him the easier accesse to a better. Say nothing though to him directly of it, till I have disposed of him I have, w^{ch}, as I told you, I cannot yet be sure to doe to my mind, nor would be soe desirous to put away, but to serve my namesake; therefore let mee heare quietely from you about it.

We expect the Duch every hower upon our coast, and therefore you may judge I am as buisy as I can bee, in ye condition I am at least. Tomorrow I hope though to bee upon ye workes again to prepare for them. Pray let me know w^{ht} becomes of Lady Richm^d,[a] and where those vacant howers are spent now that used to be passd away at her chamber.

Yrs.

Humblest services to Lady Cicilly. Pray tell mee when you intend to be married.

[a] Frances Theresa, daughter of Sir Walter Stewart, third son of Walter, Lord Blantyre, the famous beauty, who had just now become the wife of Charles, Duke of Richmond and Lenox.

THE SAME.

June 8th, 1667.

I have received y[rs], w[ch] is full of news I wonder att. I am sorry poore Dick is still soe unlucky, for luck's all.

Yesterday the enemyes fleete of about 70 sayle came to an anchor in the Gunfleete, some 4 or 5 leagues of this shore, w[ch] is as neere as well they can ride. You may easily imagine this does give us a warme alarum, especially because wee have so much warning from above to expect they will attaque us.[a] They having, as you say, soe many land forces, wee are as buisy for our defence as wee can be. My L[d] of Oxford[b] is wth us and lyes in my house. I have sent my wife to his, tenn mile of, till the alarum be over. I am, in all the hast,

Yrs.

One a clock.

THE SAME.

D[r] KYTT,   July 11 [1667].

I thanke you for the pleasant account you gave mee of y[r] tattered regim[t], and am glad your owne company is soe good. I am very confident the Duch will not attempt any more upon the river, at least soe high as Gravesend, and, though wee fortifie all we can still against them heere, yet I thinke they will have as little mind to trouble us. They doe indeed lye still wth a squadron of theyr fleete in sight, and soe wee cannot be confident. My L[d] Berkly[c] was left by the Duke on the Suffolk side, to command the forces there

[a] Four days after this the Dutch were at Chatham.

[b] Aubrey de Vere, twentieth and last Earl of Oxford. He was the colonel of the Royal Regiment of Horse, or Oxford Blues.

[c] George, Lord Berkeley.

in quallity of Lt Generall, wch quite takes away my L^d of Suffolke's ^{a} authority as Ld Leiftenant; soe I suppose he withdrawes. L^d of Oxford continues to command heere, as he did. My wife has had both my Ladyes letters, but is soe continually sick wth (I thinke) breeding, that she can do nothing but puke.

Y^{rs}, C. L.

LADY LYTTELTON ^{b} TO LADY CECILIA HATTON.^{c}

Ja. 27th [1668?].

As I am hartily sory, Madam, to heare of my Lady Thanets late distemper, soe I am infinitely reioyced to heare at the same time of the hopefull way of her parfet recovery, which I pray God to grant. I thanke your La^{ps} for the faver of acquainting me of a woman; but it is not such a servant I want att presant, but a house keeper that can preserve and still well, and for such a one the wages I give is eight pounds a yeare. If this you mention be soe qualified, you will much oblige me to let me heare suddenly for (*sic*) you. I am very sory to heare of your brother's misfortune.

I am, deare Madam,
Your most humble servant,
E. LYTTELTON.

I beg my service to my Lady. Sr Harry humbly kisses your hands. Pray both our services to Mr. Hatton.

---

^{a} James Howard, Earl of Suffolk; died 1689.

^{b} Elizabeth, daughter of Francis, Viscount Newport, second wife of Sir Henry Lyttelton. She married, secondly, Edward Harvey, of Combe, co. Surrey.

^{c} Cecilia, daughter of John Tufton, Earl of Thanet, lately married to Christopher Hatton. She was killed in the explosion at Cornet Castle, Guernsey, 29-30 December, 1672.

Sir Charles Lyttelton.

My Dᵣ Lord,[a]   Sep. 17 [1670].

The wind has bine so crosse that it makes mee beleeve this may still find you at Southampton. However, it will come time enough to tell you the greatest of it's buisnesse, that you have left nobody behind that more heartily wishes you a good voyage then I doe. I delivered yʳ excuse to his Rᵘ Highnesse, wᶜʰ I perceived he tooke very well. I heard him say yesterday (wᶜʰ will be of some consequence, it may be, to yʳ Lordship) that yᵉ Duch will have out the next yeare a mighty fleete; and last night he sayd that his regimᵗ should be all drawn together about Rochester. I have not seene him since, to ask wʰᵗ that meanes, but it must bee sure either that we are jealous of our coastes, or that they may be readie to transport to yᵗ partie wee favour, if our neighbors shall come to declare warr. I have stayd in towne this 3 or 4 days for nothing but to get an answer of my businesse about the musterring a man in yᵉ companies, wᶜʰ the Duke promises to speake in. I think I told you my Lord Craven [b] has got it. I shall not take my family wᵗʰ mee, as I proposed, they being very sickly at Harwich, as indeed they are every where, but *qui sta bene no se move.* I shall be out of towne though three weekes or a month, if the King or Duke come to Audley Inne [c] and Newmarket, of wᶜʰ I suppose there is not much doubt. The French have besieged two of the Loraine townes, wᶜʰ 'tis thought will make a brave resistance, though they cannot hope for reliefe. I heare the King has sent to Prince Charles of Loraine, to offer to put the soverainty thereof into his hands, and to hold it

---

[a] Christopher Hatton succeeded his father as second Lord Hatton, 4 July, 1670.

[b] William Craven, Earl Craven, died 1697.

[c] Audley-End near Waltham, co. Essex, purchased of the Suffolk family by Charles II., to be used as a palace. It was reconveyed to the family after the Revolution.

as his foedotarie; but its thought heele not accept it, being in the
Emperors court, and that dukedom having formerly acknowledged
none but the Emperor.   But, if he does refuse, then they say heele
give it to the Duke of Guise, as next heire of the family.

My poor Lady Mordant[a] is relapsed and I fear will dye.

Thom. Lynch[b] the King told should goe with the charrecter of
Lt. Gov., and to take ye government out of Modiford's hands; and
I doe not thinke my Lord Carlisle will get um in ye humour a
good while to be at the expence to send him after.

THE SAME.

MY DEARE LORD,   October 10, 1670.

I have been out of towne at Harwich and Newmarket these three
weekes, and at my returne I find two of y^r Lordship's, that at y^r
landing at Guernesey,[c] and another wch came to-day of 8^ober ye 2^d.
The court is still at Newmarket and are expected heere a Thursday
and Saturday.   The Duke comes a Thursday because his birthday
is Fryday; and then, if it be not too late, I will speake to His
Highnesse for ye yach for you.   I heard not of my Ladyes illnesse
till y^rs told it mee; so I sent presently to Thannet House to enquire,
and my Lady Thannet send mee word that my Lady was fairely
recovering when she left her, and that ye children are well.

I am sorry, my Lord, to find y^r civillities have beene so ill returned
at Guernesey, and am glad you have so well remembred M^r. Le
Dignieres rule: "Avec les glorieux il faut estre superbe."   Indeed,

---

[a] Elizabeth, daughter of Thomas Carey, son of Robert, Earl of Monmouth, and
wife of John Mordaunt, second son of John, Earl of Peterborough, created Viscount
Mordaunt in 1659.

[b] Sir Thomas Lynch succeeded Sir Thomas Modyford as Governor of Jamaica in
1671.

[c] As governor of the island.

there is nothing fitts them so well. I cannot yet heare of any complaint hee has made, publik or private; but, as there is ocasion, you may be assured I shall be readie to justifie y^r Lordship. His greate b^r in law, I am told, is much offended y^t my friend T[homas] L[ynch] is resolved to goe Lt Gov. of Jamaica, and that and ye lesse prospect he has of w^ht he first phancied, of ye swelling advantages to be made of y^t governement, has together stopt his pretences to goe thither himself; but I heare that he does labour to get ye government now for S^r J[onathan] Attkins,[a] wch I doe not think he can accomplish, and Lynch is making all his preparations to be gone and hopes he shall be dispatcht w^thin a month or thereabouts.

Of publik news, my Lord, I am able to tell you very little; for, though I come from ye Court, they talk there of nothing but horses and dogs. The duke told mee that he beleeved the King would draw all his regiment together about Rochester in spring, to be a guard to ye navy and ye forts upon ye river, and that the companies then may be filled up; but of this I suppose they waite the parlim^t's results for supplyes, and if they be considerable, I suppose they intend to raise more forces, hors and foot. They talk to make up ye horse two thousand and to fill up the companies. W^ht part we are like to have in ye affaires abroad I beleeve wee shall know no more then wee can guesse at, till ye parlim^t has met and given ye King mony; but you know, I suppose, there is order to fitt out 50 saile of ye greate ships, and ye Duch doe set out 80. But those, I heare, thinke y^t we shall take ye French part, who all agree will quarrell wth ye Duch; and yet ye Prince of Aurange is sent for hither by my Ld Ossory and expected every day, and ye Duke's lodgings in St James's providing for him.

I was this afternoone wth my poore Lady Mordaunt, who by mistake has beene greevously fluxed this fortnight, her phizitians for the distemper she had of her feavor and flux de ventre thinking it fit to give her such a proportion of mercurius dulcis as they did

---

[a] Afterwards Governor of Barbados.

not design should have such an operation; and, had not my Lord
bine more skilful then they, she had gone abroade when it first
began to salivate her, but now 'tis allmost over, and they say it will
doe her a greate deale of good, and they hope of her recovery. It
was reported she was dead, but its more certaine soe of S[r] John
Morton,[a] to y[e] no small sattisfaction (I doubt not) of a friend of
ours, M[r] Bronkier.[b]

I was once Major Creede's[c] prisoner. He sent my b[r] Lytt. and
mee up to Cromwell, out of Worcestershire. Hee is a civill in-
sinuating fellow, and held one of y[e] most dangerous now among
that partie.

The fanatickes met a great number y[e] last Sunday, and y[e] soldiers
beate them wth cudgells and threw dust upon the women. My
b[r] Lytt. is coming to towne. S[r] Thomas Chicheley[d] is about marrying of y[e] rich widdow Henneage; and Will. Legg e is very ill
and like to dye, and I heare this place is disposed on by y[e] M[r] of
y[e] Ordinance, but I suppose y[e] King will recommend my neighbour.
Capt. Midleton has bine dying, but I thinke is recovering.

---

[a] Sir John Morton, of Milbourne St. Andrew, co. Nott., Bart.; died in 1698.

[b] Henry Brouncker, Groom of the Bed-chamber to the Duke of York, and cofferer
to Charles II., who succeeded, in 1684, his brother William, 2nd Lord Brouncker,
the President of the Royal Society. Pepys's character of him is not flattering: " a
pestilent rogue, an atheist, that would have sold his king and country for sixpence
almost, so corrupt and wicked a rogue he is by all men's report."—*Diary*, 20 Oct.
1667. Evelyn says little better.

[c] Major John Creed, of Oundle, co. Northampton.

[d] Master of the Ordnance.

[e] William Legge, brother of George, afterwards 1st Earl of Dartmouth, Groom of
the Bedchamber, and a captain in the Earl of Oxford's regiment of horse. He here
seems to have held some office in the Ordnance, of which his brother George was at
this time Lieutenant-General. Afterwards Lt.-Col. of the Queen's Horse (1st
Dragoon Guards).

The same.

London, October 20th, 1670.

I calld yesterday at Thannet house to enquire of my Lady, who I heard was much mended, and [send] a letter from her to y[r] L[p] to tell you so; but little misse has still her ague. I wonder I see not S[r] Jonathan [a] yet, and, till I doe, I would not expect y[r] Lordship.

Wee have a mighty fleete preparing; 6 first rates, and the rest are to beare proportion. Wee talk too of raising more forces, horse and foote. Y[e] confederates of y[e] League presse us hard to give them assistance. Some think wee shall stand newters, if not take the contrairie partie. But probably that, nor anything of this, can be resolved till the parlim[t] have met, where most agree y[e] King will find his work easie; and I heare some say that many of the dissaffected partie will not come thither, because they may not seeme to vote [agst] theyr wills. The Prince of Aurang is expected wth y[e] first easterly wind.[b] His lodgings are prepared at y[e] Cock-pitt and are very fine. He will be treated w[th] all the respect and kindness imaginable, and, because it's thought fit he should take place of Prince Robert, he retires to Windsor. S[r] John Morton is alive again, so is my Lady Mordaunt; and I beleeve, al[w]aies(?) likeing, the first was not sick and y[e] later is not yet well.

So soone as I heare from you w[ht] certainty there may be of y[r] coming away, I'le speake about a yach, and probably by that time there will be one at leizure. At present, I beleeve, they are all attending upon the Prince.

My d[r] Lord, I am

Y[r] most humble servant,

C. L.

[a] Sir J. Atkins.
[b] He landed soon after. Evelyn saw him on the 4th November: "Saw the Prince of Orange newly come to see the King his uncle; he has a manly, courageous, wise countenance, resembling his mother and the Duke of Gloucester, both deceased."

CHARLES HATTON.[a]

July 13, 1671.

*   *

The absence of y[e] Court occasions a great dirth of news here. Only yesterday ther was soe great an allarum in Westminster Hall that y[e] gates were commanded to be shut. Y[e] King's Bench rose up in great disorder; but when they understood y[t] it was only a mad cowe w[ch] made all this disorder they sat down againe. But the fright in Westminster Hall hath furnished y[e] whole town wth discourse; for she, having tossed several persons in Kings street, and coming into y[e] Palace Yard towards y[e] Hall gate, several personns drew their swords; others endeavoured to seise upon y[e] officers staves at y[e] doore, to defend themselves wth. Those in y[e] hall, who saw y[e] bustle and swords drawn, were afrighted, and some cryed out y[e] fifth-monarchy men were up and come to cut y[e] throats of y[e] lawyers who were y[e] great plague of y[e] land. Some flung away their swords, y[t] they might not seeme to make any defence; others their periwiggs, y[t] they might appear to be y[e] meaner persons; y[e] lawyers their gowns; and y[r] freind, Serjeant Scroggs,[b] who of late hath had a fit of y[e] gout, wase perfectly cured,

---

Lord Hatton's brother. He was sometime Lieutenant-Governor of Guernsey and commanded a company in that island. Later he was a captain in Lord Huntingdon's regiment, now the 13th Foot. He married a widowed daughter of Chief Justice Scroggs, Elizabeth Gilby. A large number of the letters in these volumes are his; in which, in addition to mere gossip, he now and then displays the taste for arboriculture which he had in common with his brother, and in other places shows that he was well read and had more than ordinary learning. His connection with Scroggs adds importance to the letters in which he alludes to the doings of that worthy.

[b] William Scroggs, according to Dugdale, the son of "a one-eyed butcher near Smithfield Bars, and his mother a big fat woman with a red face like an ale-wife," was, at all events, a man of education, having entered Oxford in 1639, at the age of 16, where he took a degree. He was called to the Bar in 1653, and, being endowed with "a bold front, handsome person, easy elocution, and ready wit," he made rapid progress; was knighted about 1662; became serjeant in 1669, judge of the Common Pleas in 1676, and Lord Chief Justice of the King's Bench in 1678. Scroggs's dissolute character and evil conduct is notorious, and the scandal of raising such a man to

stript himself of his gowne and coife, and wth great activity vaulted over ye bar, and was presently followed by ye rest of his brethren. But none wase more frighted then a person who is more troubled wth ye gout, though he wase not cured by his fright, for it occasioned a fit of purging, as it did in several others, and physitians are of opinion y^t it is not good for ye goute. Some persons fled and barricadoed themselves up in ye lobby of ye House of Commons. This dreadfull beast I met as she wase driving towards Kings street. She wase hocked and came along very lamely. Two butchers who followed called out to every one to take care of themselves. Y^e sentinell at ye Cocke pit laughed at ye butcher for calling out and asked if he thought any body would be afraid of such a poore lame cowe. Immediately, the cowe made at him. He ran into ye entry. She followed him, flung him down. The people cryed out he wase killed; but, according to ye proverbe, she had short horns and only broke his shinns.

This story of ye cowe puts me in mind of another of a certain Deane, who was at Windsor desired to preach before ye King. He replyed: God did variously dispense his gifts; to some he gave ye gift of preaching, to others y^t of praying, and to others the gift of government, wth wch He had in a very extraordinary manner endowed him; and for proof thereof he appealed, if any man doubted of it, to ye bishop of y^t diocese, who, if occasion wase, he was confident would testify what service therby he had done ye King and ye Church; and for this it wase, he said, he wase preferred in ye Church, not for preaching, for therein he confessed he wase not a gifted or very able person, but yet in his owne parish church he cou'd doe well enout.

the Bench was too great even for those days. His ratting in the trials on the Popish plot, from the attacking to the attacked side, is said to have been caused by a sudden discovery that Shaftesbury had no influence at Court. At any rate, he made enemies of Oates and Bedlow, and, though he beat them with their own weapons, he was impeached in Parliament, and only escaped by the prorogation. It was, therefore, thought prudent to remove him in 1681, on a pension of £1,500. He died in 1683. —Foss, *Judges of England*, vii. 164.

I have now sufficiently troubled y^r Lo^{ppe} I shall therefore conclude wth my wifes humble service to y^r L^{dppe}, and both our duties and services where due.   I am very glad to heare y^r Ld^{ppe} and all y^r company are well in health and satisfyed wth ye place, and y^t my sister Hatton and Mistresse Anne have both lost their agues.

I am, my L^d,

Your most affec^t Brother and humble serv^t,

C. HATTON.

It is confidently reported y^t my Ld Berkeley [a] returnes againe very speedily into Ireland.   The Lord Renaulough [b] hath suceeeded in his proposall.   Next Thursday the King goes from Windsor to Portsmouth, and it is said that in his pleasure boate he will coast it to Plymouth.   If he doth, a gale of wind may occasion him to visit you at Gue[r]nsey.   But many are of opinion he will goe noe further then Portsmouth, ye exchequer is at soe low an ebbe.

SIR CHARLES LYTTELTON.

MY LORD,   Landguard, August 8th, 1671.

I have y^{rs} of ye 25 July, wch made us all laugh extremely at y^t part of Bruces being shot, for I should have told you Rewse, if I did not.   He is ensigne to Capt. Bennet at Hull.   Now y^t Brewse wth you does owne any thing like it, is so like himself, that you must know he is a boy that has ever had ye fame of having an excellent fancy that way to tell strange thinges of himself or any-body else.

[a] John, Lord Berkeley of Stratton, Lord Lieutenant of Ireland in 1670 and 1671.
[b] Richard Jones, third Viscount, afterwards Earl of, Ranelagh, Vice-Treasurer of Ireland. Died in 1711.

I have heard no more of Ld Windsor since he was in ye Tower, but that he was mightily complemented by visitts from all the towne, and stayd there, I thinke, about a fortnight, and, then released, came to Windsore and kissed the King's hand there. The Councill would heare nothing in favour of him. They looked upon his challenge to a person in y^t employment of L^t of Ireland^a as such an affront to ye King, as nothing should have made him presume to recent it at that rate. I doe think it was ill timed to send a challeng to one that was going to give an account of such an employ; for sure my L^d L^t, as a cavaleere as well as a L^d L^t, might very reasonably refuse a challenge, till that was over. He is going L^t againe. W^ht you tell mee of Ld Rockingham^b and Sr Norwich^c I never heard of, but from y^r L^p.

I had news last post, wch I can scarce creditt, that there is one of ye King's yachs ordered to goe to ye Duch fleete and to require theyr admirall to strike his flagg, and, if he doe not, to fire at him. The King is expected in these countreys the later end of ye month, and to be treated at Norwich by the Ld Harry Howard.^d

I am glad to find by y^r L^ps that your company is so well pleased wth Guernesey, because y^r L^p likes so well to be there; and I hope I may tell you somethinge of the like of mine heere, for, for the same reasons wch y^r L^p mentions of ye charge of doing that to settle, as other thinges, it will be inconvenient for mee to make but a short stay, and, truly, if it be not for a month to goe see my b^r, I intend not to stirr, unlesse I am commanded, till after X^tmasse. I had a letter lately, from one a little concerned to have it so, that Phill. Honniwood^e would leave Portsmouth and y^t I should be sent

---

^a Lord Berkeley of Stratton.

^b Edward Watson, second Lord Rockingham. He married Anne Wentworth, daughter of Strafford. Died in 1691.

^c Perhaps Sir Roger Norwich, of Brampton, co. Northampton, M.P. for the county.

^d Lord Howard, of Castle Rising, afterwards, in 1677, sixth Duke of Norfolk.

^e Sir Philip Honywood, Lieutenant-Governor of Portsmouth.

thither. Nothing in it would please mee better then y^t I should lye more in y^r L^{ps} way and be more at hand to doe you service.

Wee have our healths heere very well, and I beleeve it as healthfull a place as can be. I cant tell if in my last I told you that when the Queene was at Hampton Court one day rideing abroad, it raining, and my Lady Marshall [a] and Lady Gerrard [b] being in her coach, her Majestie came into ye coach and called in the two Duchesses, Buck [c] and Richmond, and left the other ladyes upon ye common to shift for themselves, wch you may beleeve was no small greife to them. As for ye story of ye silk stockings,[d] I heare now there was no such thing but an old story revived of ye last King's time, but this later goes of so many, that it is not fitt to father it upon any one in perticular, unlesse they know it better then I doe.

I am, my Lord,

Y^r most faythfull servant,

C. LYTTELTON.

Since I writt this at 11 a clock last night, my Lady Falmouth,[e] wth her daughter,[f] and Jack Bartley,[g] and Dick Niccolls,[h] &c., landed heere and came to ye fort. You may easily imagine, my Lord, w^{ht} that was to get um supper and lodging at that time of

[a] Perhaps Lady Mary Hay, daughter of George, Earl of Kinnoul, and wife of George Keith, eighth Earl Marischal.

[b] A French lady, whose name is unknown, wife of Charles, Lord Gerard of Brandon, afterwards Earl of Macclesfield.

[c] Mary, daughter of Thomas, Lord Fairfax, and wife of George Villiers, second Duke of Buckingham.

[d] This story is too indecent to print. The only interest that it has is, that it was probably the source of the anecdote of Lady Chesterfield's stockings in Grammont's *Mémoires*.

[e] Elizabeth, daughter of Colonel Hervey Bagot, widow of Charles Berkeley, Earl of Falmouth.

[f] Mary, at this time a child, afterwards married to Gilbert Coryn Gerrard.

[g] John Berkeley, second son of John, Lord Berkeley of Stratton, who afterwards succeeded to the title, in 1682.

[h] Richard Nicholls, a Gentleman of the Bedchamber to the Duke of York. He served as a volunteer and was killed in the battle of Southwold Bay, 28 May, 1672.

night; and 'twill be allmost as difficult to find it for um for 3 or 4 days more, wch they are like to stay before they can order theyr convenience to London by land, for they will no more at sea. They come from Scarborow waters. The news I tell of the Duch admirall is all false; so is y^t of ye green stockings.

Charles Hatton.

Aug. 19, 1671.

*

I received 3 red billed jackdawes and delivered them to Mr May,[a] who presents his service to you and sath the King is very much pleased wth them; for they are birds he likes soe well he desires to have many of them, and he had but one left before thes came from y^r Lo^{ppe}. I received likewise 3 gulls, for ye cariage of w^h I pay'd 3 shil:, but, finding Mr May not soe well pleased wth thes as ye dawes, I have kept one in my garden to picke up the woormes, till I hear from y^r Lo^{ppe} whither it may remaine ther. Y^e other two I sent to Mr May, who sath he acquainted ye King what birds y^r Lo^{ppe} had sent, and he wase very well pleased wth them, and, if y^r Lo^{ppe} can send any other kind of strang fowle or more dawes, it will be a very acceptable present. I find Mr May woud willingly have a gannet or some of ye barbelotts, if y^r Lo^{ppe} ever send any more birds.

[a] Baptist May, Keeper of the Privy Purse.

SIR CHARLES LYTTELTON.

MY LORD,   Landguard, Aug. 21, [16]71.

I have y^r Lordships of Augst 3^d, in wch you give mee a worse account of Mr Bruce then by y^r former, and for wch I thinke you could not be too severe wth him. His captaine has not had much better luck at home, for hee has bine lately engaged in a rencounter wth young Churchill.[a] I know not ye quarrell; but Herbert[b] rann Churchill twice through the arme, and Churchill him into ye thigh, and, after, Herbert disarmed him. But w^{ht} is ye worse, I heare y^t Churchill has so spoke of it, that the King and Duke are angry wth Herbert. I know not w^{ht} he has done to justifie himself.

My Lord, there has gone 2 yachs to the Duch fleet, neither of wch can prevaile wth um to strike. The first that went was Capt. Crow[c] in ye Monmouth; and he is now in ye Tower about it. His story is this, that being commanded to fetch my Lady Temple[d] from Holland, he passd by the Duch fleete upon his returne, when ye Admirall saluted him wth 4 gunns, wch he answered wth 3; then shot another at him, wch made the Admirall presently send his l^t aboard him, to know ye reason. Crow told him, but presently shot another shot; whereupon De Ruiter or ye Admirall presently came aboard him himself, to ask ye reason, wch he told him was to strike to ye standard. The Duch Ad. replyed, he had no such com^n, no[r] would he w^{t}hout one, and that it must be argued before his masters at ye Hague and at Whitehall, and so perswaded Capt. Crow that he had done his duty, and to leave him. It seemes that Crow had orders not to leave shooting till hee had shot downe his flag, or that

---

  [a] John Churchill, afterwards Duke of Marlborough.

  [b] Perhaps Captain Henry Herbert, afterwards, in 1678, Lord Herbert of Cherbury.

  [c] Anthony Crow.

  [d] Dorothy, daughter of Sir Peter Osborne, and wife of Sir William Temple, who had been lately recalled from his embassy to Holland.

the Duch had fired upon him againe, and either done dammage to ye yach or some of the company; and then ye Duch had broke ye articles of peace. The perticulers of w^{ht} the later that went did I have not; but Mr Bronkier writt mee this post that he was returned and could not get them to stĭike. I am told too ye King has taken notice to ye ambassador of ye affronts done him in his person, by making of pictures of him of base representations.^a

I heare that another company is sent to strengthen Sheerenesse, and that ye other guarisons will be likewise more strengthened. 'Tis I of any that lye in ye lyon's mouth, for I am ye outquarter, am worst fortified, and have fewest men. But God's above. Yet Ile write to day to put um in mind. Wee all hold out yet in excellent health, and returne the ladyes and you our humble services.

THE SAME.

MY LORD,   Sep. 26, [16]71.

Its so long since I heard from y^r L^p, that I am affraide some letters I writt lately to your Lordship, that is since I received any, have not come to you. I directed them to y^r B^r Charles. This Ile send to Mr Loving, who, for all I know, may be dead too.

I have letters from Sr T. Lynch. He is in Jamaica, and re ceived there wth all ye wellcome ye place can afford. But hee was not well, for ye gowte had seized him in a terrible manner.

---

^a Evelyn tells us that when, at Charles's request, he had undertaken to write a History of the Dutch War, and had submitted his plan, "in the afternoone his Majesty tooke me aside into the balconie over the terrace, extreamly pleas'd with what had been told him I had begun in order to his commands, and enjoyning me to proceed vigorously in it. He told me he had ordered the Secretaries of State to give me all necessary assistance of papers and particulars relating to it, and enjoining me to make it a *little keene*, for that the Hollanders had very unhandsomely abus'd him in their pictures and libells."—*Diary*, 28 Aug. 1670.

I can hope to give y^r L^p no divertion by my letters wth any news from hence. You have no doubt heard the Duch have strook theyr flaggs all to the King's yach, and y^t y^e King has declared in councell he will prorogue the parlim^t till 23 of 8$^{o^{ber}}$ come 12 month; that he has damnd the new pattent for y^e customes, upon theyr demanding an abatement in case of a warr; that Sr William Thompson and Mr Garraway[a] of y^e House of Commons, Mr Millington,[b] and another I have forgot,[c] and, since, Sr John Lowther of y^e House too is put in, are all Commissioners, and have 1,700^{li} a year each to manage the customes for ye King.

I know not too if you have heard of Harry Saville's[d] adventure at Althrop. Hee being there wth Will Russell,[e] my Lady Northum.,[f] Lady Ashley,[g] and others, one night, when all were a bed, he comes up to Lady Northum. chamber, and finding her doore open, goes in and up to her bed side in his night gowne; and, when he is there, calls " Madam! Madam!" till he wakens her, and says that he came to acquaint her wth a passion he had long had, in the dark, wch he durst not own to her in the light. She, being mightily amazed to heare his voice, rung a bell by her bed side; upon wch presently her women in the next roome began to stirr. He begd her not to discover him, and so went away. She imediately rises and goes to bed in another roome, to Lady Ashley, and acquaints her. They send for Will Russell and tell him. He goes to Harry Savill, advises him to quitt the house presently, or he would be

[a] William Garraway, member for Chichester.

[b] Francis Millington.

[c] John Upton.

[d] Son of Sir William Savile, and brother of the Marquess of Halifax. Vice-Chamberlain to Charles II., and M.P. for Newark.

[e] A grandson of Francis, fourth Earl of Bedford, and standard-bearer to the King.

[f] Elizabeth, daughter of Thomas Wriothesley, Earl of Southampton, widow of Joceline Percy, eleventh Earl of Northumberland.

[g] Margaret, daughter of William, Lord Spencer of Wormleighton, and third wife of Anthony Ashley Cooper, Lord Ashley, afterwards Earl of Shaftesbury.

affronted; wch he does to. Ld Sunderland^a and Will Russell follow him to London to fight him. The King has notice and prevents it. H. S., since, has w^thdrawn himself, ashamed for so ill a conduct, no body know whither; some say beyond sea. The King is now at Euson,^b at my Lord Arlington's. At his returne thither I intend to wayte on him for some days, if my wife be well, wch she has not bine thesse 4 or 5 days, but slept pretty well to night. I shall returne hither for a month or two, and then am not resolved whether for London or Arely. I am,

My Lord,

Your most humble servant,

C. L.

They talk of my Ld Sunderlands going embassador into Spaine. Sr Tho. Osborn c is made Treasorer of the Navy, and Sr Thomas Lyttelton^d left out. I heare not of any thing else they do for him. My b^r Nando^e goes a captain of a troope in Sr Harry Jones^f regiment of horse into France.

---

^a Robert Spencer, Earl of Sunderland.
^b See Evelyn's account of Euston. *Diary*, 16 Oct. 1671.
^c Afterwards Earl of Danby.
^d Sir Thomas Lyttelton of Stoke Milburgh, co. Salop, Bart., the statesman. Speaker of the House of Commons in William III.'s reign. He was of a younger branch of the Lytteltons, being descended from Thomas Lyttelton of Spechley, second son of Judge Lyttelton, while Charles Lyttelton claimed the elder son, William, as his ancestor. Sir Thomas had been joined with Sir Thomas Osborne in the office of Treasurer of the Navy, but was now ousted. He afterwards held the office, in 1699.
^e Ferdinando, one of Sir Charles's younger brothers.
^f Colonel Sir Harry Jones, killed at the assault on Maastricht.

THE SAME

MY DEARE LORD,   Landguard Fort, October 7th, 16[71].

*   *   *   *   *

My wive's sicknesse has kept mee at home, else I had seene the greate doings at Euston and Norwich. They say there was never any thing so fine as that at Euston. As it happens, since I must to London, its not so materiall that I went not, but its hugely necessary for mee to be at Court, to represent to them y[e] greate weaknesse of this place, and to get more men allowed for the establishment at 60, and so many as are allways sick, absent, and duty-free out of them. I can scarce keepe my guard; and if they doe not begin early to work, nay this winter, if wee have a warr in spring, this place cannot be kept w[th]out a greate force in it by any body that will attaque it. Its allmost all mens opinions we shall breake w[th] y[e] Duch. One marke they take of it is employing S[r] George Downing[a] embassador thither; another, that y[e] Spaniard have allreadie refused our men of warr to come into Mahon, the Span: and they being absolutely confederated. But wee are not like to have so much use of that port as wee have had, for the consull of Argiers writes word, not only to tell us he lives, though indeed he has bine barbarously treated, but that those people are now very desirous of peace, and will doe w[ht] they can to precure it. To make the E. India Company sattisfaction they cannot, but they have strangled 20 of those that did the injury, and there are 40 more fled. They offer too to deliver all the English slaves w[th]out ransome, and, if wee stand upon it, they will send us theyr Divan or his head.[b] This S[r] Sam. Barnardiston[c] told mee two days since, who is my

[a] Of East Hatley, co. Cambridge, Bart. He had been ambassador to Holland under Cromwell, and was very unpopular with the Dutch. On his sudden return from Holland early in 1672, his conduct there was thought so unsatisfactory that he was sent to the Tower.

[b] Peace was made with the Algerines at the end of this year.

[c] Sir Samuel Barnardiston, of Brightwell-Hall, co. Suffolk, Bart. He sat for the county in Charles's third parliament in 1679.

next neighbor, and will, when there is an election for knight in S[r] Harry North's[a] place (who shot himself dead w[th] a pistoll and left a paper in Latin to justifie himself about it), infallibly (I beleeve) carry it, though he be a pre[s]biter, and y[e] gentlemen most ag[st] him.

No doubt you heare the greater news from better hands and from those y[t] have it fresher and more at hand, yet, because I have not much else to doe, nor it may be y[r] L[p] to reade, Ile tell you w[ht] I heare. The Master of y[e] Roles has his quietus,[b] and is made Viscount Verulam; the Speaker M[r] of y[e] Roles, and S[r] Robert Adkins Cheife Baron.[c] S[r] Tho. Osborn has y[e] Tr. of y[e] Navyes place to himself, and S[r] Tho. [Lyttelton] not otherwise provided for yet. The buisnesse was thus ordred upon a dispute betweene them in y[e] buisnesse of theyr employ, w[cb] came before the Councell, and I am told that S[r] Tho. Lytt. came of these not to his discredit, though it has proved since to his losse. But this may give you a hint of theyr patrons creditt and interests, w[ch] I suppose I need not name to you. The buisnesse of the Treasury (I suppose) is but rather layd aside for y[e] present then given over, and it's probable enough, when the King returnes, youle heare of a furter effort from y[e] Duke of Buck. and L[d] Ashley, whose credit I guesse was never so high.

The levyes for France are mightily countenanced. The muster master told mee he came from mustering S[r] Harry Jones troope, and that, when it was over, S[r] Harry proposed to as many as would goe wth him to draw forth, and, because there were but 14, he was inraged, and sur le champ put out one of those that stayd out of the troope. My b[r] Nando, who I expect heere to night, is like to have

[a] Of Mildenhall, co. Suffolk, Bart. member for the county.

[b] Sir Harbottle Grimston, who held this office through Charles II.'s reign. The announcement of his peerage is incorrect; though the title was actually conferred on a descendant in 1790. Sir Harbottle married, for his second wife, Annie, daughter of Sir Nathaniel Bacon, and niece of Lord Bacon.

[c] These promotions did not take place, the Speaker, Sir Edward Turnour, Bart. had become Lord Chief Baron in May; and Sir Robert Atkyns was made a judge of the Common Pleas in 1672, and Lord Chief Baron in 1689.

most of his troope at York wth him, but his troope is completed
and waites there only his coming to march them; and they say it
will be the best for the number amongst them, or as good as any in
England, both for men and equipage.   In my opinion this had bine
a good expedition for y^r brother, who by my Lord Bellasis ^a too
might have had any recommendation he desired, as I suppose, to S^r
Harry Jones, if he arives at any employment of that nature; and it
will be the easier, its likely, to get it at home after hee has had it
abroade, rebus sic stantibus.   Mr Brounkier has bine allmost dying
of late wth a rhewmatisme from head to foot, and is far yet from
well, as he tells mee.   I gave him advise to take ye diet of milk.
The Duke of Florence,^b upon one of our men of warr's stopping a
ship in his port that would have carryed away a merchant of those
countreys that owed a greate somme of mony to an English merchant in Legorne, did not only imprison the merchant by whose
meanes the other was stopt, but after, upon some very slight oca-
sion, put Captain Beach,^c captain of one of ye Kings frigots, into a
dungeon and, I thinke, irons on his legs, wch I know not how wee
can be revenged well of; sure not by his R^{ll} H: marrying his sister,
as they talked, her picture being sent over hither, it was thought,
for a baite.   My Lord Gerards lady is dead.   My Lady Mordant is
recovered, that it may be possible for you to goe a woing to her
againe, but I doubt neither for love nor mony.   I had a letter last
night, after I writt this from London, from one who says y^t a
Duchman assured him that morning the Freneh had returned
hither 600,000^{li}, and that ye mony was all in ye Tower, and that
they were to make it up 3,000,000^{li}.^d   I heare ye horse races are
begun at Newmarket, so its probable the King will be at London a
Saturday.

My humblest services to ye ladyes.

^a John, first Lord Belasyse.
^b Cosimo III. Grand Duke of Tuscany.
^c Sir Richard Beach, commanding the " Hampshire " frigate.
^d i. e. Three millions of *livres*, the sum stipulated by the secret treaty of Dover.

THE SAME.

MY D^r ·LORD, [1671.]

I am newly come to towne, where I shall be very glad to receive y^r commandes. The news heere is but very little; all talk of a warr in springe. I am solliciting hard for mony to repaire my fort, wch I am promised. If I get it, I shall be content to goe downe and see it layd out, else I intend not to goe away more this winter. I dined yesterday wth my Ld Bedford [a] and that family at Lord Newports,[b] where wee had much of ye discourse concerning Lady Thannets [c] being poisoned, or rather that she had like to have bine so; but I cannot tell ye particulars, wch I suppose too y^r L^p has from better hands; but I perceive that my Ld Thannet [d] is not excused at all from having a hand in it. I never heard the like how they talk of him.

Capt. Herbert is going a captain in Sr H. Jones troope for France; and the Duke told mee his company shall be removed into England. They say that the French will not trouble ye Spaniard, but fall in upon ye Duch somewhere about the Rhine; and so the tripple alliance may continue. My Ld Sunderland is hastening for Spaine. I am in greate hast, but I must tell you before I conclude y^t my old Lady Peterborough [e] is dying, and my Lord Peterborough was wth much adoo perswaded to goe this morning to take her blessing. She has done pritty well all she could for Ld Mordant.

Y^r L^{ps} humble serv^t,

C. LYTT.

[a] William Russell, fifth Earl, and afterwards, in 1694, Duke of Bedford, father of Lord William Russell.

[b] Francis, Lord Newport, afterwards Earl of Bradford.

[c] See above, p. 50, note [a].

[d] Nicholas Tufton, third Earl, who died in 1679.

[e] Elizabeth, daughter of William, Lord Howard of Effingham, and widow of John Mordaunt, first Earl of Peterborough. Her two sons, mentioned above, were Henry second Earl of Peterborough in 1642, who died in 1697, and Charles, created Viscount Mordaunt in 1659, who died in 1675.

THE SAME.

London, Jan. 13, 1671[2].

*   *   *   *

The acc^t of ye Treasury and ye banquiers you will best under
stand by ye King's declaration.[a]   Sr Steph. Fox [b] is dipt 70,000^li
deepe in that concerne; for w^ht mony he had of his owne, and all
he could take up upon his credit, will be paid but 6 per cent.; for
he advanced to ye army, and ye King allowd him 10^li, or he took
orders which he had more for.   I am sorry my Lady Thannet is so
much concerned; and I heare my Lady Anne's [c] pention was in y^e
banquiers hands.

Harry Norwood [d] had allmost all he had there, and I believe y^t
was a greate deale.   He is very sick to boote wth a greate rhewmatisme from head to toe.   Robin Holmes estate in ye same condition.   I have an order for 664^li of Sr Tho. Lynches, wch is in y^e
same misfortune.   Mr Ralph Montague [e] has bine heere three
weekes and is sworne is of ye Councell; and I assure you a greate
man he is, going back though to Paris.   The army will be payd,
they make us beleeve, as formerly by Sr Stephen; and the mony
to be payd imediately out of ye Checquer.   Y^r b^r has told you you
have 20 men allowed to each company, but it will be impossible to
get ye other 20 allowd at this time.

[a] The closing of the Exchequer took place on 2nd January.

[b] Paymaster-General.

[c] Anne Tufton, Lady Thanet's youngest daughter, who married Samuel, son of
Sir Harbottle Grimston.

[d] I suspect that this is the Major Norwood, who had been Governor of Dunkirk:
" Then over the Parke (where I first in my life, it being a great frost, did see people
sliding with their skeates, which is a very pretty art), to Mr. Coventry's chamber to
St. James's, where we all met to a venison pasty, Major Norwood being with us,
whom they did play upon for his surrendering of Dunkirke." —Pepys, *Diary*, 1 Dec.
1662.   He appears to have held a post at Court under the Master of the Horse.

[e] At this time ambassador at Paris.   Lord Montagu in 1683, and Duke in 1705.
He is best remembered as "the faithless and shameless man" who took part against
Danby; and less, as the builder of the Montague House, which became the British
Museum.

Wee have certainly peace wth Algiers, as by a letter from Sr William Godolphin,^a but none expresse from S^r Ed. Spragg.^b Wee waite much w^{ht} ye Spaniards will returne to ye King of France message, that if they will sitt newters they shall have all the assurance he can give them not to molest them in any of theyr estates; and they say ye King of England and other confederates have offred to be caution. It's imagined the Duch will not dare to sett out theyr fleete this summer. The Spaniards have a very considerable army in Flanders, and they are well ordred and payd. Prince of Aurange will be generall. My b^r Nando is not yet got into France. The King gave him 200^{li}, and ye Duke 150^{li}, to equipp.

Lady Willowby^c dead, I meane L^{ds} Lady. I have asked leave to waite on ye Duke as a volonteere, but we have no leave yet. Ld Winchelsea^d and his sonne have done so too, and its granted; so has Ld Howard^e and his two sonnes. The Prince Rupert goes not to sea. Ld Sandwich^f commands next ye Duke, and ye blew flag has Sr George Arscue.^g All ye first rates, which are 6, and all ye 2^d, 9, and all the 3^{ds}, 20, and 15 of ye 4th rates, are ordred to be made readie, and officers commissioned to command them. There shall be no 5^{ths} nor 6^{ths}, only ketches and such small craft to attend the fleete and fire ships. Sr Richd Browne^h is about resigning his place in ye Councell to Mr Williamson.

^a Baronet, elder brother of Sidney Godolphin. He was ambassador to Spain.

^b Vice-Admiral commmanding in the Mediterranean; drowned in the action with the Dutch, 11 Aug. 1673. With regard to his mission to the Algerines, see his instructions printed in *Memoirs on the English Affairs,* 1660-1673, by James, Duke of York. London, 1729. 8vo.

^c Anne, daughter of Sir Philip Carey, of Stanwell, co. Middlesex, and wife of William, sixth Lord Willoughby.

^d Heneage Finch, second Earl of Winchelsea.

^e Henry, Lord Howard of Castle Rising.   ^f See above, p. 37, note ^d

^g Admiral Sir George Ayscue, or Askew; distinguished himself in the sea fight of 1st June, 1666, where he was taken prisoner.

^h Clerk of the Council; John Evelyn's father-in-law. See Evelyn's *Diary,* 23 Jan. 1672: "To London, in order to Sir Richard Browne, my father-in-law, resigning his place of Clerke of the Council to Joseph Williamson, Esq. who was admitted and was knighted."

THE SAME.

Jan. 18, [16]7½.

I writt to y^r L^p the last post but one by Mr Loving, wch I hope got well to you. Since, wee find that there is not any likelyhood of so sudden a removall among ye greate officers as was then imagined, that is to say, in ye Treasury and household. For that of the L^{t}enancy of Ireland holds, and my L^d of Essex^a [is] to goe. And I beleeve there will be another President of Wales made; not that the old one^b is dead, but they say does not behave himself well; and there has lately happened a very strange passage upon ocasion of Mr Russell's serving him a warrant out of ye Chancery, in right of my Lady Vaughan,^{c} and being put into possession by law into a house and some of ye estate, the people he employed about it being mightily beaten and wounded, some theyr eares cut of, and one his tongue cut out, and all dispossessd; wch is like to hasten it. The Irish officers, who were petitioners about theyr pay and brought over hither about it, are all forbid the court, excepting some who have eminently served ye King, as my Ld Poore,^{d} Sr Robt Byron, Nick Armorer,^{e} and Sr Will. Flower,^{f} who was Lt Col. of ye Guards.

The Ld. Arlington and ye Treasurer,^{g} in all appearance, does gaine ground exceedingly of ye other faction, and they say wthall y^t ye Duke of Buck. and Ld Ashley are fallen out. Md^{lle} Keerewell^h

---

^{a} Arthur Capel, first Earl of Essex.

^{b} Richard Vaughan, second Earl of Carbery.

^{c} Anne, daughter of Sir George Savile, afterwards Marquess of Halifax, married to John Vaughan, afterwards third Earl of Carbery.

^{d} Richard Power, Lord Le Poer, Earl of Tyrone in 1673.

^{e} Sir Nicholas Armorer; at this time held a post in the household.

^{f} An old cavalier officer. Lieut.-Col. of the regiment of Irish Guards.

^{g} Sir Thomas, afterwards Lord, Clifford.

^{h} Louise Renée de Querouaille, afterwards Duchess of Portsmouth. This is a new spelling of the name, which usually appears as Carwell.

is infinitely in favour, and, to say truth, she seemes as well to deserve it, for she is wondrous handsome,[a] and, they say, as much witt and addresse as ever anybody had. There will be presently new levyes for 3,000 men, to be sent into France and to be joyned wth ye rest of ye King's subjects allreadie there, and all to be commanded by ye Duke of Monmouth; and I heare some talk of Lockier to command under him, others of my Ld Bellassis. I beleeve I shall goe to sea wth ye Duke. I find it's well taken of mee to presse it, wch will therefore oblige mee to it; but I beleeve however there may be no action, for most are of opinion the Duch wont come out, and I doubt it may loose mee a commiss^{rs} place of ye Prize Office, wch I have else pritty well secured, unlesse I can get to be y^t com^r who is to be wth the fleete, wch Ile endeavor.

I heard an honest gentleman say yesterday, they begin allreadie to find one good effect of breaking ye banquiers in ye countrie, for it makes mony to be more plentifull there upon this account, that all receivers of publike, and allmost private, revenues that were considerable, sent up all the mony they could make into a somme hither, wch lay at interest, as long as they could wthhold it from them it was due ; and now they have not that way, neither to secure it nor make ye advantage, they are content to let it lye in the countrey; and undoubtedly, my Lord, it will inhance the value of land everywhere. I was mistaken about my Lady Anne's portion, for Mr Walter[b] tells mee shee had no mony, nor my Lady Thannet neither. He had himself 1,200^{li} there. Y^e Bishop of Durham is dead.[c] B^p Salisbury[d] and Chester[e] are named to succeed

---

[a] Evelyn thought otherwise (*Diary*, 4 Nov. 1670): "I now also saw that famous beauty, but in my opinion of a childish, simple, and baby face, Mademoiselle de Querouaille."

[b] William, son of Sir William Walter, of Saresden, co. Oxon., Bart., married Mary, daughter of John, second Earl of Thanet.

[c] John Cosin, Bishop of Durham, died 15 Jan. 1672.

[d] John Dolben, translated to York in 1683.

[e] John Wilkins, died on the 19th November of this year.

him; but the later is supposed to decline in favour, and the first, I beleeve, will be loath to be so far from Canterbury, if that see happen to be vacant, as aspiring to it and being most faire to carry it.

I heard at Court to-day my Ld Exeter,^a the Earle I meane, is dying; so is Capt. Broughton of ye Guards.

My wife is something better, and, I beleeve, if she knew of my writing now would have writt to my Lady, to whom I beseech you, my Lord, present humblest services, and to ye rest of ye ladyes.

THE SAME.

MY DEERE LORD,   Tuesday, Feb. 12th, 1671[2].

I hant heard from you since Capt. Izod came from you; but I have writt twice by way of Hampton.

The greate talk of Lambert's being sent for hither, I beleeve, proceedes from nothing but that y^r b^r borrowed my Ld Howard's coach (as I heare) for to meete Mrs Lambert upon ye roade, to bring her to towne; and I thinke hee and his wife went wth it to meete her. This Mervin Tucket^b told mee at my Lord Windsor's lodging, who is in towne. The news is come that the Queene of Spaine has signed the rattifacation of ye league, offensive and defensive, wth ye Duch.

Sr George Downing is in the Tower, for coming away in so much hast and contrary to the King's direct orders to him under his own hand. It's beleeved he was affraid the people would attempt upon him.

---

^a John Cecil, fourth Earl of Exeter, died in 1678.
^b Colonel Mervyn Touchet, afterwards fourth Earl of Castlehaven.

The Duke of Buck., they say, and my Lord Ashley are fallen quite out; and yᵉ Duke is very fond growne of yᵉ Treasurer, and says he shall be Treas. of England; but I beleeve, for all yᵗ, he continues firme in his friendship to the Lᵈ Arlington. My old Lady Moulgraive ᵃ [is] dead. Last night died Dr. Clerk ᵇ yᵉ phisitian. Sʳ Thomas Ingram ᶜ lyes dying, and Bab May is to be Chancellor. I was to night to see Thom. Grey, but could not; he was so ill. His disease a consumption and dropsy. Last night, one of Sʳ John Lewis his heires ᵈ was stollen from her mother's house in Lincoln's Inne fields by I know not who; she is sister to her my Lᵈ Huntingdon ᵉ is to marry. The mother ᶠ was married but a little while agoe in her boudore to one of Sʳ Onslow's sons of Surrey.

I know not if you know that little Osborne is knighted and married to Ned Vernon's ᵍ sister, and had 6,000ˡⁱ wᵗʰ her, wᶜʰ I feare was greate part of it in yᵉ banquiers hands. They are not yet raising yᵉ Duke of Mon[mouth's] regiment, nor yᵉ commissions delivered out. I heard to-day wee shall have two regiments raised at home, and that Fitz-Gerrard ʰ is to command one.

I am mighty cold and in hast.

Your most obedient servant,

C. L.

ᵃ Elizabeth, daughter of Lionel Cranfield, Earl of Middlesex, and widow of Edmund Sheffield, second Earl of Mulgrave.

ᵇ Timothy Clarke, physician.

ᶜ Chancellor of the Duchy of Lancaster.

ᵈ Mary, second daughter of Sir John Lewis, of Ledstone, Bart.; married to Robert Leke, Lord Deincourt, son of Nicholas, Earl of Scarsdale.

ᵉ Theophilus Hastings, seventh Earl of Huntingdon, married Elizabeth, eldest daughter of Sir J. Lewis.

ᶠ Sarah, daughter of Sir Thomas Foot, Lord Mayor of London. Her second husband was Denzil Onslow.

ᵍ Colonel (?) Edward Vernon, one of the Gentlemen of the Privy Chamber.

ʰ Colonel Fitz-Gerald, formerly Deputy-Governor of Tangier.

THE SAME.

MY LORD,   Feb. 22th, 1671[2].

I have received 2 letters from you this weeke, ye 1st of Feb. 3rd, and ye later by a reiveller, of ye 12th, whom I told I should be very readie to serve in w^{ht} I could.   He came wth Dick Beavor.[a] I read that part of y^r L^{ps} to his Royall H^{gs}, wherein you commanded mee to sattisfie him about y^r companie, wch I suppose was sufficient.   I allso told my Ld Arlington about ye quarters w^{ht} you writt.

Yesterday came ye Spanish embass: from Flanders. He had private audience to day, and, after that, ye K^g and French embass: were alone above an hower.   W^{ht} resolutions are taken a little time will show, but most beleeve wee shall have warr; and how ye matter will be ordred I know not, but I suppose they that govern think soe as that the Spaniard and wee shall still continue faire together however.

The weather being broke and ye wind westerly our ships will come quickly about, that lye at Portsmth and westward, and bring in S^r Ed: Spragg.

I had a letter lately of Nov. 29 from Sr T. Lynch; his wife brought well to bed of a boy. This day Sr Robt Carr had ye seale given him of ye Duchy [b] and took his oathes. They talk much to-day of raising new forces, they say 2 regiments of foot and a troope of horse in every county.

The King has of late forbore visiting my Lady Cle[veland]; but some two days since was wth her againe, and I suppose will continue to goe sometimes, though it may be not so often.

Capt. Izod dined wth mee to day, and my chaplin, Mr Evans, who Izod told y^r L^p was resolved to give a parsonage too when one fell, w^{ch}, if you have not greater ingagem^t, in truth, my Lord, I think he will well deserve, for hee is an honest sober man and a

---

[a] Richard Beauvoir, of Guernsey, sometime adjutant in Lyttelton's regiment.

[b] Duchy of Lancaster.

good preacher. He thinkes he shall goe to sea this summer in one of the greate ships.

The B^p of Bath,^{a} Dr Charleton, kept his consecration feast at ye Cock, for wch reason none of ye B^{ps} would goe to it. A Tuesday night there was greate maskarading at my Lady Portland's, my Lord Alesburye's, and Lady Walgrave's. I am calld away in hast and have no more to adde but that in good earnest y^r ormers ^{b} were thought most excellent meate. My humblest services to my Lady &c. And am, my Lord,

Your most humble servant,

C. LYTTELTON.

THE SAME.

MY LORD, March 22, [16]7$\frac{1}{2}$.

Since I came out of Worcestershire I have y^r L^{ps} of Feb. 24 and March 14, both wch mentioning my doing right to y^r captain, wch I shall not be wanting in.

I humbly thanke you for y^e noble present of ormers, wch my Lady Thannet sent hither. I doubt not y^r b^r has allreadie told you of ye declaration for liberty of conscience, and, since, another for the warre upon the United Provinces,^{c} and of Sr Robert Holmes his falling on ye Duch Smirna fleete, consisting of about 60 merchantmen and 6 or 7 men of warr. When he begun the fight he had but 5 ships wth him, but the next morning (I thinke) his b^r, Jack Holmes, came in wth 3 or 4 more. My Lord of Ossory ^{d}

---

^{a} A slip of the pen for Bristol, which see Dr. Guy Carleton held. Robert Creighton was Bishop of Bath.

^{b} Ormier, or oreille de mer, a shell-fish so called from its shape. Scroggs (see below, p. 115) refers to them as "those lympitts y^t were never seene in England."

^{c} The two declarations appeared on the 16th and 17th March.

^{d} Thomas Butler, the gallant Earl.

CAMD. SOC. M

in y[e] Resolution began the fight. Holmes his shipp and my Lord's
were disabled by the shotts in theyr masts and rigging very soone,
and were faine to lye by. S[r] Robert went into y[e] Cambridge,
commanded by S[r] Fretswill Hollis,[a] and fought in her. He complaines of S[r] Fretswill and Capt. Elliot, that they did not doe
theyr parts, els that they had taken them all; they of him, that
he wanted conduct, and used them ill to excuse it. Both presse
for a councell of warr, w[ch] I beleeve will not be granted; but
w[ht] faults [there] were will be rather concealed. Another thing
they impute to Holmes is, that when he was in search after y[e]
Duch he made Sprag's fleete, w[ch] so soone as he knew to be so,
altered his course and would not speake w[th] him, though he were
intreated to it by George Leg[b] who was in y[e] Fairfax. The reason
they say was because he emulated him, and that he must have
fought under his flag, and, being too confident of successe w[th]out
him, would not let him share w[th] him in y[e] victory. They tooke
a rich Smirna man and 3 others, w[ch], though I am a commissioner,
I can yet tell you no more of, for wee are not yet settled in our
buisnesse. Wee lost a pritty many men in this action, and all the
ships were notably torne. That I saw when I was wth the K[g] and
Duke the other day, at Sheereneese, where there are a greate many
brave ships in good readinesse, but not half mand; and more readie
to fall downe to them.

So soone as I have my instructions, I beleeve I shall be sent to
Harw[ch], as well to looke after y[e] Prize Office as my other concerne.
Prince Rupert is about raising a regiment. S[r] John Talbot[c] L[t]
Coll: and Andrews[d] Major, Sam Moris his sonne. The 4 companies
came from Barbados are in that regiment, and 6 more. Fitz-
Gerrard has another regiment and as many companies. His L[t]

[a] Sir Fretcheville Hollis. Both he and Captain Elliot were killed at Southwold
Bay, 28 May, 1672.   [b] Afterwards Earl of Dartmouth.
   [c] M.P. for Knaresborough. He was second to the Earl of Shrewsbury in his fatal
duel with Buckingham. See Pepys, *Diary*, 17 Jan. 1668.
   [d] Edmund Andross.

Coll. is one Butler, of Sommersetshire, and S[r] Edward Charleton is his Major.

The Duch embassador tooke leave to-day, and, I heare, assured the King that, whenever his M[atie] should have any inclinations to peace, his masters would be willing to embrace it. Blanford[a] is in France about making conditions to carry over a regiment of horse from hence. The King goes but seldome to Cleveland house. S[r] George Downing is out of y[e] Tower and has kissd y[e] King's hand. I am not able to tell you how our affaires are like to goe wth y[e] Spaniard; and its y[e] more a mistery, because I beleeve the match for y[e] Duke wth y[e] Lady of Inspurg is still on foot. Y[e] Duke of Richmond goes to morrow for Denmark. Swede will stand newters. The answer they give to those that presse them to declare wth them is, that they who governe affaires are but administrators and are desireous to leave thinges as they are, rather then to imbarke in so greate a matter, when, in half a yeare, theyr prince will be at age and may then choose w[ht] part he pleases himself. I was wth my L[d] Windsor at Wolverhamton at his new house he has bought of y[e] Deane and Chapter and is allreadie raising y[e] rents upon y[e] tennants by y[e] way of from 100[li] to 140. Harry[b] is a brave boy and much made on, and will be readie to make love to y[e] proudest of y[r] daughters.

My most humble services to my Lady &c.

My eys have bine sore a greate while and now I can scarce see.

---

[a] Louis Duras, Marquis de Blanquefort, created Lord Duras in 1673; succeeded his father-in-law as Earl of Feversham in 1677.

[b] Lyttelton's eldest son by his second marriage, who entered the army, and, much to his father's displeasure, went over to the Prince of Orange at the Revolution. He died unmarried.

FRANCIS IZOD.[a]

MY LORD,   Portsmouth, March 25th, 1672.

    *   *   *   *

l beleeve your Lordsp. hath the bad account of our late engage
ment by Sir Rob. Holmes, w[ch] the day before mett wth S[r] Edw.
Spragg as neare as betwixt Orm and Castle Cornett, and would not
suffer any of his fleete to goe neare Spragg, but stood of, and Spragg
passed through channell to the Downes, he being, as tis thought,
jelouze that Spraggs flagg should have the honour of doeing that
w[ch] he intended for himselfe.   The Dutch, makeing a running fight
one it, have disabled the St. Michaell and the Resolution and most
of our small number in a dreadfull manour.   Theire viz-adm[ll] sunke
presently, and theire adm[ll] at the mouth of the Texell, and about
12 or 14 marchants ships taken; but it is verily thought that, if it
had not beene for this proud neglecting of S[r] Roberts, they might
[have] had all with much ease and consequently put an end to this
warr.   I heare there is two redgm[ts] raiseing, on for Prince Rupert
an the other for Coll. Fitz Gerard, and wee expect to have our
redgm[t] fild to a 100 in a company.

    *   *   *

I remaine
    Your Lordsp. most obedient and most humble servant,
                        FRANC. IZOD.

SIR CHARLES LYTTELTON,

MY DEERE LORD,   Landguard Fort, May 16, [16]72.

    I have rec[d] y[rs] of May 3rd. I have bine heere this month.   The
Duch fleet lye now before us, and, both for number and quallity,
look very terribly.   I had y[e] fortune to save by a scout, w[ch] I sent

  [a] A native of Guernsey, afterwards a captain in Lyttelton's regiment.

out to spye after them, 7 of our frigots and 3 other greate ships wch lay in the Gunfleet; who, when he told were coming upon them, would hardly beleeve but they were our own fleete, and had scarce time to weigh and be gone again into ye river before they were in ye Gunfleet too; and ye next morning, they sent above 40 sayle of theyr best ships after them, wch pursued them as far as ye buoy of ye Nore, but I think did us no hurt. This afternoone they are come back again, for wee see them, to ye rest of theyr fleet, wch I beleeve are about 100 greate and small. The Duke has bine at Dover these three days; but the wind is so crosse and ye tides have bine so slack that hee could not get up hither. The Duch are now all under saile; I cannot tell if they will endeavor to get of, but I hope they cant before ye Duke has spoke wth them. For I beleeve the Duke's fleet, joyned wth ye French, to be farr superior to theires as to goodnesse, and better manned.

I am glad y^r L^p is in so good a posture to defend y^rself. I never could get sight of y^r Lftenant you brag so of, though I desired it much. I wish you could have as good an acc^t of mee, for Langor Fort stands just as neglected as ever it did, only there is more company in it; for I have lately my company made up 100 men, and I have Sr Robt Caryes company in Fitz-Gerrard's regiment quarters upon ye hill and keeps guard heere, and two troopes, my Ld Oxford's and Sr Francis Compton's.

The wind is come southerly, and the Duch are gone to sea, so that I hearken every moment to hear them at it. Of the successe I shall be sure to give y^r L^p notice as fast as I can.

My wife is wth my b^r Lytt[elton] and all my babyes; but y^r sonne in law has bine very ill of an ague, but I hope upon recovery.

Wee have 10 sayle come out of ye river into ye Gunfleet since morning, when ye Duch went thence. The same they alarumd out of it, when they came in, and, I beleeve, had bine surprized and lost, if a ketch I employd for to waite on ye Duch fleet and had bine wth them all day had not given them notice of it. The Duch pursued them however ye next morning to Sheerenesse.

THE SAME.

MY LORD,   Landguard Fort, 1 June, 16[72].

I am in so greate [haste] just taking coach to give his R^ll Highnesse ye parù bien after his late danger, being (as I suppose by ye inclosed) at Sole Bay, that I have only time to put that up and to tell you, ^wch will be ye best acc^t you can have (I suppose), of that action, when I return from thence. I may learne other perticulars, wch I shall write y^r Lords^p; only this in the meane time. I believe ther is some reason to hope, wch is ye best, my Lord Sandwich may be a prisoner wth ye Duch, not being heard of in our fleete; because I have examined one y^t was in ye James when she was a fire, who does aver that he saw my Lord and Sr Charles Herbert,^a Capt. Haddock^b and Lt Mayo, all leave ye ship and goe into my Lord's barge.

My d^r Lord, I am

Y^r most humble serv^t,

C. LYTTELTON.

Poore Thom. Bromly ^c was in ye Royall James and all his company. So was Capt. Bennet ^c and his, in ye Henry. The Duke has lost 4 captains ^d of his regm^t. It's not impossible I may get Izod a company wch I would faine doe.

---

    ^a Sir Charles Harbord, serving as a volunteer, was killed.
    ^b Afterwards Sir Richard Haddock; the only officer of the "Royal James" who escaped.
    ^c Two of the captains in Lyttelton's (the Admiral's) regiment.
    ^d Besides Bromley and Bennett, Captains Burgh and Barry were killed. By a whimsical accident the letter B. was unfortunate in the regiment on this day.

James de Havilland.[a]

My Lord,   London, y[e] 3[d] day of June, 1672.

*   *   *   *   *

On Tuesday last y[e] Dutch fleet appeared by break of day neare
Sole Bay, hoping to surprise our fleete y[t] was then at an anchor in
y[e] bay; but having beene discovered, our fleete made all y[e] speed
they could to weigh anchor, and y[e] blew squadron being next to y[e]
Dutch fleet, they fell upon it, and chiefly upon y[e] Royall James in
w[ch] was y[e] Earle of Sandwich, upon whom they sent 2 fire shipps
which he sunke, and, afterwards, having battered one of their flagg-
shipps which having yealded and which was noe sooner boarded by
y[e] English she sunk; which y[e] Dutch perceving, they sent another
fire ship, which being fastned to y[e] Royall James was burnt in
so much y[t] y[e] remainder of y[e] seamen y[t] were left alive leapd over
board to save themselves, except y[e] Earle of Sandwich and 7 or 8
more which were seene aboard as y[e] ship was on fire, not being yet
knowne whether he be dead or taken prisoner. His Royall Highnesse his ship was also sett upon by severall of y[e] Dutch shipps in
such a manner that he had 20 shott betweene wind and water, and
was so disabled that his Highnesse was faine to shift to another
ship, which being also disabled, he went to a third ship, and afterwards went againe to his owne shipp, after it was fitted againe,
severall other of our shipps having also beene much shattered and
disabled to y[e] number, as it is reported, of 14 or 15, amongst which
was y[e] Royall Catherine, the Henry, y[e] Royall Charles, &c., but
none were lost but y[e] Royall James. Severall commanders were
also killed, namely Captaine Coxe[b] (who was killed as he was
speaking with his Royall Highnesse), S[r] Fressville Hollis,[c] Cap[ne]

[a] A native of Guernsey; an agent for Lord Hatton in England.
[b] Sir John Cox, of the " Prince."
[c] In the " Cambridge."

Digby,[a] and several others, and S[r] John Chisley[b] taken prisoner. And of y[e] Dutch it is affirmed that they lost about 15 or 16 ships, whereof 3 were taken, one sinking before she was brought into harbour, y[e] other two being of 70 and 62 guns.   The next day, which was the Wednsday, his Highnesse endeavouring to engage y[e] Dutch, y[e] wind being very high and a great fogg coming at y[e] same moment did hinder y[e] engagement; but, having cleared up againe, and as the 2 fleetes were ready to engage, there hapned againe such a fogg that it was impossible to engage, and y[e] night comming on it gave time to y[e] Dutch to retire, who went towards y[e] oyster sands and soe forwards towards Flushing.   They say that they have lost Cap[ne] Everson,[c] and wee have one of their Mogen . . . . oner.[d]   This is all y[e] accompt I can give your Lord[p] at present, untill Cap[ne] White e goes over, by whom I hope to send you a printed relation of y[e] whole busines.   In the meane time let your Lord[p] be pleased to accept this from, my Lord,

Your Lord[ps] most humble and devoted servant,

J. DE HAVILLAND.

SIR CHARLES LYTTELTON.

MY LORD,   Landguard, June 4, [16]72.

I am sure I writt to you since the battle, so of that I need say no more; besides that, you will have, I question not, the printed letter

---

[a] Francis Digby, second son of George, second Earl of Bristol, in command of the "Henry."

[b] Sir John Chichely. His ship, the "Royal Catharine," was captured, but was retaken by the crew, who overpowered the prize crew.

[c] He probably means Elzevir.   [d] The letter is torn here.

[e] Isaac White, a sea captain.

of Mr Savill's^a to my Ld Arlington, wch is a better and more exact
acc^t then any body els can pretend to make it, being made from y^e
report of all ye commanders in the fleet to his R^{ll} Highness, and so
digested by Mr Savill who now executes the place of secretary, M^r
Wrenne^b being so ill he is not able, and some think scarce ever
will; and, if he don't, I beleeve Savville will keepe it.

The death of Sr John Trevor has made his uncle, Harry Coventry,^{c} who is not yet returned from his embassy,^{d} Secretary in his
place; and this I heard too by my Lord Arlington's meanes, if the
extraordinary merrit he has acquired in this embassy has not done
it alone. Some were of opinion, who I talked wth in ye flecte, y^t
Sr William may ere long get again into ye ministry too.

My Lord Sandwich's body was found last Tuesday at sea, at
least 40 miles from ye place of battle, floating upon ye water, and
was known by ye George and starr on him; though, when he first
came in, it was easie enough to know him. He had in his pocket
three ringes, one a white sapphire wth his crest and garter, and the
most glorious blew saphir that ever I saw in my life; the other was
an antique seale. He had a p^r of compasses and a compasse too.
So soone as I heerd of it, I went and brought the body hither,
wch lay in a small boate, as it was towed by ye smack wch found
him. I presently writt to my Lord Arlington of it, and gave order
to my surgeon, Mr Thatham,^{e} who is here wth mee, to prepare for

^{a} "A true Relation of the Engagement of His Majesties Fleet under the command
of His Royal Highness with the Dutch Fleet, May 28, 1672. In a letter from Henry
Savile, Esq., on board His Royal Highness, to the Earl of Arlington, Principal
Secretary of State. Published by Authority." Lond. 1672. sm. fol.

^{b} Matthew Wren, eldest son of Matthew Wren, Bishop of Norwich. He was first
secretary to the Earl of Clarendon, and afterwards admiral's secretary. He died at
this time. Sir Christopher Wren was his cousin. Savile did not get his place, as
appears by the next letter.

^{c} Anne, daughter of Thomas, Lord Coventry, and sister of Henry Coventry, was
the mother of Henry Savile.

^{d} To Sweden.

^{e} Samuel Tatham, the regimental surgeon.

CAMD. SOC.   N

ye embalming it, ^wch he has done; and, since, I had a letter from
my Lord Arlington, who commanded mee, by order from his Matie,
to embalm him and to keepe the body wth all possible honour and
decency, till it be sent for away, and gave the man that found it,
and who went wth the news himself, 50 pieces, his Majesty being
resolved to bury him at his own charge and expence, for his greate
and eminent services, especially this last at his death, wherein he
certainly made for some howers as brave and generous a defence,
before the ship was burnt, wch was not till after he had put of two
fireships, by the 3^d. His sonne ^a allso perished wth him. He was
scene by some that escaped one of ye last in ye ship, but, it seemes,
at last leapt over board, for his body seemed not to be touched w^th
the fire or powder, ^wch it could not have escaped, if he had bine in
ye ship or very neere it. I should think it was a strange misfortune
that all the small vessells and tenders upon his ship were, at that
time the Duch came upon us, from ye fleet; nor had he any of his
boates, but his barge, ^wch so many of the men leapt into as, they
say, she sunk by the ship side. He lyes now in my chappell, in his
coffin, wth black bays over it, and some black bays and scutcheons
round the chappell, wch is all the ceremony this place will afford,
till further directions. But there is nothing stranger to mee then
y^t, in all this tyme, not one of his relations nor servants are yet
come hither, to waite on him or enquire. I writt to my Lord his
sonne too ye same night.

The Duch fleet dare not goe in, for feare they should not get out
againe, all thinges at home wth them being in that confusion, y^t
they have now scarce any or no governm^t, every one shifting to save
himself as from an inundation; so strangely does the French
victoryes seeme to distract and amaze them. They have taken
Wezell, Groll, Burick, Rhenburgh, Rhez, Emmerick, and they say
Skinksconce, and by this time, it's beleeved, Utricht; beaten theyr
army; and nothing makes opposition. Last Tuesday, Monsieur

---

i. e. his son-in-law, Sir Philip Carteret.

Boreell,[a] who never went away, made meanes by Prince Rob[t] to come to y[e] King, and then, w[th] teares in his eyes, besought him to give leave to 3 of theyr states to come over to treat w[th] him, upon w[ht] termes his M[atie] should like. The King's answer was short, that he could resolve on nothing w[th]out sending to his B[r] of France; so Silvius[b] or little Aston[c] is gone, and my Lord Hallifax follows y[e] next week to y[e] French court,[d] w[th] argum[ts] to try if the French will yeeld to any accommodation w[th] them, w[ch] its thought they will not; but wee talk of nothing but peace w[th] y[e] Duch, and, to say truth, I beleeve are as fraid of y[e] French conquering them as they themselves. It's thought by this time they have as good as 5 of y[e] 7 provinces. They are the cowardliest people, and make y[e] worst defence for themselves that ever I heard of. I can tell you nothing of them from hence, but will be stale news by that time it comes to London; for every minute begets news from thence. Surely wee have a faire ocasion to proffit ourselves, if wee take it. They will submit to any termes, I doe not question, but to own y[e] K[g] of England for theyr L[d] and sovveraign, if he will undertake theyr protection; w[ch], if he doe, must bee speedy and powerfully. Wee have now the best opportunity, for our fleete is readie to set saile again, and wee have a greate many new raised forces. Some think that they will be forced to bring in theyr East India fleet into our harbours, if wee will promisse them protection, and be content to pay the customes; if not, I beleeve wee shall goe ncere to take it.

When I was last week in y[e] flecte wth y[e] Duke, I heard a fearfull murmure of y[e] French, that they did not behave themselves well in y[e] battle; and though for that they have a faire pretence, because,

---

[a] Johan Boreel, Heer van Westhoven, Dutch ambassador in England. He died in 1673.

[b] Sir Gabriel Sylvius.

[c] One of Lord Aston's family?

[d] Halifax, Buckingham, and Arlington were sent soon after this on a mission to Holland, but returned on the 21st July without effecting anything.

being to lee-ward, they could not come more into ye fight then theyr enemy would let them, yet ye same excuse, nor indeed any, will scarce serve turne for ye next day, when, being to windward, and y^t ye Duke gave ye signall to them to beare in, they would not understand it; for, if they had, in probabillity the Duch had bine lost, wee had so much the advantage both of wind and strength of them. Of this, though, I doe not find Mr Saville says anythinge.

I have y^r Lds^{ps} of ye 28th May, and humbly thank you, my Lord, for ye warrant in it; am sorry you have any sicknesse among you. I thanke God, wee are well heere; but only one fellow that died of a feavor much about that tyme as y^{rs} did, and another since was drownd. I pray God send my Lady a safe delivery of a brave boy. The Duke lost 4 of his Capts. in ye battle, I meane of his regiment; and has put in theyr places Mr Bagot,[a] Lady Falm^{ths} brother, my b^r George,[b] Vaughans L^t, old Cornwall[c] of ye house of Commons, and Mr. Churchill[d] that was ensigne to ye King's company. Poore Thom. Bromley was in ye R^{ll} James. His ensign was soe, but, wth swimming at least an hower and more, at last was taken up and is well; only his head a little burnt and his mouth hurt; his name, Wilson. I was told last night, by a letter from London, my Ld Arlington shall have ye garter.

---

[a] Richard Bagot, who was major in the regiment in 1687.

[b] George Lyttelton appears in the list of the regiment as captain still in 1687. (Harl. MS. 4847: "List of officers of His Ma^{ts} army. Nov. 1687.") In this list it is a curious fact that in one company George Lyttelton is captain and Francis Izard his lieutenant, and that the next is commanded by Captain Francis Izod with George Littleton for lieutenant. Whether by this transparent diversity of spelling they succeeded in holding two companies and drew double pay cannot now be settled. But they had two veritable ensigns, so that the two companies may be presumed to have existed.

[c] Humphrey Cornwall.

[d] Afterwards Duke of Marlborough.

The same.

My Lord, Landguard, July 2, [16]72.

No doubt you will have heard the Duke of Buck., Ld Arlington, are gone for Holland and to ye French court. There is joyned wth them in com^n the Duke of Monm^th and Ld Hallifax, wch later went before them.

A Fryday last I was aboard ye Prince in ye Gun Fleet. There was Capt. Lovell, master of one of ye yachs that went wth ye Lords for Holland. He told mee that those ships of ye Duch he met wth going into ye Brill all strook to them; that, when they came ashore, the people flockd about them, crying out, "Bless ye King of England and Prince of Aurang." When they came to ye Hague, none of ye States came to them, for they durst not shew themselves, the people there and every where being readie to stone them. But the Prince of Aurang was there, and they supt wth him. The next day they went to Utricht to ye French court, from whence I have not heard of them.

Saturday, the Duke set sayle for ye coast of Holland, and ye pacquet boate came in last night says they were there the night before; that De Ruyter was about 6 leagues of them with a great fleete, but ill manned, for they have put a greate many ashore to defend ye country. They have, wth ye rest of ye countrey not under the French power, universally declared the Prince of Aurange Governor, and ye name of States they doe no more endure then wee doe a Rump parlim^t. I cannot think why ye Duch fleet should fight us, nor wee them. We have no quarrell, sure, to ye P. of Aurange; but if our difference be not accommodated by treatie very speedily, I beleeve wee shall endeavor to ingage them or els to seize theyr India fleet. But I had rather have them subjects then prisoners, and I beleeve, if wee will accept them, the King may be acknowledged theyr protector, I meane all that have not yet submitted to

ye French; who, though, pretend they will treate of nothing w^th^out
our consent, and have sent to tell us that, if theyr be any thing
omitted in our treatie, wee shall yet insert it, that is, any townes wee
would have wee shall have them, but those are yet to take y^t they^a^
know wee can care for, at leaste to keepe, for they have not, in all
theyr conquest, one port towne, nor, by w^ht^ I heare, are likely; for
· they have so drownd all the countrey, that they can make no further progresse, it being impossible to march an army upon the bankes
above the waters, but that 100 men may defend them ^agst^ 1000;
and they say that the boores of those drownd parts are all flockd
into ye Prince of Aurange's army, wch have infinitely encreased it;
and ye townes seem all very resolute to defend themselves, under y^e
conduct of ye Prince, ^agst^ ye French.   I beleeve we hold ye French
at this time to theyr good behaviour, for, if they will not come to
such an accomodation as is reasonable, and that wee fall from
them, the other princes of Germany, Sweden, and the Spaniard
will be all upon them, and he can't get back his fleete neither.   He
asks mighty thinges: Maestricht, Breday, all the townes he has got
and Sluys, and 26 of theyr capitall ships, and that the Duch be
obliged to pay them, and all ye charge of ye warr, wch is five and
twenty millions, to be repayd him.

Sir Harry Jones' regiment, in the passing the Rhyne, swamme
all over as they were drawn up on ye side of ye river in battalia.
Capt. Pendannis and one trumpet drownd.   The Duch y^t were to
defend ye river on ye other side fled w^th^out a strooke, as soon as
they landed.   The river was as broade heere as it is at Kingston.

Lord Harry Howard is passing his pattent for Earle Marshall.

Harry Saville does but execute ye secretaryes place to ye Duke
till Robert Worden's sonne^b^ in Sweden comes over, who is then to

---

^a^ "he" in orig.

^b^ John, son of Robert Werden, of Leyland, co. Lanc.   He was created a baronet
this year.

be secretarie. He has leave to sell his groomes place,[a] and is promised the next vacancy of a groome wth ye King.

My wife is yet with Sr Harry. I sh^d be very glad to heare my
Lady were well brought to bed of a young nobleman. My humblest
services to all the ladies and him, if there be such a one.

Y^e Duke of Buck. regiment is 15 companies, and 1,500 men;
and there is to be a regim^t of seamen.

THE SAME.

MY DEERE LORD, Landguard Fort, Aug. 26, 1672.

I am just come heere from ye buoy of ye Nore, where I left y^e
King and his Royall Highnesse wth ye whole fleet, wch were in no
condition any longer to keepe the seas, they have bine so cruelly
harassed, both men and ships, by the tempestuous seasons they have
had ever since they were abroad, many of ye ships being quite disabled and the men allmost all soe sick, that they have scarce in any
ship enow well to weigh their anchors. Yet, notwthstanding, I left
them in councell upon resolving the fleete should out againe, and
that very speedily, and that some thousands of landmen should be
put on board, wth designe to land them somewhere upon the Duch;
a traine of 12 peeces, 3 morter peeces, and theyr equipage being
long since shipped in other vessells. They talked of 6000 Scotch
that are upon theyr march too for this expedition, besides some out
of Ireland, where, by the way, the new L$^{t\,b}$ has disbanded a greate
many of y^e troopes, and taken away the power and courts of y^e
presidents. It was y^e opinion of all y^e sea officers I talked ^{with},
that it would be scarce practicable to get y^e fleet out in such time
as is proposed; but I beleeve they will trye w^{hts} possible, the Prince
being to be Gen^{ll}, and ye Duke of Buck: Lt Gen^{ll}; and they say
that either Lockier (who has a regiment of Scots in this country of

[a] In the Duke of York's household. [b] Earl of Essex.

1000 men) or Fitzgerald [is] to be Major Gen[ll], and 4 troopes of
the K[gs] regim[t] to goe wth them.

I was told I should have no part in the affaire; soe I left it,
wishing them good successe. By y[e] death of Capt. Cartwright[a] my
Ca: L[t] has his company, w[ch] made [me] thinke of y[r] kindnesse and
charrecter of L[t] Izod,[b] and have got him to be my Capt. L[t], w[ch],
though it be no greate advantage for y[e] present, will be yet a
remove from Portsm[th], where he was wearie, and a feather in his
cap and somew[th] neerer a company.

I never saw people soe intollerably wearie as they are all of being
at sea, not only land men and volonteeres, but the seamen themselves.

They spoke much of my Lord Peterborows going for y[e] Arch
Duchesse,[c] the Spaniards at length having complyed in the treatie
to the K[gs] sattisfaction.

My Lord Peterborow, while I was there, went away to fight
wth M[r] Felton,[d] of the K[gs] bedchamber, upon a quarrell they had at
sea, in w[ch] my Lord gave him a cuffe o' th' eare; but the Duke sent
after them, and they were prevented.

There was a fine youth wth the King, by the name of Don Carlos,e
who the King ownes for his sonne by my Lady Greene, who has
bine bred in Flanders. They say he has a great deal of witt and is
finely bred. I have not heard from y[r] L[p] a greate while. I think
I told you, in my last, my pritty girle died suddenly in her inne.

<hr/>

[a] Sir Philip Carteret, son of Sir George Carteret. He married Jemima, daughter
of the Earl of Sandwich, and was killed with his father-in-law at Southwold Bay.

[b] Lyttelton was not so pleased to find out afterwards that Izod had served under
Cromwell.

[c] Claudia Felicita, daughter of Frederic Charles, Archduke of Tyrol-Innsbruck,
one of the princesses for whom negotiations were entered into for marriage with
the Duke of York. Another was Eleanor Magdalen, daughter of Philip William,
Elector of Neuberg. Both these princesses were married in succession to the
Emperor Leopold, in 1673 and 1676.

[d] Henry Felton.

[e] Charles Fitz-Charles, natural son of Charles II. by Catharine Peg, wife of Sir
Edward Green, Bart. He was created Earl of Plymouth; married Bridget Osborne,
daughter of Lord Danby; and died at Tangier in 1679.

as my wife was coming to mee, of a convulsion. My wife is very bigg and hastening to London to lye in; but I must not stirr hence till the fleet comes in for good and all.

My humblest services to all of ye good company. Old Lady Berksh^r dead.^a

Y^r L^ps most humble servant,

C. LYTTELTON.

My sister Lyttelton has bine very ill and is not yet, I feare, out of danger; and my poore Harry not well recovered yet. I should be glad to heare better news of y^r L^ps.

I found they are not well sattisfied wth ye P. of Aurange, because he does not shew himself more complizant to our demands.

THE SAME.

MY Dr LORD,   [November, 1672.]

I writt to you a little before I came from my fort, and twice since. I have bine from thence 8 or 9 weekes, but I have never had any letter from y^r L^p since, though I have heard you are well by others.

I have orders to quitt my fort and to march to Rochester, where I shall have, and in that countrey, all the Dukes regiment. The King allows mee, as has bine to ye former commanders there, 10^li a weeke for a table. At present, till I releeve him, Sr Jonathan Atkins is there. The Kings whole regim^t comes up to towne. Y^e Princes Dragons are gone into Northamp^t and Warwicksh^r; Duke

---

^a Elizabeth, daughter of William Cecil, Earl of Exeter, and widow of Thomas Howard, first Earl of Berkshire.

of Bukinghams are from Branford to Portsm^th. Y^e Scots are marcht to Winchester and those parts; Irish, commanded by my Ld Pore^a in Essex; FitzGerrauds in Suffolk; Sr Walter Vane's^b in ye North. There are 8 companies of the Duke of Monm^ths regiment in France reduced, and wee are sending 9 companies out of ye regim^ts heere to be joyned to ye Dukes regiment in France, and 150 horse out of ye Guards, wch Blanfort^c is to command. The news this morning was that ye Germans are passd the Rhyne by force, and that there has bine a greate many of ye best quality lost on both sides; that Liege has declared and rendred to ye Imperiallists, and that it's expected Collogue should doe soo too. The Prince of Aurange marcht to joine wth the Germans; and ye Spaniard send them all the force they can too. It's thought wee shall breake wth the Span. who joyne wth ye Duch and are sending a squadron of ships into ye W. Indies, of wch wee are dispatching a ketch to give advice to our settlements there. There is a pleasant report that the French King is designing to unite all his Xtian subjects in one profession of religion, and has, in order to it, sent to all ye Prottestant ministers he intends to abolish the worship of images, the doctrine of purgatory, that ye divine worship shall be all in the vulgar tongue, and ye Sacrament of the Eucharist administred in both kinds; that there are 32 b^ps of ye French Church wch have consented to this alteration, and, if the Pope doe not agree to it, that they will choose a patriarch to preside in that Church. This is written from the Professor of Ledein to a French minister heere who brought the letter to Sr Joseph Williamson, wch he told him: "Je le croy comme une article de ma foy." But there is none of this in any other letters from France, so it's understood but a raillery.

^a Lord Le Poer. See above, p. 76.
^b At this time Sir Walter Vane commanded the famous Holland regiment, now the 3rd Buffs. At the end of 1673 he was appointed to command the newly raised regiment, now the 6th Foot.
^c See above, p. 83.

The King makes ye banquiers beleeve that heele keepe his word wth them, and that ye checquer shall be open at X^tmasse; wch I pray God he be able to doe.

I had lately an offer to be Lt Governor of Portsmth, but wth a condition to quit my regim^t, wch therefore I desired to be excused in; and, since, I have heard this was a devise to grattifie my Ld Molgraves^a adventures to sea by giving him ye regim^t. Since, they have thought on George Leg to be Governor of Portsmth, and he will have it.^b

The King saw the Scots regim^t exercise the French way, and it pleases soe well that ye King says he likes it far better then ours, wch the Prince, Coll. Russell, and all the English officers allmost doe not, and yet I know not if wee shall not be ordred to change. I am one of ye opinion it will be for ye worse.

I met y^r brother two or 3 days since, and he told mee y^r L^p will be heere at spring, wch I shall be very glad of; but I doubt if your wives will permitt you. I writt to y^r L^p to give mee a doe, and I told you I had sent y^r brother 4^{li} of good chocolate and 6 rollittos of excellent tobacco. I heare you take both. My Ld Sandwich^c has given mee a very fine saphire ring that I told you was found in his fathers pocket. He told mee heed right to you and send mee the letter; but hee has not yet. I phancy the Dukes match wth ye Archduchesse is a little dulld, my thinkes. They speake not of it soe briskly; and I heare nothing of late of my Ld Peterboroughs going.

---

^a John Sheffield, third Earl of Mulgrave, afterwards Duke of Buckinghamshire. He showed same qualities as a naval officer; and was present at Southwold Bay on board Lord Ossory's ship, the "Victory." His solicitations for a command were long disregarded by the Duke of York, who preferred old sailors to young courtiers as his captains; but he at last had the "Royal Catharine" given to him.—See his *Memoirs.*

^b He was appointed soon after, but not immediately.

^c Edward Montagu, second Earl of Sandwich.

My wife is brought to bed of a girle 3 days since, had ill labour, and is very ill since.

Sure I told you how my Ld Fanshaw [a] was disapointed of his desire to goe to Constantinople, having long pretended to it, and, as I heare he says, upon some promisse he sh^d have it when Sr Dan. Hervey should be recalled; and I suppose you have heard too that Sr Dan. is dead.[b] My Lord Winchelsea pretended to it againe too; but both failed, for Sr John Finch ye Attorney's b^r has it; and now my Ld Winchelsea w^d faine goe to Jamaica, but I doubt not but ye King likes soe well of Sr T. Ly[nch] that he will not thinke yet of sending another.

I am,

My Lord,

Your most faithfull and humble servant,

C. L.

I had allmost forgot to tell y^r Lordsh^p that I rec^d a letter from y^r lawyer and 2 writings to seale, and I think there will be more ab^t Hatton Garden; wch I have done.

They expect any day to heare the French and German armyes are ingaged, and I think there came some news of them to y^t purposse to night, wch being not told I suspect is none of ye best.

The King had a good deale of ye French money lately, of wch the Treasurer my Ld Clifford wholly disposes, as indeed of all, for he makes the lists w^{ht} mony shall be payd every Saturday himself.

---

[a] Thomas, second Viscount Fanshawe.

[b] Sir Daniel was not dead, and served again at Constantinople.

CHARLES HATTON.

My L^d, No. 19, [16]72.

*   *   *   *

Wee have lately had a very great removall of an eminent person, ye Ld Kceper.^a   Last Saterday night, about eight of ye clocke, Mr Secretary Coventry went to Essex House wth a warrant for ye seales. My Ld Keeper was very much surprised at it, and offered to deliver ye seales wth ye purse.   Mr Secretary said he had noe order but for ye seales, but would know ye King's further pleasure concerning ye purse; and, after he had delivered ye seales to his Mat^y, he returned againe to ye late Ld Keeper and told him His Ma^{ty} wou'd speake wth him ye next morning at Whitehall, by eight of ye clocke, and y^t he must bring then ye purse wth him; wch he did.   And ye King told him y^t, in consideration of his great indisposition of body, he had thought fit to free him from y^t troublesome imployment; but, in consideration of his faithfull service, he would settle upon him a pension of 2000^{ll} per annum, wch shoud be well payd him; and, presently after, His Ma^{ty} said to my Ld Shaftsbury: " My Ld Chancellor, I deliver you ye seales," who presently came and seated himself in ye chappell, next ye Arehb^p of Canterbury, and ye next morning went to Westminster Hall, attended by all ye great officers at Whitehall, and wase ther sworne by ye Duke of Lauderdale and Ormond.   All personns were very much supprized at ye suddainness of this great alteration, ye resolution therof, it is said, having only been taken that very afternoon, before Mr Secretary went for ye seales.

Alderman Backwall^b hath been sued by severall of his creditors, and judgments granted against him.   He moved ye late Ld Keeper, upon pretence y^t he had lent all ye mony to ye King, whose

^a Sir Orlando Bridgman.   The immediate cause of his removal was, according to Burnet (*Hist. of Own Time*, i. 307), his refusal to affix the great seal to the Declaration of Indulgence.

^b Edward Bakewell, ruined by the shutting up of the Exchequer.

Exchequer wase now shut up, to grant him an injunction to stop ye proceeding of all his creditors, and for denying this it is generally reported ye scales were taken away.   But this is but guess, and y^t by ye most ignorant.

Here is a talke of severall other new officers, of wch I gave you an account yesterday by ye way of France.   I shall not now further trouble you.

I am,

Y^r truly affect Brother
and humble servant,
C. HATTON.

This morning dyed ye B^p of Chester;^{a} and it is reported y^t ye Ld Hallifax maryed Mr Will. Peirepoint daughter.^{b} Mine and my wife's duty and service where due.   Sr John Duncomb is made Chancellor of ye Exchequer.

SIR CHARLES LYTTELTON.

MY LORD,   No. 21, 16[72].

*   *   *   *   *

On Sunday last the King sent for ye Keeper and received the seale from him, and gave it to my Ld Shaftsbury, as Chancellor, who came imediately wth it out of ye King's closset, and went and put on his gowne, as formerly (sic) and readily as could be.

Sr John Duncomb was, at ye same time, saluted Chancellor of ye Checquer.

The Treasury yet continues to be managed by ye old commission, but it's thought my Lord Arlington or Lord Clifford will soone be

----

^{a} Dr. John Wilkins.

^{b} Gertrude, daughter of William Pierrepont of Thoresby, second wife of George Savile, Lord Halifax.

decl..red Treasurer. Most think my Ld Clifford, who will then be Controller. I doe not heare sayd, I know, but by common heare say, why Sr James left his master, wch is for being to greedy a^{bt} takeing fees, and, having soe much of his own affaires in hand, he could not attend his master's. My Ld Hallifax is suddenly to marry Mrs Gatty Pierpoint. Sr Will. Coventry has left ye towne and is gone to live in Oxfordshire.

No news considerable, since my last, of ye greate armyes abroad; but I believe the French is mightily streightned for provisions. Dick Lane has bine a greate while very ill wth a giddinesse in his head, but he is now somew^{ht} better.

THE SAME.

MY LORD,   London, Jan. 6th, 1672[3].

I was at Rochester when I received y^r Ldps. of Jan. 1st, in an enclozed from Sr William Scrugs, wth whom y^r b^r was at his house in Essex, wch brought mee the dire account of y^r Lps. most lamented losses;^{a} and, because his letter (for y^r brother was in y^t sorrow and trouble he could not write himself) did seeme to require my advice and service to him on this ocasion, I imediately came away and was heer that night, and this morning I waited on y^r b^r to my Ld Arlington, and after, to the King; and all this day allmost wee have spent together in takeing order about mourning and other matters necessary for the bringing my Ladyes to towne and theyr interrment,^{b} wch I hope will be to y^r L^{ps} likeing. I w^d have waited on him, truly, to Portsmth, but that there is an inevitable necessity

^{a} The death of his mother·and wife, caused by a powder explosion at Cornet Castle, Guernsey, 30-29 Dec. 1672.

^{b} They were buried in Westminster Abbey, 11 Jan. 167$\frac{2}{3}$.—Chester, *Westminster Abbey Registers*, 1876.

incumbent on mee to hasten back to Rochester, it happening soe, that there is not one captain upon y^e place, and that I have at this time more then an ordinary observation how I behave myself, wch it will be fitter another time to entertaine you w^th; for at present indeed I ought only to tell you how much all the world doth aecompany y^r L^p in the tenderest resentments you have in ye ocasions of y^r sorrow, and yet wth all doe congrattulate and allay those troubles by the strange, and allmost miraculous, deliverance of y^r L^ps own person, y^r children and sisters, wch I hope y^r L^p will take that comfort in as not to neglect ye care of them by abandoning y^r self to melancholy and greife, w^ch, you know, too much of will hurt ye living and is of no use to the dead.   But I need not preach to one soe prudent and constant as you are, and therefore I will adde no more then that I wish, wth my soule, I were at liberty to come to you or to doe any thing in ye world to divert and serve you, or that your L^p could come to mee to Rochester, where I will doe my uttmost to contribute to both, being wth extremest passion,

My Lord,

Y^r most faithfull servant,

C. LYTTELTON.

THE SAME.

From Rye Roade, abord of ye Prince, Admirall of ye Blew, commanded by S^r Ed. Spragge, May 20th, 1673.

MY DEEREST LORD,

I had soe little warning; it made mee soe buisy before I came away, that truly I had not any time to spare ; and that, I hope, will be my apollogie I did not write to y^r Lordp. before I came away.

I will now give y^r L^p an account of w^ht has past in ye fleet since I came to it, as short and materially as I can.   The next day after wee weighed from the buoy of ye Nore, being at anchor, wee saw ye Duch fleete; upon wch wee weighed and set sayle towards them, the wind being directly in our way, and came to an anchor at ye Shooe, the lesser and fire ships lying between us and ye enemy. The Duch were in sight but 28 sayle, but had another squadron at ye Long Sand of ^{aþt} 40 more. They had among them 9 greate flye boates, deepe laden, wch wee suppose they designed to have sunke in the narrowes to have hindred our coming out. Wee were 35 sayle of men of warr, and most capitall ships; but, because of the narrownes of ye place, had they attacqued us, the wind being soe faire for them, and bravely brought on theyr fireships, they had taken us at greate disadvantage or forced us to retreate; wch I think some councelled at first, but our A^d ye Prince, who never knew w^{ht} it was to goe back, resolved on ye more generous councell. In ye evening there was a very thick fogg, in wch the Duch stole away towards the rest of theyr fleet. Our lesser ships stood after them, and all the fleet followed, the wind still agst us, but it pleased God wee got all safe through ye sands, though severall ships were aground ; but it was never attempted before to turn it out of ye river wth the wind soe contrary for ye greate ships. When wee were got ab^t ye Long Sandhead, the wind was faire to bring us hither, whither wee came wthout seeing any more of ye enemy, who were retired to theyr old holes wthin ye Weelings.

The next day wee had ye Royall Charles, wch is now Admi[ral], and 7 or 8 more very considerable ships came up to us from Portsmth, and ab^t three daye since the French fleet, wch consist of 27 men of warr from 100 to 50 gunnes and seven fireships. The next day His M^{atie} and ye Duke came to us; yesternight they returned. My Lord Ossory came wth the King, and, I beleeve, wth no design to stay, for he has nothing wth him; but finding, by reason of Capt. Norberryes [a] stay soe long wth ye Straits fleet, that the ship wch is ye St. Michell and ye Rear Admiralls flag, wch he was to have com-

---

[a] Afterwards Admiral Sir John Narborough?

manded, undisposed, he bravely offred himself; and his offer was accepted, I beleeve, to ye Kings very good likeing, as I am sure it is to all the fleete's.

Soe soone as the wind favours us, wee shall goe upon ye Duch coost, and, if wee cannot ingage them in open sea, shall certainly attempt them ^wth our smaller and fire ships w^thin theyr sands. If wee succeed either way happily, wee shall land upon them; and there is ten thousand more land forces, besides these now wth us (wch are 5,000 English), that are getting in a readinesse to joyu to us, and wch will be half or rather twice as many more; his R^ll Highnesse at ye head of us. The Duke of Buck. is Lt Generall, but I doe not certainly know who is Ma. Gen. I heare FitzGerrard and Sr Tho. Morgan^a both named. It was offred to Coll. Russell, but he would accept of nothing under ye Duke of Buck.

To day Prince Rupt sent a complim^t to Monsieur d'Estree, ye Freneh Ad., that he intended to morrow to give him a visit, but that he expected, when he came abord, he should put up his flagg. The return was that he was very sorry he could not receive the honor of his High^sse favour upon those termes, for y^t he w^d not put up his flagg. Soe, I beleeve, the Prince has sent to acquaint the King, and in ye meane time will suspend his visit. The Prince has a com^n as well, and they say more absolute, from ye King of France, to command M^r D'Estree, then that of ye King to command the English fleete.

My Lord, I have told you all I can say of our affaires heere, wch it may be youle heare from better hands, and therefore will bee tired wth soe much of them from mee; but I know not when or ever I shall have ocasion to entertaine you again. W^ht ever becomes of mee, as long as I live, I am and will be eturnally

                                                                    Y^rs.

---

^a Best remembered by his not altogether unsuspicious transactions in the West Indies.

The same.

My deerest Lord,   London, 24 June, 1673.

*   *   *   *   *

By all the letters that are yet come from Holland it cannot yet be certainly resolved whether De Ruyter were killed, wch his ship going soe suddenly out of ye battle as it did gave them all the reason imaginable to suspect.

Sr Harry Jones was killed by ^a ye Duke of Monmouth, who has his regim^t there; and my b^r Nando is his Lt Coll., and his troope of horse given him by the King heere, and hee is allso of ye Dukes bedchamber, soe that he is fairely now provided for. My Ld Wil-lowby ^b is dead at the Barbadoes, and Sr Jonathan Adkins, I beleeve, a pretender to y^t governement, and, as he told mee, was formerly promised it. If it had happened at a time when my regim^t heere w^d have bine a better present to some greate man then now it is, I thinke I shd. have bine tempted to have exchanged it; yet I know not how it w^d sort wth others likeing whom I am to consider.

The laying down of ye T^{rs} staffe does not yet shew any other change but that Sr Tho: Osborn has taken it up, and seemes to be soe too wth full as good likeing (and I beleeve it in earnest) of his Majestie; and, if Mr Bronkier be a good judge, he says that the King is not soe kind to any man now as he is to him. My Ld Clifford is gone into ye countrey and intends a very private life.^c

My Ld Ormond is lately brought into ye cabinet againe. My Ld Arlington keepes his own very well, I assure you. Ile give you one by measure of it. The K^g lately, by ye greate importunity of my

^a *i. e.* by the side of.

^b William, sixth Lord Willoughby, of Parham. Sir J. Atkyns succeeded him.

^c See Evelyn's interesting account of Clifford's retirement and death.—*Diary*, 25 July, 18 Aug. 1673.

L^{ds} Albemarle, Bath,^a and, I imagine too, Ld Clifford, got the King
to order Sr Tho. Modifords release out of ye Tower; wch he will not
suffer to passe, nor does it.

My Lord, I have tired y^r L^p, and am soe myself, and have much
to doe; yet I cannot leave till I have told you I have seene y^r pritty
babies and am heartily glad they are heere, and soe I shall be to
meet your L^p heere at winter, that you may have the greater com-
fort of them and the rest of y^r L^{ps} friends and servants, of wch you
have a greate many that wish you as I doe, and you deserve abun-
dance of prosperity and happinesse.

CHARLES HATTON.

My L^d,   June 26, [1673].

     *   *   *   *   *

Sr Thomas Osborn is created Ld Viscount Osborne, of Dunblaine
in Scotland, and wase this day sworne in ye Exchequer chamber
Ld Treasurer of England.   I know you will be desirous ye most
expeditious way to be informed thereof, y^t you may congratulate
him and acknowledge his late favours to you; for he hath expressed
himself very obligingly to you in ye late businesse.   It is s^d my L^d
Clifford will retire himself into ye country.   I told you in my last
his R. H. had delivered up to his Ma^{ty} all his commissions;^b and,
at ye same time, acquainted you who were nominated commissioners
of ye Admiralty.   Fryday last, Maestricht wase surrendred upon
articles to ye King of France; 5000 foot and 1000 horse marched
out of ye towne, June ye 24th, stilo novo.   Y^e Duke of Monmouth
wth prodigious courage and great conduct possessed himself of a
half moon, after y^t ye French had been twice beaten of wth ye loss

^a John Granville, Earl of Bath; died, 1701.
^b In consequence of the Test Act.

of 1000 men and 100 officers. Sr Henry Jones was killed going
on as a volunteer wth ye Duke, his regiment not being there, wch is
since given to ye Duke of Monmouth, and his troope of horse here
in England to Capt. Ferd[inando] Littleton, who is alsoe made
Lieut. Coll. to ye D. of Monmouth reg. of horse. After ye French
had possessed themselves of ye aforesaid half moone, from their
batteries they made a large breach in ye wall of ye town; where
upon the citizens began to mutiny, and ye Fryday following, y^c
French designing a generall assault, ye burghers forced their
governor to send out, about six m ye morning, to parley, and by
eleven of ye clocke ye capitulation wase signed, and, about 1, y^e
Marquis of Louvoy entred ye town. Y^e garrison marched out y^e
next day wth bag and baggage, drums beating, colours flying, match
lighted, bullet in ye mouth &c., wth peices of canon and two mortar
peices. The French King hath confirmed ye priviledges of ye town,
and it is s^d Monsr D'Estrades will be made governor. Y^e garison
marched towards Breda, and it is s^d ye French King is marched
either towards ye same place or Bois le Duc. Certainly the losse of
soe strong a place, making resistance and yet taken in 11 dayes,
must strike a great consternation in ye Dutch who are very strong
att sea and, it is to be feared, will beate us; for we want seamen,
and are forced to take new raised landmen.[a]

Mr Schomberg[b] came to town last Monday; it is s^d he will settle
here and be made an English peere and one of ye Lieut. Gen. of y^e
army encamped at Blacke heath. Who shall be Gen. is uncertain.
Some say D. Munmouth,[c] but most thinke they will be disbanded;
if not,[c] Sr Walter Vane, it is said, will be Major Gen., but y^t is uncertain, as is ye day of generall rendevous. Ther are at present
but six reg. encamped ; Ld Northamptons, Ld Mulgrave, L^d
Worcester, Ld Vaughan, Ld Carlisle [and] Albemarle. But L^d

[a] This passage, "who are very strong . . . . . . landmen" is in cipher.
[b] Marshal Frederic de Schomberg, afterwards, in 1691, Duke of Schomberg; killed
at the Boyne. See below, p. 111, note [a]
[c] "D. Munmouth" and "disbanded; if not" in cipher.

Ogle's, Ld Peterborough's, and Sr Water Vane's are dayly expected. The match wth ye Dutchess of Insprucke is quite broken of. It is s^d ye Emperour will marry her, and y^t my Ld Peterborough is gone for Cologne to propose a match wth a daughter of ye Duke of Newburke.[a] He proposes this to delay coming to England, thereby to delay takeing sacrament. Y^e Duke has lost his esteem. God grant life to ye King. Our feares are great. We are all divided and in great confusion.[b] My Ld Wilobby is dead in Barbadoes. Who shall succeed him is not known. My Ld Arlington had a shot in ye thigh before Maestrict; it wase only a flesh wound, and he is pretty well, as is Lieut. Tufton. My sisters and neices are very well, and soe [is] my Lady Thanet, who hath lately been indisposed.

I am,

Y^r truly affect Brother

to serve you,

C. HATTON.

THE SAME.

MY L^d,   July 8, [16]73.

*   *   *   *   *

Y^e Duke of Monmouth is coming for England to command us, some say, ye army at Blackheath, though others say ye Prince shall, and y^t ye Duke of Yorke shall be generalissimo. But that is very doubtfull; and ye truth is, it is very uncertaine whither those forces will not be speedily disbanded. Monsr Schombergh is returning backe. Some say he refuses to serve under ye Duke of Buces, who,

[a] See above, p. 96, note c
[b] From "to delay" to "confusion" in cipher.

he saith, hath not been trained up in military affaires, and therefore he will not be in a subordinate command to him.[a]

I have sent you y[e] Articles of War lately published, but how they will be executed I know not. Our parliament men and lawyers doe not care to heare of martiall law; and, without that, I doe not see how an army can be governed. At Blackheath ther hath been severall mutinies. Ye mutineers are sent to y[e] Tower. The souldiers in very considerable numbers dayly run from their colours. Y[e] judges have been consulted and have declared y[t], by y[e] law of y[e] land, neither y[e] mutineers nor y[e] runawayes can loose their lives (and yet they are horriblely scandalised at the name of martiall law); and, if some are not hanged to deter others, you may imagine how y[e] army is like to be kept up.

Wee have had great alterations in our great officers at home, and more are dayly expected. It is said y[e] L[d] Arlington will buy out y[e] L[d] S[t] Albans, and be made L[d] Chamberlaine, and y[t] S[r] Joseph Williamson shall succeed as Secretary of State.[b] Others say S[r] Robert Car, and some speake of Sidney Godolphin, formerly

[a] Burnet (*Own Time*, i. 345), gives Schomberg a high character, but says that, owing to his having been in the French service, he was looked upon with suspicion by the English nation "as one sent over from France to bring our army under a French discipline, and so he was hated by the nation and not much loved by the Court. . . . The Duke of Buckingham hated him, for he hoped to have commanded the army. And as an army is a very unacceptable thing to the English nation, so it came to be the more odious when commanded by a general sent over from France." After the action of the 11th August, Burnet adds (i. 352) that Schomberg, seeing the difficulties of his position increased by the conduct of the French fleet, "made haste to get out of England, to prevent an address to send him away: and he was by that time as weary of the court as the court was of him." Sheffield, Duke of Buckinghamshire, in his *Memoirs* gives us the story of Prince Rupert firing upon Schomberg's ship, the "Greyhound," in which Sheffield himself was sailing, because he had hoisted a regimental flag. According to him also, the Duke of York used his influence in Monmouth's favour against Schomberg.

[b] Williamsom became Principal Secretary of State in September, 1674; and Henry Bennet, Earl of Arlington, succeeded Henry Jermyn, Earl of St. Albans, in the office of Lord Chamberlain of the Household, in the same year.

page to ye King. This will scarce seeme credible to you, I am
confident, considering how well my Ld Arlington at this time stands
in ye Kings favour, and that y^t this shou'd be done at his not only
choice but suit.

Y^r truly affect Brother to serve you,

C. HATTON.

SIR WILLIAM SCROGGS.^{a}

MY LORD,   Weald Hall, July ye 22^d, [16]73.

I am not quite so lazy nor halfe so ill naturd as, when I cannot
come (as I would), not to send. And I choose the rather to write
when I have nether business nor newes, that you may see tis nether
necessity nor the itch of imparting state affaires provokes this, but
a naturall felicity I take of writing to y^r Lordship, with (I confess)
ye addition of rayling at y^r brother for nether comming to Weald-
hall nor letting his wife nor y^r sisters come before he went. I know
ye excuse is important business, wch he never wants; and yet, for
all that, he is but a kind of lawyer y^t seemes farr busier then he is.
There is, my Lrd, in all y^r family such a smoothness of kindness
like a dead calme, not a wrinkle to be seene; but it carryes you no-
whether. I could wish, if it were possible, y^r Lordships example
could change that way in 'em; for I suppose that tyme and y^e
nature of y^t place has wrought off much of that sweetness w^{ch}, as in
wine, leaves it better to ye tast and stomack. And now you talke
of wine, well remembered! the last hogshead's abroach, and without
a sudden supply there is no living for mee at Weald Hall. The
woemen drink in fear allready, and you know all theire passions are
violent. Tis not a small matter will satisfy any ones desire, and

^{a} See above, p. 60, note ^{b}

heere are a greate many to be satisfyed, besides y^r sisters and Mr Hattons lady, famous at 2 in ye morning. My Lrd, by my last I wrott how you might send it, viz. to have it landed at Rainham, wch Arthur knowes, and from thence Ile send for it. Thinke not of any other stores at Guernsey but this, and let as much of it be clarrett, and as strong as you please, and more then ever you imagined.

I lately received a letter from my Lady Colster^a out of France. Her enquiryes are much after y^r Lordship with greate seeming kindness, but I suppose y^t is ye way of France and good breeding, wch is all is meant; and I know y^r Lrdship can be even wth her. Mr Hatton can give you an account how she used mee when she went away; yet I know heele mince ye matter, because it was not very much unlike himselfe. However, I, like an easy English foole, have wrott to her now, and in truth upon ye matter have desired her pardon for ye unkindness she has done mee. Such is the catiffe nature of him that should be a vassall to none but y^r Lrdship.

W. S.

My love to Arthur.

CHARLES HATTON.

My L^d,   [August] 1673.

*   *   *   *   *

I shall tell you what publicke news wee have here, and first what is said of ye late engagement,^{b} w^{ch}, by ye rashness of Sr Edward Spragg, and cowardise of ye French, had like to have proved fatal

---

^{a} Charlotte, daughter of Charles Stanley, Earl of Derby, and wife of Thomas Savage, Lord Colchester, eldest son of Thomas, third Earl Rivers.

^{b} Between Prince Rupert and the Dutch, 11 Aug. 1673.

to ye English.   The French, if they speake truth, must either
excuse their cowardise by their treachery or their treachery by
their cowardise.   You may see by ye enclosed what a faire
story they make for themselves, but I beleeve you will smile at
their policy to forbeare fighting that they might secure ye weather gage against ye next day.   It is said ye French embassador
is displeased.   Y^e narative is published in distinct relations
from each squadron.   But, to give ye more credit to what y^e
French say for themselves, he wou'd have had it inserted in one
intire narrative of ye whole engagement.   Some speake as if y^e
French doe accuse ye Prince, as well as he them ; but it is as impossible to make any Englishman suspect ye Prince his courage, as
to persuade him ye French have any at sea.   Since ye engagement
ye Dutch are higher then ever.   They say they will be content to
allow ye English ye flagge in ye narrow sea.   As for fishing in our
seas, they have as good a right to it as wee, and y^t they know
better to dispose of their money then to give it away.   But ther is
news from Kinsale y^t three of their East India shipps are brought in
thither richly laden, taken by those men of war who retooke S^t
Helena.   It is hoped this may humble ye Dutch.   This last engagement ye French behaved themselves so cowardly y^t, 27 Dutch men
of war going to engage them, they waved them, so y^t ye Dutch, not
fearing any oposition from them, deserted them and fell upon y^e
Prince.   Only Monsr Martell put himself into ye Prince his squadron
and behaved himself very gallantly, to ye shame of ye rest of his
countreymen.[a]

Sr Edward Spragge is much lamented, and would have been
more had he not clashed wth ye Prince.   He wase a very brave
commander, and very unfortunately lost.   An accidentall shot sunke
ye boate he wase in.   His men fastened him to a planke, went to
fetch another boate, and found him, when they returned, halfe

[a] "None of the French ships engaged, except one, who charged their admiral for
his ill conduct: but, instead of reward, he was clapt in the Bastille on his return to
France."—Burnet, *Own Time*, i. 352.

above water, but dead, yet grasping ye planke very hard. It is beleeved ye waves, beating against ye planke, destroyed [him] being a very weighty and full-bodyed man.

I am sure you will be glad Sr Charles Littleton wase upon soe honorable an account sent out of danger. The match wth ye Duke of Modena's sister is broke of, as it is said. Duke Lautherdale is come to town, and in better favour then wase reported. My Ld Treasurer is created Viscount Latimer, and recovered of his late sickness. Sr Robert Paston, Ld Viscount Yarmouth, his son maryed ye Lady Chanon's daughter,[a] w^ch, together wth my Ld Treasurer's interest, who is his great friend, advanced him to this dignity. I am,

Y^r truly affect Brother to serve you,

C. Hatton.

Sir William Scroggs.

Sept^br ye 12th, [1673.]

My Lord,

The worst name I can call you by; for when you were a comoner and an honest man you had plaine thoughts, and beleeved that promisses ought to be performed, and that he y^t sed: " Ile send you a hogshead " had but meanly kept his word in sending but two.

---

[a] William Paston, son of Robert, Viscount, afterwards Earl, of Yarmouth, married Charlotte Jemima Maria, natural daughter of Charles II. and Elizabeth Killigrew, wife of Francis Boyle, Viscount Shannon. He succeeded to the title.

But now you, like them y^t pretend so much to religion y^t they are above ordinances, thinke it dishonourable to y^r title to keepe y^r word, and y^t by y^r dignity you must falsifie, lest you become like that low sort of people y^t keepe faith. S^r, I am much wrongd by you in preventing mee from buying of wine at 6^l a hogshead y^t must now cost mee 10, depending very foolishly on one y^t I ought to have knowne before. I know now y^{tt} pyrates and ye daingers of seas must be y^r excuse; but why wine could not as safely come as cidyer I understand not, unless there be articles for apples but not for grapes, or y^t ye vigour of one would make it safe, but ye cowardize of wine would turne it into vinegar.

My Lrd, pray know y^t I am (though not ye best performer) yet ye greatest exacter of promises y^t will never be answered by reason, but the thing itselfe; and thinke y^t reasonable to be madè into a law y^t w^{t}soever is promisd ought to be performed, whether it can or no; for though it were sometymes impossible, yet y^t were better to condemne then suffer the excuses y^t will ever be made by [y^r] Lrdship.

I can have no better reason for establishing impossibilityes by law then my Lord Hatton, who otherwise will make all things impossible. I could willingly raile on, but can write no more then

W. S.

If hogsheads were as cheape as warrants I had received them.

To my Lady my reall service; to Saunterer, my love, like hers. In greate hast to drinke y^r L^{r}sp's health.[a]

---

[a] Scroggs must have been drinking his Lordship's health pretty freely before he began the letter, to judge from the drunken appearance of the handwriting.

THE SAME.

My Lord,   [1673]

You say very true, wine is answerd with nothing but wine. If
anything or anybody else could have donne it otherwise, it must
have bin y^r Lrdship, in whom there is much art, but in wine is
truth. Y^r present was spoild before y^r brother receivd it. We
broke ope ye coffin at his howse, wherein we found only the furniture of a coffine, corruption. Those lympitts^a y^t wer never seene
in England lack wine to make 'em tast; and I will take it y^t y^r
Lrdship keeps y^r word, that you send w^t was yet never seene in
England, when you send ye next hoggsheads. My Lrd, you must
not take it ill if I write of nothing but wine, for there is nothing I
want more, nor of wch I can better write, or more willingly—with
this difference only, that wine wrott for has not halfe y^t elegancy
as wine thankt for. I am glad to hear y^r Lrdship is like to come
over, because then you will bring wine infallibly; for you know you
must shew y^r face and see Weald Hall. In short, I rely upon you
in that matter and let Christmas take its fortune accordingly.
Having vented my passion of love to wine, my next good subject is
of railing ag't woemen, and in ye first place at y^r sisters, who, by
ye conduct of y^r brother and his lady, haunt my chamber oftener
then a pauper and with much greater trouble, for they only [do]
not give, but these plunder what others give. I want y^r company
to redress y^t too. Prethee, my deare Lrd, make hast, ...
and y^{ts} an answer to the complement you gave him that is to
much a friend to neede one, because I am all love and all yrs.

W. S.

---

^{a} Ormiers. See above, p. 81, note ^{b}.

CHARLES HATTON.

My L^d,   October 28, [16]73.

*   *   *   *   *

Monday last, ye Parliament met, and, as soone as ye doore of ye House of Commons wase open, a kinsman of ours, John Aylif^a (as is reported), rushed in and went up to ye Speaker's chaire; and ye woeman wch kept ye doore, seeing him fling something under it, imagining it had been a fire ball, cryed out: " Treason! treason!" whereupon ye doore keepers came and apprehended him wth a sabot having a great bracelet of beades passed through ye heel wth a crucifix at ye end of it, and on ye left side of ye heel of ye sabot ye King of England's armes blazoned and "utrum" writ under, and on ye right side ye King of France his armes and "horum" under written.   They kept our kinsman prisoner, till some of ye members came who knew him; and they told ye doore keepers he wase distracted, and bid them let him goe.   You cannot imagine how much this sabot is talked on, and what infinite number of people goe to see it.   I am confident it may be sold for 50^{li} to be shewn as a sight, peni apiece for every one who comes to see it; and should anyone upon those termes purchase it, they would quickly double their mony.

*   "   *   *   *

Y^r truly affectionat Brother,

C. HATTON.

<hr>

^a John Ayloffe, a lawyer, connected, not only with the Hattons, as appears by this letter, but also with the Hydes, and, through them, with James, Duke of York. He was concerned in the Rye House plot; but his name will always be remembered in connection with Monmouth's rebellion, as told in the pages of Macaulay.   His answer to James, just before his execution, will outlive his name : " You had better be frank with me, Mr. Ayloffe," said the King, " you know that it is in my power to pardon you."   " It may be in your power; but it is not in your nature," was the reply.

THE SAME.

My L^d   November 6, [16]73.

*   *   *   *

Yesterday, ye 5th of Nov. was observed with an incredible number
of bonfires. Y^e Pope and his cardinalls were, in Cheapeside and
other places, hung up and burnt in their effigies. One told me he
counted 200 bonfires between Temple Barr and Algate. The
Dutchess of Modena^a setts out of Paris to morrow. All his R. H.
his equipage lyes ready at Dover to receive her.

My sisters and neices are very well and give you their service, as
doth

Y^r truly affect Brother to serve you,

C. HATTON.

THE SAME.

[About A.D. 1675.]

*   *   *   *   *

Last Saterday morning a duel was fought at Marybone by ye L^d
Ossory and Coll. Mecarty,^b ag^t Bucly and my Ld Gerard's son.^c M^r
Gerard wase slightly hurt in ye belly, but struck Mecarty's sword
out of his hand, [and,] having disarmed him, required my Ld Ossory
to surrender his sword, who wase fighting wth Buckly and had
slightly wounded him in ye hand; and my Ld Ossory, after a short

---

^a Mary of Modena arrived in England at the beginning of December, having been
delayed at Paris by a slight illness.

^b Justin Macarty, distinguished as a Jacobite general in the war in Ireland, and
created Viscount Mountcashel by James II., in 1689. He was a son of Donogh,
Earl of Clancarty.

^c Charles, afterwards second Earl of Macclesfield.

resistance ag^t them both, wase overpowered and did deliver up his sword. The occasion of ye duel wase this: Buckly ran ag^t my Ld Ossory as he wase coming into ye bedchamber. My Ld Ossory asked him what he meant; he replyed: " My L^d, I must not chaleng you; pray doe you chalenge me?" Therupon my L^d sent him a chalenge by Mecarty. A warrant is out ag^t Buckly.

I am

Y^r truly affectt Brother to serve you,

C. HATTON.

THE SAME.

Aug. 13, [16]75.

*   *   *   *   *

Here hath been, every day since Sunday last, great disorders committed in ye city and suburbs by ye weavers; who first, in great numbers, fell upon ye French weavers, pulled down some of their houses, burnt their loomes; but, afterwards, those weavers who had loomes without engines broke open ye houses of all those weavers who had loomes wth engines, and burnt their loomes, pretending y^t one man wth an engine loome can doe more worke in one day then 10 men wth loomes without engines, and y^t therfore ther wase thousands of weavers y^t, for w^t of employment, were ready to starve, and y^t they had rather venter hanging then starving. Y^e Ld Mayor^a and Sr John Robison^b have been reproved at ye Councell board for being neglectfull in supressing thes insurrections, by wch 100 families, in and about London, have been ruined, and some men lost their lives.

*   *   *   *

Y^r truly affectionat Brother and servant,

C. HATTON.

[a] Sir Robert Viner, Bart.

[b] Sir John Robinson, Bart., formerly Lord Mayor, now an alderman.

The same.

Sep. 2, 1675.

*　　　*　　　*　　　*　　　*

Here hath been issued out a commission of oyer and terminer for y[e] tryall of y[e] weavers; and y[e] judges were to have sat yesterday, but most of them excused themselves for appearing, and y[e] court is adjourned for a fortnight. They are at Court much offended at most of y[e] judges for their backwardnesse therein.

Last Saterday, at y[e] Dukes play-house ther happened a quarrel between M[r] Scroope, who wase in drinke, and S[r] Tho: Armsstronge.[a] M[r] Scroope gave S[r] Tho. very ill language and, at last, drew upon him; wherupon S[r] Tho. drew, and y[e] first passe ran M[r] Scroope through y[e] heart, who fell down dead upon y[e] place without speaking a word. S[r] Tho. wase slightly hurt in y[e] arme, and he immediately went to Harris and told him, he being an indifferent person and one who had seen y[e] high provocation he had, he thought him y[e] fittest person to give an account thereof to y[e] King; and therefor he must immediatly take horse and goe to Windsor, w[ch] he did; and all personns who were at y[e] play say S[r] Tho. had as high provocation as possibly cou'd, and at last wase forced to draw in his owne defence. Y[e] crowner's inquest have found it only man slaughter, and S[r] Thomas hath given in bayle.

*　　　*　　　*　　　*　　　*

Y[r] truly affectionat Brother to serve you,

C. Hatton.

[a] Colonel Sir Thomas Armstrong, concerned in the Rye House plot. He fled to Holland; but was given up by the magistrates of Leyden, brought back to England, and executed in 1684. He was one of the Duke of Monmouth's party. Reresby calls him the debaucher of the Duke.

THE SAME.

MY L^d,   Apr. 25, [16]76.

*   *   *   *   *

Last fryday night, ye King told Sr John Duncomb y^t he must
resigne his place. He desired to know for what crime. Y^e King
told him y^t he did beleeve him to be a very honest gentleman, but
y^t he did obstruct his affaires by interfaring wth ye Treasurer, and
y^t he wou'd not have his Treasurer be uneasy. Sr John Ernly
is Chancelour of ye Exchequer, and some of my Ld Treasurer's
creatures, as Sr Francis Lawly and Sr Richard Wiseman, put for S^r
John Ernley['s] place, as commissioner of ye Navy. But my L^d
Treasurer told them y^t it wase by ye Duke of Yorke's meanes y^t
Duncomb wase put out, and that therfore he wase obliged not to
interpose wth ye Duke for any person to succeede S^r Jⁿ Ernley, and
y^t ye Duke hath put in Narbrough,^a a person very deserving and
qualifyed for y^t place. Idle people in ye coffe houses say S^r Jⁿ
Ernley gave money; others say. y^t he pay'd none do[w]ne, but
engages to make a match wth one of my L^d['s] daughters wth y^e
Duke of Somerset,^b and to contribute 5000^{ll} towards her portion.

Now all ye talke is who shall fall next; whither Secretary
Coventry, or ye Ld Arlington, or Sr Rob. Car,^c or ye Attorney
Generall,^d for they say all thes are under condemnation, but y^t they
will not be put out all at once; and those two who put out Sr John
Duncombe are not agreed who shall be first outed.

The Dutchesse of Portsmouth is not well; her sicknesse, it is
said, is encreased by discontent at somebody's visiting ye Dutchesse
Mazarine ^e at my Lady Harvey's house.

Y^r Lo^{pps} truly affect Brother and humble servant,

C. HATTON.

^a Admiral Sir John Narborough.
^b Francis Seymour, fifth Duke of Somerset. He was murdered at Genoa in 1678.
^c Chancellor of the Duchy of Lancaster.
^d Sir William Jones; succeeded, in 1679, by Sir Cresswell Levinz.
^e Hortense Mancini, niece of the Cardinal. She died in 1699, and, according to
Evelyn, "is reported to have hasten'd her death by intemperate drinking strong
spirits." See Lord Macaulay's description of her in chapter iv. of his *History*.

THE SAME.

May 11, [16]76.

*　　　*　　　*　　　*　　　*

Last Monday S^r Jⁿ Ernley wase sworne Chancelor of ye Excheq^r. When he tooke his oath he wase accompanyed wth Duke Lautherdale, Ld High Chamberlaine,^a Ld Marshall,^b Ld Maynard,^c Ld Arundel of Trerise.^d Not one of ye other party appeared wth him. My Ld Treasurer wase in ye court. My Ld Chancelor's^e speech wase not soe florid as it is thought it wou'd have been if his designe had succeeded of bringing in Sr Edward Deering.^f

My Ld Shaftsbury hath been much disapointed this terme;^g for my Ld Digbyes^h counsell pleaded, in arrest of judgment, y^t my Ld Shaftsbury had not in his declaration truly recited ye statute of scandalum magnatum, for ye words of ye statute are to this effect " Who ever shall say or devise any scandalous words against ye Ld Chancelor, Ld Treasurer . . . . . . , or any other great officer or peers of ye realme ; " and St Scroggs said y^t in ye declaration " contrafacere " wase put to signify " devise," wch could not have any such signification. This exception to ye judges seemed soe materiall y^t they tooke two dayes time before they wou'd give their opinion whither they wou'd grant an arrest of judgment

^a Robert Bertie, Earl of Lindsey.
^b Henry, Lord Howard, afterwards Duke of Norfolk, Earl Marshal.
^c William, second Lord Maynard.
^d Richard, 1st Lord Arundel of Trerice.
^e Heneage Finch, Earl of Nottingham.
^f Afterwards a commissioner of the Treasury.
^g A vacancy had occurred, in 1675, in the representation of Dorsetshire by the death of Colonel Strangways. Lord Digby came forward as a candidate, and was at first supported by Shaftesbury. The latter, however, changed his mind and put forward a Mr. Moore in opposition. This irritated Lord Digby so much that, when he next met Shaftesbury, he accused him in violent language of sedition, and threatened to have his head next parliament. Shaftesbury brought an action, and recovered £1,000.---Christie, *Life of Shaftesbury*, ii. 214.
^h John, Lord Digby, who succeeded, at this time, as third Earl of Bristol.

therupon or not; and then, upon debate, they seemed not to allow it as a materiall objection; and were ready to have passed judgment when S[t] Stroud[a] started a new objection y[t] y[e] words, " or any other," were left out in y[e] declaration, it not being therein said, as it ought to have been, " sive de aliis; " and therby y[e] very sense of y[e] statute wase altered. Upon this, y[e] judges have taken time to consider till y[e] second Saterday in y[e] next terme; and it is verily beleeved y[t] they will grant an arrest of judgment upon it, w[ch] will not only be very displeasing to my L[d] Shaftsbury but to severall other L[ds], who will find it more difficult to recover great fines upon actions of scandalum magnatum then they thought, and may per-happs retract y[e] suits they have begun therupon, w[ch] are very numerous. Y[e] Marq[s] of Dorchester[b] sues a man for saying, to one y[t] s[d] y[e] Marq[s] wase a great physitian, y[t] all men of y[e] Marques his yeares were either fooles or physitians. And my L[d] Mohun[c] hath an action against one for saying y[t] he wase good for nothing but to sit in ladyes chambers and thred their needles; and my L[d] Peters[d] hath brought a double action against one, y[e] first for saying he wase a pimpeing L[d] and no gentleman, y[e] other for saying, if he wou'd leave out y[e] latter words, he would prove y[e] former. My L[d] Townsend[e] hath another action. Thes severall actions hath occa-sioned several contrivances how to evade y[e] penalty of y[e] Act; and one is to plead that ther is no such Act, for, it is said, y[e] original Act is noe where to be found. S[r] Rob. Cotton, in y[e] account he hath given of what statutes were in y[e] Tower, sayes particularly, of that statute, y[t] it is not ther.

Y[r] truly affect Brother to serve you,

C. HATTON.

[a] George Strode, Serjeant-at-Law.

[b] Henry Pierrepont, second Earl of Kingston, created Marquess of Dorchester.

[c] Charles, fourth Lord Mohun, father of the notorious duellist, who himself was not undistinguished in the same way.

[d] William, fourth Lord Petre.

[e] Horatio, Lord, afterwards Viscount, Townsend.

WILLIAM LONGUEVILLE.[a]

Whitson eve, [1676].

I now grow, my Lord, strangely concernd to heare how your lady goes on with her burthen. This continued indisposition, with ye same accident of your coach overthrowne, makes mee entertaine just cause of feare. Pray spare us your letters so soone as your Lo^p has any reason to say there is an amendment. A line or two w^d bee of comfortable importance from Easton.

One Ponder, a stationer in Chancery Lane, is taken into custody about an offensive discourse hee was printing for Naked Truth, and hee is like to name Mr A. Marvell as ye author.[b]

Y^e Councill board hath been much entertaind of late about a libell called y^c Chronicle, which from y^c excise men of Herefordshire and Gloucestershire was fix't on Mr. Herbert Perrot, of ye Middle Temple; by him layd on one Mr. Radford; by Radford cast upon Mr. Bolton, an Irish student of ye Inner Temple; from Bolton againe it was remov'd to one Mr. Clarke; which Clarke also quoted Basset's man, a bookseller in Fleet-streete; and ye yong bookseller vouch't Mr. Freake, a yong barrister of ye Middle Temple. Mr. Freake yesterday denying ye booksellers oath to bee true, and refusing to bee examined upon oath against himselfe at ye Councill, was committed to ye Tower, though great bayle was offerd by his relations.

---

[a] Only son of Sir Thomas Longueville, of Bradwell Abbey, co. Bucks., Kt. He was of the Inner Temple, and an eminent counsellor at law; and was, moreover, the patron and literary executor of the author of Hudibras. He married Elizabeth, daughter of Sir Thomas Peyton, of Knowlton, Bart., and died 21 March, 1721, at the age of 82. He was buried in Westminster Abbey.—Chester, *Westm. Abbey Registers*, p. 303.

[b] See the next letter.

May 18, 1676.[a]

I have this day, my L^d, according to y^r directions, sent some cherries and given charge to ye carier to send them by Easton, when he sends ye letters. There is one pound and half of Duke cherries wch cost 3^{sh} ye pound, and 2^{lb} of May cherries wch cost 2^{sh} ye lb. They were ye best wch cou'd be got in ye market. I have also sent 2 paire of Roman gloves wch cost 3^{sh} a pair, and 2 paire of tanned leather gloves; those wth lined topps cost 2^{sh} 6^d, ye other 18^d. If y^r Lo^{ppe} doe not like them, you may return them. And wth them is ye Ld Hollis his books and a letter from ye Duke of Mon mouth,   *   *   *   I will immediately send to ye Serjeant[b] who will I am very confident be made a judge in Ellis[c] his place some time ye next terme. Y^e great minister of state is extraordinarily kind to him and assures him y^t in a very few dayes he will provide for him.

The gentlemen of Dorsetshire, to expresse how much they disliked ye verdict for ye Ld Shaftsbury, have subscribed to present my Ld Digby wth 3000^{ll}

I have by ye carier sent ye cloths wch James left wth his wife, wch are, his new coat, 4 paire of sleeves, 2 paire of cuffs, 2 shirts, 3 cravats, and a riding belt, for wch I payed 8^{ll} to redeeme them, his wife having pawned them for soe much; and I have payd Daniel 7^{sh} for his riding coate, wch wase in pawne, and he hath promised to bring it to me some time to morrow.

Of late severall persons have been examined before ye King and Counsell who have dispersed a scurrilouse libell, called ye Chronicle; and one Mr Freeke of ye Temple wase accused by a booksellers

[a] The year is accidentally written 1667.

[b] Scroggs.

[c] Sir William Ellis, one of the judges of the Common Pleas, was dismissed soon after this to make room for Scroggs, as foretold in this letter.

prentise to have delivered it to him to transcribe, though Mr Freeke denyed it, but is committed prisoner to ye Tower. Some sheets of a booke, writ by Andrew Marvel against Dr Turner's Animadversions on Naked Truth, have been taken at ye presse;^a wherin, it is said, he did much more sharply and scurilously abuse Dr Turner and ye B^p of London ^b then ever he did Dr Parker.^c

The Dutchesse of Portsmouth is gonne for ye Bath. She is of late very much indisposed. The Dutches Mazarine, it is said, is buying ye Ld Windsores house at St. James, and will soudainly appeare very splendidly.

Last night ye Ld Cornwallis^d and Mr Gerrard, ye Ld Gerrards son, being in drinke, abused ye sentinells in St James Parke, and, after, Mr Gerrards meeting Capt With's footboy, upon what provocation is not yet known, strucke him soe y^t ye boy fell down dead. Y^e sentinell cryed out murder; whereupon they both fled, but were pursued into Sr Stephen Fox his house. My Ld Cornwallis appeares and declares y^t he wase going up ye staires when ye boy wase killed; but heareing murder cryed he returned to Mr Gerrards and his servants, who said y^t their master only hit ye boy a box on the eare of wch he dyed. Mr Gerrard absconds himself, and ther appeares noe bruise on ye boy but just under his eare.

The Gazet will informe you of ye engagement between ye French and Dutch fleet, wherin De Ruiter had his heele shot of and his leg broke; and therefor shall say no more of it.

Y^r truly affect Brother,

C. HATTON.

^a "Naked Truth, or the True State of the Primitive Church," was published by Herbert Croft, Bishop of Hereford, in 1675. It drew an answer from Dr. Francis Turner, Master of St. John's College, Cambridge, and afterwards Bishop of Ely, viz. the "Animadversions" referred to above. Andrew Marvell's rejoinder, which appeared in 1676, bore the title: " Mr. Smirke, or the Divine in mode, being Certain Annotations upon the Animadversions on the Naked Truth. . . . . By Andreas Rivetus, junior, anagr. Res Nuda Veritas."

^b Dr. Henry Compton.

^c Samuel Parker, afterwards Bishop of Oxford.

^d Charles, third Lord Cornwallis.

THE SAME.

MY L^d,   May 23, [16]76.

  *   *   *   *   *

Here wase this day a general reveiw in Hide Parke of all y^e
Guards in new cloths and my L^d of Oxfords regiment. Y^e L^d
Cornwallis is put out of ye Guards, upon ye murder of ye boy in
St James's Parke, of wch I acquainted you in my last, though it
wase then reported y^t he wase killed only wth a box of ye care; but
when ye chirurgions searched ye corps it was found y^t his necke
was broke.   Mr Gerrard is gone into France; but my Ld Cornwallis
will stand his tryal, and Sr St Fox hath given in baile for his
appearance.   The enquest have found it murder.

  Mr Henry Savile is banished ye Court for speaking disrespectfully
to ye Duke of Yorke, but what were ye words I doe not know.   I
hope Andrew Marvel will likewise be made an example for his
insolence in calling Dr Turner, Chaplain to His Royal Highnesse,
Chaplaine to Sr Fobling Busy,[a] as he terms him in his scurrilous
satyrical answer to his Animadversions on Naked Truth.

  *   *   *   *   *

            Y^r Lo^pps truly affect Brother to serve you,

                                          C. HATTON.

THE SAME.

                                          May 25, [16]76.

  *   *   *   *   *

Heer is at this time great labouring pro and con. to have this
parliam^t dissolved.   The D[uke] of Y[ork], L^d Ar[lington], y^e
Prince (being influenced by ye Ld Shafts.), Secretary Williamson,

  [a] He should have said Sir Fopling Flutter.   Etherege's comedy, "The Man of
Mode, or Sir Fopling Flutter," had lately appeared, and was very popular.

and y[e] D. ot Orm[d] on one side; y[e] L[d] Tr[easurer], L[d] Ch[ancellor], Seer. Coventry, on y[e] other. Lautherdale is upon y[e] reserve, y[t] he may joyne himself wth y[e] prevailing partie. As yet y[e] King hath not declared himself, but he hath been for thes 3 or 4 dayes sufficiently teized. The L[d] Tr. and L[d] Ch., you will easily imagine, are very thoughtfull. The arguments for dissolving this parl[t] are, y[e] unpracticableness of calling y[e] parl[t] before y[e] prefixed time, and y[e] necessity of having a parl[t] assembled before y[t] time. The answer is, noe such necessity, and, if it wase, y[e] convoking y[e] p[arliament] sooner not unpracticable. The generall opinion is y[t] either this or another will be called to meet about 7[br] next; though many thinke y[e] D[uke] will prevaile to have this p[arliament] dissolved; and when he hath drunke y[e] wine he will fling away y[e] water. Hee doth of late more publickly concerne himself in state affaires then he hath done for a long time. Harry Savile is banished y[e] Court upon this acct: The Duke wase saying y[t] Burnet wase a much better preacher then any of y[e] D[rs] soe much cryed up at Court.[a] H. Savil told him y[t] he wase not a competent judge, for he never came to Court to hear any of them preach; and after, y[e] D. discoursing of y[e] necessity to have guards and soldiers to prevent tumults, H. S. told him y[t] an army had turned out Richard and he feared might turn out others, and that he hoped to see England governed w[th]out any soldiers. Though this wase insolent, yet it is much wondred that he, who hath spoke soe much more insolently to y[e] K. himselfe, shou'd be turned out for this; for it is said y[t], not long since, being in y[e] K[s] company, when they were very merry and H. S. high flown in drinke, of a sudden he seemed very melancolly, and, y[e] K. enquiring y[e] reason, he told him y[t] wee shou'd very shortly be all in confusion and up in arms, and y[t] he wase thinking what to doe wth himself, and that he had resolved to get up behind y[e] old King at Charing Crosse, and wase thinking what sport it wou'd be to him to peepe through his armes and see y[e]

---

[a] It will be remembered that Burnet stood high in James's favour at this time.

King, Will Chiffings,[a] and y[e] Sert Trumpeter (for, wth an oath, he averred he wou'd have noebody ells with him) mounted on their great horses and charging y[e] 3 nations. For this he wase only put out [of] company for that time, and the next morning all y[e] blame wase layd on y[e] wine and he pardoned.

Pray burne this letter. What I shall for y[e] future report for coffee house news, assure y[r]self I have a good author for it.

I shall write againe this day by y[e] post and therfor shall add noe more now.

THE SAME.

[25 May, 1676.]

*   -   *

Here hath of late generall outrages been committed by our military officers at Plymouth. Coll. Piper, y[e] Deputy Governor, hath been basely assaulted by one Morris, a capt in S[r] Ch. Littletons regiment, and soe wounded y[t] it is beleeved he will not recover of his wounds. Morris invited y[e] Coll. and one Capt Morgan to a collation, and, Morgan profering to sell a horse to Morris, he asked him whither he wou'd warrant him sound. He s[d]: " Yes, upon his reputation." " What ! " said Morris, " upon such a reputation as our Govr sold his ? " (It seemes Coll. Piper had sold a horse, w[ch] he warranted sound but happened to prove otherwise.) Herupon Piper asked Morris whither or noe he questioned his reputation, w[ch] certainly was as good as Morris his. Wherupon Morris giving him very foul language, Piper withdrew, telling [him] he supposed he wase in drinke, and y[t], when he wase sober, he wou'd be of another

---

[a] *i. e.* Chiffinch.

mind. Morris followed him, and, before Piper cou'd draw his sword, Morris run him through the thigh, and, making a 2 pass at him, Piper, putting by ye thrust wth his hand, is soe wounded in ye hand it is thought, if he recovers, he will loose ye use of his fingers. After this, Piper's man, coming to his masters assistance, wase wounded by Morris, who still thrusting at Piper, he catched hold of his sword and broke it short of; but, having lost much blood, he fell down, and Morris attempted to make his escape, but wase taken and committed to ye gaole at Plymouth. At Chichester, very lately, a cornet in my L^d of Oxfords regiment, quarelling wth a country gentleman, he challenged ye country gentleman into ye feild, who fought and disarmed ye cornet; after w^h, they were in appearance good friends and went together to ye tavern, wher ye cornet left him and went into ye town, called his corporal and one of his soldiers, whom he met in ye streete, to him, and commanded them to follow him; and he went to ye place wher he left ye gentleman, and, finding him ther, commanded the corporal to disarme him; but ye corporal, distrusting his command, he threatned him, and ye gentleman himselfe tooke his sword in ye scabbard, telling ye cornet y^t, to prevent his fury against his corporal, he wou'd disarme himself, and y^t he looked upon him as a gentleman who wou'd not doe a base act, and therefore he rendred him his sword, wch ye cornet snatched out of his hand and immediately run him through wth it, soe y^t he dyed on ye place, and ye cornet wase seized on and sent to ye county goale.

Y^r truly affectionat Brother to serve you,

C. HATTON.

THE SAME.

MY LORD,   June 29 [1676].

*   ~   ~   *

His [Scroggs'] condition is now much better then when I writ
last to you, for Ellis is turned out, and not only ye King and my
Ld Chancelor but my Ld Treasurer doth positively assure ye sert he
shall succeed him; and next Sunday he is to kisse ye King's hand,
for wch it is thought fit y^t he shou'd be presented to his Mat^y by y^e
Ld Chanc. who cou'd not sooner be at leisure. The Ld Treasurer
declared he wase forced to be unmannerly wth ye King in his expressions before he cou'd prevaile wth him to out Ellis; and Atkins^a
had now been outed, but y^t he prevented it by a trick; but w^t that
wase I know not.

Saterday last wase ye day for choosing sherifs in ye city and in y^e
Hall. When ye citizens were met, one Ginks, a linnen draper in
Cornhill, start up and told them y^t he thought it wase very requisite,
before they chose their officers, y^t they considered how to redresse
their greivances, wch were many, as, ye danger of their religion, the
decay of trade, wch he thought did proceed from ye prejudice by y^e
French trade, ye King of France having by his edicts prohibited all
our manufactures. He offered to demonstrate y^t ye nation yearely
lost by ye French trade 1,100,C00^ll per annum; and y^t, of late, so
many fires had happened y^t it wase not to be beleeved but that they
were occasioned by some conspiracy; and therfore he proposed y^t
my Ld Mayor might be mooved to call a common counsell to draw
up a petition to his Ma^ty, that thes greivances might by a new parliament be redressed. Yesterday, Ginks was examined by ye King
and Councell and committed to ye gate-house. In his speech he
wase by some interrupted, but by ye major part called upon to pro-

---

^a Sir Robert Atkins, Judge of the Common Pleas.

ceed, but seconded by none; and for sherifs they have chosen S^r Th. Clargies and S^r Th. Rich, lately a hosier in ye new exchange.[a]

This businesse of Ginks hath been long contriving by ye D. of Bucks. and Ld Shaftesb., ye later of whom did oppose making any such motion as yet, judging their buisnesse wase not yet ripe; but it is s^d ye D. of B. wase for putting it now to ye test, and ye miscariage hath occasioned great feuds amongst their partisans. Ginks denyes to have been incited to what he s^d by any man. But ye fanaticke party, who before were insolently high, are much crestfallen, since Ginks is clapt up and Ellis layd aside.

Mr Downs is dead. Y^e Ld Rochester[b] doth abscond, and soe doth Etheridge,[c] and Capt Bridges who ocasioned ye riot Sunday sennight. They were tossing some fidlers in a blanket for refusing to play, and a barber, upon ye noise, going to see what ye matter, they seized upon him, and, to free himself from them, he offered to carry them to ye handsomest woman in Epsom, and directed them to the constables house, who demanding what they came for, they told him a wh . . . , and, he refusing to let them in, they broke open his doores and broke his head, and beate him very severely. At last, he made his escape, called his watch, and Etheridge made a submissive oration to them and soe far appeased them that ye constable dismissed his watch. But presently after, ye Ld Rochester drew upon ye constable. Mr Downs, to prevent his pass, seized on him, ye constable cryed out murther, and, the watch returning, one came behind Mr Downs and with a sprittle staff cleft his scull. Y^e Ld Rochester and ye rest run away, and Downs, having noe sword, snatched up a sticke and striking at them, they run him into ye side wth a half pike, and soe bruised his arme y^t he wase

[a] The sheriffs were John Peake and Thomas Stampe.

[b] John Wilmot.

[c] George Etherege, the dissolute wit and dramatist. He was knighted about the year 1683. The few plays that his idle nature would allow him to write brought him into notice and obtained for him some diplomatic appointments. He died resident at Ratisbon.

never able to stirr it after.   He hath given his estate, wch wase
1,500 per annum, to his sister, and is reported ye Ld Shrewsberry^a
is to marry her.   But some say his estate wase entayled on a kins
man of his.

You see how malitious I am.   I punish myself y^t I may revenge
myself on you for y^r little scripps of paper.   We are much af-
frighted wth a report y^t part of Kimbolton Castle is burnt down w^th
lightning, and my lady's woman killed.

Y^r truly affect Brother to serve you,
C. HATTON.

THE SAME.

July 2, [16]76.

*   *   *   *   *

Here is little news since my last; only that, Fryday last, ye L^d
Cornwallis wase tryed and acquitted.   The middle of Westminster
Hall wase all schaffolded, and on ye right side of ye state (under
wch ye L^d Ch[ancellor], then Ld High Steward, sate), wase a box,
in wch were ye King, Queen, Duke and Duchess, and ye Duke of
Mexlenburg, who marryed Mad. Chatillon.^b   Ther were 31 Lords
tryers present.   1. The Ld Treasurer, 2. Ld Privy Seale, 3. Marquisse Dorchester, 4. L^d H[igh] Chamberlaine, 5. Ld Steward of
ye Household, 6. L^d of Oxford, 7. Ld Kent, 8. Ld Derby, 9. L^d
Bedford, 10. Ld Suffolke, 11. Ld Dorset, 12. Ld Bridgewater,
13. Ld Northampton, 14. Ld Devonshire, 15. Ld Peterborough,
16. Ld Sunderland, 17. Ld Clarendon, 18. Ld Bath, 19. L^d
Craven, 20. Ld Aylesbury, 21. Earle of Guilford and Lauderdale, 22. Ld Campden, 23. Ld Halifax, 24. Ld Newport, 25.

---

^a Charles Talbot, 12th Earl, afterwards Duke, of Shrewsbury.   He married an
Italian lady.

^b Christian Ludwig, Duke of Mecklenburg, married Isabelle Angelique de
Montmorency-Bouteville, widow of Caspar Coligny de Chatillon.

Ld Berkely, 26. Ld Paget, 27. Ld Maynard, 28. Ld Howard of Escrick, 29. Ld Freschevile, 30. L^d Th. Butler, E. of Ossory, 31. Ld Duras; and 8 of ye judges, ye L^d Ch. Justices, L^d Ch. Baron, Jones, Windam, Littleton, Thurland, and Bertue. Y^e counsell were Maynard,^{a} Attorny G[eneral],^{b} and Sollicitor Gen.^{c} The evidence wase ye same wch wase given in ag^t ye footmen, who were now witnesse ag^t ye prisoner and upon oath declared y^t Mr Gerrard killed ye boy by taking him by ye sholder and tripping up his heeles and flinging him ag^t ye ground, and y^t ye Ld Cornwallice wase upon ye staires when ye fact was done and ye boy at a good distance from ye staires. The summe of evidence, in breife, wase y^t both ye Ld Cornwallis and Mr Gerrard threatned to kill ye sentinell, and y^t one of them, but wch could not be proved, bid ye sentinell kill ye boy, and said: " We will kill somebody;" and y^t, presently after, Mr Gerrard killed ye boy. St Maynard said y^t ye Ld Cornw., if he did not say: " We will kill somebody," yet being by when those words were said and shewing noe dislike of them, nor endeavouring to prevent Mr Gerrards doing ye fact, he wase in law equally guilty of ye murder. The truth is, ye soldier who gave evidence did not clearly expresse himself, whither one or both said: " We will kill somebody," of wch ye Lord Privy Seale^d tooke notice twice, but ye Ld High Steward and Mr Sollicitor, who summed up ye evidence, declared that it wase only proved y^t one of them said those words.

The Ld Cornwallis made a very breife defence : y^t he wase not upon any unlawfull occasion in ye parke ; y^t ye quarrell wth ye soldiers wase over ; y^t that wth ye boy wase upon a new occasion; and y^t he did not say those words, neither wase it proved ag^t him; y^t it wase proved he did not doe ye fact; y^t it wase true, when ye fact wase done, he ran away and lost his hat, but it wase because ye corporal came immediately wth his guard and cryed: " Knock them down! knock them down!" as ye corp^{ll} himself had declared upon

---

^{a} Sir John Maynard, King's Serjeant-at-law.

^{b} Sir William Jones.

^{c} Sir Francis Winnington. ^{d} Arthur Annesley, Earl of Anglesey.

oath; and that he very[ly] beleeved, had they stayd, ye soldiers wou'd have done them some mischeife.   But, ye very next morning, he delivered himself and servants up to ye Coroner, wch ye Coroner wittnessed.

After he had made his defence, and ye Sollicitor summd up ye evidence, upon ye Ld Privy Seales motion ye L^ds withdrew for above 3 houres.   In ye interim theyr wase brought by ye Ld Cornwallis servants Naples bisquits and wine, wch wase first presented to ye Ld High Steward and, after, given about to ye Company.

When ye L^ds returned, ye Ld Treasurer acquainted ye L^d H[igh] St[eward] y^t divers of ye L^ds desired to be satisfyed in a point of law, wch wase, whither or noe, a fact being done wch wase only adjudged to be manslaughter, any person who wase aiding and assisting wase equally guilty wth ye person who did ye fact, as if ye fact had been adjudged to be murder.   The Ld Clarendon stept up and said ther wase only very few Lords, not above 5 or 6, who desired to be satisfyed therin.   The L^d H[igh] St[eward] declared ye prisoner must be brought to ye bar before any question cou'd be put; and accordingly he wase, and then ye question put; and ye judges all declared y^t in manslaughter, as in murder, all aiders and assisters were equally guilty wth those who did ye fact.

After this, ye L^ds withdrew againe and about half an houre returned, and they all acquitted him of ye murder; but six of them, ye Ld Manard, Ld George Berkely, Ld Alesbury, Ld High Chamberlaine, Ld Privy Seale, Ld Treasurer found him guilty of manslaughter; at wch my Ld Gerrard is not a little pleased, and some are soe malitious as to say it wase done purposely to declare y^t, in ye opinion of ye L^ds, Mr Gerrard wase only guilty of manslaughter. Great notice wase taken y^t ye Ld Shaftsbury, Ld Wharton,[a] and Ld Mohun sat just in ye King's sight, wispring together all ye time.

*   *   *   *

Your Lops. truly affectionat Brother to serve you,

C. HATTON.

[a] Philip, Lord Wharton, who had served in the parliamentary army.

THE SAME.

My Lᵈ,   July 25, [16]76.

*   *   *   *   *

Here is a Welshman, who pretends to cure any wound whatsoever in yᵉ bowells or any part, except yᵉ heart, in a few houres.

*   *   *

Several pigges, kidds, and chickens have, in yᵉ King's presence,
been run into yᵉ bowells and through yᵉ head wᵗʰ knives and hot
irons, and cured in a short time by this man's medicines. Shou'd
he goe unto yᵉ King of France's army, he wou'd render all yᵉ
designs of yᵉ Spanyards and Dutch ineffectuall. His Majesty is
gone to Windsor, but returns next Thursday.

Yʳ truly affect Brother to serve you,

C. HATTON.

THE SAME.

Aug. 3 [16]76.

*   *   *   *   *

The Bᵖ of Norwich is dead;ᵃ Dʳ Carew, yᵉ Deane,ᵇ is to be Bᵖ,
and my cousen Northe,ᶜ Deane. The Bᵖ of London hath complained ᵃᵍˢᵗ yᵉ Portugal Embasʳ ᵈ for licensing yᵉ translation of yᵉ
masse. About six months since, an English preist publish'd yᵉ

ᵃ Edward Reynolds; died on the 28th July. He was succeeded by Anthony
Sparrow, translated from Exeter.

ᵇ There was no dean of this name in the Church at this time. Herbert Asteley
was Dean of Norwich.

ᶜ Hon. John North, Regius Professor of Greek at Cambridge, and Prebendary of
Westminster, and, in 1677, Master of Trinity College, Cambridge. He died in
1683.

ᵈ Francesco de Mello, Conde da Ponte.

CAMD. SOC.   T

masse of y[e] Holy Trinity in Latine and English, with expositions, and entitled his booke: " Y[e] great sacrifice of y[e] new law expounded by y[e] figures of y[e] old," and had now a designe to reprint it, with all y[e] epistles and gospells in Latine and English, and had a license from y[e] Embas[r]; but y[e] booke was seized on at y[e] presse, and y[e] licence, and complained of by y[e] B[p] of London at Councell board. Y[e] Embassador wase appointed to appeare ther, but he came not; but writ to excuse himself and sent his secretary. He pretends he only licensed 100 for y[e] use of y[e] Queen's servants, but a figure of nine wase put into y[e] licence without his privity, after he had signed it, w[ch] made it for 900; and pretends that, being an Emb[or], he cannot, without leave from his prince, answer in person at Counsell board; w[ch] very plea argues that his office of Chamberlaine[a] is here incompatible wth his other caracter. It is generally beleeved he will loose his key.

The B[p] of London hath likewise made complaint ag[t] y[r] freind, M[r] Collman,[b] for printing a booke in defence of y[e] Pope's supremacy. But he denyes he ever writ any booke, and y[e] popish party say ther is noe such booke writ. It is said y[e] Duke of Yorke is much offended at y[e] B[p] of London for complaining of anyone of his servants to y[e] King, without first acquainting him ; and y[t] y[e] Duke formerly told him, if he did, he shou'd take it very ill.

It is s[d] a parson in Norfolk, when y[e] Duke wase at sea, sent him a present, w[ch] y[e] Duke tooke soe kindly y[t] he procured him a very good living; after w[ch], y[e] parson did very violently persecute y[e] fanaticke Nonconformists, and, coming up to town, M[r] Collman rebuked him and told him y[e] D. wase very much offended w[th] him, and he, pleading y[t] he only prosecuted y[e] fanaticks, M[r] Collman told him y[t] y[e] D. wase very much troubled y[t] any persons shou'd be troubled for serving God that wase w[th]in their conscience they thought they ought to doe. The parson, after this, visiting y[e]

  To the Queen.
  [b] Edward Coleman, secretary to the Duchess of York ; one of the victims of the Popish plot.

B^p of London, he told him that he had in this manner been lectured by Collman; and ye B^p caryed him to ye King, who thereupon advised ye Duke to discharge Colman, wch ye D. did highly resent from y^e ·B^p, and told him as much, and now is afresh provoked. I am

Y^r truly affect Brother,
C. HATTON.

THE SAME.

Sep 23, [16]76.

   *   *   *   *

 Your pictures will be all finished ye next week. The Queen's, Prince's,^{a} and Ld Dorset's^b are ready. I dare not hazard them in my little house, least ye sea coale smoke this winter shou'd spoyle them. Had ye Queen's picture hung a little longer at Thanet House, it wou'd have been quite spoyled, for ye cloth wase primed wth tobacco pipe clay, and it wou'd have pilled all of. As soon as the durt wase wash'd of, ye cracks appeared. But M^r. Baptist^c engages he hath secured it for ever. He highly admires my Ld Dorset's picture, sath it is every stroake of Van Dyke and of his best painting; and ye priming of ye cloath is very good.^{d} Van Dyke was very neglectfull in ye priming of ye cloths he painted on. Some were primed w^h water colours, as ye fine crucifix at M^r

 ^{a} Prince Rupert.

 ^{b} Edward Sackville, fourth Earl of Dorset.

 ^{c} John Gaspars Baptist, a native of Antwerp; settled in England and was much employed by General Lambert. After the Restoration he was engaged chiefly as a drapery painter, particularly by Lely. He died in 1691.

 ^{d} I have not been able to identify these pictures among the lists of Vandyck's works. They must have passed into other hands; and the number of replicas of Vandyck's paintings is so large as to make a search almost vain. Vertue engraved a portrait of the Earl of Dorset after a Vandyck in the possession of the Duke of Dorset.

Lillyes,[a] some wth tobacco pipe clay, as y[e] famous picture of y[e] late
King and Queen, at Whitehall, w[ch] is now allmost all pilled of, and
y[r] Queen's picture; but y[t] is now secured.   Vandyke wase much
pleased wth that priming, for it wase smooth as glasse; and he did
not live to see y[e] inconvenience of it by being soe little durable,
unlesse care be taken by some skillfull artist to fix it afterwards,
either by varnishing it on y[e] backe side with a varnish w[ch] will
passe quite through and fix y[e] colour, or else wth a strong size and
clap on another cloth.   Here is noe news.

Y[r] Lo[pps] truly affect. Brother to serve you,

C. HATTON.

THE SAME.

MY L[d],   December 14, [16]76.
     Last Monday, I received y[rs] of y[e] 9th inst., and wase very glad
to heare you got soe safe to Easton.   According to y[r] order therin,
I desired Madamoisel de la Chappell to see y[e] Lady Anne Grim
ston,[b] and accordingly she did; and I desired her to be at an hour's
readinesse, whensoever she shou'd receive y[r] orders to goe down;
but, your Lo[ppe] taking noe notice in y[r] letter when you wou'd have
her goe, made me imagine you did not designe it left this weeke.
But last night, at eleven of y[e] clocke (y[e] extremity of bad weather
occasioned y[e] delivery of y[e] letters soe late), I received y[rs] of y[e] 12
inst., wherin you desired Madamoiselle shou'd goe down as to day.
     It wase too late then, either to advertise her, or take a place in
y[e] coach.   But this morning, betwixt 3 or 4 of y[e] clocke, I got up
and wase to goe to White Hart Yard, in Drury Lane, whereabouts
in Drury Lane I knew not.   Ther wase soe great a fogg, and it

---

     [a] Peter Lely.
     [b] Daughter of John Tufton, Earl of Thanet, and wife of Sir Samuel Grimstone,
Bart.

wase soe extreemly cold, y^t betwixt my house and Drury Lane I met noe living creature; and when I wase in Drury Lane, y^t I might be directed to White Hart Yard, I wase forced to knocke up somebody, and, over against Drury House,^a I knocke at a doore, and, every body in the house being fast asleep, I wase necessitated to knocke very loud; and at last a man clapt his head out at a window, and (y^t wch wase very pleasant) he imagining I wase one of my Ld Craven's^b fire-spyes, the first words he said to me wase: " Where is ye fire, S^r, where is ye fire?" I humoured him in his errour, for feare of warme water being flung on my head, and told him in Southwarke. He then asked whither my Lord knew of it. I told him I cou'd not tell, but I wase going to informe one, who wase concerned, y^t lived in White Hart Yard, wch how to find he gave me very punctuall directions, and desired to know who it wase. But I thought it not convenient to name anybody, but left him, and found Mr. Housdan['s] house; and, when I had knocked them up, I acquainted them wth ye reason of my disturbing them.

But Mad. la Chappel would very desirously have deferred going down till ye next opportunity of ye coach, wch I thought might have been displeasing to y^r Lo^ppe; and I fully satisfyed her y^t it was absolutely necessary she shou'd goe this day, for, shou'd it thaw, perhapps ye coach might not be able to passe of a weeke, or ten dayes. And when I had prevayled wth her to resolve to goe as this day, I went to Smithfeild, and it wase but five of ye clocke when I got thither; and, when I had taken a place in ye coach, I went and fetch'd Mad^ll, and, wth an addresse to Mr. Ebriel,^c I recommended

---

^a Near the junction of Drury Lane and Wych Street.

^b William, Earl of Craven, the stout old colonel of the Coldstream Guards who was so distinguished in early life in the German wars, and was so ready to fight William's Dutch Guards when they occupied Whitehall, in 1688. He shewed great zeal in the prevention of fires in London, and was so famous for his constant attendance at them, that it was a common saying that his horse scented a fire as soon as it broke out.—Collins, *Peerage*, v. 453.

^c A saddler at Northampton who received letters and parcels for the Hatton family.

her to ye care of ye passengers, and saw her trunke delivered to ye carrier. I gave her 20 shillings in mony, pay'd fiveteene shillings for her passage, and for coach hire, porter, and breakfast I pay'd 4^sh 6^d more.

Y^r truly affect Brother to serve you,
C. HATTON.

THE SAME.

December 30, 1676.

*   *   *   *   *

We have noe publike news here. Y^r neighbour, ye Ld Exeter,[a] is turned out, by his Maties direction, from his Recorder's place of Stanford, and ye Lord Cambden[b] put in. Ther is a certaine politike squire you know, who inadvertently let fall y^t ye Lady Shrewsbury[c] wase brought to Court, therby to gaine her favour that she might endeavour to bring of her brother Westmorland and her other relations from joyning wth ye Ld Execeter. Pray God all this may advance his Maties service. I doubt it will occasion great feuds amongst y^r neighbours.

Y^e Ld Mohun is also lately given over by his phisitians and chirurgions; it is thought he cannot live many houres. He hath very generously done what he can to secure ye Ld Cavendish,[d] having signed a declaration, wherin he averrs y^t ye quarel in wch he engaged upon ye Ld Cavendish account wase fully ended, and y^t he received noe hurt therin; but afterward in [a] particular private

---

[a] John Cecil, 4th Earl of Exeter.
[b] Baptist Noel, 3rd Viscount Campden.
[c] Anna Maria, daughter of Robert Brudenel, 2nd Earl of Cardigan; the paramour of Buckingham, who killed her husband Francis, 11th Earl of Shrewsbury. Her sister Dorothy married Charles Fane, 3rd Earl of Westmoreland.
[d] William, Lord Cavendish, afterwards Duke of Devonshire.

quarrel upon his owne account, independant from y^t of my L^d
Cavendish, he received his wound.^{a} Y^e Ld Cavendish hath given
great scandal by dayly frequenting ye theater, ever since my L^d
Mohun hath layn thus desperate ill.

*   *   *

Y^r Lops. truly affect Brother to serve you,

C. HATTON.

LADY ELIZABETH BERKELEY ^{b} TO LADY HATTON.^{c}

Feb. 14, [1677?]

I had the honor of a letter from dear Lady Hatton directed to
St Johnses, and was in hopes that my thankfull acknowledgment
of y^t favour had long since given notice of its reception.   But I
perceive mine did not come to your hands.   I hope this will not
have the same misfortun, that I may not appear ungreatfull, wch is
the only thing I can ame at wth my dull scribling, since it cannot
pretend to give you any devertion, being sure you have all y^e
parliament news from much better inteligencers; yet I believe they
have not acquainted you wth Lady Alethea's ^{d} privet wedding last
Tuesday.   Mrs Katherine Grey call her out upon the pretence of
going to a play, but, wth her own consent, carried her to Sr Edward
Hungerford's, wher she was married to his eldest son whome she

<hr>

^{a} Lord Mohun partially recovered, though he appears to have died from the
effects of his wound about Michaelmas of this year.   See *Prideaux's Letters*
(Camd. Soc.), p. 57.

^{b} Elizabeth, daughter of Baptist Noel, Viscount Campden, married to Charles
Berkeley, created Lord Berkeley in 1689, who succeeded his father as Earl of
Berkeley in 1698.

^{c} Frances, daughter of Sir Henry Yelverton, of Easton Mauduit, co. Northampton,
Bart., second wife of Christopher, Lord Hatton.   She died in 1684.

^{d} Alethea Compton, daughter of James, 3rd Earl of Northampton, married to
Edward Hungerford (afterwards a baronet), son of the "spendthrift," Sir Edward
Hungerford, K.B.   She died in 1678.

had never seen but thrice. She did not acquaint her father nor
any of her friends or relations, who I think are more angry at the
proceeding then at the match, for he is a very considerable fortune
and a handsome man. My sister Northampton [a] I am sure would
have given you a more perticuler account then I can, if the small
pox had not bin in her house, wch makes her forbear writing, only
in respect to your La^p; for I thank God she is now out of all fears
for Lady Julianas being in any danger of her life or beauty. This
letter is already come to such a prodidious length that I dare hardly
increase it, tho but to beg pardon for all the errors commited by,

Dear Madam,

Y^r La^p most humble servant,

E. BERKELEY.

WILLIAM DUGDALE.[b]

Blythe Hall, neere Coleshill, 24 Febr. 1676[7].

MY MOST HONOURED L^d,

In answer to y^r Lo^pps letter (wch came to my hands this morning),
whereby I understand that Sr Edw. Walker is dead [c] (wch as yet I
have not heard from any other), I do in the first place return my
most humble thanks to y^r Lo^pp for your most kinde and noble offer
in favouring me wth your assistance for succeeding him in his place
of Garter; wch I confesse I should looke upon as an injury to me,
that any other should leap over my head, considering that my predecessors in the office of Norroy have, for many ages, been successors

---

[a] Mary, daughter of Baptist, Viscount Campden, second wife of the Earl of
Northampton.

[b] The celebrated antiquary. He became Garter and was knighted in April, 1677.
Died 1686.

[c] He died on the 20th February.

to Garter in that office, were my qualifications such as might well sute therewith. But so it is, that besides my great age (wch is now 72), whereby I am not fitt for those attendances as properly belong thereto, and the dignity of knighthood, wch for the honour thereof it will be expected I should take upon me, and wch my estate will not beare, there would be of necessity an expectance that I should remove my family to London, w^{ch}, wthout a better support than the proffits of that office will beare (my own estate being small), would be my ruine. There are also four other reasons w^{ch}, had I the happinesse to see your Lo^{pp}, I could impart to you. So that, in short, were it freely offred to me, I should decline it.

As to a perfect list of all the peeres, there are of the heraulds now at our office neere Doctors Commons who can easily fulfill what the House of Lords have thought fitt to require therein, in case they be sent to.

Touching the Lord Grey[a] (for that is his title, and by wch his grandfather, upon the judgment given in the House of Peeres, upon the dispute thereof wth Anthony Earle of Kent, grandfather to this Earle,[b] had his writt of summons, and not Grey of Ruthyn, though commonly so called), now that the dignity is descended to him by the death of his noble mother in whom it was during her life, it matters not what the Earle of Kent shall object against it, for it is sufficiently setled, as the journalls of the Lords' House will manifest (of wch I have an abstract), but, till this young Lord be of full age, he is not capable of sitting in the House of Peeres, and therefore cannot properly move the King by petition for his writt of summons. If the Earle of Kent have a minde to say anything in opposition thereof, then will be his time to do it. And when this

[a] Charles Yelverton, 14th Lord Grey of Ruthyn, son of Sir Henry Yelverton, by Susan Grey, Baroness in her own right, daughter of Charles Longueville, 12th Baron, by Susan, daughter of Charles Grey, 10th Baron. It will be remembered that Lord Grey was brother of Lady Hatton.

[b] Anthony Grey, 12th Earl of Kent.

CAMD. SOC. U

Lord Grey shall be setled in the House, according to his just right, then will be his most proper time to except against the Earle of Kent for usurping the title of L⁴ Grey of Ruthyn, whereunto he hath not any right, though de facto he useth it.

At the beginning of Easter terme I resolve (God willing) to be in London, and then to wayt on your Loᴾᴾ. And, if your Loᴾᴾ shall thinke fitt to write to me in the meane time, write your name on the backside your letter, wᶜʰ is the note whereby your letters in parliament time, and 40 days before and after, do passe wᵗʰout payment for the postage.

I heare in generall that there is great hopes of a good progress in parliament this session, notwᵗʰstanding the malevolent practises of the presbyterians and their partizans, wᶜʰ is no small joy to all good subjects in these parts.

So praying for your Loᴾᴾˢ good health wᵗʰ all happiness, I rest

Your Loᴾᴾˢ most humble and most obliged servant,

Wᵐ DUGDALE.

CHARLES HATTON.

[Feb. ? 1677.]

*   *   *   *

The Lᵈˢ in yᵉ Tower are likely to remaine ther till your Loᴾᴾˢ meet. They did, when yᵉ King wase at Newmarket, joyntly petition his Maᵗʸ, of wᶜʰ his Maᵗʸ made this observance, yᵗ it looked as if they were guilty of confederacy for wᶜʰ they were under soe close a restraine, and, if they had separately petitioned, they had been lesse suspitious of combination, and in his apprehension some deserved more favour then others; wherupon they all separately petition'd. Secretary Coventry presented yᵉ Lᵈ Shaftsburyes petition, the Ld Middlesex ye Duke of Buces, and ye Ld Suffolke ye Ld Salisburys. But all their petitiones were denyed.[a]

*   *   *   *   *

I am,

Y^r Lops. truly affect Brother to serve you,

C. HATTON.

LADY HATTON.[b]

MY DEARE LORD,   Kirby, March the 31th, [16]77.

I hope you have received all my letters this week; for I never missed any opportunity, only by the caryer. I am glad that you design to com. Your coach shall be sure to meet you at Baldock; but you must be sure to send me word what horsemen you would have, and at what time the coach must be there. I find you intend to be at Kimbolton that night. Pray be sure to send me word wheathere you will be here by dinner or not. I believe you cannot, but be sure you let me know. One of your best coach horses has been like to dye; but wee hope the danger is past. I had Shefeld with him, and all the care that can bee. I hope he will

[a] The parliament of 1677 having met after a prorogation of fifteen months, it was maintained by the country party that such prorogation, extending over a year, had in effect dissolved the parliament. In the House of Lords, Buckingham made a speech in favour of this view, and was supported by the Earls of Shaftesbury and Salisbury and Lord Wharton. All four lords were sent to the Tower. Buckingham, Salisbury, and Wharton, on making their submission, were released. Shaftesbury would not yield, and remained in custody more than a year. Echard (*History of England*, iii. 416) tells the anecdote that Shaftesbury had made some remarks about Buckingham's giddiness, which had reached the latter's ears. Shaftesbury, looking out of his window as Buckingham was stepping into his coach to leave the Tower, called out: "What, my Lord, are you going to leave us?" "Aye, my Lord," was the reply, "such giddy fellows as I can never stay long in a place."

[b] See above, p. 143, note [c].

doe well, but they say I must not venter him in the coach so farr a great whill. But one of the cart horsses will doe in the coach very well.

Poor little Susana is very ill about her teeth. I hope in God they will not be long before they be cut. Shee bares it with a great deal of patience. My Lady Rockingam[a] has been with me yesterday. I thought there had been wine enough in the house, but there is none left. But there is forteen botles of Renish and all the sherie sack that was, but noe other; so now you may the better gess what you must send down. Some sack you will need I am sure. My deare Lord, I should be very glad you would bring some chocolate along with you. I hope I shall receive a good acount of all your business, for I long to know. My daughter Nany is very well, and was yesterday at my Lord Brudnal's.[b] I believe I shall like your cook very well. Pray, deare, let Smith buy a Wesfaily ham and too or three neats tongues. I would fain get every thing pretty handsome against my Lord Manchester[c] comes. I hope I shall know the time. I am, my deare Lord, overjoyed to hear that your business goes on so well with the Bishop.[d] I long till the Act of Parliment be passed.

I received D[r] Kings letter; but I shall not need much of his phiseck, for I thank God I am much better. Smith forgot to send the pickales down; but I beg they may not faile this next week, and, with them, some oyle, about a pint will be enough, because wee shall stay noe great whill there. I return you many thanks for the oysters. I can write noe more, to morow being sacrament day. But, for God sake, make hast down, for I am weary of my life.

[a] Anne, daughter of Thomas Wentworth, Earl of Strafford, and wife of Edward Watson, 2nd Lord Rockingham.

[b] Francis, Lord Brudenell, eldest son of Robert, 2nd Earl of Cardigan.

[c] Robert Montagu, 3rd Earl of Manchester.

[d] Referring to transactions with the Bishop of Ely touching the Hatton Garden property.

WILLIAM DUGDALE.

My most honoured L^d,   Blythe Hall, neere Coleshill, 7 Apr. 1677.

By your Lo^{pps} letter dated on Tuesday last I perceive that it is his Maties pleasure that I shall have this office of Garter, though, by a letter to me of the same date from the Earle Marshall's secretary, I finde that his Lo^{pp} commanded him to let me know that his Lo^{pp} hath made choyse of me to that office, willing me to hasten up wth all convenient speed.^a

I must confesse that the news thereof hath much discomposed me, having (by reason of my age, and other inconveniences wch may befall me by undergoing this imployment,) resolved of a retired life; but, on the other side, to decline this high favour from his Matie and the like (for so I must now believe it) from my Lord Marshall I know not how, wth my safetie, to do; and therefore have determined, wth all humility, to submit to God Almightyes disposall of me herein, and, in order thereto, to be in London on Wednsday evening next; and, so soon as I can enquire out your Lo^{pps} lodging, to wayt upon you, there to present my personall thanks to you for your great favours herein; but in the meane time to intreate that you will please to stand my freind to his Matie, in case you can have any fit opportunitie so farr to represent my condition unto him (wth my most bounden thanks for this great favour), as to desire that, though many of my predecessors in this office have had the dignitie of knighthood conferr'd upon them, his Matie will excuse me therein; for otherwise I am sure that hatred and scorne will be my portion from very many people, by reason of my low estate. When Mr Camden (who was a person much my superior every way) was offred to be made a knight by K. James, he humbly declined it, though his place of Clarenceiux did in point of proffit far exceed

^a Referring to a claim set up against the Crown by the Earl Marshal to the right of nominating Garter. In the present instance Dugdale was agreeable to both sides.

that of Garter; and I hope his ^{Matie} will not thinke it more dishonour to himself to be served in this office by an esquire than his grandfather did in that of Clarenceiux by Mr Camden.

My other sute is, that his ^{Matie} will vouchsafe (by reason of my age and the infirmities incident thereto) to dispense wth my personall residence in London, considering I shall take care not to be absent from any dutie of consequence, and provide a fitt person at other times to performe whatever is requisite, as some of my predecessors have done; and lastly, whereas I am to undergo the whole service of Garter at this installation, in Easter weeke, of the Duke of Newcastle[a] and Ld Treasurer, that I may, through his speciall grace and goodness, not be abridged of the usuall fees for the same, though my patent for creation be not then passed by reason of the shortness of time. I am loath to make any one my mediator herein but your Lo^{pp}, to whom I do beleive I must owe my total thanks for whatsoever benefit I shall have by this office, for I am fully satisfyed that the character wch you have given me to the King hath been the ocasion of all this; for, as to my Ld Marshall, I know he was totally engaged to bring in Mr Lee,[b] and I beleive that the King, by such meanes as Sr Wm Haward[c] made, did wholly incline to him.

My L^d, I heartily crave pardon for this my over-boldnesse wth you, and so, praying for your good health, do rest

Your L^{pps} most obliged
servant and honourer,
Wm DUGDALE.

[a] Henry Cavendish, who succeeded to the title in 1676.

[b] Thomas Lee, Chester Herald, who declined the promotion on account of bad health.

[c] Sir William Hayward, of the Privy Chamber.

CHARLES HATTON.

October 23, 1677.

Wee are all here in town, my L^d, soe full of joy at ye declaration y^t Lady Mary is to be marryed to ye Prince of Orange y^t, tho' I have many other things to say to y^r Lo^{ppe}, I cannot refrayne from acquainting you with y^t in ye first place. Last Sunday his Ma^{ty} declared to ye cabinet counsel y^t ye match betwixt Lady Mary and ye Prince of Orange wase concluded on, and ye Privy Counsell wase summoned yesterday morning, and ther his Ma^{ty} did publickly acquaint ye L^{ds} therwth; and, presently after, ye Duke of Yorke came in and tooke his place, not as a Privy Counsellor but at some distance from ye table. And, in a speech to ye L^{ds}, he wase pleased to take notice y^t he had been misrepresented, as if he sought to disunite ye kingdome, and he declared he never did, nor ever wou'd, attempt to make any alteration in ye establish'd government of ye kingdome, either in matters of Church or State; and y^t his inclination, as well as his interest, obliged him to preserve ye peace and unity of ye kingdome, wch he shou'd ever promote, and, in order thereto, had given his consent to ye mariage of his daughter wth ye Prince of Orange. After w^{ch}, severall L^{ds} of ye Counsell made complemental speech to his Highnesse; and ye L^{ds} ordred y^t ye Ld Maior of London shou'd be acquainted wth ye mariage intended and shou'd order bonfires to be made in ye city. After ye Counsel wase up, Lady Mary declared her consent; and in ye afternoone all ye Ministers of State and L^{ds} of ye Counsell went in a body to waite on Lady Mary and ye Prince of Orange; and ye whole night wase spent in ringing of bells and bonfires and ye greatest expressions of joy wch I beleeve were ever in England, except at ye King's restauration.

This day all ye judges went in a body to congratulate ye Lady Mary and ye Prince. The Ld Cheife Justice^a made a long speech,

---

^a Sir Richard Rainsford, Chief Justice of the King's Bench, who was turned out, in 1678, to make room for Scroggs.

and how eloquent I need not say. They all kissed Lady Maryes hand, and offered to doe ye like to ye Prince; but he wou'd not permit it, but shooke them all by ye hand and gave them thanks for their compliment, told them he shou'd ever endeavour to promote ye interest of ye kingdome, and shou'd be glad to serve them in particular.

The clergy did not goe in a body, but all ye b^pps in town have separately made their compliments. The ArchB^p of Canterbury^a lies soe weake, it is thought he cannot live but a few dayes longer. Several personns are discoursed of to succeed him, ye B^p of London, Yorke, Oxford, Durham, and Winchester.

*   *   *

Y^r Lo^pps truly affect Brother to serve you,

C. HATTON.

The Ld Treasurer of all ye Ministers of State hath soly been entrusted wth ye management of ye treaty of mariage wth ye Prince and Lady Mary.^b Last Sunday, in ye morning, ye King, ye Duke, ye Prince, and my Ld Treasurer, were 3 honres shut up in ye King's chamber, ye Ld Chancelor and other ministers attending without for a long time; and they were, in ye afternoone, as long in private. The Ld Chancelor, Ld Privy Seale, and ye 2 Secretaries are ordred to draw up ye articles of mariage; and it is said ye Prince will now in a very few dayes return for Holland. My cosen Montague^c is expected from Paris in extraordinary business. To-morrow Sr Robt Howard's^d businesse shou'd come on, but he is very sicke on it, hath ye gout and cannot stand long; but it is thought he will endeavour to keepe of ye evil as long as he can.

---

^a Gilbert Sheldon, died on the 9th November. He was succeeded by William Sancroft, Dean of St. Paul's, who was consecrated 27 Jan. 1678.

^b For an account of Danby's action, see Burnet, *Own Time*, i. 408-411.

^c Ralph Montague, the ambassador to France.

^d Sixth son of Thomas, first Earl of Berkshire. He was Auditor of the Receipt of the Exchequer. Died 1698.

SIR CHARLES LYTTELTON.

London, Octo. 25th, [16]77.

I suppose you know ye marriage is declared, and how all the world has bine to complim^t Lady Mary. My Ld Chancellor came wth the Councell and made a most curious speech. I w^d he w^d lend mee his tongue, for I am just agoing my self to her to say as well as I can. I assure you every perticular about ye court allmost does so, or els I s^{hd} not show my parts that way.

The Duke told ye Councell that he had a great while thought this ye most convenient match for his daughter, and therefore desired it; and hoped it w^d sattisfie concerning him, that he never had any intentions to innovate religion in the state, and he did promisse them he never would.

They will be married privately, and I doe not heare of any preparations of private persons to be fine at ye wedding, tho' I heard there was; and that drew me partly to towne to day, to doe as others did.

His birth day is ye 4th or 5th of No^{br}. So probably then; els stay till ye 15th, wch is ye Queene's. Lady Mary is well pleased wth it, I can assure you. Y^e P. has wooed hard for ye time; but to day he waites on ye K^g to Windsor. Y^e Duke is heere, because they expect ye Duchesse to cry out. She was grumbling last night. God send her a brave boy and you another. Mine, I thank God, is well, but wee thought wee should have lost him wth ye gripes.

About a fortnight hence I hope wee shall be settled in towne

My humblest services to my Lady. I am glad you like the nurs, her fault is to be mity proud and passionat.

Charles Hatton.

8 Nov. 1677.

I am very glad, my L^d, y^t, at y^e same time I heard y^e ill news y^t you have of late been indisposed, you wase pleased to assure me your distemper wase (as you thought) going of. But I am very impatient, my L^d, till I heare you are perfectly recovered; and therefore I beg of you I may y^e next post heare from y^r Lo$^{pp e}$, my just concerne for whose welfare will not permit me, till I am fully assured of y^r perfect recovery, to joyne in those publicke demonstrations of joy wth wch our streets are filled here, for y^e joyfull news y^t y^e Dutchesse of Yorke wase brought to bed last night, at 10 of y^e clocke, of a son,[a] and ye Lady Mary married to ye Prince of Orange. Y^e marriage wase celebrated at St James very privately last Sunday night, about 10 of ye clocke, in Lady Maryes chamber, by ye B^p of London. None of ye English nobility, except ye Ld Treasurer, Duke of Albemarle, and Ld Ossory, permitted to be present. The Lady Mary is not adopted ye Kings daughter, as wase reported.

* * * *

Y^r truly affect Brother and servant,

C. Hatton.

Sir Charles Lyttelton.

My Lord, London, No^{br} 10th 77.

I came hither yesterday wth all my folk, and to settle, I hope, for a long while; for 'tis very chargeable removing, and the refitting my house undoes me. You must have heard before this ye Duke has a sonne. His name is Charles. Y^e K^g, Prince of Aur., and his two younger sisters, Lady Ann and Izabell,[b] gossips. Y^e Duchess of Buck, I heard, was intended to be one, but whither she were

[a] Charles, who died on the 12th December following.
[b] That is, the two younger daughters of the Duke of York; Princess Anne, afterwards Queen; and Isabella, a child born in 1676, who died in 1680.

put of, and so, to avoyd ye affront or by chance, went out of towne that day, I know not; but goe she did. The P. is a very fond husband, but she a very coy bride, at least before folkes. Thev goe away a Fryday next.

The P. has given her very fine jewells, one ring of 10000^{li}, wch D[ick] Bevoir says he saw, and a necklasse of 8000^{li}, and many other good jewells. She is gone to ye play to-night in these and all ye Duchesses jewells.

Lady Ann is sick and, its feared, may have ye small pox.

Sr Robt Howards businesse wase heard yesterday in Councell. I cannot tell w^{ht} was resolved on certainly concerning him; for some say ye thing will be left to ye law; but others that when he was sent for in, my Ld Chan[cellor] told him the K^g was very well sattisfied wth my Ld Treas^r proceeding, but very ill wth his, but, in confidence of his better conduct for ye future, hee was graciously pleasd to continue him in ye exercise of his place. If he be left to ye law, w^{ht} is sworn against him by Sr Will. D'Oyley[a] will, it's thought, put him out of office. Sr Gab. Silvius, I heare, is married yesterday to Mrs Howard,[b] ye mayd of honor, and I thinke one of my wives sisters will be in her place, the Queene wthall saying a very gracions thing, that she would not be wthout one of them till they were otherways disposed of.

It may be, you have not heard, and 'tis no greate matter youle say, that Mr Ropier[c] is married to Mrs Walker,[d] ye mayd of honor;

[a] Of Shottisham, co. Norfolk, Baronet.

[b] Sir Gabriel Sylvius married 1st, a daughter of Charles Peliott, Baron de la Garde; and 2nd, Anne, daughter of William Howard, a son of Thomas, first Earl of Berkshire. This second marriage took place on the 13th November. The bridegroom was double the age of the bride; a difficulty in the way of the match which was smoothed by Evelyn: " I was all this week composing matters betweene old Mrs. Howard and Sir Gabriel Sylvius, upon his long and earnest addresses to Mrs. Ann her second daughter, mayd of honour to the Queene. My friend Mrs. Godolphin (who exceedingly lov'd the young lady) was most industrious in it, out of pitty to the languishing knight; so as, tho' there were greate differences in their yeares, it was at last effected."—*Diary*, 11 Nov. 1677.

[c] Francis, son of John Roper, 3rd Lord Teynham.

[d] Anne, daughter of William Walker, of Bringwood, co. Hereford.

and she is now of ye bedchamber. My sister Phill. is offred a pritty
good match too, wch it may be will be accepted too.

I know not if I have told you my boy's name is Charles.

Upon a report Mr Brounkier was dying, Sr Steph: Fox got himself sworn Cofferer, upon ye decease or other vacancy of Mr Ash:^a
and Mr Brounkier.

Ye Prince of Aurang goes away a Fryday next.

CHARLES HATTON.

November 22, [16]77.

*   *   *

Noe Arehb^p is yet declared. The persons most spoke of are, y^e
B^p of London, ye A^p of Dublin, ye D^n of Pauls,^b Sr Lionel Jenkins,^c
ye B^p of Oxford, but those who are not friends to ye Coventry
family oppose him. The Deane of Pauls wase nominated when the
B^p of London^d wase ye sole candidate ; and they who were not
freinds to ye B^p of London nominated ye D^n of Pauls, not out of
kindnesse to him, but, in opposition to ye B^p of London, sett him
up as a person highly qualifyed, beyond exception, both for y^e
gravity of his yeares, his profound learning, exemplary piety, approved prudence, and recommended above most others in one circumstance very considerable, that he wase without ye dependences
of relations, hath noe nephews and neices to provide for; and some
say it is as convenient for ye Church of England y^t alterius orbis
papa shou'd have noe relations as it is for ye Church of Rome y^t
papa Romae shou'd have none. But, if ye B^p of London misses it,
he hath gained this great fame: y^t he wase judged most worthy in

---

^a *i. e.* Colonel William Ashburnham, Cofferer of the Household.

^b Sancroft, who was appointed next year.

^c Prideaux (*Letters to Ellis*, p. 54) notices the rumour that Jenkins was to go
into orders for this purpose.

^d Henry Compton.

ye vogue of ye greatest of ye King's protestant subjects. It is very wonderfull that soe many shon'd appeare soe zealous for him; but ye popish party are full as zealous for ye Arehb^p of Dublyn. Y^e general report amonst ye yulgar yesterday wase y^t ye B^p of London wase Arch^{bp}; ye B^p of Rochester, B^p of London; my cosen North,[a] D^n of Westminster; and Dr Outram,[b] B^p of Rochester.[c]

The Prince of Orange and Princesse set saile down ye river last Monday, and, after they were got as far as Margetts, were driven backe to Sherness, where they now are.

Last Saterday ye coronation of Q^n Elizabeth wase solomnised in ye city wth mighty bonefires and ye burning of a most costly pope, caryed by four persons in divers habits, and ye effigies of 2 divells whispering in his cares, his belly filled full of live catts who squawled most hideously as soone as they felt the fire; the common saying all ye while, it wase ye language of ye Pope and ye Divel in a dialogue betwixt them. A tierce of claret wase set out before ye Temple gate for ye common people. Mr Langhorne[d] sath he is very confident ye pageantry cost 40^{ll}.

It is reported ye D. of Buces supped wth ye King at Nell's last Munday night.

Y^r Lo^{pps} truly affect Brother to serve you,

C. HATTON.

[a] See above, p. 137, note ^c.

[b] William Owtram, of Christ's College, Cambridge, the celebrated divine; he was a prebendary of Westminster.

[c] John Dolben, Bishop of Rochester, was also Dean of Westminster.

[d] Richard Langhorne, the lawyer, one of the unfortunate victims of the Popish plot.

THE SAME.

November 27, [16]77.

*   *

The news of ye commotions in Scotland is now almost quash'd,
but ye forces ordred to march into Northumberland are not recalled.
It is heare said y^t Duke Lauderdale's interest declines ther. The
Marquis of Athol ^a and several others, whose freindshippe he thought
to have gained, are now his declared enemies, to awe whom it is
reported y^t he writ hither for succors, as if he feared an insurrec
tion, of wch ther is noe just cause of apprehension, as is now generally
given out. But many intelligent persons are not without their
feares thereof, ye presbyterian party ther being very potent and
insolent.

The Prince of Orange went from Sherness to Canterbury, and
staid ther till yesterday. The wind then coming southerly, he went
to Marget and put out to sea; but ye wind presently chopt about
easterly, soe y^t it is to be feared he will be driven back againe.

It is now generally reported y^t we shall not of a long time have
any Arehb^p of Canterbury declared, his Mat^ie designing to have
commissions appointed for ye management of ye temporalities; and
ye Deane and Chapter of Canterbury are by law of course, during
ye vacancy, ye guardians of ye spirituallities. This night, my L^d of
Oxford comes to town to preach to ye parsons' sons, who, next
Thursday, keep a great feast.^b His coming to town of a soudain
occasion'd a discourse, as if it wase in order to be Arehb^p. My L^d
Pembroke ^c hath, in a duel last Saterday night, wounded one

---

^a John Murray, Marquess of Atholl, Keeper of the Privy Seal of Scotland.

^h The festival of the Sons of the Clergy, held at St. Paul's, was first instituted
about 1655.

^c Philip, 7th Earl of Pembroke; died in 1683.

Vaughan (husband to my Ld Ross his first lady ^a) in ye belly, and it is thought he cannot recover. The quarrel wch occasioned it wase at Lockett['s]; and·ye next morning my Ld Pembroke sent, as it is reported, Mr Billinsly to let Vaughan know he was in drinke and to desire him to forget what had passed; but Vaughan, not content therwith, came at six of ye clocke againe to Lockett's and sent to my Ld Pembroke to challenge him out, who tooke Mr Billingsly for his second, and they two fought in ye moonshine behind Lockett's house wth Mr Vaughan and a kinsman of his; and it is s^d Vaughan run my Ld Pembroke down, and, when he wase upon my L^d, my L^ds footman came and cut Mr Vaughan over ye hand soe y^t he was disabled, and, as soon as he was got up, my L^d run him into ye belly. But others say my L^d wounded Vaughan fairely; but he hath been in soe many unhappy buisnesses y^t people are very apt to raise and credit all reports to his prejudice.

My Ld Renalaugh ^b hath a promise graunted him to be gentleman of ye bedchamber. The Lady Frances Villers ^c is dead, and ye Lady Harriot Hide ^d hath her place.

Y^r Lo^pps truly affect Brother to serve you,

C. HATTON.

^a Anne, daughter of Henry Pierrepont, Marquess of Dorchester, and wife of John Manners, Lord Ross, afterwards 9th Earl of Rutland. She was divorced in 1668. The case was brought in the House of Lords, to give Lord Ross power to marry again, and so to form a precedent for the King's divorce from the Queen and subsequent marriage with Miss Stewart. Charles had the good sense to abandon the project.

^b Richard Jones, 3rd Viscount, and 1st Earl of Ranelagh.

^c Frances Howard, daughter of Theophilus, 2nd Earl of Suffolk, and wife of Sir Edward Villiers, knight marshal of the household.

^d Henrietta, daughter of Laurence Hyde, afterwards Earl of Rochester.

The same.

*   *   *   *   *

Satterday last, ye Commons voted: That ye league offensive and defensive wth ye States Gen^ll and ye articles hereunto relating are not pursuant to their addresses nor consistent wth ye safety and good of this kingdome.

Sr Robt Sawyer, ye Speaker, not being judged by ye Court soe capable of serving ye King as Speaker to ye House of Commons as Mr Seymor,[a] it wase thought fitt y^t Sr Robert shou'd be sicke and therupon desire to be dismissed, and for his cure he wase promised 3,000 ginnies. Sr Robt therupon, tho' he was very well on Sunday night and is soe this day, yet yesterday morning he wase soe very ill y^t he desired by a letter to ye House y^t they would please to dismiss him; and, that wch made it ye more comicall, he desired ye prayers of ye House, and wase therupon prayed for in the House; and, after, Mr Seymor, upon ye King's recommendation, chosen, and approved of by his Ma^ty.

This day ther hath passed 2 votes in ye House of Commons, wch hath much disturb'd ye Court and it is thought may occasion a sudden prorogation, if not dissolution, of ye Parl^t.

(1) That an addresse be made to ye King y^t he will be pleased to remove ye councellors y^t advised him to make y^t answer to their addresse, ye 26 of May last and ye 31 of Jan. last, or to either of them.

(2) That an addresse be made to ye K. y^t D. Lauderdale be removed from his Councell and presence.

Y^r L^pps truly affect Brother to serve you,

C. Hatton.

[a] Edward Seymour, of Berry Pomeroy Castle. See Macaulay's character of him in the fourth chapter of his *History*.

Sir Charles Lyttelton,

My Lord, Bruges, May 18th, 1678.

Before I came out of towne I had really so much buisnesse that I could not write to you.

I have bine about 10 days landed in this countrey and heere the next day after, where wee have allarums all day long wth ye French troopes that appeare in sight of ye towne, the French King lying wth a mighty army, they say 60,000, and I beleeve it little lesse, w^thin 6 or 7 leages betweene this and Gaunt. Our feare of theyr coming hither is a little of for ye present; not that we know any other design they are going upon, but wee imagine, till it be resolved at London if wee shall have peace or warr, they will act nothing especially ag^st this place, where the King of Englands forces lye. Wee are at present 28 companies, and expect 3000 more this weeke, and there is 12 companies of the Guards at Ostend under my Lord Howards command. The forces heere are under mine, and I beleeve will continue so while they stay heere, because I am ye eldest collonel, and a gen^ll officer can't come heere to be commanded by ye Governor, whom no coll: of ye Spanish force will receive orders from. My Lord, wee are in a mighty mist w^ht our buisnesse is heere; this place is not to be defended nor worth it, and wee have possitive orders, upon no pretence or order of ye Governor (whom I am to obey in all thinges els), not to draw out any of the forces to any other place; wch he has pressd mee so hard to doe, that, to sattisfie him, I have bine forced to write to ye King expressly about it. Dam is a very strong fort about a mile hence, and, as it were, ye cittadell to·this place, where they have but few men; and they would fain have had mee sent some, but I could not w^thout orders.

My Lord Midleton,[a] who commanded heere before I came, is still heere and has lately had his breviat sent him to command as collo-

---

[a] Charles, 2nd Earl of Middleton, Secretary of State under James II.

CAMD. SOC. Y

nell.   This is a very greate towne and many people of ye best
quallity in it, it being one of ye refuges left for ye rest of ye countrey, theyr estates being all under the power of y^c French; w^ch
makes them very poore.   I am undone wth making my equipage to
come hither and wth the charge heere to maintaine it.

The Duke was kind to mee before I came away, and makes mee
beleeve it shall not rest upon him if I be not made a brigadeere, if
wee march into the field; wch I doe not thinke wee shall, because
wee all expect peace.^a   Some talk our buisnesse is to establish the
Prince of Aurange.

CHARLES HATTON.

MY LORD   June 18, 1678.

*   *   *   *   *

The day Sr Will. Scroggs came up as L^d Ch. Justice into West
minster Hall, I met Mr Longuevill ther, and he then very politickely
advised me to desist now from going so frequently as formerly I did
to ye new Ld Cheif Justice his house; for it might occasion y^c
like report, as formerly ther wase of y^r Lo^ppe, y^t I went a suitor to
Mrs Gilby.^b   I gave him sufficient assurance, as I thought, y^t, if
ther was any such report, it wase as groundlesse as y^t of y^r Lo^ppe
had been; but I told him I did not thinke it reasonable to follow
his advise in desisting from going to ye L^d Ch. Justice, for, by y^c
same reason, I must forbeare going to any house wher there wase a
young woman unmarried; for I never of late went to any such

---

^a It will be remembered that at this time the treaty of Nimeguen was in course of
negotiation.   The French made difficulties about evacuating the towns which they
held, when Charles, with unexpected vigour, suddenly took active measures, sent
troops to Holland, and entered into a league with the Dutch.   This brought matters
to a crisis, and the peace was signed in August.

^b Sir W. Scroggs' daughter.

place, but it wase reported I went a woing; and my cosen Roan, being at Kirby, hath raised a great report y^t I went soe frequently down of late only in designe to court her. But because I wou'd not follow Mr Longuevill's advise, whenever he comes, according to his politicke way of spreading of news, he wispers it about as a great secret, injoyning all persons to privacy, y^t I goe every day to ye L^d Ch. Justice his house to court Mrs Gilby; wch is every word true alike, for my indisposition of late hath kept me from going thither but very seldome, and Mrs Gilby hath not been in town thes six weekes. Almost all ye last terme I wase in Northamton-shire. Before ye end of ye terme all Sr William Scroggs his family and Mrs Dos and Mrs Dol. and Mrs Mary Phetiplace went to Weild Hall and designed to stay ther till Michaelmas. But, as soone as he wase declared Ld Cheife, ye Saterday following, he went down to Weild Hall, designing to receive ye sacrament in ye Weild church; and, businesse obliging him to leave his servants here in town, he desired me to goe down to be a witnesse for him, as I did; and, ye Monday following, he brought up his lady and daughter Anne, left his daughter Gilby and ye rest of his family (who desired me to give y^r Lo^ppe their service) at Weild Hall. Had it not been for an accident, I had not seen her thes 2 months, nor, in all probability, shall not thes four months. I must needs say I thinke her a very good woman, but she hath one damnable fault, and an unpardonable one: no portion except 3 boys, wch y^r Lo^ppe wants; and I desire not to meddle with ye mother, except y^r Lo^ppe will take ye boys.[a]

*   *   *   *   *

I shall now give you ye best account I can how Sr William Scroggs came to be made L^d Ch. Justice, for I am sure you will be very desirous to know it, and am certain you will keepe secret what I shall say, soe y^t neither I nor any personells shall receive any prejudice by what I shall disclose to you. Last Whit Sunday, he

---

[a] Qui s'excuse, s'accuse. He married her, the boys notwithstanding.

wase sent for up to to town to confer wth His M^{ty} and ye Ld Treasurer and to receive instructions for making a speech for ye King to ye Parl^t, who wase to meet ye Thursday following and had, a little before, for their peevishnesse, been prorogu'd by his Ma^{ty}. Sr William made a speech, but their were in it some expressions ag^t popery, wch were by one person disliked and therfore ye whole speech rejected. Ther were 3 speeches made for His Mat^y, one by ye Ld Treasurer, one by ye present Ch. Justice, and one by Sr Will. Temple, wch last wase approved of at ye cabinet and wase ye speech ye King spoke, wch I sent you in print; but, tho' the Ch. Justice speech wase not spoke, yet his Mat^y and ye Ld Treasurer were very well pleased wth him, and, great complaint being made of ye un-activenesse of ye late L^d Ch. Justice, who most commonly slept on ye bench, ye King told Sr Will. Scroggs that ye next remove of ye L^d Ch. Justice he wase in danger to be promoted; and ye Ld Treasurer discoursing wth him to ye like effect, and y^t it wase very requisite, as soone as ye Parl^t wase up, it wou'd be necessary to give ye L^d Ch. Justice his quietus. Sr William told ye Ld Treasurer y^t, if it wase done immediately after ye rising of ye Parl^t, ther being now such jealosies of an arbitary governm^t, people wou'd not beleeve that ye L^d Ch. Justice wase lay'd asyde for his incapacity for ye place, but that it wase only to make roome for him who wou'd better serve a turn; and this wou'd beget in ye people a pre-possession agst him, and he shou'd not be soe well able to doe the King y^t service, as if he wase put in during ye Session of ye Parl^t; for then people wou'd be apter to beleeve y^t ye late L^d Ch. Justice wase solely remooved for his incapacity. This reason did worke ye good effect wth my Ld Treasurer for wch it wase designed, and he approving thereof effectually pressed ye King immediately to remove Rainsfort. And ye Ld Chancelor presently after complaining to ye King of ye wcekenesse of ye King's bench, by reason of ye inactivenesse of ye L^d Ch. Justice, and y^t Twisden wase quite antiquated and Wild [a] very infirme, and moving ye King to allow

[a] Sir Thomas Twisden and Sir William Wilde, Judges of the King's Bench.

thes 3 pentions and put others in their places, the King said he wou'd not pay 15 judges and have but 12 in service, but he wou'd for Scrogs his sake give 1000^{ll} a yeare, and immediately ordred Rainsfort to be removed.

*   *   *   *   *

Last Saterday, ye House of Commons voted y^t they wou'd receive noe proposall for mony this sessions after this day. Yesterday, they tooke into consideration the charge of ye navy, and how to raise ye 200,000^{ll} for wch they stood engaged to ye King; but w^t they determin'd therein I cannot yet informe you. It will be time enouf by ye next oportunity. I suppose you see ye vote of Parl^t for disbanding ye army; but yesterday orders were issued out for several companies and troopes out of severall new raised regiments to march for Ireland. Perhapps you may wonder y^t ye Parl^t did allow but 200,000^{ll} for disbanding ye army; bnt they did comput that that, added to ye poll bill, wou'd be sufficient; for ye paymasters gave them an accompt that ye pay of ye army to ye last of May amounted

to	.	.	.	.	.	.	.	. 194,806 19 7
Clothing ye foot .		.		.	.	.	61,405 3 0
Clothing ye horse		.		.	.	.	18,270 0 0
Clothing ye dragons			,	.	.		12,480 0 0
Clothing ye grenadiers			.				1,600 0 0

For paying y^c forces, field .and staff officers,
from ye last of May ex. to last of June
inst. 51,125 5 0

339,687 7 7

Deductions.

For discharge of clothing, 2^d per diem foot, 6^d horse,
    2^{sh} 6^d grenadiers and dragons   .   .   .   22,000^{ll}
Deductions for ye clothing in June .   .   .   .   8,451^{ll}

30,451

The total charge of ye army, from y^c time of
raising to ye last of June incl. .   .   . 309,236 6 9
Wth deduction for cloths, wch amounts to   .   30,451 0 0

makes total 339,687 6 9

Sr Robt Car is turn'd out of ye Councell, and had been out of his
place of Chancelor of ye Dutchy but his patent is durante vitâ.
His crime is, appearing very high in ye House of Commons for y^e
bringing in Sr Will. Ellis in opposition to Sr Robt Markam, return'd
burghess for Grantham,^{a} and befreinded by my Ld Lindsey^b and
his kindred.   Sr Will. Ellis is nephew to Judge Ellis, looked upon
as a disafected person, and Sr Robt Car wase commanded by y^e
King not to endeavoure to bring into parl^t a person disafected to
ye governm^t, that he might gratify his owne private animosity agst
my Ld Lindsey and his relations.   But Sr Robt wase very violent
for Sr Will. Ellis, notwithstanding his Maties command.

I will not beg your pardon I can write noe more but for having
writ soe much.   I doe and hope you will excuse me considering
how indisposed I am to everybody ells.   I am

Y^r truly affect Brother to serve you,

C. HATTON.

THE SAME.

July 11, [16]78.

*   *   *   *   *

Yesterday, a soldier wase hanged at Tyburn for running from his
colours, tryed and condemned at y^c Sessions.   Here is great rumour
againe of war.   When my Ld Morpeth ^{c} went to put his regiment

^{a} Sir Robert Markham sat for Newark; Sir William Ellis for Grantham.
^{b} Robert Bertie, 3rd Earl of Lindsey.
^{c} Edward Howard, Lord Morpeth, afterwards 2nd Earl of Carlisle.

aboard for Flanders, above 200 run away; but they retooke 150. A L^t lay'd down his commission and went and harangued ye soldiers, told them he thought he and they shou'd have been employed in an actuall war agst France, but he now feared the designe was to enslave their own country, and he wou'd not be an instrument therin, and advised them to consider well what they did; upon wch they flung down their arms and run away. My cosen Montague is come over to vindicate himself agst severall accusations lay'd to his charge by ye Duchesse of Portsmouth and ye Duchesse of Cleavel^d, who accuses him of too great kindnesse wth her daughter Sussex^a and taking her out of ye monastery in wch she had placed her and putting her into another. The Earle of Plymouth^b is to be made a Duke and mary ye Lady Bridget Osborne, ye Ld Treasurer daughter. The Parl^t will have a recesse ye next weeke. I send you ye votes, and am

Yr Lo^{ppe}

truly affect. Br. to serve you,

C. HATTON.

MARY HATTON.^{c}

DEAREST BROTHER,   July ye 17, [1678.]

*   *   *   *   *

My designes, as you know, are broke, since a peace is absolutly determined. The K. consents to disband the army, onely that in garrisons, in Flanders, to stand till peace is determined generaly. Sr Robert Carr is turned out from being Chancelour of the Dutchy. He was too much a freind to Ld Arlington to stand. The next

---

^{a} Anne, married to Thomas Lennard, Earl of Sussex.

^{b} Charles Fitz-Charles. See above, p. 96, note ^{c}. He married Bridget Osborne, but did not become a duke.

^{c} Sister of Lord Hatton. She resided in France; and belonged to the Sisterhood of the Filles St. Thomas.

news he gives me is a pleasant storry that begings thus: Daincourt, Lady Gray,[a] and M[is] Smith walked still on. In the Park, the first left them, and going home in her chair, the L[d] of Monmouth mistaks the Lady Gray and gives her a billet. When she came home, she gives it her husband, who was angry with her, least y[e] L[d] should be displeased at the misfortun of his billet; he caryes it presently to him, beggs his pardon in the mistake. The L[d] beggs his, lest he should take the giving of the letter ill to his wife. And thus much for lnglish news.

What I have to aquaint you w[th]all of Paris news is our cosin Montagues being gon last Monday post towards Ingland, opon my Lord Sunderland's being sent hither ambassador, which bussness they say my Lady Cleavland has intrigued, out of revenge to the ambass. for being soe jealous of her for one Chevalier Chatillon [b] as to wright it wheire he thought it might doe her most prejudice, which she being advertised of, and attributing to it the cold reception she found when she was laitly in Ingland, has, as they say, acussed him of not being faithfull to his master in the imployment he gave him here; [c] too which there is another particular that dus much agravate her, and that is that, whillest she was in Ingland, the ambas. was every day with her daughter Sussex, which has ocationed such jealously of all sides that, for the saffty of my Lady Sussex, it is reported the ambass. advised her to a nunnery, and made choice of Belle Chase for her, where she is at present and will not see her mother. The Chevalier Chatillon is a person of quallity, young and handsome, but noe istate, and therefore &c.; pour la

---

[a] Mary, daughter of Charles Bennet, afterwards 2nd Lord Ossulston, and wife of Ford Grey, Lord Grey of Werke. It will be remembered that this is the Lord Grey who made such a sorry figure in Monmouth's rebellion.

[b] Alexis Henry, Marquis de Chatillon.

[c] Two of the Duchess's letters to Charles II., relating to her unseemly quarrel with Montague, are in the British Museum (Harl. MS. 7,006, f. 171; Add. MS. 21,505, f. 32), and are printed by G. S. Steinman in his *Memoir of Barbara, Duchess of Cleveland.*

bigotte, si elle ne peut courrir, quelle trotte, with which French proverb I will now eaise you of this trouble, and onely begg one favour more of you, that you will, ever beleeve me, what sincerly I am,

Deare brother,

Y^r most affec. sister and humble servant to command,

M. H.

Deare brother, I am not afraid of y^r getting the small pox, but for God saike have a care of coming neare those that have the feavour.

THE SAME.

Sept. ye 6th [1678?].

* * *

It comes in my mind to aske you if you have, in England, stel penns; because, if you have not, I will indevour to gett you some by one that told me of them, and did asseur me neither the glass penns nor any other sorts are neare soe good.

* * * *

The Duchesse of Mon[mouth], laitly arrived at Paris, went yesterday towards Bourbon. She dus gaine upon all that visitts her here for her tender hart to the Romain Catho. in Ingland. Doctor Goffe taks ye care of all her affaires here.

Y^r lo^p most affec. sister and humble servant to command.

Sir Charles Lyttelton.

MY LORD,   Jan. 21th, [1679].

It was last night' resolved to stop the proclamation, and that
the Councell shd. meete to day to consider if ye Parlimt. should sit
ye 4th of Feb.; but I am told just now, it being 1 a clock, that the
Councell does not meete to day, but there is order given for the
execution of Ireland, and Grove's to be on Fryday next, but not
Pickering.^a

Last night, after being examined by ye Councell, ye K^g being
present, my Lord Aston^b was committed closse prisoner to the
Tower.   Mr. Fowler denyes the knowledg of any thing concerning
the plot, and says he was not like to be trusted, being allways a
profest enemy to the Jesuites.   News came this morning that
Ralph Montague is taken in a disguise at Dover, where he was
endeavoring to get into France.   He hired a small vessel in ye river
and went aboard it as a servant to his own man, and, the wind
being ag^st them, hee put into Quinborow and so went over land to
Dover.

The same.

MY LORD,   Jan. 28, [1679].

I have y^rs of the 27th, since my last wch told you of ye dissolution.
I doe not know any thing considerable to tell you, but that I doe
not heare ye K^g concernes himself much ab^t ye elections of new
members; wch makes all those of ye Court at a stand if they shall
pretend or no; and I am sure many think utterly to decline it, tho'

---

^a William Ireland, a Jesuit priest, and John Grove and Thomas Pickering
servants in the Queen's Chapel, victims of the Popish plot.
  ^b Walter, 3rd Lord Aston.   Dugdale, the informer, had been his bailiff.

I beleeve some of them have interest enough to carry it; yet I am like one of those that have never bine married and w^d faine put my neck into ye noose, and soe, betweene you and I, am trying if I can creepe in at Harwich, wch I am in some hope to succeed w^th.

A Sunday nighte there happened a terrible fire in ye Temple lane. Pump Court is all burnt downe, and all behind the Divell Tavern, they say 200 houses. All Sr Francis Winnington's writings are lost; soe are a greate many others, and Mr. Ashmole's fine collections of medells.[a] But that wch is much more consider able then all these, I feare my Ld Feversham[b] is killed by ye fall of a peece of timber upon his head. He was opened this morning and they have resolved to trapan him, and are not w^thout hope; but it is a dangerous matter.

I am in so greate hast, my L^d, I can scarce tell w^ht I write; but you are used to it, and so I hope will excuse mee.

My Ld Brudenall is out npon bayle.

I sh^d say a greate deale for ye honour of my Lady's letter, but I can best expresse it in silence.

No disbanding of forces yet.

THE SAME.

MY LORD, Jan. 30, 167⅞.

There is found in my Ld Aston's house, among other papers, an indulgence, and a letter of my Ld Staffords wch tells him ye plot is discovered and they are all undone, but that he will hasten into Shropshire to allay the feares of theyr party. This a friend of mine

[a] See Evelyn's letter to Pepys, 12 Aug. 1689, wherein he mentions Elias Ashmole's collection of " all the antient and modern Coins of this kingdome, which were very rare, together with severall Medalls of our British, Saxon, and other Kings."

[b] Louis de Duras, lately succeeded to his father-in-law as Earl of Feversham.

saw in a letter from Thom Lane, who was by ye K^g's command appointed to search ye house.

Since my last, ye K^g has spoke to severall to use theyr interests to get into ye House againe, but yesterday there was a report that ye judges had given theyr opinions the parlim^t cannot be dissolved but when they were to meete or sitting, and that ye writts allreadie given out are illegall, and that no writts can be given out legally, till 40 days after ye dissolution, to call a new one; but all this I beleeve was but talk.

My Lord, my brother Lyttelton has ingaged mee to trouble y^r L^p in a little concerne of his, wch is this: the minister where he lives, having a very factious parish, and many of them refusing ever to come to church but going to conventicles, he proceeded to excommunicate some of them; wch has caused such a malice and combination against him that they will never leave him, joyning in a common purse to persecute him wth continuall law suites, not only to ye disgust but utter ruine of ye poore man; and, there being a tryall to be this term before my Ld Cheife Justice Scrogs, I sh^d, and so w^d my brother, take it for a greate favour, if y^r L^p w^d give my L^d a hint only, wch I know will be enough from y^r L^p, that Mr Waldron (for so is his name), ye minister, may not be oppressed by a company of fanatick rogues, he desiring nothing but equall justice and a faire end of the businesse. There is one of ye Masters of ye Chancery, Sr Lacon Child, who does set um to work and uphold them in it, upon a particular malice wch tis too long to give your L^p the trouble of. My Ld Feversham is trepand and is like to doe well after it.

W^{ht} I have told you of Ld Aston's letter, ye Duke told mee this afternoone he had enquired of some of ye Councell that had read ye letter, and that it containes nothing to that purposse wch Lanes does import.

It's my L^d Ch: Justice Scroggs.

The same.

My Lord,   Feb. 7th, 1679.

Yesterday one came to mee, a friend of y[rs] who I am enjoyned not to name, and desird mee to tell you that it had bine told at y[e] Cock pit y[t] M[r] Montague was going to lye at Kirby, and that it was privy you w[d] appeare concerned for his election,[a] and that I shd. therefore caution you of it, as a matter w[d] give y[e] K[g] and my L[d] Tr[r] greate offence; w[ch] I am apt truly to think it may, he being at this time so signally under his Ma[ties] displeasure.

My L[d], I thank you for y[e] assurance y[r] L[p] gives me of going to my L[d] C[hief] J[ustice] myself, w[ch] I will therefore venture to doe.

The news is that y[e] B[ishop] of Brandenburg has taken and killd upon y[e] place 8,000 of y[e] Swedes army, and driven the rest ab[t] as many more into an island, where they will be all at his mercy.

Yesterday morning M[r] Bedloe,[b] after being up and debauching all night, fell a railing to his guards of theyr captain, L[d] Grandison, and his L[t] Howard, and gave them very vile language, and sayd L[d] Grandison had married his sonn to a whore[c] (meaning M[rs] F. Gerald), and that she was y[e] Duke's, and that he had put her upon him, and that y[e] Duke himself was a rogue and a raskall, and that he had told him so to his face twenty times. Of this y[e] Duke and they made a complaint last night in y[e] Councell, and 2 of y[e] guards made oath. Bedlo was examined; he sayd he did not say so, but, if he did, it was in his drink, and asked pardon. So I think he was dismissd w[th]out any reproofe, that being looked on as some sort of sattisfaction. The meaning I suppose is, that there is to be a tryall to-morrow ab[t] y[e] murder of S[r] Ed: Godfrey, and

[a] He sat for Northampton.

[b] William Bedloe, the informer.

[c] Edward Villiers, son of George, 4th Viscount Grandison, married Catherine, daughter of John FitzGerald, of Dromana, co. Waterford.

Bedlo is a maine wittnesse; so the Councell was not willing to doe
any thing to weaken his evidence, and that the people may have no
pretence to say it is a trick on purposse.

My L^d Tr^r has writt to Litchfield to choose S^r Ch: Wheeler;
but I heare he is like to doe no good. My b^r is invited to it; but
he is not yet fully resolved to stand, for he is unwilling to stand so
in opposition, as to be at vast expence, as he was ye last time, and
to be in doubt wthall of carrying it. For his last letter seemes to
say there are severall pretenders. He might have bine K^t of y^e
Shire for Worcester wth lesse charge, I ^{1}magine; but my Ld Windsor at first seemed to oppose him for S^r Fr. Russell. Since, S^r
Francis refusing to stand, my L^d wd. have had my brother; and he
then, being so farr ingaged for Litch:, w^d not quit them.^{a}

Sr John Wordens lady dead of ye small pox.^{b}

Sr Nicolas Cary is chosen againe for ye place he served before.^{c}
Not a farthing yet at Mr Kingdom's office.

Our forces in Flanders cant stirr till ye weather changes.

Mr Peppys^d is chosen at Harrwich wth Sr Anthony Deane; but I
beleeve he does not resolve to accept it, if he be chosen at Portsmouth.

THE COUNTESS OF MANCHESTER^e TO LADY HATTON.

11 Feb. [1679]

I am very much concernd to heare of the loss of your little girl.
I thought it had bine grown very stronge, but I suppose it twas

^{a} He was elected for Lichfield.
^{b} Lucy, daughter of Dr. Osbourne, and wife of Sir John Werden, Bart., of
Leyland, co. Lanc. secretary to the Duke of York.
^{c} Sir N. Carew, M.P. for Gatton.
^{d} Samuel Pepys.
^{e} Anne, wife of Robert Montague, 3rd Earl of Manchester, and, after his death in
1682, of Charles, Earl of Halifax. She was the daughter of Sir Christopher
Yelverton, Bart., of Easton Mauduit, co. Northampton, and was thus the aunt of
Lady Hatton

somethinge concerninge the teeth. I hope God will soone make it up by sendinge you a son. I give you a thousand thankes for your kindnes to y⁰ girls. Kattes illness was a feaver, and left her soe weake and fante that she will be some time before she can stirr any wither.

I hope to see you aganest the parlimᵗ in towne, wᶜʰ will now bee very quickly. I suppose you have all the news from your bro[ther], who is a great man amongest the ladyes. He comes sometimes to us; and I am forced to putt him out of doores att night, he is such an etternall sitter up att nights. I am just now come from takeing y⁰ oathes and subscribing y⁰ Test in y⁰ Court of Chanserie, as all the Queen's servants are to doe. Yesterday the 3 men acussed by Prance was condemned,ᵃ att wᶜʰ the people made y⁰ grattes[t] show of satisfaction imaginable. My Lady Gerard ᵇ was in the Citty taken (in a chaire) to bee y⁰ Dutchess of Portsmouth, and called the French whore; and soe many gott about the chaire as much frighted [her]. But some wᵗʰ her told who she was. Sʳ Jhos: Williamson was told by the Kinge one Sunday morninge he was noe longer fitt for yᵗ employmᵗ as the Kinges afferes att this time was, and y⁰ secretarie's plaice given to my Lᵈ Sunderland. He is promised to have y⁰ 6,000ˡˡ given him he payed for it, together wᵗʰ 2,000ˡˡ Sʳ Floyde is to pay for his plaice.ᶜ He was much surprised, not in y⁰ least expecting it. Tis said y⁰ orther will bee removed to. I begg my servons to your Lord, and remaine

Your most affectionat aunt and servant,

A. MANCHESTER.

ᵃ Robert Green, Henry Berry, and Lawrence Hill, condemned for the murder of Sir Edmond Bury Godfrey, on the evidence of Miles Prance, who, to save his own life, took to the trade of informer.

ᵇ A French lady, whose name is unknown, wife of Charles, Lord Gerard, afterwards 1st Earl of Macclesfield. She did not show the presence of mind which Nell Gwyn is said to have displayed on a like occasion in assertion of her Protestantism.

ᶜ Sir Philip Lloyd (who is more than once in these letters called Floyd), one of the Clerks of the Council.

SIR CHARLES LYTTELTON.

MY LORD,   [4 March, 1679]

That on ye other side is a coppy of ye K^{gs} to ye Duke, who, in obedience to it, went away yesterday wth ye Duchesse. It was known to but very few the night before y^t ye Duke wd. goe; tho' it were guessed he wd. not stay long after her. There is gone wth him my Ld Peeterborow, Ned Griffith, Fortrey, Coll: Worden,^a and some under servants. The rest will soone follow. It's sayd they goe first into Holland, and after to Bruxelles, to reside; but I phancy theyle land at Ostend.

I went after them yesterday to Eerif, where they went aboard ye yacht, and tooke my leave. I beleeve they are still there and like to be so yet, for the wind is directly ags^t them, and little appearance of a sudden change; but I beleeve they will endure it.

This is news enough in conscience, my L^d, for once; therefore, wth my humble services to y^r L^p, I kisse y^r hands.

Y^r humblest servant,

C. LYTTELTON.

It was once intended Lady Anne sh^d have gone wth them; but since, that was altered by order of Councell, as I heard.

My B^r is returned hither, and is so for burgesse of Litchfield.

---

^a Edward Griffin (as he is called by Chamberlayne in the *State of England*) and Thomas Fortrey, Grooms of the Bedchamber of the Duke of York; and Colonel Robert Werden, his Comptroller.

CHARLES HATTON.

My L^d,   March 4, [16]7⅘.

*   *   *   *   *

Here is very prodigious news, wch noebody wou'd beleeve till they saw ye event. The Duke of Yorke is gone beyond sea, set forward yesterday. Last Saterday, it wase reported y^t ye Dutches and Lady Anne designed, as yesterday, to goe for Holland, to visit ye Princess of Orange, and it wase wispered y^t ye Duke wou'd follow; but ye Lady Anne went not, but ye Duke and Dutchesse set out yesterday. Severall bishopps were lately wth his Royall Highness, to endeavour to convert him, but he told them plainly he wou'd neither be of their religion nor pretend to be of it. The King, it is said, therupon told his Highness y^t, if he did not return to ye Church of England, he must for some time withdraw himself beyound sea, or els ye parl^t wou'd be soe incensed as to press wth great violence the passing acts of parl^t to ye utmost prejudice of his Royal Highnesse, who then desired his Ma^{ty} y^t, for ye securing ye succession of ye crown to him, his Ma^{ty} wou'd in Counsell declare and have it entred y^t he wase never marryed to any person but Queen Catherin; and accordingly his Ma^{ty} did soe declare last Fryday in Counsell. It is said y^t, at ye Duke's further request, his Ma^{ty} write ye enclosed letter.

Y^r Lo^{pps} and my sister Hattons

truly affection^t Brother and humble serv^t,

C. HATTON.

I shall take care about ye apricocke trees.

Lord Grey of Ruthyn.[a]

My Lord,   [8th March, 1679.]

I cannot omit this opportunity of giving you some account of us,
for tho' there is no matter happen'd of extraordinary consequence,
yet it will be a satisfaction to your expectation to know what has
occurred.   There is but very litle encouragement to invite your
Lordship amongst us; we have but bad omens.   The King recommended S[r] Thomas Meres for Speaker, but the Hous chose M[r]
Seimaur, whom the King refused.   He put my Ld. Chancelour to
some litle disturbance, who was only provided for the formality of
his refusing it; but he said no more [than] that since he was
unanimously chose by the Hons, if he had his Majesties roial approbation, he would endeavour to serve them to his power.   But he
was commanded to desist, and the House to choos a new Speaker
presently.   They on their return voted it their undoubted right
and priviledg, proffering to produce presidents where the Speaker
has acted without having had the King's approbation.   They beg'd
farther time to consider of it, and the King granted them till Tuesday, till when we are adiourned.   In all this proceeding there has
not bin a dissenting vote.   The court party is in some distress,
since S[r] John Earnely is their only Speaker.   They are all resolved
to venture an hundred dissolutions rather then not ruin my Ld.
Treasurer; and M[r] Powel[b] told them that they might, by the last
parliment and the countreys new elections, see that a dissolution
had only turu'd out those that were wholly prejudicial to the
nation's interest; and that, the oftener they changed, it would produce more clearly that effect.   He will find his enemies increased
in our House, since he has shewed so much ingratitude to the Duke,

---

[a] Charles Yelverton, 14th Baron, died in May.

[b] Henry Fowle, M.P. for Cirencester, Speaker in the Convention Parliament of
1689, and afterwards Master of the Rolls.

and yet, as they say, has not at all mended our councels. If they bring new articles, sending of the Duke away is likely to be one, dissolving the last parliment contrary to the councels advice, and the denial of the Speaker, since the King told him the night before that he was the last man he would refuse for that imploiment.

My Lord,

Your Lordship's most affectionate,

humble servant,

GREY RUTHIN.

* * *

CHARLES HATTON.

Mar. 8, [16]7⅞.

I suppose, my L^d, y^r Lo_{PP}e may be desirous to be informed fully of all ye parliamentary proceedings since ye houses met, and I am very confident you have much better intelligenc then I can give, yet perhapps I may here have heard some circumstances, and thos not inconsiderable, wth wch y^r corispondents may not have acquainted you. I shall therfore let you know what I heare from ye most intelligent personns of my acquaintance. Last Thursday morning there wase a rumour as if Sr Thomas Meeres, not Mr Seimor, wase design'd by ye court to be Speaker of ye House of Commons, who, as soone as they were return'd to their House, after ye enclos'd speeches were finish'd, ther wase a short pause in ye House; and then Birch^a start up and said, he beleeved, noe person being recommended to them, y^t his Ma^{ty} resolved to leave them to make a free choice of their Speaker, and, for his part, he thought noe man soe fitt and acceptable to ye House as Mr Seymor. Where-upon, Sr Thomas Lee, Sr Richd Ingoldsby,^b and all y^t party did, in a very tumultuous way, take Mr Seymor and carry him to ye chaire.

a Colonel John Birch, M.P. for Weobly.

b Members for Ailesbury.

Sr John Ernly attempted to speak, but ye tumult wase soe great
noebody cou'd be heard. Mr Secretary Coventry is very ill and
wase not ther. As soon as Mr Seymor wase in ye chaire, he gave
ye House thanks for their favour to him, and did, after ye usuall
manner, endeavour to disable himself, and told ye House, if they
wou'd not excuse him, he wou'd move his Ma^{ty}, and he' hoped he
wou'd; and y^t it would be ye only thing in wch ye King and y^e
House wou'd disagre.

All ye ministers of State seem'd much surprized, as soone as they
heard ye news y^t Mr Seymor wase chosen Speaker; and yesterday
morning ther was a report y^t his Ma^{ty} wou'd not approve of M^r
Seymor; who, when he wase, at three in afternoone, presented to
his Ma^{ty}, he did not, according to his promise and y^e usuall forme
of speech, desire his Ma^{ty} to excuse him; but only said y^t y^e Commons, according to his Ma$^{ty's}$ command, had made choice of a
Speaker, and did present him to his Ma^{ty} in y^t capacity, of whom
shou'd his Ma^{ty} in his royall wisdome approve of, he wou'd endeavour, according to y^e utmost of his abilities, to serve him. After
short pause, y^e Chancelor, who seemed surpris'd at y^e manner of
Mr Seymor's speech, told him his M^{atie} had other services to employ him in, and therfore he cou'd not admit of him to be Speaker,
but commanded ye Commons to returne to their House and make
choice of another Speaker.

As soone as ye Commons were return'd, they expressed great
disatisfaction y^t his Ma^{ty} had refused to approve of ye Speaker they
presented to him, declaring it to be a high breach of their priviledge
and wthout any precident; y^t never any but one person wase refused,
and y^t only by reason of a sudden sicknesse fallen on him. In their
speeches they did much reflect on ye cheif minister of state, as if the
refusall wase advis'd by him, for y^t, on Thursday night, his Ma^{ty}
declared himself very well satisfyed wth ye choice of Mr Seymor,
but ye next day refus'd him. After some debate, they adjourn'd it
till nine this morning, y^t precidents might be search'd.

This morning, his Ma^{ty} sent to acquaint the House y^t he wou'd give them till Tuesday morning to make choice of a Speaker. Mr Seymor wase not in ye House. This day Sr Thomas Meeres and Mr Powell were nominated, but ye House seemed peremptory resolved to adhere in their choice of Mr Seymor, but have adjourn'd ye debate till nine next Monday.

This beginning looks ill, tho' I find many are of opinion y^t this storme will blow over, y^t they will choose a third person, not Sr Tho. Meeres, wth whom they seeme much disatisfyed. But it is feard they will begine wth impeaching ye Premier Minister d'estat, to whose advise ye Duke's departure wase attributed, and therby he gain'd great applause; but now ye high flown blades say, it wase ye Duke's feares, least he shou'd be accus'd by ye Ld Bellasis and others, made him desirous to leave England, and y^t ye letter wase only a contrivance to disguise the true occasion of his departure; that this refusall of ye Speaker is a contrivance of ye L^d T^r to secure himself by occasioning a rupture betwixt ye K[ing] and P[arliament], wch it is to be feared, if they proceed in thes heats, they themselves will soudainly occasion.

The L^ds in ye Tower^a have petitioned to be speedily brought to a tryall; as it is thought they will, if ye Parl^t continue.

> Y^r Lo^pps truly affec^t Brother to serve you,
> C. HATTON.

I am my sister Hatton's very humble servant.

WILLIAM LONGUEVILLE.

MY LORD   11th of March, [1679].

The Commons have not as yet agreed what to doe in this new started question about their Speaker. The King too day, in answer

---

^a Lords Powis, Stafford, Petre, Arundel of Wardour, and Belasyse, imprisoned for the Popish plot.

to their Representation (that's ye word now), told them that too
much time had been allready lost, and that hee wisht them to goe
doe as hee had advised them.   Upon returne from Whitehall with
this his Ma^ty's short discourse, some speeches were made in that
house, many old stagers inclining to comply wth ye King's former
advise, and to wave Mr Seymour in order to ye choosing of some 3^d
person; Mr Powle or S^rt Gregory ^a are thought of, Sr Thomas
Moore's unlikely.   But, after all, and that they might sleepe upon
the point, ye Commons adjourned till too morrow eight a clockc.
All our towne expected a prorogation, if not a dissolution, too day,
for the barges of state lay out all ye morning, and other directions
for ye solemne attendance made ye guessers busy.

Mr Langh[orne] was not offerd a pardon in my commission; but
my Ld Bridgwater ^b and Essex were with him afterwards wth one in
their order, yet have gaind no more then I did; y^t 's nothing.
Tom Langh[orne] was at mee last night to send to your Lo^p to
come up to meet wth my Ld Longf[ord] about his brother, and this
hee said was at his brother's desire.   I told him his brother sayd
no such thing to me, and I conceivd that, tho your Lo^p and twenty
lords more should intercede, there would bee no good done thereby
in the condition the citty and nation are in, having respect to 's
popery.

The Savoy is this day search't and dugg into by those who are
to find 2 or 3 hundred thousand pounds there, the plot money men
say lyes there hid.

*   *   *   *   *

Y^e Duke is not gone as you have herd, if I am informed rightly;
but some think ye ministers want him againe to beare a load, and
others wish y^t hee were recalld for ye nation's satisfaction, who
thinke him worse abroad then heere.

^a Serjeant William Gregory, appointed Speaker
^b John Egerton, 2nd Earl of Bridgewater.

Your B^p of Peterborough ^{a} is reported to bee dead suddenly. Sunday last a fire or two broke out in y^e citty; two houses in one place were destroyed, in y^e other only a fright. How these began is y^e quære.　＊　＊　＊

Your Lo$^{p's}$ most obliged
and most faithfull serv^t,
W　L.

CHARLES HATTON.

My L^d,　　　　　　　　　　　　　　　March 18, 167$\frac{8}{9}$.

Every howre doth here produce fresh news. I will acquaint you wth y^e most considerable I heare, wch is, y^t my Ld Treasurer hath obtained leave of y^e King to keepe his staff till y^e 26th inst., and is created Marquisse Danby,^{b} and y^t y^e Treasury is to be managed by commissioners, but not those I named in my last, but ye Ld Arlington,^{c} Sr John Ernly, Sr Edwd Deering, Mr Lawrence Hide, and Mr Sidney Godolphin, and Harry Guy to be secretary; tho' many thinke ye House of Com. will oppose y^t ye present Treasurer shou'd name his successors, and his freinds doe much blame him for drawing by any empty title a greater envy on him.

Yesterday, St Gregory wase presented to his Ma^{ty} as Speaker. In his speech he tooke notice y^t he had made his excuse to ye House, but they wou'd not accept thereof; but he submitted himself to his Ma^{ty}. Y^e Ld Chancelor in his speech to him (in answer to his desire y^t his Ma^{ty} wou'd candidly interpret his transactions) s^d that he might be assured y^t what his Ma^{ty} had created by his power he wou'd protect by his kindnesse. As soone as y^e

---

^{a} Joseph Henshaw, died 9th March, 1679.

^{b} The design to create him Marquess of Caermarthen was entertained at this time, but was abandoned. He obtained the title under William, in 1689.

^{c} Essex, not Arlington.

Commons were withdrawn, ye Ld Shaftsbury fell very severe on my
Ld Chancelor for y^t expression, and s^d it was cnouf to renew ye late
unhappy difference, and desired it might not be entred in their
books. My Ld Chancelor excused himself by alledging y^t he wase
put upon making his speech extempory, and moved y^t neither the
Speaker['s] nor his speech might [be] cntred in ye journal, but
only y^t ye Speaker wase presented and approved of by his Mat^y;
and soe it wase ordred by ye House. But my Ld Shaftsbury fell
severely on my Ld Treasurer, taking notice of ye report y^t he wase
created a Marquisse during ye time he lay under an impeachm^t
from ye Commons of Engl^d of being a traitor, and moved y^t y^e
House wou'd petition his Mat^y not to doe such an act as might
allienat ye affection of his subjects. But ye Ld Hallifax opposed
his motion, saying his Lo^{ppe} had been impos'd on by a flamm
report, for it wase impossible to imagine y^t ye King cou'd ever be
prevailed upon to doe an act soe ungratefull to his people.

It is reported y^t ye Duch^{ss} of Portsmouth hath been wrought
upon by ye Ld Rannelaugh and Mr Seym^r to act ag^t ye Treasurer,
ye Ld Rannelaugh being dist[a]sted ag^t ye Treasurer for designing
to turn him out of his place in Irel^d and put ye Ld Plymoth in.

I shall send ye wine and tobacco according to y^r command. This
day, Mr Kingdon gives me fresh assurance he will very soudainly
supply you. I am my sister Hattons and y^r Lo^{pps} very humble
serv^t and most affect Brother,

C. HATTON.

The Duke of Yorke is gone from ye Hague to Brussells.

THE EARL OF DANBY.

My L^d,   28 March, [1679.]

I know not whither those unfortunate circumstances I am under
may not make this seeme an unseasonable application to y^r Lo^p for

so great a favour as I now presume to beg of you; but, if I may have creditt wth y^r Lo^p to bee beleeved in what I say, I know honour will then bee a motive to grant my request, as what one peer might hope for from another.

Yo^r Lo^p knows I am impeached by the House of Comons, for high treason &c., and my charge is as well known as my impeachment, wherein the 4 first articles are those wch are pretended to bee the treason. The first and third of them are grounded upon a letter I writt by ye Kings comand to Mr Montagu, as his Matie has alwaies own'd, and is subscribed under his hand. The second is my raising of an army and maintaining itt (wch every body can answer and is as much concern'd in as myselfe) and not takeing security of ye paymaster; wch was done. The fourth is my concealeing the plott wch ye King discovered to mee, besides that I was the sole cause of Coleman's papers being seized, wch has discovered more of ye plott then anything else; so that, in truth, I am only accused for haveing obey'd ye King's comands about ye letter, and ye matter of that letter aggravated to be called treason, though all my councill att law have declared nothing in the letter to bee treason, though construed in ye worst sense and without ye true interpretation of itt. Yett, such is my hard fate, that as I am impeached for my obedience, and I call God to witnesse for nothing else that I know, so I am like to be condemn'd also by my obedience. For his Matie, from an apprehension of this giveing too great an interruption to ye publique matters at this time (but I thinke truly more out of kindnesse to mee, beleeving that ye torrent of ye House of Comons would ruine mee by theire violence), did command mee to absent myselfe when my comittment was orderd by the L^{ds} on Monday last, though they had given mee till the Thursday following to putt in my answer. This absenting did exasperate ye L^{ds} to passe a bill of banishment ag^t mee, if I did not appeare by a day not named; and ye bill was sent to ye Comous yesterday, who imediately threw itt out of theire house for being too moderate and are com'd to a second reading of a bill of attainder against mee; so that my humble request now to

CAMD SOC. 2 B

y^r Lo^p is, that you would bee so generous and charitable as to come up and give mee y^r assistance against such a cruelty, if y^r Lo^p shall find true what I say: and, if you do not, I will not only loose all my honour and reputation wth y^r Lo^p but will consent to your joyning against mee when you are here.

I hope y^r Lo^p will forgive this tedious trouble where itt is of so great importance to,

My L^d,

Y^r Lo^{ps} most humble and obedient servant,

DANBY

CHARLES HATTON.

Apr. 15, [16]79.

*   *   *   *   *

Yesterday ye L^{ds} passed ye bill of attainder ag^t ye Earl of Danby, in case he comes not in by ye 21 inst. It was carryed by 3 votes. 6 B^{pps} went out of ye House as soone as ye L^{ds} went to voting, all who seemed inclinable to have ye bill passe but wou'd not give their votes, because it wase for taking away life. Y^e Ld Shaftsbury moved y^t all ye rest wou'd goe out. But they stayed in and voted ag^t ye bill, viz. Canterbury, London, Rochester, Bath and Wells Ely, Worcester, Landaf. Y^e B^{pps} who went out were, Durham, Exeter, Bristow, Carlisle, Chester, Lincoln.

*   *   *   *

Y^r Lo^{pps}

Very affect Brother to serve you,

C. HATTON.

THE SAME.

My L^d,   July 10, [16]79.

     *   *   *   *   *

This day his Mat^y declared in Councill, at Hampton Court, his resolution of dissolving this parl^t and calling another, ye 7th or 8th next. From thence you will conclud, I doubt not, y^t Mr Langh[orne] must not expect mercy. He petitioned wth all submission and made a most ample declaration of his loyalty, but, because he denyed to be conscious of ye plot, his petition was rejected; and it wase declared that, unless he discovers ye plot, he must expect noe mercy.

Mr Pepys and Sr An^w Deane^a wase bailed yesterday, and, if my L^d Ch. J[ustice] hang 500 Jesuits, he will not regaine ye opinion he hath therby lost wth ye populace, to court whom he will not act ag^t his conscience. He gives you his service, sath he hope you will meet him according to y^r promise at Oxford, and he designs from thence to make Kirby in his way home; sath he will come with all his family and retinue, and ther examine ye business of ye swappe, and, unless you have V. and B. in ye country, he beleeves you will want witnesse. Whatever you doe him, he sath you will find it very difficult to convince Mis Anne.

The D. of Monmouth I expect to-morrow by ye Hampton coach to receive ye accompts from Guernesey. I hope wee shall get of pretty well. One of ye commissioners advises me to put a good face on it and take notice of any irregularity.

I will enquire of Mr Ashmole when venison will be most wellcome to him.

---

^a They were accused of supplying information to the French respecting the English navy. Moreover, Pepys was suspected of popery. See his correspondence of this period.

I have as great a rarity almost as ye booke he hath of Dr Dee, wch wase burnt; for I have a letter from Penning (who wase to have 60^{ll} per annum of my fee farm rents during his life), dated June ye 29th, 79, and I am able to prove he hath been dead allmost a twelvemonth

I am y^r Lo^{pps} truly affect Brother to serve you,

C. HATTON.

THE SAME.

M^y L^d,   July 15, [16]79.

Mr Langhorn wase yesterday executed. It is generally said he dyed very couragiously. It is most certain he did, wth great asseveration, declare he knew nothing of ye plot. He had prepared a solemn declaration of his ignorance therof, and design'd to have read it; but ye sherif, as soone as he wase in ye sledge, demanded what papers he had, and tooke y^t from him; but I heare it will soudainly be printed, and by ye next I designe to send it you. The substance of it wase ye same wth his declaration herein sent, wch wase caused to be printed by one who wish'd better to Mr Lang horn's party then ye Protestant religion. I guesse it wase ye same person who told him y^t Whitbread^a assented to ye discovery of their lands.^{b} Since y^r Lo^{ppe} went away, I have often been wth Mr Langhorne. He delivered me a letter, directed to ye Ld Langford^c and y^r Lo^{ppe}, wch I wase to deliver to wch of you I saw first. I have delivered it to my Ld Langford, who told me it wase an intimation

---

^{a} Thomas White or Whitebread, Provincial of the Jesuits in England; lately executed.

^{b} Langhorne was respited for a short time that he might make a return of the Jesuits' property in England. His information was not so full as had been expected; he was therefore executed.

^{c} Francis Aungier, Earl of Longford.

how he designed to dispose of his estate. He engaged me to assure y^r Lo^ppe he dyed a true honorer of y^r Lo^ppe, and made it his request, if his son Richard escaped, you wou'd please to entertain him as y^r servant; W^ch he wou'd not doe but y^t he wase most confident he wou'd serve you faithfully. And he desired of my Ld Langford and y^r Lo^ppe y^t all his books, writings, and manuscripts whatsoever, might be given to his said son Richard, if he shou'd not be con-demn'd. And he further desired me to acquaint y^r Lo^ppe y^t it wase his earnest request y^t ye last Midsummer quarter rent in Hatton Garden might be pay'd to his brother, for ye maintenance of his son in prison, and y^t you wou'd please to order Mr Monteage soe to pay it; but he wou'd not have his wife nor my Ld Langford know it. And y^t, as for his daughter, it wase his desire she shou'd have noe dependence on her mother, but y^t care might be taken to free her from ye tyranny of her mother, y^t in a few months she wou'd be of age to choose a guardian, and y^t he had acquainted her soe and advis'd her to choose ye Ld Langford or y^r Lo^ppe

*　　　*　　　　　*　　　*

Y^r Lo^pps truly affect Brother to serve you,

C. HATTON.

THE SAME.

My L^d,   Aug. 26, [16]79.

I know all the King's loyall subjects must be extreemly alarumm'd at ye news of his M^aties illnesse, and be very desirous to know all ye circumstances therof, and y^t noe person will be more concern'd then y^r Lo^ppe; and therfore I shall give you ye best account I can receive therof.

Last Wednesday his Ma^ty play'd at tenis, and, after y^t he had been in bed and rubb'd, he walked a long time by ye water side.

Y^e next day, he found himself indispos'd, and on Fryday morning he had a very great chillness and nummness in all his limbs, especially his leggs and shoulders, and his head much indispos'd and heavy. On Saterday he tooke some manna wch purg'd him 16 or 17 times. On Sunday he wase better, but on Monday morning he had a very ill fitt. Severall physitians sent for from henc. He wase blouded 12 ounces, after wch he vomited, wch did affright ye physitians, and purg'd. But last night he rested very well, and wase well this morning. If it prove an ague, his Mat^y resolves on his well day to come to town. Orders are sent to have his lodgings at Whitehall got ready, without faile, by to-morrow night. But if his Mat^y continues well, as it is to be hop'd he will, and as we have all reason to pray he may, he will not, it is thought, come to town soe soudainly.

The Privy Counsell, wch wase adjourn'd till ye 2^d of 8bre, is now I am inform'd, summon'd to meet again soudainly and sit twice a weeke.

*   *   *   *   *

Y^r Lo^{ppes} truly affec. Brother to serve you,

C. HATTON.

SIR CHARLES LYTTELTON.

MY LORD,   London, Aug. 28th, [16]79.

I have bine 4 or 5 days at Sheene.^{a} A Tuesday I was at Windsor. I saw ye King, who was then very weake. He has a

---

^{a} Perhaps on a visit to Shene Abbey, Henry Brouncker's house, which afterwards became his own, as Evelyn tells us, in his *Diary*, 24 March, 1688: "I went with Sir Charles Littleton to Sheene, an house and estate given him by Lord Brouncker; one who was ever noted for a hard, covetous, vicious man, but, for his worldly craft and skill in gaming, few exceeded him. Coming to die, he bequeath'd all his land, house, furniture, &c. to Sir Charles, to whom he had no manner of relation, but an ancient friendship, contracted at the famous siege of Colchester 40 yeares before. It is a pretty place with fine gardens, and well planted, and given to one worthy of them, Sir Charles being an honest gentleman and souldier."

tertian ague, and has had 4 fits; the last was more gentle, yet held him from 9 on Tuesday night till noone yesterday. The lodgings are here prepared for him, so soone as he is fit to remove; but I feare that will not be a good while. I pray God give him better health. All thinges yet are quiet, and I hope they will continue so. To-morrow I goe againe to Windsor, and, as I have ocasion, will give y^r L^p a further account.

Harry told mee my Lady's brother Yelverton has this feavor wch rages terribly in these parts. My Ld Lauderdale has 14 or 15 in his family down of it. I wish you better health where you are. My humble services to my Lady.

CHARLES HATTON.

September 2, [16]79.

Last night, my L^d, about nine of ye clocke, his Royal Highnesse came to Sr Allen Appsley's^a house, in St. James Square, and lay ther, and early this morning went for Windsor, where he wase received by his Mat^y wth all possible demonstrations of joy. The Duke wase not expected here by any of his servants, as may very probably be imagined; for, after his arrivall, all their letters were countermanded from ye post house. It is said that his Ma^{ty} ordred ye Ld Privy Seale^b and Ld Feversham to acquaint ye Duke wth his illness, and at ye same time let ye Duke know he neither had nor wou'd doe anything wch shou'd be injurious to him; and y^t his Highnesse did, immediately upon notice of his M^{tys} illnesse, take post. Now ye entertainment of ye town is to enquire: "Who goes for Windsor?" that being ye mesure ye disafected personns take to judge how other personns stand affected.

---

^{a} Sir Allen Apsley, an old Cavalier. Falconer to the king, and almoner to the Duke of York.

^{b} Arthur Annesley, Earl of Anglesey.

The personne[a] you enquired after wase, last Saterday, in town. He came y[e] night before from Windsor, where his Mat[y] wase very extraordinarily favourable to him. As soone as he saw him, he tooke notice to him how ill y[e] people had used him in his absence; " But," s[d] he, " they have used me worse, and I am resolv'd we will stand and fall together." The other replyed, he hoped they shou'd stand but not fall; for his part, he wase resolved to deport himself wth all y[e] courage and loyalty befitting y[e] dignity of y[e] place his Mat[y] had advanc'd him to. His Mat[y], being in bed, call'd him to y[e] bedside and gave him his hand to kiss, renewing to him y[e] assurance y[t] he wou'd stand by him. He wase resolv'd to have gone this weeke to Windsor againe, but I suppose he will not now make such hast.

I am very glad to heare of y[e] probability of seeing y[r] Lo[ppe] in town soe soudainly. I wish to Heaven you had been here now, least it be interpreted y[t] you come not to congratulate his Mat[ies] recovery but to wellcome his Highness upon his arrivall. His stay here is variously discours'd of. Some say he will fix here, but his own servants give out y[t] he will not stay above 8 or 10 dayes.

His Mat[ie] is very well. His physitians were S[r] Alexan. Frasier, D[r] Dickeson, D[r] Mickctwait, D[r] Needam, D[r] Lower, and D[r] Yerbrow.[b] D[r] Micketwait is knighted; he is President of y[e] Colledg, who are very much pleas'd y[t], tho his Mat[y], when he was well, seemed to slight them, yet now he wase sick made use of none but physitians of y[e] Colledge. It is reported his M[ty] got his illnesse at Portsmouth, where severall of his attendance fell sicke, amonst y[e] rest S[r] Jonas Moore, who, in his returne from thence, dyed in an inne on y[e] road. His son succeeds him in his place.

*   *   *   *   *

Y[r] Lo[pps] truly affect Brother to serve you,

C. HATTON.

[a] Chief Justice Scroggs. His favour at Court at this moment was due to his conduct in the trial of Sir George Wakeman, the Queen's physician, which took place in July.

[b] Edmund Dickenson, John Micklethwaite, Sir Caspar Needham, Richard Lower, and Henry Yerbury.

The Countess of Manchester to Lady Hatton.

Sept. 8th, [1679].

*   *   *

I was two dayes att Windsor, and had the fortune to bee ther when the Duke first come. It was a great surprise, if not to all, to ye greater number, the Kinge having sent before to him not to come. But he did noe question expect to finde him much worse then he found him, for yt daye he begane to walke about the hons. Ther are severall oppinions wether he will goe back or noe; and, till the Kinge remooves from Windsor, I suppose he will not stir. About the 15 or 16 of this moneth the Kinge speakes of New-markett. The docterrs are much against it, and, if he goeth not thither, I beleeve will stay ye longer att Windsor. My Lady Montrose a is going to morrow for Ireland. She seems much pleased and willing to goe. Her sister goeth wth her. My Ld of E. was not kinde to her, made ym pay for ther board, and went the next morning after she was married away into ye country, and left her husband to gett her a dyner as he could. I wonder how people can doe such thinges. My Ld Halifax is become soe great a courtier as never is from ye Kinges elbow. Thus you see how men change their mindes upon ocasions. The D. refused Sr Tho. Armstrong to kiss his hand, and, 'tis said, is very coole to ye D. of Monmouth. Thus I have told you all the news I know, and only begg my service to your Lord, and remaine,

Your affectionat Aunt

and servant,

A. Manchester.

---

a Christian Leslie, second daughter of John, Duke of Rothes, and wife of James Graham, third Marquis of Montrose. Her sister was Margaret, Countess of Rothes, who married Charles Hamilton, fifth Earl of Haddington.

CHARLES HATTON.

My L^d,   September 13, [16]79.

Wee are all here in a great amazment and astonishment; and you will be noe lesse, when you heare y^t ye Duke of Monmouth is turned out of all command and banisht ye 3 Kingdoms. This day he is gone to Windsor to surrender his patents. He came from thence last Thursday night late, and this news yesterday morning, like gunpowder set on fire, did in an instant run over ye whole city to ye generall amazement of all people. All ye phanaticks and male-contents cry up ye Duke of Monmouth as ye great confessor for ye protestant religion. The best account I can receive of ye occasion of his banishment is, y^t ye D[uke] of Y[orke], being pressed by his M^{ty} to returne into Flanders, declared a great aversion thereto, and an absolute unwillingnesse to leave ye D[uke] of M[onmouth] here in soe great power and authority, and therefore, for his satisfaction, ye D[uke] of M[onmouth] wase banisht. But, if y^t be ye true reason, it is thought he will yet stay, for many are of opinion ye D[uke] •of Y[orke] will now stay here, tho' some say he will certainly goe next Wednesday. By ye next post I shall be able more satisfactory to informe you.

It is reported ye Duke of Buccs and E. of Shaftsbury will be secured. I am very confident you will soudainly heare very sur-prising news, but what I am not able to informe you as yet. Ther wase inserted in one of ye late printed Intelligence that ye city had sent ye Recorder^a to welcom his Royall Highness. Hereupon Sr Tho. Player^b and some of his party went to expostulate wth ye Ld Mayor,^c who denyed y^t ther ever wase any such thing, and y^t he who printed y^t intelligence wase fled, but, if he cou'd be seized, he shou'd be made exemplary. It is said S^r Th. Player termed y^e

^a Sir George Jeffreys, afterwards the Lord Chancellor of infamous memory.
^b Chamberlain of the city, a violent Exclusionist.
^c Sir James Edwards.

Duke an enemy to [yᵉ] city, and one who by yᵉ Parliament had
been declared soe to yᵉ whole nation, and tooke notice to yᵉ Lᵈ
Mayor that it had been reported yᵗ he shou'd have said, had his
Matʸ dyed of his late illnesse, he wou'd immediately have proclaın'd
yᵉ D[uke] of Y[ork] king; wᶜʰ yᵉ Lᵈ Mayor denyed, declaring he
wou'd stand and fall by yᵉ protestant interest. Sʳ Tho. Player did
likewise presse that, during yᵉ Dukes stay in England, a stronger
guard of yᵉ militia might be upon yᵉ watch every night, wᶜʰ wase
referred to yᵉ lieutenancy and caryed in yᵉ negative; but yᵉ Lord
Maior ordred yᵉ constables every night to double their watch.

     *   *   *   *   *

Yʳ Loᵖᵖˢ truly affect
Brother to serve you,
C. HATTON.

THE SAME.

My Lᵈ   September 18, [16]79.

    *   *   *   *   *

I sent you word in my last of yᵉ Duke of Monmouth's being
banisht yᵉ 3 Kingdoms, and his commission of generall being taken
from him. He was sent for last Munday to Windsor; and it wase
reported his Matʸ had changed his mind, and yᵉ Duke of Monmouth
wase to stay in England; at wᶜʰ news, here in Westminster, ther
were great bonefires made for joy; but ther is noe such thing. His
Matʸ is resolved he shall goe. He sath it is not out of any unkindnesse to yᵉ Duke of M[onmouth], but for conveniency to his affaires,
for yᵉ Lᵈ Shaf[tesbury] and yᵗ party did put yᵉ D[uke] of M[on
mouth] upon solliciting their concerns and countenancing their
designs. Yᵉ D[uke] of Y[ork] will not goe till yᵉ other be gonne;
and it is reported yᵉ D[uke] of M[onmouth] will goe next Munday,
and yᵉ D[uke] of Y[ork] Tuesday or Wednesday.

Yesterday his Mat^y came to town. He is very well, and it is said
he will goe next weeke to Newmarket. In my last I told you perhapps both Dukes might stay, and you might heare of other great
alterations. But ye councells, I heare, are changed, and y^t they
will both goe. This day his Mat^y commanded a list to be brought
him of all foot and horse officers now in command.

Y^r freind in Chanc[ery] L[ane]^a wase 3 or 4 dayes at Windsor,
and highly caress'd by all ye favoritts of both sex. He dined wth a
great Dutchesse;^b and ye Master of ye Horse came in and said he
durst scarce yet drinke any wine, but called for a glasse and begun
y^r freinds health to ye lady. If he cou'd by deed of intayle secure
to himself ye court favour, he wase very happy; but every day
shews how fickle it is, and I feare thes concessions to all parties will
encourage them to make fresh demands.

I am y^r Lo^pps truly affect Brother to serve you,

C. HATTON.

THE SAME.

My L^d,   September 25, 1679.

Yesterday ye Duke of Monmouth went for Utrect, and this day
his Royall Highness for Flanders. Y^e Parl^t is prorougu'd till y^e
30th of Octob^r. To-morrow his Mat^y goes for Newmarket. Ther
wase a report that his Royal Highness wou'd have dined wth y^e
Artillery Company, but he did not. I find most personns doe
much wonder ye Duke of Yorke shou'd, under thes circumstances,
return to Flanders, for those who most desired it are not pleased at
all wth it now y^t ye Duke of Monmouth is gone; but some personns,

---

^a Scroggs.

^b He no doubt means the Duchess of Portsmouth; and by the "Master of the
Horse" he refers to the Duke of Richmond, her son, then a child of only seven years,
for whom that office was held in commission, after the disgrace of Monmouth.

and it is said ye most considerable, thinke y^t, by ye Duke of York's absence, his ^Maties life (wch God preserve) is most secure from any attempts of ye Popish party.

It is said ye reason of ye prorogation of ye parl^t is in hopes y^t, before ye end of ye next month, a firme league may be concluded wth ye Dutch, wch is thought will be as acceptable to ye English nation, as it is distastefull to ye French, who have, and still doe, wth great earnestness oppose it. Ther is a rumour y^t ye Earle of Shaftsbury will be put out of office [a] before ye parl^t meet, but I cannot find y^t it is credited by any judicious personns. This is certain, ye E. of Hallifax and Essex are quite lost in ye opinion of ye men of Shaftsbury.

*   *

Y^r Lo^pps truly affect Brother to serve you,

C. HATTON.

SIR CHARLES LYTTELTON.

MY LORD,   Octob^r 21, 1679.

I am so angry wth you for y^t news, tho' it be very good, I can scarce find in my heart to thank you for't;[b] but I am very glad my Lady is well rid on't, and so 'tis wellcome; and, for all I know, the next weeke you will make mee ye like compliment.

I have bine at dinner wth ye Duke, at ye military feast, of wch I have only to say, wch is very true, that one side of a very long table was filld allmost entirely of noblemen, and ye other side, a greate part of it, wth my Lord Mayor and Aldermen, and five or 6 tables

---

[a] He was deprived on the 15th October of his place as President of the Council.

[b] No doubt he refers to the birth of a girl to Lord Hatton, who seems to have received repeated blessings of daughters when he hoped for sons. A letter from one of his sisters, on another occasion, announces the birth of " a very lusty garle, which she [the mother] is very sorry for, but hopes you will forgive her!"

more of ye best cittisens, and ye hall so crowded as I never saw at
any feast, and all the signes of welcome and sattisfaction y^t could be
desired; and this was so to ye Dukes sattisfaction, y^t it gave him
ocasion to say to mee, since he came away, this was pritty well for
a poore banished man but so little a while since; and all the bal-
conies were full to see him passe by as he came back, amongst w^ch
were Mr Oates and my Lord Howard^a in a balcony together.

There is one has sworne to-day that Mr Oates sayd it would
never be well in England till the monarchy were elective.   This, I
think, is sworn to before my Lord Ch. Justice Scrogs, and my L^ds
warrant is out for another who will sweare to ye same thing.   When
that is done, my Lord will give out his warrant to bring Mr Oates
before him; and he will commit him.   Say nothing till you heare
further.   The Duke goes a Monday.^b   Heele lye at Stamford, I
suppose ye 3rd day.   You shall know more perticularly time enough.

CHARLES HATTON.

My L^d,   Oct. 21, 1679.

    *   *   *   -   *

The Parl^t is prorogued till ye 26 of Jan.; and very few beleeve
they will then meet.   Sr Will. Jones hath resigned up his office as
Attorney Generall; Mr Sollicitor Finch declines it, soe advised by
his father.   Ther wase a report Sr John Temple wou'd be Atturney,
but I am confident he will miss of it; for his Ma^ty declared he nor
ye son of noe rebel shou'd, and y^t he wou'd never trust any of y^e
brood of a rebell.   The Recorder of London^c is much discoursed as
likely to be Atturney Generall, and truly I have reason to thinke

  William, 3rd Lord Howard of Escrick.
  ^b To Scotland.   ^c Jeffreys.

he will be. He hath, in great perfection, ye three cheif qualifications of a lawyer: Boldness, Boldness, Boldness. Ther is a report y^t my Ld Chancelor is likely to loose ye seales, w^{ch}, it is said, will be given to Sr Lionell Jenkins; and y^t Tom Cheeke [a] will be put out of ye Tower and Coll. Leg succeed him; but I heare this only from publicke fame.

This day y^e Duke of Yorke dined wth y^e Artillery Company. It is said he goes for Scotland next Tuesday, y^e 28th inst. In my next I will informe you more particularly and what road he goes. If y^e doe comes to-morrow, my L_d Ch. Justice will be very well pleas'd; but, if it failes, I dare never appeare more in Chancery Lane. He stands, I verily beleeve, as well at Court, if not better then ever he did. I shall shortly send you a speech of his ^{wch} he designes to speake, in his vindication from y^e slanders put on him, ye first day of ye terme.

I am y^r Lo^{pps} truly affect Brother to serve you,

C. HATTON.

THE SAME.

Nov. 1, [16]79.

*   *   *   *   *

Here is a counter plot of ye papists lately discovered by one Willoughby,[b] wch doth strangely surprise all people and hath been examined into by ye lords of councell for thes three or four dayes last past. This Willoughby is called by ye name of Dangerfeild and two or three other names. He hath been twice pillor'd, and committed all manner of villaney. He wase brought by Collⁿ

---

[a] Captain Cheeke, Lieutenant Governor of the Tower.
[b] i. e. Thomas Dangerfield.

Hassell[a] to M[r] Secretary Coventry, under pretence y[t] he wou'd discover a plott of y[e] presbiterians, of w[ch] he discours'd of in generall terms and undertooke to discover severall particular persons, provided he might have y[e] Secretaries warr[t] to search all houses he suspect'd to harbour y[e] presbiterian conspirators; but M[r] Secretary did not thinke fitt to grant him such a wart, not knowing what ill use he might make therof. Hereupon this Willoughby inform'd the officers of y[e] custome house y[t], at one Coll[n] Mansell[b] (who belongs to y[e] Duke of Buces) his lodging, ther wase severall prohibited goods, wherupon an officer came to search, and Willoughby (as after discovered) conveyed a packett of letters behind y[e] bed's head, and then directed y[e] officer to search ther, wher they were found, but directed to Coll[n] Mansfeild. The letters had noe name, but discoursed of a plott to be cary'd on by y[e] L[d] Shaftsbury, Essex, Hallifax, y[e] Duke of Monmouth. Upon strict examination all this wase found out to bee a forgery, and now, upon stricter examination, Willoughby sath he wase put upon this contrivance by y[e] Lady Powis[c] and y[e] L[ds] in y[e] Tower; y[t] y[e] L[d] Arundull and Powys propos'd to him 3000[l] to kill y[e] King, and accused y[e] L[d] Castlemaine to have blam'd him for not accepting y[e] money to doe soe glorious a worke. Hereupon y[e] L[d] Castlemain is sent to y[e] Tower.

Here is newly come out y[e] Earle of Danby's case writ by himself, w[ch] I have here inclos'd sent you.

I am y[r] Lo[pps] truly affect Brother to serve you,

C. HATTON.

---

[a] Colonel James Hallshall, one of the King's cupbearers.

[b] Roderick Mansel. He published a Narrative of the Meal Tub plot, in 1680.

[c] Elizabeth, daughter of Edward Somerset, Marquess of Worcester, and wife of William Herbert, Earl of Powis.

Sir Charles Lyttelton.

My Lord,   No. 6th, [16]79.

Y^r Cousine, Lady Powis, is sent to the Tower, there being many ill thinges proved agst. her by her practisses wth this Dangerfield. The particulars I am not well enough informed to give you; but, in generall, there is enough proved to shew they had a base designe to put a plot upon ye presbiterians, and to have made them in a design to doe w^{ht} the papists are accused of, to destroy the King and the government. But I beleeve 'tis like to fall heavily on them; for, by seeming so base in this, they give ocasion to be thought capable of ye rest they stand charged wth. My Ld Peterboro' has bine examined in Councell abt. this, and hee has answered, as I heare, to sattisfaction. He ownes a correspondence wth this Dangerfield, that hee brought him to ye Duke and was recommended to him by my Lady Powis. My Lady Powis denyes every thing. Some would turn this practisse of Dangerfield wth the D[uke] to ye D[uke's] prejudice; but I hope they may have theyr ends, for ye D. cleared his hands soone of him by saying he medled in no such buisnesse, and bid him goe to ye K^g; so he was brought to him by James Hallshall, who ye K^g told ye Councell told him, when hee first brought him, that he was a pickpocket and rogue; and Dangerfield in his narrative says, when he was in ye Tower wth the Lords, they bid him not to treate any further wth Halshall, for y^t heede discover ye cheate and tell ye King.

Dr Jasper Neeham [a] is dead of the feavor.

My humble services to my Lady. Sr Robt Peyton [b] was burnt last night in ye citty wth ye pope.

---

[a] Sir Caspar, or Jasper, Needham.

[b] M.P. for Middlesex. He was mixed up in the Meal Tub plot; and, from being a violent opponent of the Court, was accused of making overtures to the Duke of York. He was, in consequence, expelled the House in December, 1680.

CHARLES HATTON.

My Ld November 6, [16]79.^{a}

*   *   *   *

Willoughby's discovery makes a great noise here. He declared
to have had several meeting[s] wth ye Lady Powys at one M^{rs}
Cellier house,^{b} a midwif. Upon search of ye house, a booke wase
found, wherein wase writ ye names of ye officers and managers of y^e
pretended presbyterian plott; and it is reported that his Ma^{ty} compared it and found it exactly to agree wth a list delivered to him by
ye Duke of Yorke, and hereupon, it is said, my Ld Shaftsbury wase
this day sent for to come to ye King, and y^t a yatch is ordred to
fetch over ye Duke of Monmouth.

*   *   *   *   *

My Lady Powis is committed prisoner to ye Tower upon Wil
loughbies information y^t she wase ye greater contriver of ye pretended presbyterian plott. She declared she never had any in-
timacy wth Willoughby; but my Ld Peterbrough, upon examination
before ye Councell, declared ye Lady Powis recommended Willoughby to him, and gave great testimonialls of his integrity.

Y^r Lo^{pps} truly affectionat Brother to serve you,

C. HATTON.

THE SAME.

[November, 1679.]

*   *   *   *   *

Here wase a report y^t Ld Shaftsbury wou'd be sent for to Councell
againe and restored to favour, but ther is noe such thing. Y^e
occasion of ye report wase, he wase required to give an account to
ye Councell what Willoughby had ever discoursed to him.

^{a} Erroneously dated '78. ^{b} Elizabeth Cellier.

Last Sunday wase a hot debate at Councell, whither or noe a proclamation shou'd be put forth to ascertain ye session of parl^t at ye day appointed. It wase much pressed by my L^d of Essex that ye King wou'd put forth a proclamation, but opposed by ye Ld President,[a] Ld Chancelor, B^p of London.

Yesterday Sr Will. Waller[b]. discovered a treasonable plot ag^t his owne person, but his witnesses were not men of such reputation to be credited. Monday next, being Queen Elizabeth's birthday,[c] Sr Rob. Peyton and ye pope are to be burnt together in effigie before ye King's Head,[d] nere Temple Bar, were Sr Robert's club wase kept; but they of ye clubb have contributed 10^{ll} a peice for his effigies to be burnt, wch will cost 100^{ll}.

The same.

My L^d,   Nov. 29, [16]79.

In my last I told y^r Lo^{ppe} that ther wase a report y^t ye Duke of Monmouth wase sicke in Holland; but it wase a double mistake, for he wase very well then and in England. For, last Thursday night, about ten a clocke, he came privatly to Capⁿ Godfrey's house, in Covvent Garden, and stay'd ther till one ye next morning, and then he went to his owne house; ye report of wch wase immediatly bruited abroad, and ye bells in all churches rung all ye morning incessantly, and bonnefires presently kindled in severall places, and great acclamations in all streets: " Joyful news to England, ye Duke of Monmouth return'd !" I say not this by hearsay from

---

[a] The Earl of Radnor.

[b] One of the Middlesex magistrates who had to investigate the Meal Tub plot.

[c] 17th November.

[d] The King's Head tavern, at the bottom of Chancery Lane, the head-quarters of the King's Head Club, afterwards called the Green Ribbon Club, from the colour of its badge.—See North's *Examen*, 572.

others, for I heard those expressions and saw ye bonnefires. The truth is, it is very difficult to expresse fully ye prodigious acclamations of ye people, nor can any one credit them who wase not an eye and eare witness. Last night ther wase more bonnefires, I am confident, then ever wase on any occasion since those for ye restoration of his Ma^ty. I seriously protest I am most confident y^t ther wase above 60 betwixt Temple Bar and Charing Cross. The rabble being very numerous stopp'd all coaches, even my Ld Chancelor's, and wou'd not let him pass till he cry'd: " God bless ye Duke of Monmouth ! " They made most other personns come out of their coaches and cry: " God bless ye Duke of Monmouth ! " And to severall personns they offer'd kennel-water, and told them they must drinke the Duke's health in y^t, or pay for better liquor. I mention what fires I saw, and I am very credibly inform'd y^t in most other streets ther wase as many. But, tho' his Grace was thus triumphantly receiv'd by ye people, he wase not soe at Court; for, yesterday morning early, he went to wait on his Ma^ty, but cou'd not be admitted into his presence. At eleven a clocke my Ld Fauconbridge[a] wase sent from his Ma^ty to forbid him ye Court, after wch Sr Stephen Fox, at ye desire of ye Duke, went to his Mat^y to acquaint him y^t ye Duke came into England only to cleare himself to his Mat^y not to be a traytor, as he was attempted to be represented by ye pretended presbyterian plott. His Mat^y reply'd he wase confident y^t ye Duke wase according to his commands return'd; if he wase not, he wou'd never see his face more; y^t by the Duke's owne acknowledgment, he had been in town severall houres before his Mat^y knew of it, and he did not know but he had been severall dayes. Sr Stephen Fox return'd wth this message to ye Duke; but he peremptory declar'd he wou'd not goe backe; at wch his Mat^y wase highly displeas'd, and last night sent for all ye officers of ye Guard and commanded them not to obey any orders they shou'd receive from ye Duke of Monmouth who is still in town, visited by very few, except those who are

---

[a] Thomas Belasyse, Viscount Falconberg.

neerly related or depend on him. I heare not of any noblemen, except ye Ld Shaftsbury and ye Ld Wharton, who were this day wth him at his house in Hedge Lane, as I wase inform'd by one who saw them ther. When ye Duke went from ye Hague, he wase only attended on by Coll^n Langly and one servant (ye only persons who came hither wth him), and pretended he wou'd goe for Cologn. Mr Vernon and ye rest of his attendants are left at ye Hague.

* * * * *

Y^r Lo^pps most affect Brother and servant,

C. HATTON.

SIR CHARLES LYTTELTON.

MY LORD,   London, Nov. 29, [16]79.

I have rec^d y^rs of ye 23, and am sorry you w^d be so ceremonious wth mee, when you were so tired wth writing to more purposse.

Y^e D. of Monmouth came to his lodgings at ye Cockpit a Thursday night (but some suppose he was in town the day before). He writt to ye King, as sone as he came, to acquaint with his being there and to excuse it w^thout his leave; because he had bine charged in ye Councell to have bine in a presbyterian plot, and that he was to head an army agst. his Ma^ty. The K^g writt back to him he was indeed surprized at his coming, and that he hoped no body els knew of it, and w^d have him return imediately w^thout further discovery of himself. Then ye Duke writt againe that he came to justify himself, and that he c^d not return wth honour till he had done so; but, if his Matie pleased to send him to the Tower, or put any other confinement upon him, he was ready to obey him and answer any charge agst. him. The K^g then sent Capt. Godfroy, to tell him hee w^d write no more to expostulate wth him, but he expected to be obeyd. For all this he stirrd not. The next morning the King, being told he was still at ye Cockpit, sent my

Lord Faulconbrigg to him, to be gone; and 2 or 3 messages passᵈ to and againe. The Kᵍ at last commanded him possitively to leave the Court; so he told yᵉ company wᵗʰ him of it (for the roome was full all the morning), and imediately went away to his lodgings in Hedge Lane by yᵉ Mues. The King sent my Lord Mattsfield, alias Gerrard,ᵃ to him in the afternoone, to tell him out of greate tendernesse he gave him till night to be gone; but hee stayd, and the bonfires were kindled againe all over this part of the towne. I know not wʰᵗ they were in yᵉ citty; but, yᵉ night before, they were every where, and began to be lighted, the bells ringing, &c., about 1 a clock. So the Kᵍ, at night, sent for Coll: Russell and all the cheife officers of yᵉ Guards, hors and foot, to command them to receive no orders from yᵉ D. of M., wᶜʰ as eldest Coll: before they ought to have done. Thus it stood yᵉ last night; only I shd. have told you that there was huge resort to his house in Hedg lane, after he came thither, as well as to his lodgings in yᶜ Cockpit. Some have phancied that yᵉ Kᵍ knew of his coming, and all this is but a feint; but they will find they are mistaken and yᵉ Kᵍ is in good earnest.

There has bine lately a meeting of severall Lords at yᵉ Swan in Fish Street, to consider of yᵉ state of yᵉ nation. I heare they em ploydᵒne Manly, a phanaticque brewer and brother to Sʳ Roger at Portsmouth, to goe abᵗ wᵗʰ a petition, in yᵉ citty, for subscriptions; but he was every where refused, so they resolve on another way by addresse.

I am assured by those that I think are well advised, that my Lord Mayor himself and the most considerable cittisens have given yᵉ Kᵍ full assurance of theyr duty to him, and I doe not feare but they will bee as ready as can be desired allmost to discountenance and suppresse by theyr authority any popular commotions, wᶜʰ one may not wᵗʰout reason be jealous of at this time.

The Duke has bine mighty well recᵈ by yᵉ Scots upon yᵉ borders; but, when yᵉ letters came, he was not at Edingbourgh.

ᵃ Lord Gerard had been lately advanced to the title of Macclesfield.

There came nobody over wth ye D. of M. but Langley, and his barber. Godfroy was heere before.

I doubt not you have heard of my Ld Thannet's death,^{a} and my Lady Jane Clifford's.^{b} Jack Hervey ^{c} is not like to last long after him.

My Lord, its now 9 at night. Y^e D. of Mon: is still at ye Mues. Y^e D^{sse} has bine earnest wth him to submit to ye K^{gs} pleasure and be gone. He has resolved, it seemes, by other councells. The K^g is so offended, he sent for ye D. of Albemarle from New Hall, and hee this night kissd the K^{gs} hand, to commande ye troope of Guards. All his other places, it's thought, will be disposed of. God blesse ye King and keepe us in peace.

CHARLES HATTON.

My L^d, December 11, [16]79.

* * * * *

Fryday was sennight, ye addressing lords were with ye Ld Maior,^{d} endeavouring to perswade him to call a common councell, and on ye Monday following ye Ld Huttington,^{e} Clare,^{f} Shaftsbury, Wharton, Grey,^{g} Howard of Escric, Herbert of Shirbury,^{h} North and Grey,^{i} all went againe to dine wth ye Ld Maior upon ye like designe. It

^{a} Nicholas Tufton, the third Earl.

^{b} Jane Seymour, daughter of William, 2nd Duke of Somerset, and wife of Charles Boyle, Lord Clifford, eldest son of Richard, 2nd Earl of Cork, and 1st Earl of Burlington. She died on the 23rd November, and was buried in Westminster Abbey.—Chester, *Westminster Abbey Registers*, 198.

^{c} John Hervey of Ickworth, ancestor of the Bristol family.

^{d} Sir Robert Clayton.

^{e} Theophilus Hastings, 7th Earl of Huntingdon.

^{f} Gilbert Holles, 3rd Earl of Clare. ^{g} Ford, Lord Grey of Werke.

^{h} Henry, 4th Lord Herbert of Chirbury.

Charles North, Lord North and Grey of Rolleston.

happened y^t that wase one of ye dayes of ye sitting at Guildhall, after ye term, of ye two Chief Justices and ye Cheif Baron, who are ever of course invited to dine wth ye Lord Mayor, and were wth him then when ye Ld Shaftsbury, &c., came in. Presently after ye L^ds were come in, ye Ld Mayor told ye Lord Cheif Justice he wase unexpectedy surprised by those lords. Y^e Ld Cheif Justice replyed, he verily beleeved all personns ther were surprised, for he wase confident ye l^ds did not expect to meet ye judges, nor ye judges ye lords ther, nor did his Lo^ppe, because he heard they had been wth him ye Fryday before. My Ld Maior answered, it wase true they were, but their reception wase soe cold he did not expect they wou'd have come againe. At dinner time ye lords placed themselves all on one side of ye table, leaving ye other side free for ye judges, and therby it happened y^t ye Cheif Justice wase placed just opposite to ye Ld Huttington and in view of ye Ld Shaftsbury, who, at ye beginning of dinner, drunke to ye L^d Ch. Justice; after wch they two had much discourse, ye L^d Ch. Justice taking notice y^t he had seen him at Oates his tryall, in wch ther were reflections on ye Ld Danby, as if he had, by his agents, endeavoured to invalidate ye testimony of Oates and Bedlow, as to ye Popish plot. But, at ye same time, Dangerfeild did upon his oath declare he went by order of ye Lady Powis to one Mrs Downing's house, over ag^t Spring Garden (where ye Ld Danby did use to meet Oates and Tongue, and did ther with them contrive ye Popish plot), and to enquire of Mrs Downing how often ye Ld Danby had been ther with Oates and Tongue, and y^t it did seem by what Mrs Downing told Dangerfeild y^t ye Ld Danby had been ther wth Oates and Tongue, which if soe, his endeavour-ing to invalidate ye testimony of Oates wou'd scarce be credible. Y^e Ld Shaftsbury replyed he did not well understand what Danger-feild said as to y^t, and y^t it made nothing to ye tryall. W^th such like obliging discourse ye L^d Ch. J[ustice] entertain'd ye Ld Shafts bury all dinner time.

After grace wase said, ye Ld Huttington desired leave of ye Ld Maior to begin a health, and begun ye Duke of Monmouth's health;

w^{ch}, when it came to ye L^d Ch. J[ustice] he pledged it, expressing withall a great honour for ye Duke, and, after, desired leave of ye Ld Maior to begin a health, and then drunke to my Ld Huttington ye Duke of York's health. The Ld Huttington replyed: "And con·fusion to Popery!" The Ld Cheif J. answered: "Yes, ye Duke of York's health, and confusion to Popery!" Y^e Ld Howard said y^t wase a contradiction, wch ye L^d Ch. J[ustice] denyed, saying ye Duke might be a papist but he cou'd not conceive how he cou'd be Popery, wch when he wase proved to be, he wou'd cease drinking his health immediately.

Upon ye L^d Ch. J[ustice] drinking this health, all ye L^{ds}, in a great scuffle, rise from ye table and went into another roome; whither ye L^d Ch. J[ustice] singly of all ye judges followed them, and told ye Ld Shaftsbury y^t he had sent him a message by Sr James Hayes, wch his Lo^{ppe} said wase never delivered. Therupon ye L^d Ch. J[ustice] told him y^t it wase, y^t he did extreemly wonder how his Lo^{ppe}, after he had soe often extoll'd him in severall speeches in ye L^{ds} House for ye great services he had done ye nation, shou'd, unheard, soe far condemn him as to move to have him displaced, when he wase in ye midst of his circuit, upon a suggestion wch wase every title a ly. The Ld Shaftsbury told him he was a plaine spoken man and he liked him ye better for it, and begun: "Y^e, old L^d Ch. Justice his health!" Y^e L^d Ch. J[ustice] asked him if he meant Hales's. He replyed, noe; but his, before Wakeman's tryall. He said he wase ye same now as before, and, making several pro-testations of his uncorruptness therin, ye Ld Shaftesbury said he wase satisfyed he had noe mony but said: "I was offred 10,000^{ll} if I wou'd have used my endeavours to save Wakeman." To wch ye L^d Ch. J[ustice] replyed, he must say what he thought he never shou'd, y^t then his Lo^{ppe} wase in y^t an honester man then he wase, for he never being proferred any mony therin cou'd not refuse it.

The Ld Howard asked ye L^d Ch. J[ustice] why he did not give

as great credit to Oates and Bedlow in Wakeman's tryall as in all
ye tryalls before. He replyed, because Sr Phi. Floyd^a had in-
validated at ye tryall the testimony of Oates. The Ld Howard
then said: " If Oates and Bedlow be not to be beleeved in all they
say, and if the Queen be not a traytor, our business is at an end."
The L^d Ch. J[ustice] replyed, he woud serve noe end nor hang
Wakeman to prove ye Queen a traytor, nor wou'd ever be a papist
nor a rebbell.

After he had thus teised them for 2 or 3 houres, he left them.
They wou'd faine have been rid of him sooner, y^t they might, w^th
my Ld Maior, have fallen upon ye business of ye day, and advised
him to goe try his causes; but he told them he wou'd first try over
that cause. This business hath occasioned various discourse here,^b
and therfore I thought it wou'd not be unpleasing to you to have
a full and true acct therof, to prevent y^r misinformation.

I have this day sent you 2 qts. of juniper water, Ricaut's Turkish
History,^c and Dr. Stillingfleet Vindication of ye right of b^pps judging
in capitall causes,^d in answer to ye Ld Hollis,^e wth wch I am very
confident you will be highly satisfyed, and be much surprised at y^e
prodigious ability of ye D^r in a point of learning on a subject to

---

^a Sir Philip Lloyd, Clerk of the Council.

^b Luttrell, in his diary, under date of December 1679, thus notices the affair: " The
beginning of this month the two cheif justices, the Lord Shaftsbury, Huntington, Gray,
and others dined with the lord mayor, where they drank very plentifully; and some
words were spoke about the acquittall of Sir George Wakeman, which occasioned
much heat, Scrogs taking it as a reflexion on him."

^c " The History of the Turkish Empire from 1623 to 1627." By Sir Paul Rycaut.
London, 1680, 4to.

^d " The Grand Question concerning the Bishops' right to vote in Parliament in
cases capital, stated and argued from the Parliament Rolls and the history of former
times, with an enquiry into their peerage and the three estates in Parliament."
London, 1680. 8vo. The question arose out of the bishops voting on Danby's
impeachment. See Burnet's History, i. 460, 463.

^e " Letter of a Gentleman to his Friend, showing that the Bishops are not judges
in Parliament, in Capital Cases." By Lord Denziel Holles. London, 1679, 8vo.

wch most men must have thought him a great stranger; and wth them I have sent Oates his narrative of ye conspiracy of Knox and Lane.^a Ag^t page 8 you will [see] an information soe horribly blasphemously reflecting on his Mat^y, y^t ye Court wou'd not permit it to be read, but yet it is now publish'd by ye authority of Oates; nor have they who have ye power to doe it courage enouf to question ye publishers. But ye L^d Ch. J[ustice], if his brethren will stand by him, will instruct ye stationer and printers to be more cautious how they publish such blasphemous slanders ag^t his Mat^y

*   *   *   *   *

THE SAME.

MY L^d,   December 18, [16]79.

I spoke this day to Staunton himself and he promised he wou'd not faile this day to cary down the juniper water and Ricaut's history, Oates Narrative, and Dr Stillingfleet ag^t my Lord Hollis.

I cou'd not get Colemans tryall nor Reading's^b this weeke, but will not faile to send them you the next, wth Sr Will. Temples last booke^c by wch he hath not made himself soe popular as by his late speech in Councell, last Fryday. He [was the] first who spoke ther ag^t ye issuing out a proclamation for ye proroguing ye parl^t till 9^{cr}; but all ye L^{ds} of ye Councell (except ye Ld President, Duke Lauderdale, Marquisse of Worcester,^d and Ld Sunderland, who were silent

---

^a "An exact and faithful Narrative of the Horrid Conspiracy of Thomas Knox, William Osborne, and John Lane, to invalidate the Testimonies of Titus Oates, and W. Bedlow, by charging them with a malicious Contrivance against the E. of Danby," &c.. London, 1680, fol.

^b Nathanael Reading was tried on the 16th April, 1679, for attempting to tamper with Bedlow. He was sentenced to a fine of £1,000, and to the pillory.

^c Miscellanea, by a Person of Honour. London, 1680, 8vo.

^d Henry Somerset, afterwards Duke of Beaufort.

and said nothing) declared ther opinion ag^t it. Sr Will. Temple said ye prorogation of ye parl^t wase a business of y^t weight y^t it wase very requisite his Mat^y shou'd heare it fully debated at Councell before he tooke any resolution therin; that all princes of great fame and renown did never attempt any business of great moment but upon mature deliberation wth their Councell; and his Mat^y himself had declared to the whole world that he wase resolved, when he first constituted this present Councell, he wou'd act nothing but by their advice; but, if his Ma^{ty} did now thinke that ther wase any person ther whose advice wase not fit to be asked, he humbly moved his Mat^y they might be dismissed, tho' he wase the first man, and that his Mat^y wou'd permit none to be thereof but such on whose councell his Ma^{ty} cou'd rely in all affaires of soe great a concern as ye prorogation of ye parl^t wase; to wch if any ther present wou'd advise his Mat^y, he humbly moved they wou'd publicly ther declare their reason, that after a mature debate his Ma^{ty} might know what wase most advantagious to his service to be done.

My L^d of Essex seconded Sr William Temple and told his Mat^y y^t, without a soudain supply from his subjects, his ^{Maties} revenew wase soe anticipated, and soe many branches soudainly falling of, it wou'd not be sufficient to support ye necessary charge of ye governm^t; nor cou'd the L^{ds} in ye Tower be brought to a tryall, and consequently ye Popish plot be throughly examined but in parliam^t.

The Ld Privy Seal, Ld Hallifax, Ld Fauconbridge, Ld Cavendish, Ld Bridgewater, Mr Powle, &c. did all speake to ye like effect. Y^e Ld Chief Justice North[a] moved y^t, shou'd his Ma^{ty} thinke fit to prorogue ye parl^t, that yet it might not be for soc long a time as till 9er. The Ld Chancelor spoke soe earnestly ag^t ye prorogation y^t his Mat^y commanded him to desist, for he wase fully resolved to prorogue ye parl^t. Thereupon ye Ld Chancelor said he wou'd say nothing more, but only as to ye manner; and then seconded what

[a] Sir Francis North, Chief Justice of the Common Pleas; afterwards Lord Keeper and Lord Guilford.

my L^d Ch. Justice North had moved. But ye King told him, if he proceeded, he wou'd rise out of ye chaire; and then noe more wase spoke on ye subject, and ye proclamation is out.

* * * * *

Y^r Lo^{pps} truly affect
Brother to serve you,
C. HATTON.

SIR CHARLES LYTTELTON.

MY LORD, Jan^{ry} 1, [16]⁷⁹⁄₈₀.

This to wish you and my Lady a good new yeare. I had like to have made an ill end of ye old one, for yesterday as I was passing ye ferry at Richm^d, my hors leapt over board wth mee on his back into ye river, and presently turud on one side and mee of his back, my feet hanging in both stirrups. But, what wth ye flounsing of ye hors and my own endeavors, I soone was free; but then was so intangled wth a p^r of greate French bootes and many cloathes, I was not able to turn myself as I lay on my back; but yet kept myself above water, till Thom Brok leapt out of ye boate and pulld mee up, being then not out of my depth. And so I got well ashore, and my hors swam a greate way down ye river, till at length he found ye way too to ye shore, and neither of us, I hope, ye wors. For my own part, I neither then nor since have found ye least cold by it.

Heere is no other news y^t I heare of. Some talk there is of ye Dukes coming back; but I beleeve there is no such thing, nor like to be quickly, for, as I told you before, 1 beleeve he is thought to be more able in y^t post,^a for ye present, to serve ye K^g and himself. I was going yesterday to make the Provost a visit at Eaton.

---

^a In the government of Scotland.

THE SAME.

MY LORD,   Jan. 10, [1680].

Yesterday S^r Ro. Peyton was sent to ye Tower; his warrant was
for high treason, being accused by Mr Gadbury^a and Mrs Celleer for
saying, if ye K^g had died at Windsor, that he would have bine at y^e
head of 20,000 men to oppose ye Duke's title; and that, if ye Lord
Mayor and sherriffs would have offred to proclaime him, they shd.
have bine killd; and they wd. have declared for a commonwealth.
Now how he came to say this to them is supposed to bee, because
he was treating wth them to come about to ye Duke, and sayd that
to set a value on his interest and service; but they speak further to
day of Mr Gadbury's discoveries, for they talk that hee has charged
my L^d of Peterborow wth high matters, and that my Ld Peeterborow is sent for up.

Sr Steph. Fox gives as yet but little comfort as to ye clearing us
to January, as he pretended he w^d doe; and wee are terribly affraid
they will only pay subsistance. 'Tis worse in all other payments,
ye navy, ordinance, and every where, so y^t 'tis allmost miraculous
the government does yet subsist, wch sure it cannot doe long at this
rate. Nor doe I see any hopes of releese, but from a parlmt., and,
to say truth, not much from thence; tho' ye Duch breaking of all
treatie wth ye French, and being, they say, willing to conclude wth
us (when ye King can give um any assurance to make good his
treaties, wch they cannot beleeve he can but by a parlimt.), its
possible they may be so gratefull to them that it may put um in so
good humor to give ye King mony (wch God grant), and the King
such councell as may support his tottering condition.

Sr Tho: Allen^b has quitted his place in the navy, being tired
wth ye clamors. Mr Hethor^c is in his place, and Mr Brisbain^d is
secretarie of ye Admiraltie.

^{a} John Gadbury, one of the chief witnesses in the Meal Tub plot.
^{b} Comptroller of the Navy.
^{c} Thomas Hayter became assistant-comptroller. ^{d} John Brisbain.

The same.

My Lord,   Jan. 13, [1680.]

I think you have judged very rightly of ye proposition you say has bine lately made you, and that ye accepting it, at least upon such termes, now would but make you uncapable of rendring ye thing fit for you heereafter; nor can I see anything so charming of y^t kind, beyond what you have allreadie, to make oneself uneasie for.

I am glad the petitions have no more encouragement among you; but this morning Sr Gilbert Gerrard,^a wth Frank Charlton,^b a sonn of Ireton,^c and ye sonn of another traytor, and Oates and Bedlow and 2 or 3 more came to Whitehall, and had ye boldnesse to present a petition, in ye name of all ye inhabitants of Westminster and Southewark, his Maties most loyall and humble subjects, Sr Gilbert being spokesman upon his knees; and he would have sayd more, but ye K^g bid him hold and sayd hee would have them to know that hee was the head in ye government, and that it belonged to him to judge when 'tis fit to call ye parlimt., and that they were not competent judges of it nor concellors to advise him, and y^t he was sorry to find one of his name and family at ye head of such a route. To wch Sr Gilbert offered to reply; but ye K^g w^d not heare him, and so went away wth ye petition under his arm and carried it into his closset. It contained a huge role of papers, being the reall or pretended subscriptions of many thousands.

My Ld Huntington, Shaftsbury, Gray, and Howard's names were to it, and no other Lords. To morrow, I heare Mr Oates and Bedlow are to accuse my Ld C. Justice at the Councell, or rather y^e former accusation to be heard.

---

^a Of Fiskerton, co. Lincoln, Bart., M.P. for Northallerton.

^b Francis, son of Sir Job Charlton, of Ludford, co. Hereford, Bart.

^c Harry Ireton, who married a daughter of Henry Powle, of the House of Commons.

Charles Hatton.

My L^d,   Jan. 15, [16]$\frac{79}{80}$.

I wonder to heare you have not yet received y^e puttee. I sent it last weeke wth y^e life of Mr Hobbs ^a writ in verse by himself; and, being to suppe y^t night at my brother Perrots, I writ in y^e morning, and sent my letter by y^e carier. This day I have sent y^e stockings you writ for, w^{ch}, if they are not to y^r liking, pray return them. I shall take care of melon seeds and Dic Beavorr vines.

*   *   *

At Hampton, last Tuesday, Sr Gilbert Gerrard and Mr Charlton wth ye wooden legge, wth about 5 or 6 factious citizens of noe great note, presented ye London and Westminster petition to his Ma^{ty}, who wou'd not permit ye petition to be read, telling them he knew what it wase, and y^t he wase ye head of ye governm^t and wou'd summon and dissolve parliaments as he thought fitting, or to y^t effect, and severely checkd Sr Gilbert Gerrard, telling him he did not expect one of his name wou'd have appear'd in such a business. Next Tuesday a common councell sitts, where it is expected ye petition will be promoted.

The commission for justices of peace will soudainly be purg'd all England over; it is beginning at London and Middlesex. Sr Gilbert Gerrard, Sr James Hayes, Dr Chamberlain, and severall others are expung'd.

Yesterday ye roof of ye Tennis Cote in ye Haymarket fell down. Sr Charles Sidley being ther had his skull broke, and it is thought it will be mortall. Sr George Etheridge and severall others were very dangerously hurt.

Next Saterday all ye priests in ye gaoles about London will be brought to their tryall, amonst them poore Starkey. Yesterday S^r

---

^a " Thomæ Hobbesii Vita Carmen." London, 1679, 4to. An edition in English was published this year.

George Carteret dyed. Sr Robt Payton is accused by Gadbury and Mrs Cellier for saying, had ye King dyed at Windsor, ther were 20,000 men in a readinesse to have seized upon ye Tower and set up a commonwealth. The factious personns of his gange, who lately reviled him as an infamous villain, now mightily commiserat him, as if his accusation wase only to carry on ye pretended Presbiterian plot; for in truth they are in great feare Sr Robt Payton shou'd bring them into ye scrappe.

*   *   *   *   *

Y^r Lo^{pps} truly affect Brother to serve you,

C. HATTON.

THE COUNTESS OF MANCHESTER.

MY LORD,   Whitehall, Jan. 23th [1680].

I received both your letters att Leez, and soe neare my comeing back that made mee defere till now wrighten. Mr Riggby hath bine wth us this Christmass att Leez, wher my Lord hath concluded wth him to travell wth my son and to goe about next Michelmass. I suppose he designes he shall stay abroad till he bee neare of agge, wch will bee four yeare att least, if nothinge should ocasion a more sudden returne then yet wee can foresee. As to w^t your L^{dsp} saith concerning him, he was gone that morning towards London when I received your letter, and that made me defere wrighten till I had acquainted him wth it, wch I did yesterday. I suppose he will returne himselfe his acknowledgm^{ts} to you for your thoughts of him, but I guess by his discours that he will bee unwilling to take any liveing of noe greater value. He, I suppose, was informed that Willbee was at least 120^{ll} a yeare, and the nebourhood of Kerby was ye greattes temptation; besides, beeing to bee abroad soe long wth Charles, att his returne I hope my L^d may have it in his power to doe as well for him, he haveing a great many very good liveings in his gifft; and truely I find his preaching, wch I never heard till this time at Leez, and his conversation, may very reasonably deserve a good one, espeshallie if he performes his dutty to my son abroad, wch I hope he will.

As to w^t neues this plaice afords, tho I suppose you have it from better hands, yet I will tell you how much pleased wee are here att Court wth the citty, and that the pett[it]ion^a was not received att the Comon Councell, tho it was by a very few voices carried against. They first declared it twas legall and the right of ever[y] man to adress that way to the Kinge, and that a parlim^t was very needefull to those purposes, but that, believing it twould procure a more certane sattisfaction w^thout, and more ready way to have ther desiers granted.

Wee are told here that the Dutch have absolutly refuced the French league and will agree wth us, into wch league the greattes part of christendome are willingle to entter, to humble the Kinge of France, if they can, att least that he might not greatten his con-quest, wch is expected he will doe next summer. 'Tis thought the Kinge may have given the Dutch some privat assurance of assist-ance, wch makes it hop'd wee may not bee long w^thout a parlim^t Next Munday, beeing ye day for the prorogation, is impatiently expected, to see ye event of peoples hopes.

Here is strange neues from France. A great many people of the best quality accused for pois[on]ing.^b Madame de Sowison^c

---

a This lady's spelling is sometimes consistent. Petition appears as "pettion" more than once.

b This word has proved too much for the writer. She first wrote *possing*, which she then rejected in favour of *poising*.

c She means Madame de Soissons; Olympie Mancini, widow of Eugène Maurice de Savoie, Comte de Soissons, and the mother of the famous Prince Eugène. Her sister, the Madam de Bullion of the letter, was Marie Anne Mancini, married to Godefroi de la Tour, Duc de Bouillon. They were both accused in the scare which followed the Brinvilliers and Voison poisonings. Olympie fled, and, according to Saint Simon, was suspected afterwards of poisoning the young Queen of Spain. Her sister was acquitted.

(Madame Mazerine sister) hath made her escape. She is said to have bine the death of her husband. Severall more wch was ingaged in that first murder, to secure her owne saffety, she hath sent after him. Madam de Bullion, another sister, is secured, and a great many more. The Marechall de Luxsomberge^a is in ye Bastill, a paper under his owne hand being found, a contract made to the divell upon three accounts: one, never to loose the Kinge's favour; to bee allwayes victouris and never hurt in battall; and allways prosperous in his love. Sesak that was here, ye great gamester, he hath done ye same thing, that he may winn allwayes att play. It makes as much discours in France as our plott doth here, and ye Kinge is much concern'd ther about it. I begg your L^{dsp} pardon for ye length of this trouble, and remaine,

Your most humble servant,

A. MANCHESTER.

Since I writte, this day, about noone, Mr Thinn,^b Sr Walter St. John, and Sr Edward Hungerford, wth two or 3 orther gentlemen, presented the petti[ti]one from Wiltshiere. Y^e K. received y^m but ruffly, asked y^m from whens it came. Beeing told, he said that nether the grand jury nor justices hands being to it, he wonderd gentlemen would owne anything from a rabble; that it twas his right to call parlim^{ts} when he thought it conve[ni]ant, and was ye judge of it, and should not doe it y^e sooner for this way; and soe left y^m.

---

^a François Henri de Montmorency-Bouteville, Maréchal Duc de Luxembourg.
^b Thomas Thynne, of Longleat, M.P. for Wilts, a follower of Monmouth. He was murdered in 1682 by assassins hired by Count Coningsmark.

CHARLES HATTON.

My L^d,   Jan. 27, 16$\frac{79}{80}$.

*   *   *   *

Y^e parliament wase yesterday prorogu'd to y^e 15th of April.   Y^e
reason of shortening y^e prorogation you will see in y^e King's speech,
wch much displeases y^e factious petitioners, whom in truth nothing
will please.   Coll. Mildmay ^a wth others presented a petition from
Essex.   His Mat^y gave him a severe checke when he receiv'd it,
and told him he remembred 40 and 41.   Mildmay insolently reply'd:
"And I remember 59 and 60."

Here is much discourse y^t ye Duke of Yorke is coming out of
Scotland.   Y^e factious give out y^t it is to breake ye Dutch league.

I will by ye carrier, wth ye tobacco, &c. send y^r Lo^{ppe} ye L^d Ch.
Justice his answer in print,^b wch came out without his leave and
hath prevented his publishing it with some observation of what
passed at ye tryall.   I acquainted you wth ye most materiall passages
some few dayes before ye tryall.   Dr Oates told ye L^{ds} of ye Councell
y^t he wou'd not positively say it, but he beleeved he shou'd be able
to prove y^t my L^d Ch. J. danced naked.^c

*   *   *   *

Y^r L^{pps} truly affec^t Brother to serve you,

C. HATTON.

---

^a Henry Mildmay, M.P. for Essex.

^b "The Answer of Sir William Scroggs, K^t, Chief Justice of the King's Bench,
to the Articles of Dr. Titus Oates and Mr. William Bedlow."

^c This recalls Jeffreys' drunken prank, as told by Reresby, how he and the Lord
Treasurer Rochester " stripped in to their shirts, and had not accident prevented
would have got upon a sign-post to drink the King's health."   The articles presented by Oates and Bedloe do not contain the charge specified above; but one item
states, " That the Lord Chief Justice is very much addicted to swearing and
cursing in his common discourse and to drink to excess," a charge which was
probably true enough in all particulars.

SIR CHARLES LYTTELTON.

MY LORD, Jan. 31, [1680.]

Major Dorrill[a] died this morning: S[r] Bowcher Wrey is Major, and Harris[b] has y[e] Company. I am Gov[r] of Sheerenesse. To night my Lords Russell, Cavendish, S[r] Harry Capell, and M[r] Powell came to y[e] King in y[e] bedchamber, and desired leave to quit theyr places in y[e] Councell. S[r] Steph. Fox told mee too to night that M[r] Vaughan,[c] upon pretence of his sicknesse, has quitted his place in the Admiralty, and that S[r] Tho. Lyttelton comes into his place; of w[ch] I am very glad.

Wee have lost an E. India ship upon y[e] rocks at Scilly.

My poore wife and sonne are both very ill. My wifes disease, I think, is vapors; but Harry has a very ill feavor hangs on him and allso does much affect his head; so hee was let blood to night, and D[r] Needham says, had y[e] most feavorish blood that he has seene of so young a child. He is much better after it, and, if hee rest well to night, I hope will doe well. I shall be very glad to heare my Lady were recovered, and that y[r] L[p] and children are well.

THE SAME.

MY LORD, Feb. 28, [1680.]

Wee are running now as fast as wee can into a confederacy wth all y[e] German princes, Spaine, Holland, &c., agst. France; and this I take to be in hearty good earnest, and I doe assure you,

[a] Nathaniel Dorrell, Lyttelton's major.
[b] Edward Harris.
[c] Edward Vaughan, one of the commissioners of the Admiralty, was succeeded by Sir Thomas Lyttelton.

from very good hands, the Duke has set that matter very much forward since his coming hither. S[r] Gabriel Silvius is sent as Envoye to y[e] Duke of Zell, and S[r] Robt Southwold[a] to the Duke of Brandenburg. It's hoped this will be so gratefull to the nation y[t], when y[e] King shall think fit to call y[e] Parlimt, they may meete in better temper.

The young gallants are tilting every day. Yesterday S[r] William Poultney's[b] sonn and young Warcup and theyr seconds, a sonne of my Lord Whartons and one Oglethorp (not he of y[e] Guards) fought. Wharton was hurt in y[e] side, and Poultney disarmed Warcup. This morning my Lord Plimouth and S[r] George Huet;[c] my Lords Cavendish[d] and Mordant[e] were theyr seconds. I think y[e] same adventure happened in this ocasion; for they say one of y[e] principalls, my Lord Plimouth, was disarmed, and my Lord Mordant hurt in his sholder. The quarrell was upon some idle messages that passed in y[e] park by an orringe wench that, they say, reported lyes to one another to make herself sport. The King is not so angry for y[e] battle as for y[e] idlenesse of y[e] ocasion.

Harry, I thank God, does recover.

THE SAME.

MY LORD,   London, March 16, [1680.]

By reason of my wife and children being at Chelsey and y[e] Court at Newmarket I am little heere; w[ch] is y[e] reason I have not

---

[a] Sir R. Southwell.

[b] M.P. for Middlesex.

[c] Sir George Hewett, of Pishobury, co. Herts, Bart.; afterwards created Viscount Hewett.

[d] Lord William Cavendish, afterwards Duke of Devonshire.

[e] Charles, Lord Mordaunt, afterwards 3rd Earl of Peterborough.

troubled y^r L^p lately. I am very sorry to find by y^r L^ps last my Lady has her ague againe; yet, if I might advise, I w^d not be discouraged, but use ye same medecine againe; for I cant heare it does any body harm. Y^e K^g took a p^d of it by all ye doctors direction, who first declared it ye best and very innocent medicine; at w^cb Frazor swore a greate oath: "Have wee bine railing at it so long, and must wee now commend it as ye only thing to ye King?"

I dont know, my Lord, if you heard y^t, before ye K^g went, he told ye Duchesse that, there being no articles by any publike treaty for her marriage to allow her ye use of a priest, she could not by law keepe any about her, nor he give them protection if she did; so desired her to send them away, as I heare she does.

*　　　　*　　　　*　　　　*　　　　*

Y^e young Duke of Hanover^a is expected heere very soone and is much talked of for a husband for Lady Anne; whose charrecter is y^t he is a prottestant, very young, gallant and handsom, and indifferent rich; and they say it will stand well wth ye Kings affaires, in relation to ye alliances he is making with the other German princes. Y^e Princes of Orange has bine dying allmost, but is now abroad again. Y^e phizitians, they say, had so tamperd wth her, abt. her being wth child, that they had allmost killd her.

THE SAME.

MY LORD,   March 18, [1680.]

*　　　　*　　　　*　　　　*　　　　*

Yesterday there was a greate meeting of ye malcontent lords at may Ld Wharton's. Among them was my Ld North, tho' hee be looked on now as a renegade, because he has kissd the Duke's hand; and I was told y^t yesterday my Ld Shaftsbury sayd that my L^d

---

^a Afterwards George I. of England. He was at this time in his twentieth year; and married, two years later, the unhappy Sophia Dorothea of Zelle.

North (it was to himself) was suing my Ld Grey for an estate and an earldom (that of Tancreville) wth it.   He ownd y^t of ye estate, but not of the earldom.   My L^d Sh. sayd there were other ways of getting an earldom.   To wch North replyed, his L^p had found out such, but he could not.   I shd. tell you that, before this meeting broke up, my Ld Shafts: desired that it might be kept up among them weekely, so my Ld Kent^a desired ye next might be at his house.

But if my intelligence dont faile mee, and I have it from a greate man, they are dissappointed of another rendevouze; for Frank Charlton went to my Lord Mayor to tell him those lords intended to come to dine wth him (wch was done a purposse to keepe up theyr credits in ye citty wch has mitily fallen of late, especially since ye King and Dukes supping there).   My Lord Mayor sayd, while he had the honour of being Mayor, he kept a publik table, and it was ever open, especially to all men of quallity.   But after reflecting wth himself, or by others advise, he sent for Charlton and told him, if hee had not allready sayd anything to those Lords, he desired that he would excuse it; but Charlton pretended he had allready invited them.   Then my Ld Mayor sayd that hee had considered of it, and it was absolutely ye interest of ye citty to live faire and well wth ye Court, and that, so long as he had ye honour to serve it as theyr cheife magistrait, he w^d endeavor to keepe it so, and therefore thought it might not be well understood to entertaine these L^{ds} who are all there together, and therefore desired he would uninvite them, for he c^d not bid them welcome.

I pray God give my Lady better health.

I am told y^t Mr Finch,^b my L^d Ch. eldest son, is run high into ye popular way; and there is some tattle as if his father w^d be layd aside and my L^d Ch. Jus. North^c in his place, and Sr Will. Jones^d made Ch. Justice.

[a] Anthony Grey, 11th Earl of Kent.   [b] Heneage Finch, Solicitor-General
[c] He succeeded on Nottingham's death in 1682.
[d] The late Attorney-General.

CHARLES HATTON.

April 27, 1680.

*   *   *   *   *

Yesterday Mr Secretary Coventry resigned up ye seales, and his Mat^y delivered them to Sr Lionell Jenkins. The business for wch ye judges were commanded to attend his Mat^y wase as your Lo^{ppe} guessed. Sr Gilbert Gerrard and all ye judges were called into ye councell chamber, and his Mat^y tooke notice of a report y^t Sr Gilbert had seen a black box wth a writing in it, asserting y^t his Mat^y had been maryed to ye Duke of Monmouth mother, and asked Sr Gilbert whither he had ever seen any such pretended paper. Sr Gilbert declared he had not. His Mat^y said he was well assured y^t ye report wase false, but, it being a business of soe great concern, his Mat^y required Sr Gilbert to answer upon oath whither he had seen any such paper or not; at wch Sr Gilbert scrupled very much, asserting y^t by law noe such question cou'd be put. But ye judges did every one of them seriatim declare y^t that board was a proper place of judicature of state affaires, and y^t, this being a businesse of such high concern to ye state, Sr Gilbert ought, if required by ye board, to answer upon oath, wch at last he did and declared he had never seen any such paper.

His Mat^y said he had once before made oath in y^t place y^t he never wase marryed to her, and did againe declare he never wase; but he wase resolved to sift strictly into ye occasion of y^t report and required all ye L^{ds} of ye Councill and all ye judges to declare what they had heard of any thing relating to y^t matter. They all answered they never had heard anything, except my L^d of Essex, who named a gentleman who had lately discoursed wth him of that matter. Whereupon it wase ordred y^t ye gentleman shou'd be sent for and examined by ye Secretaries of State.

Just before this affaire wase agitated in ye Councill ye Duke of Yorke wase called in and stayed all ye time.

Y^r Lo^{pps} truly affectionat brother to serve you,

     C. HATTON.

Sir Charles Lyttelton.

My L^d,   London, May 22, 1680.

I have y^{rs} of ye 17 from Guernesey. I did not thinke [when] wee parted I sh^d so soone have bine sent after you as I am like to be; for the K^g has bine pleased to tell me I shall goe to command in Jersey in Sr Laneere's ^a place, and Coll. Churchill ^b has ye Duke's regimt. and ye gov^mt of Sherenes; and Laneere comes in Sr Richd Dutton's place in ye guards, who is to be Govr of Barbadoes.^c This world is a vaine, transitory, uncertain thing. My comfort is, I am allmost at my journey's end, and if this be my last stage I am not unhappy to have so honorable a retreate to think w^{ht} I have bine doing these 50 yeares, of wch Ime sure I can give but an ill account to my family, and I doubt a wors to God Allmighty.

My Lord, I doe not expect but to find this remove much to my losse in point of profit, and therefore did w^{ht} I might to oppose it; but the fates have determined otherwise, and I submitt, not wthout some sattisfaction and hopes that it may prove to ye best. I intend to goe as soone as I can conveniently, and to take all my family wth mee. I hope I shall see y^r L^p heere first; and think it very unlucky y^r L^{ps} absence, whose advise and conduct in this affaire w^d have bine so usefull and necessary to mee.

I am, my L^d,
Your humble serv^t,
C. Lyttelton.

My humble service to all y^r good company.

---

[a] Sir John Laneere, Governor of Jersey
[b] At this time lieut.-colonel of Lyttelton's regiment. These removes did not take place.
[c] This appointment was made.

The Bishop of Oxford[a] to Lady Hatton.

MOST HONORD MADAM, May 27, [1680].

As you have the satisfaction at present of being in hourly expectation of my Lord's arrival, I hope you will speedily have the more real enjoyment of his personal presence, the notice whereof will be exceedingly welcome to me. Your being tired with your stay in town, and your longings for the diversions of Kirby, are particulars wherein I fear you have not many rivalls. In this world every one makes his own contentment and misfortune by the desires wch they take up and the ends wch they propose to themselves. The greatest part of your sex, having fild their minds with the gaities and entertainments of the town, would look upon a return to the country as being thrown into a goal or the being buried alive. But your Honor, having renounct in your judgment as well as baptism the pomps and vanities of the world, that think your family and devotions the best employment of your time, your Lord, your children, your own conscience, and Almighty God, the most desirable company, think London to be the wilderness and place of torment. And may you still retain the same apprehensions, and pass thro this world of guilt and vanity without contracting the sulliage and infection of it. The solemnity of Whitsuntide now approaches, and while other ladies fit and dress themselves to appear at court, the play house, or the park, you will put on the better robes of innocence and piety, the wedding garment wch may render you a guest for the table of your God.

I am sorry to hear of your brother Hatton's misadventure, but London is a place where there is so ready help that 'tis to be hoped he will be soon recovered. The Provost of Eton[b] has almost finisht

---

[a] John Fell, better know as the active Dean of Christ Church; became Bishop of Oxford in 1676, and died in 1686.

[b] Dr. Richard Allestree, who died in 1681.

his course at the Bath, and upon Teusday next purposes to be returning homeward. I beseech Almighty God to give your Honor health and mercy and blessing, and, with infinit respect, remain, honord Madam,

Your most faithfull serv^t in our Lord,

Jo. Oxon.

THE SAME TO THE SAME.

MOST HONORD MADAM   July 3, [1680].

I perceive it lies upon your mind that you are a person remarkable for misfortunes; therefore I pray let us consider the thing a a little first, whither your observation be truly made, and then whither it ought to be matter of trouble to you. As to the former part, I think it not evident that any thing singularly calamitous has befaln you. It is very sure that you have lost several of your neerest relations before you attaind to a full age; but surely this is no unusual thing; for children to be orphans, and of a numerous family several to dye early, is the event of every day. On the other side, to how many is it exceedingly unfortunate that their parents have lived long, have wasted the fortunes, disgraced the families, and debaucht the manners of their relations, so that the life of parents and kindred is very far from being in itself a blessing. But, dearest Madam, the friends which you have lost were persons of vertue; and is that the calamity that, when you had received the benefits of education and example from them, Almighty God took them from this miserable world to give them the rewards of eternity? Do you envy them their happiness? Or do you count it an injury that you have not them continued here to their infinit disadvantage, so long as it would answer your convenience? Tho your dear father lived not long after you could understand the tenderness due to that relation, it pleasd God to continue your incomparable mother till you were not only fully instituted in all christian duties but till you were married and put into obligations of leaving father and mother; and indeed, if you remember well, you had, even in my most honord ladies life time, a prospect of being calld to attend your husband at Guernesey. And I pray think, had that bin the case, nay had you bin settled at Kirby and my lady but at Easton, would you not for a great part of your time be deprived of each other?

In like manner I could reason with you concerning my dearest Lord, your brother.[a]   But to go forward, let us consider whither the loss of friends be the only calamity of the world. What think you of poverty; what think you of sickness; what think you of being debaucht in vice? When you number your misfortunes, I pray put on the other side your blessings and advantages, and con sider that whatever ill of any kind you are freed from, whatever blessing is continued to you, is the meer bounty and free mercy of a gracious God. Whatever innocence you have that may recommend you to His favor is itself the greatest of favors.

And now, dearest Madam, let us consider the second point, whither, taking it for granted that you are this remarkably unfortunate person which you esteem yourself, this ought to be so much resented by you.   I am sure, upon all the mesures which christianity teaches, afflictions are placed under a better character; we are told it is the mark of sonship, the sign that we are not bastards, nay, that we are children whom the Father of spirits loves and chastises. Accordingly we are commanded to think it all joy when we fall into diverse temtations, to rejoice and to be exceeding glad, and be assured therefrom that great is our reward in Heaven. If you have any argument to justify your grief and trouble, I pray let me hear it, and let us debate the matter at large.   But if upon an equal view your condition be not extraordinarily calamitous; that if it be tis sent by an alwise and gracious Providence that designs it for your real and certain advantage, I hope you will be so just to that

[a] Charles, Lord Grey of Ruthyn, who had died of smallpox in 1679. .

Fatherly hand, and so just to your own interest, as with cheerfull-
ness to acquiesce in your condition and resolve yourself to be, as I
verily believe you are, very happy. I will not lay before you the
large receits wch you have had from God's hand, of fortune, honor,
understanding, education, friends, health, and the like; but I will
tell you why I think my Lady Hatton very happy. She is removed
from the infectious conversation of the town, where the precious
time designed for the great purposes of eternity is to be wasted in
impertinent and uncharitable visits and unseasonable meals; where
the estate designd for the infinit emprovements of charity is to be
wasted in gaudy furniture, expensive dressings, and ridiculous
equipags; where the reputation, our best tresure next to innocence,
must be in perpetual hasards, and is impossible by any care or fore
cast to be preserved entire. And she is also in the station where
Providence has placed hir in the country, where she has free opportunities for devotion and retirement into hir own soul, for frugal
care of the interests of hir family, for charities to hir poor neighbours, and retird from the stroke of malicious tongues; and with all
this dares be alone, dares look into hirself, and esteems a conversation with God and vertue superior to all the frolics with men or vice.
    My most honord Madam, cast up your accounts, and, when you
have don so, tell me plainly whither you would change your condition with any of the gay ladies of the age, nay, with any one
whom you know in the whole world.   And if upon just reflection
you cannot pitch anywhere to better your condition, then determine
whether you ought to be dissatisfied with that wch is assigned you.
God Almighty bless you in all your interests and relations.
            I remain, honord Madam,
                    Your most faithfull serv^{t} in our Lord,
                                            Jo. Oxon.
    I shall be glad to hear that my little Lord and Kitty^a are well at
Eton.

    ^a Lady Hatton's two young brothers: Henry Yelverton, now become, by the death
of his elder brother, Lord Grey of Ruthyn, afterwards Viscount Longueville; and
Christopher.

Charles Hatton.

My L^d,   July 15, 1680.

*   *   *   *

One Douty, who wase once page to my Lady Shrewsberry and, after, gentleman of ye horse to ye Duke of Buces, and hath purchas'd a very good estate and built a very fine house in Yorke buildings, did some time since take coach at ye new Exchang for Westminster, and, it being very rainy, ye coachman was not content wth a shilling for his hire but gave very ill language; and Mr Douty therupon struckt at him wth his hand, ye coach[man] therupon whip'd him, and Mr Douty drew out his sword and run him thro. But the coachman, it wase thought, was cured, went abroad, got drunke, fell into a feavour and dyed. Mr. Douty, out of confidence to escape, brought himself upon his tryall and wase found guilty of willfull murder.

*   *   *   *   *

Y^r Lo^{pps} truly affectionat brother to serve you,

C. Hatton.

Sir Charles Lyttelton,

My Lord,   July 27, 1680.

I humbly thank you for y^r favorable enquiry w^{ht} becomes of mee; wch I had sooner given y^r L^p an acct. of, but that I was rambling abroad at Richmond on ye post days.

I am not like to goe to Jerzey at all nor yet to Rochester, the yeare being so farr spent and ye sickly time coming, wch is a good pretence enough for my wife not to leave London.

The news is y^t my Ld Ossory is very ill of a feavor. His phizitians this morning despaired of his recovery, but to night they have some hopes.

My Lord Mulgrave and Lumley [a] are come back from Tangier, where they stayed but 4 days, finding y[e] truce made, and, as they beleeve, y[e] Moores willing to prolong it or els they would never have made it, for they w[d] have played theyr cannon when they had 20 planted. S[r] Palmes Feirbon [b] sayd wee c[d] not have kept y[e] town 2 days. But he thinks theyr design is to give us leave to build the mole, or els to make a new treaty wth us to furnish them wth guns, &c., as they want. But my L[d] Lumley tells mee that there is no part 40 yards of y[e] wall w[ch] does not so command the place, that wth a musquet one may not shoote from one end of it to y[e] other. This, he says, when they told y[e] King, he sayd he was in the condition of a man that had lived severall yeares wth a wife who had preserved her fame, and, at last, one telling him he took one abed wth her, he could not tell how to give credit to. W[ht] councells will be taken heereupon I cant tell, but they have for the present given orders that y[e] men w[ch] were drawne out of y[e] troopes here should be all sent for back and theyr horses and furniture be delivered to y[e] new raised troopes, y[e] K[g] allowing 18 and 15[li] for a hors. Who will goe com[dr] in cheife I cant guesse, if they confine theyr design to send an army, for L[d] Ossory wont be capable of it.

I am told S[r] John Laneere wont keepe Jerzey, and yet I beleeve it will never fall to my lott; w[ch] if it be so, one may guesse my friends' interest is not so good as it has bine. I think to goe to morrow to Windsor.

The same.

MY LORD,   Aug. 3[d], 1680.

If you have a mind to rubb up y[e] memory of y[r] old loves, I can help you a little in it; for, tother day, in shifting of a cabinet that

---

[a] Richard, Lord Lumley, afterwards Earl of Scarborough.
[b] Sir Palmes Fairborne, Governor of Tangier, was killed in the siege this year.

was y^r friend's I found abundance of y^r letters to her about that subject, wch I hant yet disposed of.

There was indeed a talk of my Lord Mulgrave, but I beleeve on no other ground then there is of some others, as ye M. of Worcester, my Ld Sunderland, my Ld Essex againe, and others. Yet I doe not think my Lord Ormond will be presently removed,[a] tho' I beleeve his sonne[b] was a great appuy to him, as he was to my Ld Chamber lain,[c] whose interest he did both mightily support; for hee was in very good credit at Court, as he was every where else, wch makes his losse ye more to be lamented.

When I was at Windsor, I found by Churchill (who is ye only favourite of his master) that his pretence to my com^{ds} heere is not given over, so consequently mine to Jerzey; and I beleeve they will in time bring it about, and ye better now, because Laneere has lost a greate friend of my Ld Ossory, and that it was he wch first put ye stopp to y^t buisnesse. My Ld Mulgrave told mee that ye acct he had brought of ye state of Tangier is direct contrary to w^{ht} had bine formerly sent by the govern^r and Mr Sheeres[d] and ye officers, and that it is signed by them all, wch is, in short, that ye town is not to be kept, unlesse there be an army of at least 6000 foot and 1000 hors, to force a passage out of ye town through theyr entrenchm^{ts} and then to entrench themselves to countenance the working ye fortiffications; but how this can be done, if ye Mores have such an army to oppose them as they have, I cannot comprehend. I doe not know nor heare if any body is named to succeed my Ld Ossory in that employ.

Whenever it will be most convenient to y^r L^p to send mee up some venison, it will be seasonable for mee so it does not come ab^t ye 17 of August; for then I must be at Sherenesse, to attend y^e

[a] He remained Lord-Lieutenant of Ireland, on his present appointment, till 1682.
[b] The Earl of Ossory had just died.
[c] Lord Arlington.
[d] Apparently formerly an attaché to the embassy in Spain and resident at Tangier. " A good ingenious man, but do talk a little too much of his travels," says Pepys.

King.   If it come next week, it will be very welcom, especially ab^t
ye beginning; for it may be ab^t ye later end I may be going thither
to prepare thinges.

My humblest services to my Lady, who I am mighty glad to
heare, by a letter I saw to ye Provost, is breeding.   I wish her L^p
better health wth it 'tho', and that she may bring you a brave boy.

CHARLES HATTON.

My L^d,   Aug. 26, [16]80.

*   *   *   *

Here is great lamentations for ye death of Cap^n Bedlow, who
dyed at Bristow of a feavour occasioned by drinking cyder whilst
he wase very hot, having rid post.   My Ld Cheif Just. North,
whilst he wase sicke, wase at Bristow in his circuit, and, at his
desire, went to him and caused one of his clerks to write down all
Bedlow said to him, part of wch I am credibly inform'd wase to this
effect: That all ye evidence he had given wase exactly true; y^t he
had not injured any person in his whole life malitiously or de-
signedly; y^t ye Duke of Yorke wase privy to ye plot to bring in
popery, but cou'd never be brought to consent to ye King's murder;
that ye Queen wase no further guilty to ye plot, but in assisting y^e
preists wth money to advance popery.   This is all I can, wth any
ground of credibility, tell you he said to my L^d Ch. Just. North.
But he did say a great deal more; and some say he accused y^e
Marquise of Worcester and others.   The well affected (as they are
called) to ye protestant religion at Bristow were at ye charge of his
funerall.   The motto on his scutcheon wase: " Testimonium, quod
vivens exhibuit, moriens confirmavit."   This minds me of a very
extravagant inscription, considering ye times, y^r acquaintance y^e

late B^p of St Asaph ordred by his will to be put on his grave stone, wch concluded: " Oh vos transientes domum Domini, orate pro conservo vestro, ut inveniam misericordiam in die Domini." ^a

*   *   *

Y^r truly affect Brother to serve you,

C. HATTON.

SIR CHARLES LYTTELTON.

MY LORD, London, Sep. 9, 1680.

The Duke declared at my Lord Berklys last weeke, where he dined, that he was very much for ye parlim^{ts} sitting, and hoped and did not doubt but ye King intended it.

There is a foolish report goes about, and tis beleeved, but tis fals, that ye Duke shd. allude to a chase he had at a stagg and bringing him to a bay, that whilst he was hunting of beasts men hunted him, and that, tho' they shd. bring him to a bay, and, after, kill him, as that stag was, he would stand it; and that this discours was to my Ld Castlehaven,^b wthin ye K^{gs} hearing.

A footman of ye Duke's was killd yesterday at Windsor by a footman of ye K^{gs}, who formerly served the Duke of Monmouth. I know not anything of ye quarrell.

The D. of Mon. came hither a Tuesday night, out of ye west. I heare there was some shabby people went out to meete him; w^{ch}

---

^a " Dr. [Isaac] Barrow, late bishop of St. Asaph in Wales writt this epitaph and desired it might be fixed on his grave: ' Exuviæ Isaaci Sancti Asaphi Episcopi in manum Dei depositæ, in spem lætæ resurrectionis per Christi sola merita. O vos intrantes in domum Domini, orate pro conservo vestro, ut inveniam misericordiam in die Domini.' This is much talk'd off for its tendency to popery."—Luttrell, i. 52.

^b James Touchet, Earl of Castlehaven.

he was so ashamed of, he drove as hard as hee c^d to be ye lesse observed; and tho', at Exeter, there came in wth greate numbers of people, yet few of good rank among them.

My Ld Carlisle^a is come back; so is ye Court hither for a few days.

If you have not seen Mrs Celliers narrative,^{b} tis well worth it.

THE SAME.

London, Sep. 14, 1680.

My Ld Carlisle does pretend to goe back to Jamaica; but, it may be, he has to keepe it in commendam and to goe by his deputy. There is not the least reall ground for such phansy of my Ld Salisbury;^{c} nor doe I beleeve it likely you will ever see y^t Comn in a single hand againe. I beleeve ye country was not very fond of my Ld Carlisle; and I heare hee commends the countrey, and he has no reason to ye contrary, for he has had better health and more mony then I beleeve he ever saw of his own before.

The greate matter that has bine lately at Court is, whither the Parlim^t shall be calld in Ireland. There were severall acts sent from hence (as all are, to be approved on by ye L^t and Councell), wch are so aproved on and desired may be passd in Parlim^t; among w^{ch}, one is to put all the papists out of ye Parlim^t, and another, to

---

^{a} Charles Howard, Earl of Carlisle, Governor of Jamaica.

^{b} "Malice Defeated, or a brief Relation of the Accusation and Deliverance of Elizabeth Cellier, wherein her Proceedings, both before and during her confinement, are particularly related, and the Mystery of the Meal Tub fully discovered," &c. She was tried, on the 11th of this month, for libel in publishing this paper, was found guilty, and was fined 1,000l. and pilloried.

^{c} James Cecil, 3rd Earl of Salisbury. Lyttelton seems to be referring to the Treasurership.

give ye K^g mony to build ye forts, buy stores &c., for ye safety of ye kingdome; wch is soe necessary, that there is scarcely a whole carriage for a gun in ye kingdome and but very few guns, not 150 of culverin weight in ye whole, and but very few of ½ culverin, but 400 barrells of powder in ye publique stores. My L^d L^t presses earnestly ye Parlim^t sitting, and undertakes, if they may, and those acts passe, they will give 50,000^{li} for 4 yeares for those uses.

My Ld Essex mitily opposes this, so does Sunderland, Hide, and Godol:, and others. My Lord Chamb[erlain],^{a} ye Secretary Jenkins, and Coventry, are for it. Ld Cham: and Essex have bine very high about it. He told Essex that it was very strange hee sh^d goe change his note since he was L^t, for then he pressd nothing so much as a parli: sitting, to put the k^{g}dom into a posture of defence, and that one might easily guesse at the change, wch is supposed to be that they w^d have my Ld Ormond leave it in that disorder, and that he wch succeeds may have ye honore to establish it; and that ye K^g may have ye least need to doe this by parlim^t, S^r . . . .^{b} O'Sheene bringes a project, wch is supported by those persons, to encrease ye revenue 24000 a yeare, wch ye other party say is no greate offer and will be done however, tho' ye parlim^t doe sitt and give ye 200000 proposed. There is huge endeavors to remove my Ld Ormond; but I heare ye K^g says he will be firm to him.

I was told last night that wthin this week wee shall heare news will please us all. I had it from no ill hand.

They talk ye P. of Orange will be heere at ye session of ye parlim^t. Wht w^d you say, if ye D[uke] sh^d make some resignation of his pretences to ye P[rince] or, if he has sonns, as that he sh^d govern till they come to age? But these are but visions, w^{ch}, it may be, my L^d, you can see clearlier into. I cant but hope the Duke has not bine so long thinking w^{ht} to doe, but he has resolved of some thing to put himself out of ye storme wch will certainly fall on him in ye posture he now is. I pray God he may goe to church, &c.; but truly I doe not hope it.

^{a} Arlington. ^{b} Torn away.

THE SAME.

MY LORD,   Octo. 12, 1680.

There has bine some of the greate Lords to persuade the Duke to w^{th}draw, perticularly my L d of Essex. They say too, Sunderland, Hallifax, and ye Chancellor; but he possitively says he will not flye, nor goe w^{th}out the K^{gs} command; and I heare the King will not, nor be advised to command him. W^{ht} will be the event, God knows. In the mean time, the K^g and Duke seeme both in good humour, and, if they will be firm, I beleeve they are safe; and for my own part, I think they cannot but together. For, if hee shews he can part wth his brother, w^{ht} may not be presumed upon after?

A Sunday, my Ld Mayor brought the new sherriffs^a to bee presented and knighted, as the custome is; but ye K^g refused to see them, and told my Ld Mayor his reasons. Perhaps he is dissattisfied in theyr proceedings, as in theyr choyce of theyr under sherriff Goodenough,^b who does take a greate deale of paines to make furies of disaffected and phanatical people.

The Queen is pritty well; so is the Duchesse.

The D. of Buck. has bine very ill wth the feavor, but is now well againe, that is, has lost his fits wth ye help of ye jesuites powder.

THE SAME.

MY LORD,   Octo. 14 [1680].

This morning, the talk in ye galleries was that ye result of ye Councill last night (where they were so private they turnd out y^e

---

^b Slingsby Bethell and Henry Cornish.

^a Richard Goodenough; who afterwards changed sides, and was one of the witnesses against Cornish in his trial in 1685.

clerkes) was the proroguinge ye parlim^t for 10 days, and that, in the meane time, ye Duke will goe to church, receive ye sacram^t at St. Martins, and take all the tests. I feare this is to good for us yet. But I beleeve wee shall heare something better for him then bannishing and ruine, wch he has bine of late so threatnd w^th

Ever y^rs.

THE SAME.

My LORD,   London, Octo. 19, 1680.

I doubt whither this will find you at Kirby, or that you may not be on ye roade hither to be at ye opening of ye parlim^t. Yesterday, the Duke ownd hee would goe by sea to morrow wth ye D^sse and all his Court for Scotland. He was pleased to tell mee the K^g sayd it was for his service, so he submitted; but I beleeve tis ag^st his judgment and inclination, as much as can be.[a] Some think that they wch have advised this way, to save themselves rather then him, will be mistaken.

ANNE MONTAGUE [b] TO LADY HATTON.

Novem. 1, [1680].

I am very much obliged to you, deare Madam, that you are pleased to be concerned for my health, which I thanke God I have very well againe, and, for the creditt of Leezs, recoveryed it there, or els I should not have had it in this place, for much companey

[a] James remained in Scotland till March 1682.
[b] Anne, daughter of Robert Montague, 3rd Earl of Manchester. She married George Howard, Earl of Suffolk.

when one is not well makes one the worse, for I never see the
towne fuller. For I was to see the new play, the Spanish Frier,[a]
and there was all the world, but the Court is a letell dull yet; the
Queen beeing sick, there is noe drawing roome. I believe she will
see companey before her brith day. I doe not heare of much
finnery, and what I.shall have will not deserve that nam; but, if it
will be any devertion to your La[ps], you shall know it. But the
greatest new that is now is the death of L[d] Ogle[b] of this new
feaver,[c] and much lamented for by all his relations and his lady
extreamly. There is great providing of her husbands, and sevearll
named. She has 2000[l] a yeare gointer, and she must give 20000[l]
to my L[d] Newcastill for it, in those (sic) power it is now to make
his daughters great fortunes, and thay doe stand in need of it. S[r]
William Clifton was to have had one of them, but now it is quite
of, as it is with M[is] Chifings; and she is talk of for one of S[r]
William Goring['s], which will doe well, he beeing of her owne
religion and has a good eastate. My L[d] Huntingtower and his lady
is to bee in towne very sundenly. Thay made her very great
presents, and she was extreame fine. M[r] Newport is now very
sundenly to be marryed to the other sister.[d] I am very glad my
cousine Anne Hatton's ague is gone, for it is but and ill com-
pangione. I heare her pictur extreamly comended. My sister
Katte presents her servis to your La[ps]. She is at present in this

---

    [a] The Spanish Fryar, or the Double Discovery; a tragicomedy by John Dryden,
founded on a novel called "The Pilgrim," by S. Bremond.
    [b] Henry Cavendish, Earl of Ogle, eldest son of Henry, 2nd Duke of Newcastle.
He married Elizabeth, only surviving child of Joceline Percy, 11th Earl of
Northumberland. After his death she was contracted, if not married, to Thomas
Thynne, of Longleat, who was murdered in 1682. She afterwards married Charles
Seymour, Duke of Somerset.
    [c] Evelyn, in his Diary, mentions the "new fever" as the cause of death of Mrs.
Godolphin, 8 Sept. 1678.
    [d] Lionel Tollemache, Lord Huntingtower, afterwards Earl of Dysart, married
Grace, daughter of Sir Thomas Wilbraham. Bart., of Woodhey. Richard Newport,
afterwards Earl of Bradford, married her sister Mary.

place, but goes to Leezs in a day or to. I disir my servis to cousin Hatton, and am very much, deare Madam, your

humble sarvant,

A. MOUNTAGUE.

The young Lady Northumberland [a] is very ill that thay feare she will not live long. I wish your La[ps] was hear to shew your fine manto, and of your owne work, which good husfrey I cannot brage of, but am to have one very sundenly, for it is about; and it is a cheery coulerd satten embroderyed with silver thick and a letell black, and to be lined with black villvet. My pettcoat to it must be a rich gold and silver stufe, which thare is the finest now that ever I see, and a brode lace at the bottom.

THE COUNTESS OF MANCHESTER TO LADY HATTON.

MY DEARE NEICE, 7th Desem. [1680.]

I should often have writte to you, but y[t] my L[d] Hatton tells mee he writts every post, and therefore I doubt not but by him you have all that is done heare. I am very sensible you must have a very mallincolly time, espsshally your L[d] being obliged to stay. I am very much obliged to him for y[e] favour of his companye, for I see him often. This last week hath bine wholy taken up wth y[e] tryall of my L[d] Stafferd,[b] w[ch] hath bine 5 dayes allready, and this day being only in order to the judgm[t] made mee not soe curious as to goe, y[e] rest I was att being concern'd to heare how this horride

---

[a] Elizabeth, daughter of Thomas Wriothesley, Earl of Southampton, and widow of Joceline, Earl of Northumberland; here styled *young* to distinguish her from the Earl's mother, who was still living

[b] William Howard, Earl of Stafford; beheaded on the 29th December. "Lord Stafford was not a man belov'd, especially of his own family," is Evelyn's remark. All the peers who were his relatives, except the Earl of Arundel, found him guilty.

plott was made out, together wth w^t evidence they had against him, wch was soe well prooved that I believe not many was unsattisfied, except those that out of favour to some of the parity might wish it orther wayes. The scandall laid upon ye wittnesses was much taken offe, and, untill I heare w^t ye L^{ds} have done, I will say noe more as to my oppinion. I cannot but looke upon it as a wonderful providence of God Allmighty that hath discover'd this designe, or ells our religion and liffs, for ought I know, had bine in great danger. I pray God deffend us yet. Heare is great indeavours made by one sort of people att least to change his sentence to banishm^t; but most thinke y^t cannot bee done by ye L^{ds}. I pray God direct y^m, for it tis a very criticall time.

*   *   *   *

Your most affectionat Aunt and servant,

A. M.

Yesterday, being Munday, when I writte the orther part, ye L^{ds} spent the whole day in debattinge, but to day they proseeded to sentence, and he was quitted by 32 and found guilty by 54. Apon w^{ch}, sentence was given as a traytor, mittigated by ye Kinge to ye loss of his head.

CHARLES HATTON.

My L^d, 28 December, [16]80.

This morning I kissed his M^{aties} hand, and shall, in a day or two, have my commission for Capⁿ Sheldon's company,^a the obtaining of wch I must and doe attribute solely to y^r Lo^{pps} favour in interceeding in my behalfe soe pressingly in ye 2 letters you sent yesterday. My Ld Thanet and my Ld Feversham (who presented me to his Matie) both present their service to y^r Lo^{ppe}, and have engaged me to

^a In the forces maintained in Guernsey.

excuse their not writing; and my Ld Feversham pressed mee, wth great earnestness, to be sure to acquaint you y^t his Mat^y is very desirous you wou'd not faile, if possible, to be here either Monday or Tuesday morning, as soone as ye House sitts.[a]   I am

Y^r Lo^{pps} &c.

C. HATTON.

[a] The Exclusion Bill was before them.

END OF VOL. I.

CORRESPONDENCE

OF

THE FAMILY OF HATTON

BEING CHIEFLY LETTERS ADDRESSED TO

CHRISTOPHER FIRST VISCOUNT HATTON

A.D. 1601—1704.

EDITED BY

EDWARD MAUNDE THOMPSON.

VOLUME II.

PRINTED FOR THE CAMDEN SOCIETY.

M.DCCC.LXXVIII.

WESTMINSTER
PRINTED BY NICHOLS AND SONS,
25, PARLIAMENT STREET.

[NEW SERIES XXIII.]

COUNCIL OF THE CAMDEN SOCIETY

FOR THE YEAR 1878-79.

CORRESPONDENCE

OF

THE FAMILY OF HATTON.

SIR CHARLES LYTTELTON.

MY LORD,   London, July 2ᵈ, 1681.

*   *   *   *   *

This morning, yᵉ Kᵍ surprized every body that is not a Privy
Counsellor by coming by 8 a clock to town, and sat imediately in
councell. The matter was, my Lord Shaftsbury was seized by a
Sarjeant at Armes (Mʳ Deerham) this morning in his bed and
brought to yᵉ Councell, and, after having bine examined, was committed to yᵉ Tower upon a warrant of high treason, wᶜʰ was sworn
agˢᵗ him by four persons. The Judges were sent for to yᵉ Councell,
and they all declared wʰᵗ was sworn ᵃgˢᵗ him to be high treason.
The persons that have sworn are one Haynes,[a] who my Lord
Shaftsbury had so much appeared to get a pardon for, one Rouse,[b]
formerly a clerk, as I heare, to Sʳ Thomas Player, and Turbervill,
and another[c] I know not. They say, too, that Turberville has

[a] Bryan Haynes, one of the principal witnesses against both College and Shaftesbury.

[b] This is a mistake. John Rouse was himself proceeded against, but the grand
jury threw out the bill. He was afterwards executed for his part in the Rye House
plot.

[c] Edward Turberville and John Macnamara.

VOL. II.   **B**

sworn that all he sayd of my Ld Stafford was fals.   They talk too
that Dugdale is come in, too, to sweare on that side.   It was sayd
that there are warrants out for severall others.   My L^d of Essex
was named; but I beleeve there is no such thing as to him, because
I saw my Lord goe out of town this afternoone towards his own
house, wth 5 or 6 of servants wth him on horsback; and I beleeve,
by his equipage, he came to town but this morning.   The King
returnd to Windsor after dinner.

Plunket^a and Fitzharris^b were both executed yesterday.   Plunket
is generally pittied and beleeved to dye very innocent of w^{ht} he was
condemned.   Fitzharris left a paper behind him to be given to his
wife, in w^{ch}, I heard the K^g say, he says that w^{ht} he sayd in his
examination before ye 2 sherriffs, when he was first taken, was
dictated to him by the sherriffs, that is, as to ye Queen, ye Duke,
my Lord Danby, and ye K^g himself.

William Longueville.

My Lord,   9 July [1681].

Yesterday the bill of enditement ag^t Colledge^c was preferred to
ye grand jury at old Baily; and Dugdale, Smith,^{d} Haynes, and
Macknamara, as also Sr Wm Jennings, were witnesses of his declaring
a plott ag^t ye King at Oxford, and of his professing treasonable
designes, &c.; wch being heard in ye court, ye jury did afterwards
catechise in private, but on what grounds satisfyed I have not yett

---

^{a} Oliver Plunket, titular primate of Ireland, the last victim of the Popish plot.

^{b} Edward Fitzharris, the author of the Libel.

^{c} Stephen College, the Protestant Joiner.

^{d} John Smith, commonly called Narrative Smith, being the author of a Narrative
of the Popish plot.   He was sometime rector of St. Mary's, Colchester.

heard, but ignoramus was found. The Duke of Monmouth, Earles of Salsbury, Essex, cum aliis, Mr Ralph M[ontagu], and such like, were all there. Then came ye point whether ye habeas corpus for L^{ds} Shaftsbury and Howard[a] should bee granted, and ye judges (9 of them being there) declared it could not bee, as ye Tower not being within their commission of oyer and terminer. Upon ye Statute 3 Hen. 8 for correcting pannells of juryes, there was a paper printed, as also of another statute of Hen. 4, in Rastall at large; and ye judges in that could not doe ought by reason of ye statutes meaning only gaole delivery, whereas ye jury was returned on ye oyer and terminer commission. It is thought ye bills of inditement against ye L^{ds} were not preferred by reason of Colledge's case. Y^e sollicitor Whitacre[b] was committed yesterday to ye Tower. Fitzharris his last papers were very odd ones.

THE SAME.

MY LORD,   26 July [1681].

*   *   *   *   *

The joyner is like to bee tryed by a speciall commiss^n at Oxford, and after him ye L^{ds} businesse comes on. My Lord Dorsett[c] is upon going beyond seas, as thought y^t hee may bee out of ye way when ye tryals come on. Tom of Ten Thousand or ye Protestant Squire[d] is most in talk for Lady Ogle, by ye meanes of ye Duke's Mr Bret.[e] Y^e Duke is like to returne after his parl^t over in Scotland. Y^e poore protestants[f] are to bee collected for next weeke

----

[a] Lord Howard of Escrick had been committed to the Tower for contriving Fitzharris's libel.

[b] Edward Whitaker.   [c] Charles Sackville, 6th Earl of Dorset.

[d] Thomas Thynne.   [e] Richard Bret.

[f] The Huguenots who had escaped from persecution in France.

here, and yᵉ Councill sitt oft about them, vizᵗ in debate whither y
King may dispense with yᵉ lawes about not exercising trades
whereto they have not been prentices; if hee does, or does not, dispense with the lawes for them without parlᵗ, what will follow?

*   *   *   *

Your Lops. most obedient servant,

W. L.

Sir Charles Lyttelton.

My Lord,   London, Augnst 2ᵈ, 1681.

*   *   *   *   *

I came but last night from Windsor. The P. of Orange, when
he was heere, had addresses of all parties to him, Lᵈ Russell, Sʳ
Will: Jones, &c. He was invited to dine at Guidhal, wᶜʰ he
accepted; but yᵉ Kᵍ sent in yᵉ morning to forbid it, wᶜʰ was a
greate disappointment to them, and I believe very dissatisfactory to
yᵉ Prince; but I beleeve that, since his coming to Windsor, the Kᵍ
has put him at ease, and I hope ye P. is so wise to take no party
but yᵉ King's. He leaves the Kᵍ to-morrow and lyes at Arlington
house at night; yᵉ next night goes to Newhall, and next day to
Harwich, where hee embarques for Holland.

There was to be a meeting yesterday, in yᵉ afternoone, of all the
ministers, that is to say, my Lᵈ Hallifax, Hide, and Seymore,ᵃ and
yᵉ 2 secretaryes, wᵗʰ yᵉ P. of Orange, yᵉ Spanish and Duch Ambassador. Yᵉ Spanish has made a chart of all the French conquests
and pretentions, and this, by yᵉ Kᵍˢ desire, to expose to them; wᶜʰ
I doubt not he did, and I wish they may take such resolutions
upon as may be for yᵉ generall good of Xtendome, before it be too
late.

ᵃ Edward Seymour.

The phanatickes say they doe not yet discover if ye P. coming be to help or betray them.

Y^e Popish L^ds dined all wth ye L^t of ye Tower the other day; and the others are kept closs, but yet they have ye liberty of theyr wives and servants to come and goe at pleasure; wch I think is an odde way, for it hinders no correspondence. I heare y^t my Ld Shaftsbury is very confident he shall turn y^t batterie upon my Ld Hallifax; but it's good to ride ye fore hors.

THE COUNTESS OF MANCHESTER.

Whitehall, Aug. 2 [1681].

Haveinge recieved soe lately from my neice ye acount of her miscariage I hoped the danger had bine quite over, wch gave mee ye greater surprise when I found by your L^dsp letter she had bine soe very dangerously ill. She is of soe thiun and delicate a constitution, that I shall be very impatient untill I heare ye hopes you give mee in the later part of yours of her recoverie againe conferm'd. I pray God she may live, and, in His time, bring a son into your familly, tho I shall hope she will gaine a perfitt health before she proove wth childe. Your L^dsp care and kindness she hath soe often founde, that all must be fully sattisfied nothing could bee wantinge was to be had in order to helpe. Wee have lost lately soe many relations out of this family, I cannot but be frighted wth the least rumore of illness in one soe very neare unto mee, and for whom I have soe tender an affectione, wch she justly merritts from mee.

I came wth my L^d last weeke to this place, and designe w^thing two dayes to returne to Leez. His bisnes was to take Epsom watters, that he might not grow to fatt, and to buy some little mourninge, made mee take this oppertunitie. The towne is very unpleasent, and ye small pox very mortall, besides a most dangerous feaver of wch many dye in few dayes.

The Prince of Orange came to Arlington house one Thursday night. The two sheriffs waitted upon him and invitted him to dyner to my Ld Mayor on Satterday, wher was a very great enttertanem^t designed. One Friday night my Ld Hallifax, Ld Hide, Mr Semour, was wth him [and] very much importuned him not to goe, but, not saying they came from ye King to him, he continued resolved to goe; at w^{ch}, Mr Semore goeing that night to Windsor, the next morning the King sent ye Prince a letter and comand to ye contraie, and that he should come to Windsor. Thus, att ten a cloke, the Prince sent his secretarie wth ye letter to my Ld Mayor, and soe the feast and citty ladyes in all ther glory was disapointed. He went away to Windsor; but this is all ye discours. He goeth some time this weeke away. Here is nothinge more, and I shall conclude this trouble by begging your L^{dsp} to believe I am,

My L^d, your faithfull servant,

A. M.

Lady Ogle, 'tis said, will certanly marrie Mr Thinn, if it be not allready done. The young La: Rochester^a is dead suddenly of an apoplexie.

WILLIAM LONGUEVILLE.

My Lord,   [30 Aug. 1681].

Your asse was one of ye best my wife thinkes that ever shee mett with, and I hope shee will give my Lady an account of ye favour in sparing of it by all possible acknowledgm^{ts} and by taking care to shew her amendm^{ts} very soone after ye using of this milke.

^a Elizabeth, daughter of John Mallet, of Enmore, co. Somerset, and widow of John Wilmot, Earl of Rochester.

I have beene at Putney all this day almost, and so want ye news of ye noone (if any bee). 'Twas last night agreed Dr Oates had left Whitehall, but whither of himselfe or turnd out some few made a doubt. Earle of Gerrard or Macclesfield was dismissed ye bed-chamber, but of ye Earle of Manch[ester] it is a quary as yett. Y^e Ld Mordaunt is restored to ye King's favour. Ld Conway (a 6 weekes widdower) hath marryed againe, and 'tis one Mrs Stowell and 15000^li, if report say true.^a The Cockpitt hee hath taken of ye Earle of Danby. Some 3 bills were (or were like to bee) found at ye sessions in being, viz. against Whittaker, Rous, and ye fore-man of ye jury wch would not find Colledge his bill. His name I forgett; and 'tis thought ye pollicy herein is to render them fitt for the London petty juries, by wch Colledge w^d scarce have been cast. Y^e poore fellow is not like to live longer then too morrow. Duke Lauderdale is ill of a feaver and sent for D^rs hence too day. Some say Ch: Just: Pemberton is not easy in his place^b; y^t his Ma^ty meanes not for Newmarket; and y^t a speciall commission of oyer, &c. shall bee for ye L^ds indictments. I present my wives most humble thanks and service to your Lo^p and my Lady and also the like from,

My Lord,

Your Lo^ps ever obedient servant,

W. L.

---

^a Edward, Earl of Conway. His third wife was Ursula, daughter of Colonel Stowel.

^b Sir Francis Pemberton, Chief Justice of the King's Bench, was removed to the Common Pleas, in 1683, and immediately afterwards dismissed.

My Lord,   London, Octo^br 11th, [16]81.
        *   -   *   *   *

I am sorry to heare you have no other thoughts of coming hither
but upon ye tryall of ye Lords, wch I doe not heare anything so
much sayd of as to conclude when that may bee. It has bine
much talked of, as if my Lord Shaftsbury was offred to be set at
liberty, if he would but promise to retire to his house in Dorcet-
shire; and Thom Thinne told mee, the other day, at Richmond
(who, by ye way, lyes there to be w^thin ye sent of my Lady Ogle,
for he does not yet visit her, nor is like to doe so, till she comes
hither, wch will be the last of this month, when her mourning is out.
Y^e next day sheele open her doores to all pretenders; tho' I think
it is scarce to be doubted but she has entertained Mr Thin's addresses by 3^d hands, and is too farr ingaged to him to receive any
other), that his house was making ready to receive him there.
But I am told from one that best knows, my L^d would be well
content to take a further journey to be quit of ye Tower; and that
he has offred to goe to Carolina^a upon those termes, and has bine
refused.   And the King says, if it were any body els, tho' he knew
he were guilty and c^d prove it upon him, he could grant w^ht he
desires, but to him he knowes that if he sh^d, he w^d say ye condition
was exacted from him and that it was a force put on him.

The same.

My Lord   London, No^hr 10, [16]81.
        *   *   *   *   *

My Lady Ogle went up yesterday wth her grandmother to ye old
Change, and there slipt from her, and 'tis not yet known who is

---

^a See Christie's *Life of Shaftesbury*, ii. 419.

gone wth her, nor whither she is gone. But, last night, Dick Bret came to ye King and told him hee had waited on him before to acquaint his Ma^{ty} that she was not married to Mr Thin, but now he was come to tell him she is married to him. The King sayd she had bine unworthily and basely betrayd by her friends. They say she raild much at them of late to some she durst trust, in that they have abused her in making her beleeve he had 20,000 a yeare, was of a better family, and but 23 yeares old. He has never layn wth her since he was married, not so much as spoken to her, nay, scarce seen her, and says she never will. Besides, I heere my Lady Trevor will prossecute him as married to her daughter, and says she can prove it.[a] If it be but a contract, they say 'twill breake ye marriage wth Lady Ogle. They say y^t Thinne has given bonds for vast summes of mony to her friends upon this account. Dick Bret and Harry Howard, they say, are deepe in, and they talk of others, who I dare not name for feare of ye statute; but I beleeve that's a scandall.

It's a greate secret yet, but I am told that my Lady Portsmouth is shortly going into France for her health.

The King dined to-day abord ye Mordaunt.

The Same.

My Lord, No. 22, [16]81.

      *   *   *   *

Tis expected that y bill of my Lord Shafts. will be brought to ye grand jury a Thursday; but tis such a return of a jury that one can hardly expect anything but ignoramus from them. I was told to day that it has bine considered ab^t bringing the bill into ye Marshals court; but I beleeve there is nothing in it.

---

[a] Ruth, widow of Sir John Trevor, sometime Secretary of State. Reresby received an affidavit in this matter on the 2nd January, 1682, as he tells us in his *Memoirs*.

We have had a greate deale of puther and bloody threatenings about a paper set up in the coffee house, but no fighting; and I beleeve they are come of a little dully.

There is one of the finest poems come out of Absolon and Achitophel that ever you read, wherein there is a greate many charracters of all y⁰ great men of both sides. Pray send for it. Tis Dreydon's they say; and no doubt, upon y⁰ presumption, some body will fall upon him.ᵃ

A chambermaid of my wife's, a very homely wench, is to be married a Thursday to one Sʳ William Milward, a man of 800ˡⁱ a yeare. I am heartily sorry to heare my Lady is not well. I feare Kirby is too moist for y⁰ winter season for so delicate a complexion.

THE SAME.

MY LORD,   No. 29, [16]81.

My Lord Sh[aftesbury] is bayled, and all the others, Howard, Willmore, and Whitacre.ᵇ My Lᵈ Sh., after, went y⁰ back way very privately home, whither out of modesty not to shew himself to y⁰ populace, or that he thought they were prevented by y⁰ strict order my Lᵈ Mayor had taken to prevent all seditious concours of y⁰ people, is a question. There is a very lying partiall accᵗ come out of y⁰ proceedings at y⁰ Old Baily; but there will be one very suddenly by authority, wᶜʰ cᵈ not so soone passe y⁰ presse, because the judges are to examine it, and they are too busy at this time. It's beleeved wee shall have a parlimᵗ and an act of oblivion pass to quiet all.

ᵃ The cudgelling which Dryden had got in December, 1679, was still fresh in people's memory. Rochester had been roughly handled in the " Essay on Satire," the joint production of Dryden and Mulgrave, and took his revenge in this way.

ᵇ Lord Howard of Escrick, John Wilmore, and Edward Whitaker.

THE SAME.

MY LORD,   London, De. 6, [16]81.

I begin to be of y^r opinion, as to the parlimt. and ye act of oblivion; and the rather, because I have a little more then ordinary reason to beleeve ye Duke will be sent for.

Y^e Du^{sse} of Portsmth does certainly goe into France after X^{t}masse, and, tho' it be by advise of her phizitians, yet she is in doubt, it's sayd, she shan't return. But, to confirm her to ye contrary and of the King's constant goodnesse towards her, my Lord Hallifax is lately reconciled to her interest, at least so farr as to visit her and attend ye King in her lodgings, wch formerly he never would, and this too, they say, by ye King's possitive command. And as a further and more unquestionable proofe of her power, her son[a] is declared Master of the Hors, and Oglethorp[b] is in Armstrong's place; wch puts ye D. of Mon: too beyond all hopes of being ever restored, so he must be either Cesar aut nullus. I was told by one lately, as an argument of his being very low in pocket, that his fine set of coach horses were offred to be sold to ye person y^t told it mee.

I am sorry y^r brother is so ill in his affaires, and doubt he may loose his company by his conduct, and see no remedy.

The person you have sent for to y^r daughter is ye same Charlot would have recommended, and is a very ingenuous young woman and draws finely.

---

[a] The Duke of Richmond.

[b] Theophilus Oglethorpe and Charles Adderley were commissioners for the office of Master of the Horse, during the Duke of Richmond's minority. Oglethorpe was also a lieutenant-colonel in the Duke of York's troop of the Guards. Sir Thomas Armstrong had held the same commission in the King's troop of the same regiment.

My L[d] Grafton [a] has y[e] command of y[e] Guards,[b] in Russells place too, and I heare he has 6000[li] for it.

S[r] Rob[t] Carr has lost 5 or 6000[li] upon severall matches at Newmarket.

THE SAME.

MY LORD,   Jan. 3[d], 1681[2].

I shall send my trunkes abord y[e] yach a Thursday, and in 3 or 4 days I hope at furthest wee may sayle. The Duke of Monm[th] and L[d] Sunderland are both forbid to come into Whitehall, and the King has told M[r] May [c] and some others that they must forbeare theyr company or not come into his presence.

My L[d] Sunderland used to come to y[e] Duchess of Portsmouth, when y[e] King sat down to dinner; so yesterday, when he came, the Duchesse delivered that message herself and sent her woman to my Lady Sunderland,[d] that she should be glad if she met her in a third place, but that the K[g] had commanded her not to see her in her own lodgings. Y[e] D. of Mon: used to come to M[rs] Crofts [e] lodgings at night.

There has bine severall angry messages passd between the D. of Albemarle and y[e] D. of Monm[th], about words the D. of M. sh[d] say concerning the troope of Guards; and they say that y[e] D. of Albemarle would have made a quarrell to bring it to a duel, but y[e] Duke avoyded it.

George Leg has his com[n] for Master this day.[f]

I am in hast.

[a] Henry Fitz-Roy, natural son of Charles the Second, by the Duchess of Cleveland.
[b] The First Foot Guards.   [c] Baptist May, keeper of the privy purse.
[d] Anne, daughter of George Digby, Earl of Bristol, and wife of Robert Spencer, Earl of Sunderland.   [e] Monmouth's mistress.
[f] George Legge, afterwards Earl of Dartmouth, Master of the Ordnance.

The same.

My Lord,   Jan. 5, 1681[2].

I goe abord a Saturday.[a] Its ye generall talk of a parlim^t to meete some say at Norwich; but most at Oxford, in March or Ap^{ll}.

My Ld Arguile,[b] it's beleeved, is heere ; his case is thought very hard, and ye proceedings agst him vigorous; and all imputed to ye Duke's severity, and so made use of by those that dont love him, as an argument w^{ht} wee may expect from his governm^t heere. But Arguile is not much pittied, being looked on generally as a very ill man to ye Crown, and who has made use of ye King's favours heeretofore to do very greate injustices to others.

My Ld Preston[c] was sent by ye K^g to bring in ye Morocco embassador to-day,[d] and he himself is to goe into France suddenly to releeve Harry Saville, and Saville is to be a Comr of ye Admirallty, so is Sr John Chichely, wch makes ye number 7.

I saw the Moores at theyr lodging. Y^e ambassador is a white man, and his cloths white; ye rest are all in scarlet, I think.

I am y^r L^{ps} most humble servant.

[a] For Edinburgh.

[b] Archibald Campbell, 9th Earl of Argyle. It will be remembered that he was at this time condemned to death, but escaped into Holland. Halifax's words, as quoted by Lord Macaulay, will recur to the memory : " I know nothing of Scotch law, but this I know, that we should not hang a dog here on the grounds on which my Lord Argyle has been sentenced."

[c] Richard Graham, Viscount Preston, Secretary of State under James II.

[d] See Evelyn's account of the audience, in his *Diary*, 11 Jan. 1682.

The Duke of York.

Edenburgh, Jan. 27, 1682.

I would not lett this bearer, S[r] Charles Littelton, returne with out a letter from me, to lett you know how sensible I am of the assurences you gave me of your stedynesse to me, by the letter he brought me from you. 'Tis but what I had reason to expect from you, having known you so long, and that you never yett made one fals step to his Ma[jesty] and the Crowne. If others had followd your example, things had not been in the condition they are, nor I heare; but where so ever I am, you may depend upon my being a true freind to you.

James.

William Longueville.

My Lord,   28th Feb[y], [1682.]

*   *   *   *   *

The jury too day were halfe English, halfe strangers. One jury tryed all. Count Coningsmark[a] was quitted; but an appeale c[d] not bee entred by some of Mr. Thin's kindred. See Magna Charta c. . Y[e] jury were thought hugely partiall. S[r] W[m] Roberts was foreman. The other 3, vizt. Wortz y[e] Capt. y[e] Lieut[t] Sterne, and y[e] Polander,[b] were found guilty. Though they 3 pleaded not guilty, yet in effect they ownd all when they made their defences.

[a] Charles John, Count Coningsmark, accused of the murder of Thomas Thynne.
[b] Their names, as given in the *State Trials*, were Christopher Vratz, John Stern, and George Borosky alias Boratzi. See Reresby's account of his capture of Vratz, in his *Memoirs*, 12 Feb. 1682.

The Count hit upon ye humour of protestantcy, and told them of his ancestors and of himselfe, and how happy hee was to bee tryed by a protestant jury and in a protestant countrey. The Count is at large, but under bayle, wch were Sr Nathan^l Johnson (his friend and interpreter), last yeare mayor of Newcastle as I think, Major Oglethorpe, &c. Lady Ogle is not like to appeale him; and none else can, unlesse yong Bainton,^{a} who is but from his sister, and so, claiming by a woman, cannot. Nor can any other, since hee that is nearest cannot. This law I have not exactly look't into, but in a bookseller's shop and over a pint of wine heard it talked off. Pray, my Lord, forgive this broken account, but I hope it may bee, as meant, accepted from,

My Ld, your Lops most obedient,

W<small>M</small>. L.

S<small>IR</small> C<small>HARLES</small> L<small>YTTELTON</small>.

M<small>Y</small> L<small>ORD</small>,   March 11, [1682].

I have a letter from Scotland, wch says they expect the Duke back very quickly; and tis very much beleeved heere that it may be so, but I think that it w^d be no good complement to ye Duchesse to send for her hither and him back, unlesse it be to fetch her. He is dayly expected at Newmarket, because he sent an expresse to tell ye K^g he w^d come abord ye yach a Monday night. I intend to goe to Cambridg, and the next day to Newmarket, and come away the same night, because I despaire of lodging.

---

^{a} Son of Sir Edward Baynton, of Bromham-Baynton, co. Wilts. by Stuart, sister of Thomas Thynne.

I saw yᵉ exccution yesterday of the German capt. &c. The capt. died very boldly and unconcerned,ᵃ neither did he, as I cᵈ heare, before or then own that yᵉ Count was privy to yᵉ murder. The other 2 shewd to be very penitent, and, tis thought, cᵈ discover nothing of yᵉ Count's practisse.

My Lᵈ Hollis's lady is dead.ᵇ

THE SAME.

MY LORD,   London, July 8ᵗʰ, 1682.

The Lord Mayor's party think they had a greate day of it yesterday; for, after a long debate by councell on both sides, the Court of Aldermen judged it to be in yᵉ Mayor to adjourn or call yᵉ court for election; and there was 14 alder: agˢᵗ 7, and so yᵉ court is adjourned for another pole to Fryday next.ᶜ

Yᵉ Kᵍ is gone to-day to Windsor, but will be back, tis sayd, a Thursday. Sʳ John Finch arrived last night from Turkey, and this morning my Lᵈ Chanc: brought him to yᵉ King, and he made yᵉ Kᵍ a mighty rich present of a cimeter and dagger. The dagger was hilt and sheath of entire jaspars, set wᵗʰ rubies of great value. The Duke had presents too of yᵉ same kind, wᶜʰ were very rich.

ᵃ "He went to death like an undaunted hero," and he "told a friend of mine that he did not value dying of a rush, and hop'd and believ'd God would deale with him like a gentleman" are Evelyn's remarks. Reresby tells us that he had led a forlorn hope at Mons.

ᵇ Lucy, daughter of Sir Robert Carr, and wife of Francis, 2nd Lord Holles.

ᶜ The Lord Mayor was Sir John Moore. The dispute was about the election of sheriffs, the Lord Mayor favouring the Court candidates.

The two Bantam embas[sadors][a] desired it, and were knighted to-
day, and had each y[e] sword w[ch] did the deed. They were but
ordinary swords.

THE SAME.

MY LORD,   London, Aug. 14th, 1682.

 *   *   *   *

The privy seales are not yet disposed of,[b] *i.e.*, they were not last
night, but the talk gives um to M[r] Seymore, and an earldom w[th]
them. But there is whispered yet greater changes: That y[e] Duke
of Monmouth will be restored to y[e] K[gs] favor and to y[e] M[r] of y[e]
Hors place too. Y[e] D[sse] is every night at y[e] Duchesses court and
very kindly rec[d], and she and her Lord were, too, never better
together. Nay, I heare that Shaftesbury has offered himself to y[e]
Duke, and not wth out hopes of being rec[d]; for y[e] Duke made him
a wise and no unkind answer, that he had bine an open enemy, and,
when he had reconciled himself to the King, he would be the first
w[d] take him by y[e] hand, as he had done my Lord Sund[erland].
It's thought that my L[d] Shafts: is affraid he shall be left alone, for
that Essex, Montague, and others are making conditions for themselves. I c[d] tell you other stranger matters yet in hand, but 'tis
enough at a time.

[a] Evelyn saw them, 19th June, at Lord Berkeley's, and has handed down a minute
account of their appearance as they sat before him, "cross-legg'd like Turks, and
something in the posture of apes and monkeys."

[b] Arthur Annesley, Earl of Anglesey, had been called upon to surrender the privy
seal on the 8th of the month. His MS. diary, which is preserved in the British
Museum, Additional MS. 18730, contains this entry: "9 Aug. In the evening
delivred the privy seale, upon the King's warrant of y[e] 8th under the signet, to Sir
Leolin Jenkins. . . . The Lord be praised, I am now delivred from Court snares."
He was succeeded by Halifax.

My Lord,

The Duke of M[onmouth], I heare, has entered into a new cove-
nant wth those of his party never to quit them, and is gone into
Cheshire to be treated there by my Ld Matlesfield,^a Whitley,^b
Booth,^c Lewson,^d and all that party who have long expected him,
and where there is not such another gang of phanatiques in y^e
kingdom, and its like is ye reason why the King resolved of putting
a guarrison into Chester Castle.   The King does not come to town
till Munday next, and then he goes the same day to Chatham, down
ye river ; so I goe a Saturday to be at Sheerness as he passes by.

The King is mightly pleased at Winchester, and ye toun has
made him a present of ye Castle for a place to build upon, and y^e
B^p has given him timber and ye gentlemen will bring it ; so he is
resolved to build, there being stone enough on ye place.^e   The
Duke says tis abundantly better place for all sort of pleasure then
Newmarket, and then 'tis neere ye forrest for hunting.   But you
must know there is a faction in this business too, ye Whig party
being lords at Newmarket, as hunting, got houses and possest themselves of ye best conveniences there.   The K^g, however, goes to
Newmarket in October; they say, not till ye sherriffs are decided.

The apprentices have bine mutinous ab^t St Giles's and w^d have
puld down a house, so y^t ye Guards were faine to come, and some
of them are taken and put into prison.   The privy seales are not
like to be disposed of yet.   They were promised 1st to Lord Halli:
and, after, to Seymore, as I am told; so, till something els happen,

---

^a Charles Gerard, 1st Earl of Macclesfield.

^b Colonel Roger Whitley, of Peele, co. Chester.

^c Henry Booth, son of Lord Delamere, who succeeded to the title and was one of
the leaders of the northern rising at the Revolution.

^d William Leveson Gower.

^e The buildings, begun by Charles, are now the barracks.

that both may be sattisfied, it may be they will remaine in ye K^{gs} hand. The Duke appeares for Ld Hamilton's ^a having ye garter, but ye D^{sse} of Osnaburgh has writt to P. Rupert, her brother, to propose a match wth Lady Ann and her son; and some say ye K^g inclines so far to it, heele reserve ye garter for him.

My Ld Monmth goes not to Chester till Thursday. The K^g sayd to my Ld Noel^c at Winchester y^t, if ye D. of Mon: w^d have submitted himself to him, as he ought, he sh^d have willingly received him; but for my Ld Shafts, he w^d not doe him that injury who, while he remaines wth ye other party, is ye noble patriot of his country, ye Prottestant Lord &c, and, when he sh^d come in to him, he w^d be ye fals and popish traiterores Ld Shafts[bury] &c.

I pray God send my Lady a good delivery and a brave boy.

The Com^{rs} of ye revenue of Ireland are now named. My Ld Longford^d is ye 1st. Y^e rest are unknown persons.

THE SAME.

MY LORD, Sep^{br} ye 23, 1682.

*   *   *

The Duke of Monmth was taken into custody by Sarjeant Ramsey, on Wednesday night, at Litchfield, and is coming up wth him, and, 'tis believed, will be sent to ye Tower ; and there is a comⁿ sent doun into Cheshire to enquire into some other proceedings there.

*   *   *   *   *

The D. of M. was brought to night to ye Secretary's office. He

---

^a William Douglas, Earl of Selkirk, who, on his marriage with Anne, Duchess of Hamilton, was made Duke of Hamilton. He received the Garter.

^b The Electress Sophia, whose husband, Ernest Augustus, Elector of Hanover, was also Duke-Bishop of Osnaburg.

^c Wriothesley Baptist Noel, son of Edward, Viscount Campden, afterwards Earl of Gainsborough.

^d Francis Aungier, Viscount Longford.

refused to be examined by him, because he sayd, having his habeas corpus, he was no longer a prisoner by his warrant, and so went out of ye roome into ye court; but, before he went away, he was served by ye same sarjeant wth a new warrant to take him again into custody, till he found good baile to keepe ye peace and to answer Mr Attorney ye 1st of ye term.

The sherriffs were bound to the good behaviour.

THE SAME.

My Lord,   Sep. 26, [1682].

The D. of M. is bailed. The K^g by ye Vi: Chamb.^a letter has forbid him coming into ye park or any part of Whitehall, as well when his Mat^y is out of town as in it. The K^g is very angry wth him and resolved to take every way to undeceive ye world that think he is not; and there is a com^n of oyer and terminer gone down, they say, into ye countreys to make enquiryes w^ht has bine done there. There is one much talked of, and that is, that there were severall baskets of blue ribons given out at my Ld Dela-meere's,^b where he was most highly treated; and ye names of those that had them taken and put into a book.

THE SAME.

My Lord,   No^br 30, [1682.]

                                                  *

Yesterday Prince Rupert died; he was not ill above 4 or 5 days. An old hurt in his leg, wch has bine some time healed up, broke out again and put him into an intermitting feavor, for wch he took

----

^a Henry Savile succeeded Sir George Carteret as Vice-Chamberlain.
^b Sir George Booth, who had been created Lord Delamere. Died in 1684.

ye jesuites powder, but he had a pleurisy wthall upon him wch he concealed, because he w^d not be let blood, till it was too late and when his blood was all corrupted. He died in greate paine. He made a will, and my Ld Craven^a is one of his executors or trustees. The K^g sent to him to secure his jewells, wch he sayd he had done, and, so soone as ye will was opened, his Mat^y sh^d have a further acc^t.

THE SAME.

MY LORD,   Jan. 30th, 168⅘.

*   *   *   *   *

There is another thing wch is now as much talked on: the new orders ab^t ye bedchamber, since the K^g is come into these new lodgings.

No body except ye Duke, Ld Ormond, and I think Hallifax, the 2 Secretarys of England, and ye Secretaries of Scotland are to come into ye bedchamber wthout leave first asked; nor are they to ask leave, if the King be in the closset. None under degree of nobleman or privy councellor may ask leave at all, unless he says he has huisnes wth ye King.

My Ld Chamberlin^b w^d have come in, when ye K^g was in his closset; but ye page told him he c^d not. He, notwthstanding, came in and desired my Ld Bath^c to inform the pages he was not to be kept out. My Lord sayd, he did not know he was, and commanded the page to let him in. Thereupon my Lord Arran^d told Chamb: the page had done his duty, and he ought not to come in wthout leave; upon wch there grew high words between them. The K^g

---

^a William, Earl of Craven.

^b Lord Arlington.

^c John Granville, Earl of Bath, Groom of the Stole ; died in 1701.

^d James Douglas, son of the Duke of Hamilton, and a gentleman of the bedchamber.

has determined ye cause ^ag^st my Ld Cham: so as that he is not to come in w^thout leave, nor ye Lord Steward,^a who does not therefore come in but as he is one of ye Ministers, i. e. I suppose of ye Cabinet.

My Ld Shaftsbury is certainly dead^b in Holland; and his relations, as Ld Hallifax, Coventry,^c Plimouth,^d (who came to town lately) &c., are in mourning for him.^e

---

THE SAME.

My Lord,   Richmond, June 30th [16]83.

I humbly thank y^r L^p for ye warrant you have sent me for ye venison and for ye letter, since, by b^r George, by whom I am very glad to heare my Lady is so well, tho' sorry to heare she has miscarried.

It's probable y^r L^p has ere this heard some thing of the discoverie of a new Presbiterian fanatique plot, no lesse then to murder ye K^g and ye Duke and destroy ye Gov^mt

There is an oylman who lived neere Smithfield (by name Keeling^f), by religion, as he told ye Councell, he has bine of all sects, at last an Anabaptist and a mighty boutefeu in all ye seditions and commotions of ye citty, is ye person at whose suite ye Lord Mayor was arrested. This man came to M^r Se: Jenkins and told

---

^a Duke of Ormond.

^b He died on the 21st January, 1683.

^c John, 4th Lord Coventry.

^d Lord Windsor, lately made Earl of Plymouth.

   Shaftesbury married Margaret, one of the daughters of Lord Keeper Coventry; Halifax was the son of Anne, another daughter; and Lord Plymouth married Halifax's sister.

^f Josiah Keeling.

him ye K^{gs} person was in danger of an assassinate, y^t he was touched in conscience to give him notice to prevent it; wch Mr Secre:, giving no greate credit to, seemed to slight. So he came 2 days after and soe pressed the eminent danger the K^{gs} life was in, y^t M^r Se:, enquiring more strictly into ye matter, had from him a very large discovery of a most dangerous hellishe conspiracy to murder the King and ye Duke, as they were to come last from Newmarket, at a place neere Stansteed; and wch was prevented only from taking effect, wthout God's infinite providence, by ye fire wch happened in Newmarket, and so hindred ye conspirators from being ready to assemble (they being to bee 40 in number) and put theyr damnable mischief into practisse, wch yet he sayd they pursued the same design as he sh^d passe between Windsor and Hampton Court; but he said they waited till ye King and Duke sh^d come together, for they durst not attempt on him alone, because the Duke w^d be left alive to revenge it. He frankly told all the conspirators names, wch you will find, I doubt not, in ye proclamation, and among ye rest Coll: Rumsey,[a] who I beleeve you cannot but know. He has since rendred himself at the King's discretion, and, as he tells Halsey,[b] who was much of his acquaintance (and to whom he writt after he was in the messengers hand, to desire so to speake wth, who had ye K^{gs} leave to doe), that hee had not come in but y^t he found it impossible for him to escape, being so closely pursued. When he was brought to ye King, he fell on his knees, sayd he neither deserved nor expected pardon who had bine such a villain to so good and gracious a prince, and from whom he had rec^d such large benefits; but that he w^d doe w^{ht} he c^d to make amends, while he lived, by a cleare confession of all he knew of ye practisses designed either agst his person or gov^{mt}; and that he w^d conceale no man he knew guilty, nor accuse any falsley to save his life.

---

[a] Colonel John Rumsey, or Romsey, an old parliamentary officer. He turned King's evidence.

[b] Perhaps a slip of the pen for Colonel James Halsal or Halshall, Scout-Master General. There was also Thomas Halsey, M.P. for Hertfordshire.

There is allso one West,[a] a lawyer of the Inner Temple, come in too, or rather indeed forced in (as they say) by his father in law, an honest man had found him out who was of greate trust among all those people. These have discovered abundance of persons and thinges, and there are warrants out to apprehend them, who are many of them fled. Algernon Sidney is taken, and Wildman, and they are in y[e] Tower; and, since them, my L[d] Russell out of his own house, and my Lord Grey, who has since made his escape at y[e] Towre gate from the Serjeant at armes, through treachery or folly, because he w[d] take no guard wth him, and was asleep, if not drunk, or pretended to be so, when he went out of y[e] coach. The sarjeant was Deereham,[b] formerly my L[d] Chamberlan's gentleman of hors, and my quarter[mr]. My Lord tooke boate and got into Southwark, whither he was closly pursued, but not taken. The K[g] is so inraged at it, he has not only turnd y[e] sarjeant out of his places, but sent him to y[e] Tower, and commanded he sh[d] be put into y[e] dungeon, and sayd he sh[d] rot there. Hee was 3 days there. But y[e] L[t] came to y[e] K[g] and sayd he w[d] perish if he were not presently removed, for y[e] water and mud came in so upon him, he stood up to y[e] knees in it; so y[e] K[g] gave leave he sh[d] be removed.

The Lords were confronted by y[e] wittnesses when they were examined, and, as I was told by a greate man (the King sayd it to), my L[d] Russell c[d] not deny his knowledg of y[e] gen[ll] plot of a rebellion and going into armes, wh[ch] was to be y[e] 3[d] of No[br] last. As to y[e] murther of the K[g] and Duke, he was not charged wth. My Lord Russell was sent to the Tower in one of y[e] K[gs] barges with a Capt of the Guards and a guard of soldiers. The Duke of Mon:, L[d] Grey, Armstrong, and Ferguson,[c] L[d] Shaftsburys chaplain, a

---

[a] Robert West, turned King's evidence.

[b] Henry Dereham.

[c] Robert Ferguson, the busiest of "fanatical knaves." "Violent, malignant, regardless of truth, insensible to shame, insatiable of notoriety, delighting in intrigue, in tumult, in mischief for its own sake, he toiled during many years in the darkest mines of faction." Pilloried thus by Macaulay, and branded as Judas in "Absalom and Achitophel," he is in a fair way of being notorious for ever. He escaped to Holland, to be at the bottom of any mischief that was brewing.

Scot, are mightily searcht after. There are a greate many more fled, and warrants out to search for them. There were 3 shutes of the silk armes taken at Umfreville's ª house, wth some new muskets and collars of bandeleeres filled with powder, and a bag of bullets. He was not found, but is since, as I heare, taken. He was a greate man in all juries in ye Popish, or rather Oates's, plot, It was asked Keeling if Oates knew of ye K^{gs} being to be murdered or anything of the plot; but he sayd he thought he did not, for they beleeved him such a rogue they w^d not trust him. There is orders gone into all countreys to disarme all that are looked on as disaffected to ye gov^{mt}.

I am told this morning, ye Duchesse of Mon: was delivered of a dead child, and that 'tis thought she can't live.

There was a com^n sealed yesterday for the tryals of the traytors; and I heare my Lord Russell will be first tried, tho', it may be, more of them together. As I heare more, I shall give y^r L^p an acc^t.

Mr Trencher ^{b} is in ye Tower too, the same who first brought in ye Bill of Exclusion of a popish successor. My Ld Russell was ye next that brought it in and carried it up to ye Lords, as you may better know then I. Sr Robt Clayton brought it in againe to ye H. of C. at Oxford.

The Bishop of Oxford.

My honord L^d,   [5th July, 1683.]

I have now by me your lordships fifth letter, and now, tho I answer the number, want a hundred more to make a just return for the kindness. The frequent hearing from your Lordship and my

---

ª Charles Umfreville, arrested and examined before the Council for unlawful possession of arms.

^{b} John Trenchard of Taunton, made Secretary of State in 1693.

good Lady is an unspeakable refreshment to me, which in this age
that understands no reason of commerce but the prosecution of the
ends of gain or pleasure will be lookt upon as extravagance, but
will be absolvd by your better judgement of things, who know how
solicitous the resentments of friendship are and whose charity as
well as interest in.them makes you concerned for their relief. We
have had no notice of the fire wch your Lordship mentions to have
bin at Roan, no more than I perceive your Lordship has of the
diabolical design lately discoverd against the King's life and the
government, the prevention of wch we owe, next to God's mercy,
to the fire which was lately at Newmarket.ᵃ The villany is so
direfull that one would think it could not enter into the hearts of
any who had the shape of men, and it passes belief that such men
as the Lord Russell, the Lord Grey, the Duke of Monmouth &c.
should be privy to it. Very few daies will bring those that have
not secured themselves by flight to their trial. God grant that others
may be deterrd from the like villanies, and that they, if it be
possible, may repent of them, and, however it fares with them at an
earthly tribunal, escape at the greater wch awaits them. I add my
praiers for all blessing to your Lordship and family, and remain,

    My honord Lord,

        Your most humble and affectionat ser^{vt},

                Jo. Oxon.

SIR CHARLES LYTTELTON.

My L^{d},   [10 July, 1683.]

    I have only time to tell you I rec^{d} y^{rs} ye last night. Besides
w^{ht} I have told you of ye plot, my Ld Brandonᵇ and young

---

ᵃ Which occasioned Charles's unexpected return from Newmarket, and was said to
have disconcerted the plans of the conspirators.

ᵇ Charles Gerard, Lord Gerard of Brandon, eldest son of Lord Macclesfield. He
was put on his trial, in 1685, and was found guilty, but was allowed to redeem
himself.

Mr Hambden^a were both sent yesterday to ye Tower, and my Ld Howard of Escrick taken out of his house. He had concealed himself in his chimney. So soone as he came to ye King, he fell a crying bitterly, and desired pen and paper that he might recollect and discover w^{ht} he knew; so has bine writing his narrative ever since. Last night my Ld Essex was sent for by a sarjeant at armes, Coll: Oglethorp and 30 hors. They met him coming to town. He lay all night in my Lord Fevershams lodging, and this morning, after being examined, was sent by water to ye Tower. The K^g is very displeased wth him. He is charged, as I heare, to have signed an association.

Mr Forbus was taken last night   I desire, my L^d, you will thank y^r keeper (for I thanked you in my last) for ye bravest buck y^t ever I saw, tho' I have had many good ones from you.

My most humble services to my Lady and Mrs Hattons.

THE BISHOP OF OXFORD.

MY HONORD LORD,   [12th July, 1683.]

The conveiance of letters from you has of late bin very propitious, every week having brought me those assurances which I with all imaginable concern desire to receive. Tis to be doubted, when the autumn gusts and winter long nights come on, there will be a more interrupted correspondence; but, if the execrable design against the King and government be fully discoverd and broken, there will

---

^a John Hampden, grandson of the patriot. He pleaded guilty, when brought to trial in 1685, and made abject submission ; and escaped with his life on paying a heavy bribe to Jeffreys. He committed suicide in 1695.

probably be such a turn of mens minds as may persuade the calling
of parliament before the third year is expired, which will have one
desirable effect: the bringing back your Lordship to your friends.
The discoveries come on so fast that there will want prisons to
secure malefactors, and innocent men begin to fear least the really
guilty should attone for treason by perjury and revive the old trade
of evidence, laying their plot at their neighbours dorcs.   The King
does very advisedly hasten the trials that the jealousy of the people
may be removed, who think every thing, however real, to be a
trick, and that his person may be in some safety by the terror of
severity.   We wonderd at the Lord Russell's being engaged in so
black a design, a man neither needy in his fortune nor extravagant
in his manner; but that wonder is encreast since the Earl of Essex
is in the Tower.   One would have thought it impossible that the
son of the Lord Capel, after wealth and honor heaped upon him,
should design the subversion of the government.   Tis less strange
that Lord Howard of Estrick, Lord Brandon, Lord Herbert of
Cherbury, Mr Wharton,[a] Mr Hambden, and others of the like forme
should engage in such an affair.   The best ont is, a few daies will
give us light.   May they also give security to the King and
government.

When your brother Grey is come to you, your Lordship will soon
observe what we may expect from him.   Mr Pullen's [b] characters
are, I doubt, not much to be depended on.   There must be a fault
somewhere besides in my Lord, if, after so many months stay in
France, no progress has bin made in the language.   My young
Lord of Manchester [c] was expected at London on Wednesday last.
For ought I know, it might have been well if my Lord Grey had
accompanied my Lord Preston [d]; any thing had bin preferable to

---

[a] Thomas Wharton, afterwards Marquess of Wharton.
[b] Octavian Pulleyn, Lord Grey's tutor.
[c] Charles Montagu, 4th Earl, afterwards Duke, of Manchester.
[d] To Spain.

loitering in English company at Paris. With my wishes of all health and blessing to your Lordship,

I remain, my honord Lord, your

Most humble and affectionat ser^{vt},

Jo. Oxon.

I send by this conveiance to Southampton five dozen of bottles of our ale. I wish this hot weather permit it to come in good order to you.

SIR CHARLES LYTTELTON.

My L^d,   July ye 14th, 1683.

Yesterday morn: my Ld Essex cut his own throate in ye Tower wth a razor wch he asked of his man that waited on him, having never a penknife to give him. He had asked for a penknife every day since he came thither. He did it in ye close stoole roome, while his man was gone down; but his page was in ye roome. He eate his breakfast well and was not perceivd to be in any disturbance of mind; but, ye day before, he had sent to desire my Ld Clarendon might speake wth him, wch he did, and he made prottestations that he knew nothing of any design to murder the King, but he sayd nothing to vindicate himself from being in other designes upon the governm^t. The K^g happened to be in ye Tower at ye same time this happened, to view ye new fortifications. The news was presently carried to the Old Baily, where was upon theyre trialls my Ld Russell, Hone, Rowse, and Capt. Blagge,^{a} a seaman, who were all found guilty, and who none of them made but very weake defences. My Lord had nothing but to call some persons to give an account of what they knew of his life, to make him unlikely to bee in such wicked designes he stood charged wth. The wittnesses ^{agst} him were my Lord Howard, Rumsey, and Shepp-

^{a} William Hone, John Rouse, and William Blague. The last was acquitted.

heard,[a] a merchant, at whose house there was some of theyr con-
sults, and who was to be the treasurer to receive and pay all mony.

M[r] Booth,[b] my L[ds] son, was brought to town last night and sent
to y[e] Tower. There has bine a good ·quantity of armes taken at
Chester, in Hodg Whitleys son's house, and this inscription on
them: Sultan Bantam; all new armes in chests.

My L[d] Salisbury[c] was married yesterday to y[e] younger daughter
of rich Bennet [and his] sister to S[r] George Downings sonne.[d]
S[r] John Babor's son has run away wth S[r] Thomas Draper's[e]
daughter. There are a hundred gentlemen of quality, of w[ch] my
L[d] Salisbury is one, who have offered themselves to be put into a
troope, under y[e] command of my Lord Ossory[f] or who his Ma[ty]
pleases, to attend his Ma[tyes] person at theyr own charge.

- - -

WILLIAM LONGUEVILLE.

MY LORD,   Thursday, 19th of July, 1683.

*   *   *   *   *

As to the plott, y[e] prints tell your Lop. as much as I know
allmost. Poore Earl of Essex hath done what one would have
thought his great vertues, his reading, and above all his religion
should never have sett in. And his poore lady hath added to that
huge affliction that his personall estate in London is y[e] bailiffe of

[a] Thomas Shepard.
[b] Henry Booth, son of Lord Delamere.
[c] James Cecil, 4th Earl of Salisbury, married Frances, daughter of Simon Bennet, of Beechampton, co. Bucks.
[d] Catherine, daughter of James, 3rd Earl of Salisbury, married George, son of Sir George Downing, who succeeded to the baronetcy.
[e] Baronet, of Sunninghill, co. Berks.
[f] James, son of Thomas Earl of Ossory ; afterwards Duke of Ormond.

Westminster's, and his fine library and all his goods (of great value) at Cassiobury are claimed by the new Earl of Salsbury, as Abbot of St Albans, wthin which liberty Cassiobury is a little mannour. Ld Russell is sayd (how truly I know not) to expresse himselfe that two ladyes are more in misery then his: the Lady Essex,^a and ye Lady Howard of Escrick^b as being such an one's wife. On Friday (i. e. too morrow), at Tiburne, dye ye 3, Walcott,^c Hone, and Rous; and on Satterday, ye Ld Russell on a scaffold in Lincolns-Inne fields. This Ld Russell eates little, drinks tea much, is very composed and resolute, as I am told. But Walcott sayes hee is meane, in that hee denyes his share in the plott, for that he had his full share therein. This Walcott never denyed it but in a course of law, to see if legally there was proofe ag^t him. His teachers, hee sayes, misguided him. I shall bee here yett about 10 dayes. Wheresoever I shall be you have mee,

My Lord,

Your Lops. most obedient servant,

W. L.

GEORGE LYTTELTON.^d

My Lord,   London, July ye 21, [16]83.

My duty tyes mee to give you what I know, though you have all by better hands; but the present is that on Thursday the Prince of Denmark made his entry att Whitt Halle, and next week for Windsor wheire the maridge is consumated. Yesterday 3 of the plotters were exequted att Tiburne, videlisett Walcott, Hone, and

---

^a Elizabeth, daughter of Algernon Percy, 10th Earl of Northumberland.

^b Frances, daughter of Sir James Bridgman, of Castle-Bromwich, co. Warwick.

^c Colonel Thomas Walcott.

^d Brother of Sir Charles Lyttelton and a captain in his regiment.

Rowse, and this morning Ld Russell was beheaded in Lincolls Inn Fields. Theire was ten companyes of ye Guards draune round the scaffold, with ye Kinges troope devided into 4 squadrons, a squadron in each angell. Theire will be noe further trialls till ye judges returne from theire serquts. I now begg your Lordships favor of my humble duty to.my Ladey and the rest of the good fameley.

Your Lordships most
obedient humble servant,
G. LYTTELTON.

SIR CHARLES LYTTELTON.

MY LORD,   London, July 21, [16]83.

I have just now rec^d y^{rs} of ye 16 wth ye inclosed to my brother, and have only since to tell you that my Ld Russell was beheaded this morning. He sayd not much, but that he did not design to murder ye K^g nor' ye gov^{mt}, but to keepe out poperie. He sayd the evidence ^{agst} him was true, as to ye place and company he was in, but he tooke that to be but misprision, for wch he did not ask God or ye K^g pardon, for that I can heare. I saw him die at a distance and he seemed very stout. The hangman gave him 3 blows, besides sawing wth ye ax, before he cut his head of. He came to ye scaffold in his own coach, wch was not in mourning nor his livery; himself was in black.

Doctor Tillotson,[a] Dr. Burnet, and ye sherriffe was wth him.

The P. of Denmark is a handsom fine gentleman. They say

---

[a] John Tillotson, at this time Dean, afterwards Archbishop, of Canterbury.

heele be married a Tuesday at Windsor. The Duke gives him place heere yet.

My brother[a] Ruthen died yesterday and I am going to his funerall. He died of a feavor and wanted 5 or 6 months to be at age. Yet I hope his signature will be good.

WILLIAM LONGUEVILLE.

MY LORD,   7th of Aug[t], 1683.

 *   *   *   *

Wee have had a deplorable fire, whereby 2 staire cases were most suddainly burnt in y[e] Temple, and no deeds, monyes, clothes, or anything but y[e] lives of a few, could bee saved. S[r] Thomas Robin son, our treasurer, leaping out of his window one paire of stayers, was bruised, being grosse ; so y[t] w[th]in an houre hee dyed, and was just now buryed. Hee had an iron chest now found, and y[e] gold and silver in it melted thought neere 10000[l], and his office L[d] Pemberton hath 6000[l] to take for it. One Glyde, at whose chamber, a ground roome, it is thought to have begun, was burned. M[r] Lloyd, y[e] B[p] of Peterborough's brother, in y[e] next chamber, escaped in his shirt. M[r] Williams and one lodging wth him for a night are both burnt. This was below y[e] Kings Bench buildings.

L[d] Dartmouth is reported gone to visit your island, as also Jersey, &c.; and on his return it's sayd hee will goe out wth 13 sayle, and towards Tangier most believe. Our plott is nothing more known then it was, unlesse M[r] Charlton[b] have added to it by any discovery, hee being newly taken. The tryalls are abroad 1st too day, but I have not yett had time to read them. L[d] Delamere hath made y[e] application to y[e] King most winning on his Mat[y] of any of our great men that I heare of. L[d] Suffolk,[c] you heare, hath been humbling

[a] Brother-in-law.
[b] Francis Charlton.
[c] Charles Howard, 3rd Earl of Suffolk.

himselfe too, as Earl of Kent,[a] Macclesfield, &c. I hope with your Lop., this mistery of iniquity being well and providentially discovered, wee may have a good government y[e] better hinged and established.

My Lord, I present my humblest duty to my Lady, and wish your Lop. and all your family all happinesse, being ever,

My Lord,

Your Lops. obedient servant,

W L.

SIR CHARLES LYTTELTON.

MY LORD,   London, Aug. 14, [16]83.

Since my last, my L[d] Conway is dead, and has left his dowager[b] vastly rich, they say his whole estate for life and 1000[li] a yeare for ever and all his personall estate. I am told, since I came hither that wee shall have a parlim[t] call'd suddenly. My Lord Grafton is the most mortified creature in the world, because y[e] command of y[e] fleete was taken out of his hand and given to my L[d] Dartmouth who is undoubtedly gone to bring away y[e] forces from Tangier; but I cannot be well assured if his orders be to ruine the place or put it into another hand. His taking Dr. Trumball,[c] a civillian, wth him lookes as if he had some publike treaty to make.

M[r] Castyres[d], a Scotch preacher, was brought up to day. He was taken in y[e] north, neere my Lord Thannets interest, as his b[r] Sackville told mee to day. The Councill met this afternoone to examine him. You will find this Castyres name in y[e] declaration, among those that are fled.

---

[a] Anthony Grey, 11th Earl of Kent.
[b] See above, p. 7, note [a].
[c] Afterwards Sir William Trumball, Secretary of State.
[d] William Carstairs.

I think I told y^r L^p that ye Prince was not installd, because he had not ye K^g of Denmarkes leave to leave of the Elephant; wch it seemes was not thought of, but must be had before he can weare ye garter.

The news from France is that ye Turkes made an assault in six places upon Viena at a time, and were beaten of wth greate losse; and they have since removed theyr camp a league of ye town.

WILLIAM LONGUEVILLE.

My L^d,   18th of August, 1683.

＊   ＊   ＊   ＊

Y^e French are now feared in Flanders. Y^e Ld Dartmouth and ye fleete are going, few know on what designe; I don't. No trialls are yet coming on that I heare of. One Casteers, a Scotch non-conformist parson, was taken in Kent, and one Westlake,[a] a lawyer, at Exeter, and are come up in custody. I was at ye Tower yesterday wth my L^d of Danby, having not been there since your Lop. remembers ye time; and hee was pretty well and ye same good company, and temperate in what hee sayd of those gone thence afore him, i.e., ye dead. I saw yong Brandon &c at their windows, their lodgings being very close, as I understand. Major Bremen is layd where E. of Essex did his worst, so I could [not] see ye roome, ye which I would have seen, because heere is a divided world whither ye Earle killed himselfe or was killed. Hence judge of ye party.

＊   ＊   ＊   ＊

Your Lops. most faithfull, humble servant,

WM. LONGUEVILLE.

[a] Hugh Westlake.

SIR CHARLES LYTTELTON.

MY LORD,   Richm^d, Octo. 2^d, 1683.

*   *   *   ~   *

Since the Court returned to London, wee have severall new Judges, 2 C[hief] Jus[tices], Sr G. Jeoffryes of ye Kings Court, and Sr Will: Jones^a of ye Com: Pleas, Mr North^b of Chester, and Ned Herbert^c, my Lady Mordaunt's brother, of North Wales.

The cittyes complyance ab^t ye charter has not gone down wth them so glib as was expected, wch has kept ye K^g, I think, a little longer from Newmarket; but, I heare, they will come to at last, and ye K^g will goe for a few days, tho' w^thout the ladyes, to theyr greate dissappointm^t. But there is so little lodging, the town being not yet rebuilt.

*   *   *   *   *

There is news come of a 2^d victory the imperiall forces have obtained over ye Turkes, wth the totall overthrow of all theyr forces and a mighty slaughter, and treasure taken; and that, since, the Xtians have beseeged Newhawsell^d and another towne, I think tis Buda.

I have had a very sore losse at Jamaica, my good friend Mr Long being dead, it having broke all my designes of settling a plantation there; for Sr T. Lynch advises mee to w^thdraw ye little stock I had sent thither in order to it, and I have accordingly desired him to make returnes of it as he can. I had a faire prospect, as I thought, of making a provision for my younger children from thence; but now they must depend upon Providence, wch will be more sure.

---

  ^a Sir Thomas Jones.
  ^b Roger North ?
  ^c Sir Edward Herbert, son of the Lord Keeper, was made Chief Justice of Chester.
  ^d Neuhäusel, in Hungary.

I heard by somebody ye other day, it was my Ld Cardigan^a who lives heere, that you are coming back. I have it often in my thoughts a fit husband for y^r daughter, and methinkes you cannot choose a better party for both sides then my Ld Grey;^{b} or why not my Ld Manchester ? But these you cannot escape the consideration of, and therefore I had as good have sayd nothing. Y^r daughters fortune is much more considerable by ye no remote possibillities she has of an encrease of it, not only from y^r L^p but her uncles, who are none of them married.

Pray, my L^d, present my wifes and my humblest services to my Lady, &c.

THE BISHOP OF OXFORD TO LADY HATTON.

MOST HONORD MADAM, [2 Nov. 1683.]

Your good Ladyship was so obliging to write two daies together, and I am desirous to transcribe that pattern; for, tho I would mortify all other ambitions, I can not quietly permit myself to be outdon in kindness. It is a bold attemt to think to equal my Lady Hatton in the expressions of friendship, but I should deserve to forfeit that relation, did I not endeavor to answer the obligations of it in punctual, tho imperfect, returns. I should be glad to hear that my Lord your brother had left Paris and begun his journey for Italy, while the weather favours travail and the Alps have not the cold of winter added to their snow.

Your honor was pleasd to enquir of a book calld the Beauty of Holiness,^{c} pretended to be writen by the author of the Whole Duty of Man, whither it were really wrote by him. To satisfy your Ladiship herein, I am to let you know that some artifice has bin

---

^{a} Robert Brudenell, 2nd Earl of Cardigan.

^{b} $i.e.$, Lord Grey of Ruthyn.

^{c} " A Discourse concerning the Beauty of Holiness." London, 1679. 8vo.

usd by several writers to make their labours more passable by a
pretence to this title; and yet, to justify themselves, if a more strict
enquiry be made into it, one of them cald his book, The Duty of
Man; another, The Whole Duty of Man, Gatherd out of the
Scriptures; another, A Supplement to the Whole Duty of Man; so
that, when the future writings of the first author which refer to his
precedent book are questioned, tis answered that they refer to the
book cald The Duty of Man, and not The Whole Duty. The
second saies that he refers to that book of his that gatherd the whole
duty of man out of Scripture, and not the other; and the third, if
he chance to write a farther supplement, will have to say for himself
that he only referd to the former supplement, which he plainly
owns not to have bin writen by the same hand which wrote the
original book. Thus, Madam, you see what little arts there are in
the world to deceive without saying downright untruths, to the
second of which I think your enquiry refers. Within few weeks all
the genuine writings will, I hope, be finisht in one volume, that will
in some measure for the future supersede the like frauds[a] I must
not end till I have wisht your dear honor all comfort, health, and
blessing, and desird you to present my respects to your good sister
and daughter, assuring you that I am and ever shall be, honord
Madam,

Your most faithfull serv[t] in our Lord

Jo. Oxon.

---

[a] " The Ladies Calling" and other works by the author of " The Whole Duty of
Man" were published in 1684, with an introduction by Fell, in which he mentions
the imitations referred to above.

ELIZABETH MONTAGU [a] TO THE SAME.

Nov. 27, [1683].

Did I not beleive, dear Madam, that you have better intelligence of all the news then I can give you, I should oftener venter to trouble your Ladyship with my letters; so that, that being the reason of my silence, I hope your Ladyship will forgive the not writing, since I designe it as a greater kindnes to you, dear Madam, then the contrary. My Lady and all hear was mighty glad to hear that you was breeding, and shall be very much pleased to have that good news confirmed from your Ladyship, and when we shall have the satisfaction of seeing you all in London again. I see my cousin, Jane Hatton,[b] often, so I know by her how all our frinds doe at Guersney.

Now as to news: M[r] Sydney has been tryed and found guilty and condemed, but when he is to be execuetted I know not. The Duke of Monmouth surrenderd himself to the King, and was receivd by him and Duke as well as he ever was. What he has discovered is not known. The Attourney was ordered to putt a stop to all proceedings against him. He goes to court just as he usd to doe. I beleive your Ladyship knew my Lady Killdaire,[c] who, pore woman, is dead of the small pox, which she got with being with her Lord who has had it. She is a great lose to her son. The other night Lady Mary Garett [d] and her women and some other of her compainions was at a tavern, whear they had musick; and after some time they went away and would not pay the musick; and so thare was a quarrell amoungest them, and some of the fiddlers was killed,

[a] Daughter of Robert, third Earl of Manchester. She married Sir James Montagu, Lord Chief Baron.
[b] A sister of Lord Hatton.
[c] Elizabeth Holles, daughter of John, 2nd Earl of Clare, and wife of Wentworth Fitz-Gerald, 17th Earl of Kildare.
[d] Mary, daughter of Charles Berkeley, Earl of Falmouth, and wife of Sir Gilbert Cosins Gerard, of Fiskerton, co. Linc., Bart. She was divorced in 1684.

and thoes that did it was taken, and one of them was the Ladys
women in mans cloaths, who was a Friench women; and she is
much concerned and tells many storys of her lady, who thare is a
warant from my Lord Chief Justice to take; but I fancy she will
not be easly found, for, if she should, it is beleived she will be
punished. They say the women will be hanged. My Lady and my
brother and all heare gives thare humble servies to my Lord and
your Ladyship and cousen Hattons. I will now releas you, dear
Madam, with the assurance of my being

Your Ladyships most humble sarvant,

ELIZABETH MOUNTAGUE.

WILLIAM LONGUEVILLE.

My L^d,   Thursday, ye 6th of Dec^r, 1683.
          *   *   *

Our publick goes untowardly wth ye mobile, who doe so raise up
spiritt by reason of ye Duke of Monmouth as is not fit for mee to
expresse. 2 councells were held yesterday; and now his Grace is
fully pardoned, hee is resty, and ye last plott is gone and never was,
as say some. Mr. Sidny doth dye too morrow, as most doe say.
       *   *   *   *   *

Your Lops. most faithfull and humble servant,

W. L.

THE BISHOP OF OXFORD.

MY HONORD LORD,   [14 Dec., 1683.]

In my last I gave your Lordship notice of the calamity which
had befalln me in the loss of my sister, which every day I have new

occasions to be sensible of. It will be a relief to me to hear that all is safe with your Lordship and my good Lady and the blessing which she gives you expectation of.

The late changes at Court have put all men at gaze. The Duke of Monmouths return and pardon and favor with the King and great applications made to him were the wonder of a week; and, after that, his being forbid the Court and discharged from his lodgings at the Cockpit are as unexpected a turn upon the other side. There are not such tides in the sea wherewith you are encompassed as there is in Court interest and favor. Your Lordship hears that Mr. Sidney died with the same surliness wherewith he liv'd; and indeed mens deaths are seldom better then their lives. I beseech Almighty God to carry your Lordship with an entire vertue and honor thro this naughty world; and, after all your afflictions, to return to you in mercy and comfort.

I remain, my honord Lord, your

Most humble and affectionat ser^{vt},

JO. OXON.

SIR CHARLES LYTTELTON.

MY Dr LORD,   Whitehall Dec^{br} 17th, 1683.

I have bine so much at Richm^d of late that truly I have had little opportunity to write you any thing of that has passd heere, till I knew you had it from other hands, tho' the various metamorphoses of the D. of M[onmouth] (and in that of the Court too) might have employed severall hands to describe it. His coming in was a huge surprize to ye standers by, and his reception wth the usual goodnes and indulgence of the King But all this wth himself sudenly disappeared, for, upon his refusing to sign an acknowledgm^t

of his having had a share in ye late conspiracy, he was commanded from Court (his pardon being sealed), and accordingly he retired and is, I think, at present at Moore Park. The K^g has since made a narrative in Councill of his confessions before he recd him to grace, and of w^ht passd since, and commanded it to be all entered into ye Councill book.

THE BISHOP OF OXFORD.

MY HONORD LORD,   8 Jan., [1684].

The northern parts of England are by God and nature liberally stor'd with fuel; else, your daughter would have an ill time of it this very cold season in hir wintering in the north. Notwithstanding the severity of the last year, it was in no degree so fatal as this has prov'd already, every day bringing news of persons who in several places have bin overwhelmed in snow or otherwise perisht with cold; but tis to be hoped that what is violent will not be of long continuance, and the return of the sun will restore us to more treatable weather.

This Christmas has produced an alteration in my family. A little before the holidaies, Colonel Macartie, uncle to the Earl of Clancartie, brought a letter from my Lord Sunderland, signifying his M^aties pleasure that the young Earl should keep his Christmas at London with his uncle. No sooner the poor creature came up but he was married to my Lord Sunderland's daughter, and is finally remov'd from hence.^a   Such extraordinary proceedings are not

----

a Donough Macarthy, Earl of Clancarty, was at this time only fifteen ; the bride, Elizabeth Spencer, only eleven. They were separated after the ceremony, and did not meet again till 1698. Their romantic story is well known through Macaulay's *History*. See also Burnet's *History of his own Time*, i. 601.

usd to be very fortunate. If heirs of families can be thus disposd of, parents have little security either of their children or estates.

It seems Sr John Churchill has put an end to the contest about the Mastership of the Rolls. If he can hold it for the same terme his predecessor did, twill be a very gainfull emploiment to him.[a] But your Lordship sits by unconcerned and pities those that toil to be miserable and envied. That you may have the blessing of content and self-denial is praied for in your behalf by, my honord Lord, your

Most humble and affectionat ser^{rt},

JO. OXON.

I am apt to think that my Lord Prestons journy is only to agitate for supplies of mony, which letters are not prevalent enough to procure. Since Sr George Wakeman was my Lord Grey's doctor, tis well his ailing was only the jaundice, wch every nurse can prescribe to. The exercise of a journey is the surest remedy for that distemper; and Bruxels will make a more thorow cure then the knight.

THE SAME.

MY HONORD LORD, 25 Jan. [1684].

The weather is such that there is little likelihood my letters should come to your hands. However, I cannot forbear to write and repete my wishes of health and comfort to your good Lordship and lady. I do not hear of any likelihood of a parliament to call you

---

[a] He died in 1685. He was a cousin of his namesake the Duke of Marlborough.

over this spring, but you have another occasion wch I hope will be successfull.

Tis said that the misunderstandings of the two great men at Court grow every day higher, and that the Earl of Anglesey has lately bin called before the King and Counsel for charging the Lord Howard for accusing the Duke of Monmouth falsely, the Earle saying that the Lord Russel was murtherd. My Lord Anglesey, being requird by the King to answer whither he had said such things, desired to be excusd, saying that what was suggested was only private discourse in his own house. There is a subpena issued out against the Duke to summon his appearance, but tis not likely to be servd, it being not known where he is. Tis thought that the Lords in the Tower may speedily have their liberty. There is no news yet of the fleet at Tanger. The charge of their work, its thought, will be double to what it was estimated. Captain Herbert,[a] who was lately admiral against Algiers, is made Rear Admiral of England for his life. Your Lordship hears I presume what executions the French make in the Spanish Netherlands, and how Amsterdam and some other towns belonging to the state oppose the levies for their assistance. Also, how the Electoral College advise the Emperor to a peace with France, and how the King of Poland has bin disobligd by the Emperor designing to make a separate peace with the Turks. The league between the Dane and French is said to be renewed, and how far that may extend is not well known. I pray God bring peace out of this discord and confusion, and give comfort and blessing to your Lordship and family.

I remain, my honord Lord, your

Most humble and affectionat serv^t,

Jo. Oxon.

---

[a] Arthur Herbert, who took such a distinguished part in the Revolution ; afterwards Earl of Torrington.

The same to Lady Hatton.

Most honord Madam,   25 Jan. [1684].

You will allow me to give myself the satisfaction of constant writing, tho I am deprivd of that of hearing. The severity of cold continues still upon us; but I look down upon it as one of the worst effects of the rigor of the season that all commerce and intercourse are frozen up. We are told strange stories of several streets built upon the river of Thames that have joined Southwark to London. I should be glad if the practice could be emproved to make a road to Guernsay and join it unto our continent, that there might be an easier passage for letters to you and for your honors return to us. In the meantime this new city upon the river is a lively embleme of the designes and business of this world, where the foundation is water and the first thaw drowns the whole fabric. That your honor may build upon the unmoveable foundations of piety and vertue, wch no change of weather or affairs can undermine, is the praier of,

> honord Madam,
> Your
> Most faithfull ser^vt in our Lord,
> Jo. Oxon.

Sir Charles Lyttelton.

My Lord,   Richm^d, June 14, [1684].

I was yesterday at Hampton Court, where there was a Councill. There was Mr Constable, Mr Chidleys^a Secretary, who took Arm-

---

a Thomas Chudleigh, English minister at the Hague.

strong.   He gave this acct. of it: that he had bine wth him, my
Ld Grey, and others, at Cleve; so has ever since had some notice
w^{ht} became of them.   And, so soone as Mr Chidley knew y^t
Armstrong was come into Holland, he got an order from ye States
to apprehend him where he then was, and demanded of him to
assist him in the executing it.   He made some scruple; but he
telling him he w^d get 500^{li} by it the K^g had promised, wch he was
ready to pay him, the rhetorick prevailed; and he, wth 3 more,
went immediately to his lodging into the roome he was in, and
Constable layd hold on him and s^d: " This is the man."   Another
in ye roome wth him drew his sword, and Armstrong put his hand
towards his; but they presently tooke away his sword and the
others that were wth them shuffled away and were some of his gang,
but there was no order to seize them.   Armstrong presently
pretended a great neede to goe-to ye privy, and it happened there
was one w^{th}in ye roome.   Being permitted to doe so, he threw
2 papers into it; wch being perceived, they seized w^{ht} els he had
about him, and, after, recovered these 2 papers, wch were found to
be one a letter to y^c Duke of Brandenbourgs secretary and another
to a Frenchman who was secretary to my Ld Montague when he
was Embassador.   I think his name is Fallazy or some thing like
it, and where he is I know not; but they were both from ye D. of
Monmouth to recommend Armstrong's worthines to theyr care and
protection; which I heare the King has so much the more reason
to take offence at, that the D. of Monmouth gave Armstrong the
worst charrecter to ye King in ye world, when he was last wth y^e
King
    Armstrong, when he was taken, pleaded it was contrary to ye laws
of nations for to seize him under another dominion, for w^{ht} he had
done heere; and the rather, being a naturall subject to the States,
as being born at Nimeguen, and his mother a Duch woman (and so
it was).   However, they put irons on him and brought him to y^e
Hague; and there had 12 of an English yachs crew came well
armed, and carried him away to Scedam, and so abord ye yach.

His wife and daughters presented a petition at Windsor. The K^g said he had pardoned him twice and kept his councill into ye bargayn, that was, he had taken no notice of w^{ht} he knew of his being pensioner and spy to Cromwell.[a] They petitioned, as I heare, the K^{gs} Bench yesterday, to take of ye outlawrie; but it was thrown by, and 'twas said there yesterday he w^d receive his sentence to-day.

It's true the Pope took M^r D'Estree,[b] the French Am: at Rome, by the hand and lead him to an altar, where he kneeled down and prayd God would make his M^r sensible of the innocent blood and all the miseries he had brought upon the Xtian world, or, in his due time, revenge it on him; and in ye consistory they had a consult if he sh^d not be excommunicated, there being 14 cardinalls for it; but the Pope s^d he w^d yet wayte Gods leizure to give him further time to repent before he w^d proceed to so severe a sentence. The French fleete is gone out againe, and tis beleeved to bombard Barcelona.

I heard yesterday my Ld Brudenel[c] w^d buy the M^r of ye Hors[d] place of Ld Dartmouth.

---

[a] Burnet also mentions this, that Charles alleged that he refused mercy to Armstrong for this reason. The story was, that he had been sent by Cromwell to assassinate Charles. He left papers with the sheriffs to refute the charge.

[b] Cardinal César d'Estrées.

[c] Francis Brudenell, son of the Earl of Cardigan.

[d] He means Master of the Ordnance.

DR. EDMUND KING.[a]

MY LORD,   Hatton Garden, June 21, [16]84.

The consideration I have had of your Lord^ps melancholia,[b] together wth my owne and illnesses y^t had attended me, has often prevented my writing to y^r Lord^p to aske how you doe, tho' God knows you have been often in my thoughts on many acc^ts, and perhaps as kind wones too as can be conceivd in the breast of one in my sphear. My Lord, there is noe body shall be glador then my selfe to hear of your Lord^ps health; and, if I durst, I would advice you to all things lawfull for your health and comfort in this world, wch may be soe manag'd as not to hinder those of the next. Your Lord^p is certainly to consider some things a little sooner under your circumstances then others of yor quallities. Will yor Lord^p pardon me if my affection outruns my judgment (in your Lord^ps thoughts), if I deserve y^t censure when I shall tell you your Lord^p I beleive will doe well to have an eye to the support of yor familie, and look upon y^r glass how the sand runs, and give me leave to say I know a Lords granddaughter who is about 19, finely aecom-plisht, bredd by the Countess of K——, her grandmother, 5 or 6000^li certaine, or therabouts. Beautie inough, nay, a large share, vertue, and hono^r unspotted. Those y^t have her in care, I am sure, will be glad a time might be thought fitt to be admitted into y^r Lord^ps thoughts. Ill say no more nowe, till I hear whether yor Lord^p will bear this hint from him y^t has noe end but true love for yor Lord^sp and am certainly yor Lord^ps faithfull sarvent.

---

[a] The physician who was present when Charles the Second was seized with the fit which preceded his death. King bled him and restored him to consciousness, a service for which a thousand pounds was awarded to him. It appears, however, from the Bishop of Oxford's letter of the 7th February, 1686, that the reward was never paid, but that King received knighthood instead, which, as the Bishop observes, was equivalent to fining him a hundred pounds. He was a Fellow of the Royal Society.

[b] Lady Hatton had died in May.

I am not asham'd of my name, but will not now write it; yet I hope y[r] Lord[p] knowes my hand, tho' in this place smaller than usual.

My Lord, if I have adventur'd to be reprov'd, pray doe it tenderly, or I shall be extreamly troubl'd.

WILLIAM LONGUEVILLE.

Tunbridge, Aug[st] the last, [1684].

* *

Yesterday my L[d] Rochester (now L[d] Presid[t]), having been here 3 or 4 dayes, tooke his lady hence. Hee was to my thinking in a good humour, played at nine pins and took y[e] other usuall courses whereby this place is entertaining. Hee has 16000[l] given out of y[e] L[d] Grey's estate.[a]

* * ☀

My L[d],
Your Lops most faithfull and
obedient servant,
W[m] LONGUEVILLE.

[a] Ford, Lord Grey of Werke.

THE SAME.

MY L^d,   27th of Sept^r, 1684.

The King last night gave an end to ye commission for ecclesiasticall matters.   Chiefe Justice Jefferyes was then also admitted of
ye caball.   Sr Robert Wright^a hath ye fame of succeeding Judge
Wyndham,^b but I know not of a certainty that it is fixed on him.
One justice Baily, of Wapping, was committed by ye Chief Justice
for kidnapping.   Y^e Scotch discovery^c and some confessions doe
reach great men there, and more I can't say.   Y^e Countesse of Pem-
broke^d last night first presented herselfe to ye Queen, and wth competent assurance.   Mr Browne,^e ye clerke of ye L^{ds} House, is dead,
and Matt. Johnson is now Clericus Parliamentorum.   Y^e Bp. of
Winton^f is reported dead; Mr H. Coventry not like to live;^g
Mr Guy^h to have left his last mistresse.   An odd libell is sayd to
be abroad about Earl of Essex his death,ⁱ wch I never saw nor desire
to see.   I think I tire your Lop., so humbly take leave.

^a He was made Baron of the Exchequer.
^b Sir Hugh Wyndham, of the Common Pleas, died on the 27th July, 1684.
^c Of a plot supposed to be connected with the Rye House plot in England.
^d Margaret, daughter of Sir Robert Sawyer, sometime Attorney General, lately
married to Thomas Herbert, 8th Earl of Pembroke.
^e John Browne.
^f Dr. George Morley.
^g Henry Coventry died at the end of 1686.
^h Henry Guy, afterwards Secretary to the Treasury.
ⁱ This seems to be a pamphlet with the title of " Hue and Cry after the Earl of
Essex's Murder."

Sir Charles Lyttelton.

3 Feb., 1685.

Yesterday, as ye King was dressing, he was seized wth a convulsion fit and gave a greate scream and fell into his chaire. Dr King, happening to be present, wth greate judgment and courage (tho' he be not his sworn phizitian), w^{t}hout other advise, imediately let him blood himself. He had 2 terrible fits, and continued very ill all day, and till 1 or 2 a clock at night. He had severall hot pans applied to his head, wth strong spirrits. He had the antimoniall cup, wch had no greate effect; but they gave him strong purges and glisters, wch worked very well; and they cuppd him and put on severall blistering plasters of cantharides. It tooke him abt. 8 a clock, and it was eleven before he came to himself. He was not dead, for he expressed great sense by his grounes all ye time. At midnight there was little hopes; but after, he fell a sleepe and rested well 3 or 4 howers, and S^r Ch. Scarboro^a told mee he thinkes him in a hopefull way to doe well. His plasters were taken of this morning, and the blisters run very well; only one is yet on his leg, wch is very painfull.

He found himself ill when he rose; and those abt. him perceived it (but he s^d nothing) by his talking and answering not as he used to doe; and he went into his closset in his gown, and stayd half an hower alone; and Thom Howard^b desired Will Chiffing to goe to him, but he w^d not let him come in, and as soone as he came out the convulsion seized him, and he fell into his chaire. The phizitians conclude the sore on his heele was ye gowte, and the applying plasters to it repelled ye humor to his head.

Tuesday, 7 at night.—The Kings head is not yet opened, that is, ye plasters of cantharides to raise blisters not yet taken of.

His mouth and tongue and throate are inflamed wth ye hot mede

---

^{a} The physician.　　　　^{b} Groom of the Bedchamber.

cines, and is y⁰ cause he has bine twice let blood since noone; but the 2ᵈ time was because yᵉ 1ˢᵗ was unsuccessful; and he bled not above 2 ounces, wᶜʰ was by Pierce, yᵉ 2ᵈ time by Hols, and then he bled 9 ounces.

The phizitians were wᵗʰ yᵉ Councill this afternoone, and told them they beleeved his Majesty in a condition of safety.

My Lᵈ Alington^a died a Sunday. Sʳ Thomas Vernon is dead too of yᵉ Kᵍˢ distemper. The ports are all stopt, and expresses gone to Scotland and Ireland, as to all the Lᵗenancies in England. All is very quiet heere, wᶜʰ God grant may continue and yᵉ King recover.

WILLIAM LONGUEVILLE.

My Lᵈ,   3ʳᵈ of Feb^ry, [1685].

Yesterday, when yᵉ King was dressed, hee fell very suddainly down of an apoplecticall fitt or of convulsions (at our end of yᵉ towne I have nothing certain), and Dʳ King then present and having his lance did presently bleed him, which did much good and caused him to recover somewhat of sence. All the day various reports went of his mending and growing worse, as apprehensions &c. are among us. But this present day began with yᵉ good news of his Maᵗʸˢ very good night and amending, as much as in so short a time could be hoped. Yᵉ Ld Allington, Constable of yᵉ Tower, dyed suddainly, and our King was mencioning of it when hee was himselfe taken. My Lᵈ Keeper on Sunday evening told mee that hee was much pleased wᵗʰ your Lops. catalogue, and that hee would ask yᵉ favour of seeing some of them. But (my Lᵈ) you have I think in that neglected [the] study over Easton House

---

* William, second Lord Alington.

doore, somewhat more considerable to a law student or judge, if you can find opportunity to looke for ye same.

Mr. Fanshawe will write your Lop. word how happily things goe on still at court; and how considerable Dr King is like to bee, I believe many wayes your Lop. will heare, for ye Duke was, and is, fully bent for expressing his thanks to him for the good successe he hath had.

I am in much hast, but allwayes,

My L^d,

Your Lops. most obedient servant,

W. L.

SIR CHARLES LYTTELTON.

MY LORD,   Feb. 5th, 8 at night, [1685].

The K^g has bine very ill, allmost since 12 a clock last night. He had indeed some intervale and gave good hopes of amend^{mt}, w^{ch}, ever since dinner, have bine dashd; his disease being, as is supposed, fallen upon his lungs, wch makes him labor to breath, and I see nothing but sad lookes come out from him. I come just from above to tell you this, wch will flye but too fast to one that loves him so well. God Allmighty comfort and preserve him and ye kingdomes.

WILLIAM LONGUEVILLE,

My L^d   From Ld Keeper's, Saterday, the 7th of Feb. [1685].

. You will heare of our King's death yesterday about 12 at noone.
I am, by Ld Keeper's order, to tell your Lop. that this evening
orders were for proclaiming of King James in Guernsy and Jersy.
Y^e King's body was opened too day in the presence of 20 physitians
and others, and found infinitely full of blood in severall parts, as if
drowned wth blood.   His now Mat^y hath declared hee will protect
ye Prott religion, ye Law, and satisfyed many; wch will be in print.
All officers are as they were yett.   My Ld Keeper doth advise your
Lop. to come up immediately.   In hast,

My L^d,
Your Lops. &c.,
WM. LONGUEVILLE.

SIR CHARLES LYTTELTON.

Whitehall, March 6th, [1685].

. Mr de Laune,[a] the P^{sse} of Oranges secretary, who came hither wth
Mr Overkirk[b] and was sent back by ye K^g to ye Prince wth some
conditions upon wch the K^g w^d receive the Prince into his confidence, is now returned.   The K^g insisted that ye Prince sh^d absolutely abandon the D. of Mon:, and command all that depend or
favour him out of ye States dominions, and cashiere 6 officers of his
army who were named of that number.   The P. has absolutely
resigned himself and them to his Mat^{ies} pleasure.[c]

[a] Abel Tasien d'Allonne.

[b] Henry van Nassau, Heer van Ouwerkerk, made Master of the Horse by
William III.

[c] See Burnet's account of this, i. 29.

This night Marshall de Lorge[a] had publike audience of theyr Maties, in quallity of envoy. The K^g received him sitting in a chaire wth his hat on, contrary to the custom, as they say, of ye late King, tho' that has bine ever the way of receiving our envoys in France, not only by the K^g himself, but by ye Dauphin and Monsieur. This day the Prince of Denmark rec^d the news of his mother's death.[b] The K^g has touchd twice this week, and the service performd by his sworn chaplains. Tis sayd heereafter, before he heales, he will, after ye practisse of Ed. the Confessor, goe to confession and receive the Sacram^t, and, after the healing, retire to pray after ye form he used.

It may be, you have not heard that the King commanded Herbert ye Adm: to take his wife[c] again, and that he told a young Lord of greate quallity, when he came to kisse his hand, y^t he must not expect any further favour or countenance from him, while he continued to live in so much unditifullnesse towards his father.

The Lord Doncaster[d] was presented to night in ye drawing roome to ye King and Queene.

THE BISHOP OF OXFORD.

MY HONORD L^d, June 23, [1685].

We are here full of the good news from Scotland, and hope rebellion is a plant which will not thrive better in England. However, we go on to raise in this place[e] our voluntier militia, consisting of two troops of horse and six companies of foot, wch will be

---

[a] Guy Aldonce de Durfort, Duc de Lorges-Quintin, Marshal of France, envoy to congratulate James on his accession.

[b] Queen Sophia Amalia, consort of Frederic III.

[c] His first wife, Anne Hadley. The reader will be reminded of Macaulay's account of the conversation between James and Herbert on conscience.

[d] James, son of the Duke of Monmouth who was also Earl of Doncaster.

[e] At Oxford. Fell was very energetic in raising volunteers in the University.

settled in very few daies, and we shall not be sorry to have put ourselves to needless trouble. My Lord Argile will, I hope, be able to
give the King a true account what charitable prince it was that
assisted him with such a quantity of arms and mony, that just retri-
bution be made for so liberal a benefaction. If it please God that a
good account be given of the Duke of Monmouth and his party, tis
to be hoped there will be no cause for your Lordships being commanded to Guernesay, but that you may be permitted to stay among
your friends in England and attend your own occasions. My Lord
Grey, I presume, is in the west, where I heartily wish he may light
into a good sort of acquaintance. Some of the young noblemen of
the town who are gon down, will, I doubt, be of as little use to the
public service as they will be to him. God Almighty give a good
issue to this concern of the State, and prosper your Lordship in your
private interests, which is heartily praied by,

My Lord,

Your Lordships most humble and affectionat ser^{vt},

Jo. Oxon.

THE SAME.

My honord Lord,   [25 June, 1685.]

I hope my Lord Grey, who applies himself to your Lordship to
be furnisht with mony to raise his troop, dos also crave your advice
and assistance in the choice of his officers and soldiers, men of such
fidelity and courage with whom it may be fit for him to hazard the
great state of life and fortune.

It is an odd piece of pageantry that the late Duke of Monmouth
should assume the stile of King; [a] besides the extravagance of the
claim, it is not popular with his party, who are all averse from kingly
government. So that I am apt to think tis don upon the notion

<hr width="30%" align="left" />

[a] He was proclaimed at Taunton on the 20th June.

that there is some legal security to them who fight for a king, however frail his title be. But where the whole transaction is madness, tis a vain thing to seek for the reason of what is don. I pray God as good an end may be put to ours as is to the Scotish rebellion. It is not easy to guess, unless there be great expectations from London, what should encourage such a handfull of men to wait till they are overlaid by numbers from all parts of the nation. A foreign aid, tho of our next neighbour, cannot give encouragement of having timely relief.

I am very sorry to hear that your daughter is indisposd upon her going abroad, but hope the inconvenience suddainly past over, and has left no other effect behind besides caution for the future. Methinks one of the two holidaies which now happen should give a vacancy for a meeting in your Lordship's affair, that you may have the satisfaction of some kind of prospect into what is likely to be don. That all your concerns may have blessing and success is earnestly praied by, my honord Lord,

Your Lordships
Most humble and affectionat ser^{vt},
Jo. Oxon.

THE SAME.

MY HONORD LORD, June 28, [1685].

It will be high time that somewhat be attemted upon the rebells by the King's forces, for it is an unaccountable thing that they should be sufferd to ramble up and down for several weeks without any notice taken of them, or so much as a single troop falling upon their rear. Whatever bystanders think of it, neighbor princes will imagin that we ar a very easy prey to an invading army, who cannot make head, in three weeks time, to a desperate man who landed with only an hundred and fifty with him; but I hope this reproach shall proceed no farther, and that rebellion will be as short livd in England as it has bin in Scotland.

I perceive the parliament is not yet adjourned, and your Lordship has not hitherto any instructions whither you are to go to Guernsey or Northamptonshire. It is a great satisfaction when our choices are fixt by our superiors, for then, whatever the event be, we can justify ourselves, as to the world, so also, what is of more moment, to our own consciences. If your Lordship be commanded to your government, you have a sister and daughter who will not regret to bear you company, and, if you think fit to leave your daughter behind, God be thankd she has that vertue and prudence which may supersede your fears of hir miscarriage in your absence. Tho, considering the tenderness of a young ladies fame in this malicious world, which no guard of innocence or caution can secure, and also considering how boundless a parents fears will be in the behalf of an only child that is far off, I am apt to think your Lordship may in the close resolve not to part company. Whatever you conclude upon, I beseech Almighty God to give it blessing. I remain

My honord Lord,

Your most humble and affectionat ser^{vt},

JO. OXON.

THE SAME.

MY HONORD LORD,   Jul. 12, [1685].

It has pleasd Almighty God to put a happy end to the two rebellions of the north and west, and disappoint the expectation of ill men among our selves and in our neighbourhood. While others entertain themselves with jollities and boastings, it will be our duty to look up unto that Providence which only can give and preserve peace to governments and render it a blessing. I am sure the poor Church of England is infinitly concerned to recommend hirself by all offices of devotion and duties of religion to that overruling power and goodness she entirely subsists by, and, having a conversation in heaven, be also the care of it.

     *   *

I remain,

My honord Lord, your

Most humble and affectionat ser^{vt},

Jo. Oxon.

THE SAME.

MY HONORD LORD,   Jul. 19, [1685].

The manner of the D. of Monmouths death is matter of great mortification to me. Tis a strange instance of obduration and being given up to strong delusion that a dying man should think himself sure of salvation, and yet not think it necessary to repent of murther, rebellion, and adultery, or own himself to have bin guilty of them, notwithstanding the most manifest notoriety of fact which fix those guilts upon him. We, who partake the same human frailty, have great reason not to be high-minded; but fear, considering that whatever befalls any other may happen to us, and that nothing can distinguish or make secure but the grace and favor of Almighty God, out of which men may sin themselves to such a degree as to believe themselves saints when they are incarnat devils, and take themselves to be secure of heaven when they are sinking into the pit of hell.

   *   *   *

I remain, my honord Lord,

Your Lordships

Most humble and affectionat ser^{vt},

Jo. Oxon.

Sir Charles Lyttelton.

My Lord,   At Taunton, Octob^r 7th, [16]85.

I thought it unreasonable to divert you wth ye entertainem^{ts} of this place, wch have bine nothing but complaints of ye violence of our predecessors to ye country in all kinds, both as to the persons as well as goods, such as I have scarce known practissed at any time in our former civill warrs, and wch I cannot but beleeve wee shall heare more of, when ye parlim^t meetes; and of the execution of so many of ye traitors heere, 18 at one lump, and all quartered, and more every day in other parts of ye country, wch will be to ye number of neere 300 ;[a] and most of theyr quarters are, and will be, set up in ye townes and highways, so y^t ye countrey lookes, as one passes, allready like a shambles. You may think w^{ht} it will be, when all is done. Those who suffered here were so far from deserving any pitty, at least most of em, and those of ye best fashion (unlesse, to speake more charritably, it be most greevous), that they shewd no shew of repentance, as if they died in an ill cause but justified theyr treason and gloried in it.

The Bishop of Oxford.

My honord L^d,   [20 Dec., 1685.]

I am exceedingly glad that your affair goes on so prosperously

---

[a] The exact number of rebels whom Jeffreys hanged, as stated by Lord Macaulay, was three hundred and twenty. The condemnatory remarks of Lyttelton are of peculiar significance in the mouth of a courtier. Macaulay has not overcoloured his vivid picture of the Bloody Assizes.

with my Lord Notingham;[a] but it was some surprize to me to be told it by the public news letter. This is a peculiar way of publishing the bans of matrimony and, if it can obtain, will supersede the use of an Act of Parliament against clancular marriages. Your daughter, if she can comport with the temper of a grave husband and denie hirself those gaities which may be decent for the wife of one who is of hir age, may promise to herself as much happiness in this disposal as is to be had in this world. But little things lead to great, and, if herein she can comply and render hirself a meet helper, she will not want any sober enjoiment or real satisfaction.

I wish my Lord Clarendon good luck with his honor,[b] which to me seems sufficiently hazardous. His son's match seems very desirable, but it comes often to pass that rich widows prove poor wives;[c] and I am told there are several pretensions to the personal estate of M[rs] Whitmore, w[ch] may make a better dividend among the lawiers then the executor of kindred. If the condition of those other officers who are cashierd[d] be no worse then M[r] Cook's, they will not be in ill circumstances by the loss of their commands. I pray God fit us for the more necessary duty of obeying, and preserve to us our laws and our religion. I add my heartiest praiers for the continuance of all blessing to your Lordship and family, remaining,

My honord Lord,

your most humble and affectionat ser[vt],

JO. OXON.

---

[a] Daniel Finch, Earl of Nottingham, afterwards Secretary of State. His first wife was Lady Essex Rich, daughter of Robert, Earl of Warwick. His marriage with Anne Hatton, referred to in this letter, took place on the 29th December, 1685. He was born in 1647, and was therefore twenty-one years older than his bride.

[b] As Lord-Lieutenant of Ireland.

[c] The match did not come off. Edward Hyde, Viscount Cornbury, afterwards third Earl of Clarendon, married Catherine, daughter of Henry, Lord O'Brien, eldest son of the Earl of Thomond.

[d] "Several of the officers, military and civill, that appeared in the house of commons in this present parliament against the king's interest are (tis said) dismis'd their several places and commands; as, Sir Stephen Fox, lord Manchester, capt. Cook, capt. Browne and others." Luttrell, under date of 13 Dec. 1685.

THE SAME.

MY HONORD L^d,   [7 Feb., 1686.]

I was in hope that the practice of duelling had bin forgot; but, if it be resum'd, tis to be doubted this little intervall of late will only give a greater appetite and the recommendation of a fashion newly reviv'd. This instance happening where an example is not likely to be made is the more unfortunat, for without severity a stop will not be put.ᵃ The age of the young lady whom your Lordship mentions is no objection, unless there have bin some personal obstacle which has kept one from a husband till two or three and twenty years are over when there was a portion of 20000ˡ. Tis easy paiment of 1000ˡ to Dʳ King to quit scores by a knighthood, wᶜʰ in truth is the fining him a hundred pound. In the mean time, tis well that a good officer is remembred at Court after a year is past, and that respit, which by the doctor's means was given, proved of greater importance then could be easily imagind.

I am, thank God, still upon my legs, and continue to go to church without inconvenience. I pray God perpetuate the happy opportunity.ᵇ Adding my praiers for the health and prosperity of your Lordship and family, I remain,

My honord Lord,
Your
Most humble and affectionat ser^{vt},
Jo. Oxon.

ᵃ He refers to the Duke of Grafton's duel, mentioned by Luttrell under date of 2nd February :—" The same day also the Duke of Grafton fought a duel with one Mr. Talbott, brother of the Earl of Shrewsbury, and killed him ; and Mr. Wharton, one of the lord Wharton's sons, killed an Irish man the same day."

ᵇ He died on the 10th July.

ALICE HATTON.

[The 3 Feb., 1687].

You had heard from me last post, dearest Brother, but by a misstake my letter was forgott to be sent, wch I fretted extreamely att, but was born for misfortune of all kinds, and I am sure it would be ye greatest to me in ye world to give y^r L^{dp} the least occation to beleeve y^t any thing can ever make me omite paying all the duty and respect that is due to ye best of brothers. Ld Nottingham designes to goe to Nor[thampton] on Tuesday next, in order to see Ld Banbery's^a house, wch he has a minde to buy. He was wth me yesterday, to settl my answer, wch I must, it seems, put in, for they will heare of nothing till that be done; and an inventory of every thing must be sett down, w^t they doe not demand as well as w^t they doe. When they have had all, I hope theyl be satisfied, and I must bare the loss.

Captain Hatton has had an unfortunait accident hapnd at Carlile. I have not heard a perfect relation how ye quarrell began, but, in short, Livetenant Gorge Comley^b has killed Majoer Morgan,^{c} that dined wth y^r L^{dp}, at his tent, and ·tis said nobody was by when it was don but Captin H. There are two papist offisirs put into theire places.

Lady Manchester and all ye young ladies very well, present theere servis to y^r L^{dp} and my deare sister. She is this day gone to a weding feast. Ld Colrain's son married to a marchants daughter in ye Citty.^{d} Ld Montagu's^e son, if not dead, is given over by ye d^{rs}.

---

^{a} Charles Knollys, self-styled Earl of Banbury.

^{b} Lieutenant of Charles Hatton's company.

^{c} Major Jenkins Morgan, of the Queen Dowager's Regiment of Horse.

^{d} Hugh, son of Henry Hare, second Lord Coleraine, married Lydia, daughter of Matthew Carlton, of Edmonton.

^{e} ? Francis Browne, fourth Viscount Montague.

The death of y^e lettl Princess, Lady Anne,^a is a great aflection to y^e Princes. L_d Grey has had another loss, besides his plate. His pag has picked his pockett of severall guinneys, but his L^dp has only had him whyped for it and still keeps him. Ld Manchester does not come from Venic till after Easter, and will not be in England soe soon as Aprill, as was expected. The Dean of Paul's^b presents his servis to y^r L^dp. I find he is very well enclined to leave St. Andrews, but, soe many parswades him against it, he is not yet resolved w^t to doe. Lady Ann Grimston in towne, and her neighbour La[dy] Wyseman^c come to her house againe. It seems La[dy] North^d was conserned in making ye match for Mr Spencer. She invited them both to her house, and when they met she locked them in a rome together. There are many surcomstances too long to trouble your L^dp wth from, my dearest Brother,

Y^r most truly af^et sister and
most obedient servant,

A. H.

L^d and La. Nottingham humbly beg y^r blessing. My servis to deare pretty Miss Bety. Ld N. will write next post.

The little Prences^e has not ye measells but a feavour, and was last night in great danger.

---

^a Anne Sophia, daughter of the Princess Anne, born 12 May, 1686, died 2 Feb. 1687.

^b Edward Stillingfleet ; Bishop of Worcester in 1689.

^c Elizabeth, daughter of Dudley, Lord North, and wife of Sir Robert Wyseman, Dean of the Arches,.

^d Catherine, daughter of William, Lord Grey of Werke, and wife of Charles, 5th Lord North and Grey.

^e Mary, eldest daughter of the Princess Anne. She died a few days after this, on the 8th February.

THE SAME.

March 8th, [16]8$\frac{6}{7}$.

I am soe troubled for y^r being ell, my dearest Brother, I dont know w^t to doe. I have had soe many aflictions of this kind, y^t I cant but dread this wch would, I am sure, be y^e greatest y^t ever can happen to me in y^e world. If it be God's will, as I pray night and day, to restore you to health againe, w^t ever ellse God pleases to lay upon me, I will never repine, but thinke myselfe happie soe long as I have my dearest brother Hatton. I am sorry my ugly letter gave you any disturbance. If I doe not heare next post of y^r being better I will come downe, and please God to see you, w^t ever becomes of me. Ld Nott: is now at Milton, and left this letter to be sent to y^r L^{dp}. Tis a great blessing to us all that y^r L^{dp} will take care of y^rselfe. Y^t ye remedies you use for ye recovery of y^r health may be succesful shall be ye dayly prayer of, dearest Brother

Y^r most af^t sister to serve you,

A. H.

Lady Nott begs y^r blessing.

THE SAME.

Easter Even, [26 March, 1687].

It was ye kindnest thing in the world, dearest Brother, to let me heare from you last post; for, in earnest, I am soe conserned for my poor sister H[atton]'s confinement to hir chamber, y^t my thoughts are never at rest but when I heare from you. It would be a melancholy thing to be allwayes in a chamber and have nothing to

VOL. II.   K

doe, but pretty Miss Betty makes it not soe I hope to her dear
mama.   I am mighty glad she breeds her teeth soe well.

There was yesterday a vast crowed at Whithall to heare D[r]
Sharp.[a]   Y[e] Bishop[b] went from thence to y[e] King's Chaple, and
was there till ten a clock at night, and a Maunday Thursday went
along wth B[ishop] Laban[c] all y[e] time he washed y[e] poor mens feet.
Tis said Nell Guin is dead.[d]   Y[e] King has seazed on hir estate and
jewles for hir son, but, unless he will change his religion, he's not
to have any thing, w[ch] he is yet very unwilling to.   Lady Nott.
askes y[r] blessing and my dear's, whose humble servant I am, and,
dearest Brother,

Y[r] most aff[ct] sister to serve you,

A. H.

SIR CHARLES LYTTELTON.

MY LORD,   March 29, 1687.

Last night, M[rs] Ogle told mee she heard you were fallen very ill
again, and that she more doubted it, because she had not heard in
3 posts from my Lady; w[ch] y[rs] of y[e] 26 I rec[d] to day undeceived us
in.   M[r] Ambrose Brown, a captain in my L[d] Plimouths regim[t], was
this day wth y[e] K[g] a greate while, in his closset, and, after, dismissed
from his employm[t], so that you may find that matter is not yet over.
M[rs] Nelly has bine dying of an apoplexie.   She is now come to her

---

[a] John Sharp, Dean of Norwich, afterwards Archbishop of York.   Lately sus-
pended for his sermon against Popery at St. Giles's.   Luttrell records that " Dr.
Sharp, Dean of Norwich, preached at the chapel at Whitehall before the princesse of
Denmark."

[b] Probably Nathaniel, Lord Crew, Bishop of Durham.

[c] John Leyburn, Bishop of Adrumetum and Vicar Apostolic in England.

[d] She died on the 14th November of this year.

sense on one side, for ye other is dead of a palsey. She is thought to be worth 100000^{li}; 2000^{li} in revenue, and ye rest jewells and plate.

Coll: Cornwall ^{a} is ab^t to deliver up his com^n, pretending afaires ab^t his wife's fortune in Holland.

Will: Forrester,^{b} who married a sister of Ld Salisbury, is sent for by a privy seale. He is at ye Hague, and his wife wth him.

My L^d, have you not seene D^r. Burnet's letters of his travells,^{c} of wch many hundred copies are seized? I am glad my Lady is well. I have ye cramp, so I can scarce hold my pen.

Sir Edmund King.

My Lord, June 9th [16]87.

Tho' its near a 11 at night, and I fear the post is going, I cannot forbear to send you a peice of news, odd and unusuall. Ther was a rich Spanysh ship coming from the West Indies y^t was sunck three score years agoe, laden wth gold and silver. Duke Albemarle,^{d} S^r Jo[hn] Narborough,^{e} Sr James Hays, and another, gott a pattent from the late King, on tearms to gett all the gold and silver they could from the bottom of the sea by any art y^t ever they have been 10 years a trying, and gott dyvers (men used to it) out of the West Indies, and found this ship, and gott her up and safe into the river, worth two hundred and 50 thousand pounds in gold and silver. Duke Albemarle's share, 2 eights, is 40000; Sr James Hays as

^{a} Henry Cornwall, colonel of one of the regiments of Foot.

^{b} Sir William Forester, of Dothill, co. Salop, married Mary Cecil, daughter of James, third Earl of Salisbury.

^{c} " Some Letters containing an Account of what seemed most remarkable in Switzerland, Italy," &c. Amsterdam, 1686, 8vo.

^{d} Christopher Monk, the second Duke.

^{e} The admiral.

much, 40000; and others proportionable. The King reserv'd a 10th
for himselfe. It's certainly true; youl heare it more at large
quickly.

Pray excuse
Y^r humble servant,
ED. KING.

The news came yesterday morn, at 3 a clock; and I beseech you
present my humble service to my Lady Hatton. They are working
on another ship.

<h3 style="text-align:center">DR. SAMUEL FREEMAN.^a</h3>

MY LORD,   July 7th [16]87.

*   *   *   *   *

The last occurrence y^t has been y^e subject of y^e towntalke was y^e
Pope's Nuncio's^b public entrance into Windsor y^e last Sunday. His
Matie desir'd y^e Duke of Sommerset^c to attend at it; but hee desir'd
to bee excus'd, and is dismist his places for refusing. The L^d Bp.
of Durham's and Chester's^d coaches were, as its comonly said, in y^e
traine. Some of ye dissenters are very brisk upon ye dissolution of
ye parliament, but I am of opinion ye popish interest will not find
y^t assistance from them, when a new one is to bee chosen, as is
expected, Some of y^m say they'l never let go ye Test. The govern^{rs}
of Charter-house, on Midsummer day, refusd ye King's mandate to
admitt an old man, a papist.^e What ye issue will bee is not known.

^a Of Clare College, Cambridge ; B.A. 1664, M.A. 1668, S.T.P. 1685. Rector of
St. Paul's, Covent Garden ; and afterwards Dean of Peterborough, in 1691. Died
14th Oct., 1707.

^b Ferdinando, Conte d'Adda.

^c Charles Seymour, sixth Duke.

^d Thomas Cartwright, lately Dean of Ripon. Died 1689.

^e One Popham. The firmness of the Duke of Ormond, who was one of the
trustees, frustrated the design. See Macaulay's account of the affair.

Nothing is done as to Magdalen Colledge since ye sentence. This day three weeks they are again to appear before ye commissioners, and to prove their information against Mr. Farmer's ^{a} morals by witnesses. My Lord Grey is expected every day. I hope hee will not stay in town, ye small pox being very much in it. I humbly thank y^r Lordship for ye honour of y^r letters and all ye undeserv'd favours to, My Lord,

Y^r Lordship's very much oblig'd serv^t,

SAM. FREEMAN.

SIR CHARLES LYTTELTON.

MY LORD, At y^s Camp [Hounslow], July 13th, [16]87.

I rec^d ye news of my Ladys bringing you a son wth all ye joy I c^d have done for my heire, and wish you a long and sollid comfort in it. I had done it ye last post, but that ye K^g surprized us in drawing us out unexpectedly to our armes; and, indeed, we can, while we stay heere, promisse little time to ourselves. To morrow, the K^g treates ye 2 Queenes heere. The Guards will be all drawn into ye field from London, and we shall make 4 lines of hors and foot, and have abundance of fireing and fireworkes. Wthin 2 or 3 days, I beleeve, the fort may be finished. It's a curtain of 2 half bastions, ab^t ye bignesse of Sherenesse, wth a ravlin before ye curtain; and this is to be attacqued in form by ye whole army, and will take up some days. The D. of Albemarle dined heere yesterday wth ye K^g, and says his ships are now all sailed to Portsmouth, and he will be soone there to embark. My Ld Faversham is gone to Sr John Raisby's,^{b} not to Welbeck, in order to a treaty wth Ld Newcastle for his daughter.

^{a} Anthony Farmer, the King's nominee for the presidency of Magdalen College.

^{b} Sir John Reresby. See his Memoirs for a long account of his negotiations for the match between the Earl of Feversham and Lady Margaret Cavendish, daughter of Henry, Duke of Newcastle ; which ended in nothing but a quarrel between the Duke and the Duchess.

Ld Dumbarton ^{a} is gentleman of ye bedchamber in Ld Som^{ts} place.

THE SAME.

MY LORD,   At Portsmouth, August 30th [1687].

I have y^{rs} of ye 22. The K^g came hither by yach from South-ampton this morning, and was treated by my Ld Gainsborgh ^{b} at dinner, as he has bine every where in his progresse; but had no present at Bristol but ye provisions for his table wch they of ye town sent in. The K^g one told me heard him tell Mr Pepys that he w^d build a fort to command the river some miles from ye town, and shewd him where it shd be upon ye chart. He has viewd all y^e for-tifications heare, new and old, and bine abord ye Royall Charles to see ye working of a new engine of Sr Sam: Morland's, and is now gone abord againe; and to morrow, very early, comes ashore heere, and touches above 300 people y^t are heere for ye evill, and goes after to ye B^p at Farnam ^{c} to dinner, and to bed to Windsor. I shall start wth him towards Sherenes, taking Tunbridg (as it is) in my way; and, wth as much dispatch as I can, hasten home. My wife is yet at Tunbridg. My 10 companyes, I feare, are to stay heere all winter. I have lately bine acquainted wth Chappell, and, if those who succeed him be as discreet as I phancy he is, you and they will be at ease.

Mr Blaithwait ^{d} shewd me a letter to night from before Buda, that ye Turkes have put in 600 men into ye town and that none of theyr mines have had any effect.

^{a} George Douglas, Earl of Dumbarton, Commander of the Forces in Scotland.
^{b} Edward Noel, fourth Viscount Camden, created Earl of Gainsborough. Died in 1689.
^{c} Peter Mew, Bishop of Winchester.
^{d} William Blathwayt, Secretary at War.

Dr. Samuel Freeman.

My Lord,   September 8th, [16]87.

I am very sorry yr Ldship should meet with any discouragement
in so pious a work as yr church affaire is. I wonder much at
Mr D[ean] of [Paul's] proceeding in this matter. 'Twas to be
wishd yt all ye out-parishes had many more churches in them,
answerable to their greatness and number of inhabitants; and yt any
incumbent should he displeasd to see the necessities of his people
reliev'd in a matter of so high a nature seemed to me to be very
unaccountable. Mr D[ean] comes but seldom to town and makes
very short stayes; yet I saw him about 3 weeks since, but he say.d
nothing of it. Yesterday I din'd with my Ld. Bp. of London, at
Fulham, and amongst other things told his Ldship yt you had begun
yr church in Hatton Garden; and hee replyed yt hee was very glade
of it, and wished yt there were more such good works begun. When
I see ye Deane of St. P[aul's] next, I think to give him an occasion
to discourse of it; and then its likely I may be able to send yr
Ldship his objections against it.

I beleeve yr Ldship has an account sent you of ye Kings reception
at Oxford. 'Tis at large in this days gazett, but nothing in it of
what he sayd to ye fellows of M[agdalen] Coll. I saw an account
of it from Dr Aldridge,[a] Sub-deane of Xts. On Sunday, about 3
in ye afternoon, his Matie sent for them and askt ym why they did
not obey his mandate and admitt ye Bp. of Oxford[b] president of
their coll.; and when ye senior of ym began to give his Matie an
account, the King took him up short and sayd hee would heare
nothing from them, and thrice at least repeated yt hee was their king
and would bee obeyd, and then bid them goe to ye coll. and immediately choose ye B. of Oxford, or els hee'd make ym feel ye weight

Henry Aldrich, Dean of Christ Church in 1689.
b Samuel Parker. Died in 1688.

of a prince's hand.   They were noe sooner got to their coll. and
deliberated a short time, but 19 of 21 resolvd on this answer: That
they were extremly sorry y^t his ^{Matie} requird of them impossibilities,
y^t they were precluded by their former election, and, ye place being
full, they could not putt an other in it.   What will bee ye issue is
not yet known.   The young students began to mutter very much
at his ^{Maties} wordes to ye fellows of Mag.; but, bateing this rough-
ness to y^m, his ^{Matie} shewd himself very gracious to ye rest of y^e
university and mightily pleasd with his reception, saying he would
ever protect y^m and hopt to be as kind to them as any of his predecessors had been; bid them not bee griev'd y^t hee had given ease
to ye dissenters, saying y^t humility and charitie were ye soul of y^e
Xtian religion, and hee hopt y^t their eye would not be evill because
hee was good.

Here is lately come out a very seasonable and excellent Letter of
Advice to a Dissenter,[a] writt impartially and with a great deale of
witt and strength.   They are mightily catcht up and are sent farr
and neare.   I hope y^r Ldship will meet with one of y^m in ye country.
I had sent one, but y^t it is too big to come in a letter.

The reformation of ye companies in London sticks for ye present
and some think y^t they are discouragd to proceed.   Whether there
will bee a parliament or no they say is very doubtfull.   At my
Ld. of London's yesterday they talkt of my Ld. Grey's selling of
his horses and hounds, and of his intention to goe again for some
time beyond sea.   The Bp. told mee hee wishd his freinds would
perswade him to stay.

*   *   *   *   *

Y^r Ldships most obligd humble serv^t,

SAM. FREEMAN.

---

[a] " A Letter to a Dissenter upon occasion of his Majesties late gracious Declaration of Indulgence."   London, 1687, 4to.

Thomas Tramallier.

My Lord,   Jesus College, October 27th, 1687.

On Thursday last in the afternoon came hither the Ecclesiastical
Commissioners, viz., the Bishop of Chester, the Lord Chief Justice
Wright, and Baron Jenner;[a] and the next day in the morning they
went to Magdalen College chapel; but that place not pleasing them,
they remov'd to the college hall, where, according to a citation putt
up on the college gate two days before, appear'd before them the
President, Dr Hough,[b] the Fellows, with the rest of the Society.
Their commission was first read, empowring them to visit the
universitys, particularly Magdalen College, the same in effect,
mutatis mutandis, with the general commission of that court; and
then the Bishop of Chester made a speech, or a charge, consisting
for the most part of upbraiding reflexions upon the loyalty and
behaviour of the college towards his Mat^y, with some exhortations
to submitt to the King's mandate. In the afternoon they mett
again; when Dr Hough declar'd to them in his name, and the name
of the society, that he own'd their authority so far as it agreed with
the laws of the land and ye statutes of the college, and no further;
telling them withall that it was a hard thing they should undergoe
a visitation at so short a warning. This declaration of submitting
no otherwise to their visitation, as also of the hard measure he had,
he afterwards confirm'd, among other arguments, by the oath he
had taken as President, which is indeed very solemne and express,
and other statutes of the college, which they are all sworn to
observe; giving them an account of ye whole transaction, but particularly of the methods they had us'd to avoid their falling under

---

[a] Sir Thomas Jenner, Baron of the Exchequer.

[b] John Hough, afterwards Bishop, successively, of Oxford, 1690, of Lichfield and
Coventry, 1699, and of Worcester, 1717. Died in 1743.

the King's displeasure. In the mean while the commission order'd several papers to be read, concerning that affair, both from the ecclesiastical courts and the college; askt questions to and fro, especially about the coming in of some of their presidents by mandates, to which suitable answers were return'd; and call'd for ye books and registers, with other instruments relating to the estate of the college. One thing I must not omitt, because indeed it was very singular: when Dr Hough insisted upon their obligation to observe the statutes of ye coll: and told them it was his resolution, by God's help, to doe it, the Bp. askt him, why then they did not read mass, according to the statutes of the college? To which the D^r answering that, besides that mass contain'd several impietys, it was contrary to the laws of the land, the Commissioners desir'd him to shew them to what law; and the Acts of Uniformity being instanc't in, they all profess't they could see no such thing in them. But all this was but skirmishing in respect of what was done on Saturday.

That morning then the Commissioners, according to their adjournment, sate in the college common room, whence all people were turn'd out; but being lett in again, after they had closeted the D^r for about an hour, the sentence of the Ecclesiastical Court was read thrice by the Bishop; which was to this effect: That he was declar'd no President, and was forthwith to deliver up the keys. To this he answer'd that he was perhaps the only instance in England, since the Restauration, that was turu'd out of his property without a legal tryal or so much as a citation; and that he could not, nor would not, part with his right.

In the afternoon the fellows were called in, and being ask't one by one, whether they would comply with the King's mandate for the Bp. of Oxon, that being read to them, they all unanimously refus'd it but two, Dr Tho. Smith, and Charnock.[a] It happn'd a little before, as Dr Hough was protesting against the proceedings of

[a] Robert Charnock. Executed, in 1696, for sharing in the Assassination plot.

the Commissioners, and appeal'd to the King and his courts of justice, that the people gave a hem; for which they thought fitte to bind him over to Westminster in 2000^{li} bail. They talkt once of committing him; though he told them that by depriving him they had discharg'd him from looking after the college; and with [that] all the Fellows offer'd to take their oaths that they were no way concern'd in it. My Ld Chief Justice was pleas'd to say that if the civil power could not keep us civil, the military should. It was a rude thing, without doubt; and therefore it was since condemn'd by a programma from the Vice Chancellour.

On Tuesday morning they sate again; but it was in order to admitt the Bishop of Oxford; which being not to be done by the Fellows, they did it in the person of his chaplain; who, as his proxy, took the oaths, and was afterwards putt in possession of the President's lodgings; but not without breaking open the doors, Dr Hough retaining still the keys. It was expected the sheriff of the county would have bin concern'd in it, with the posse comitatus, or that ye three troopes of horse, which have been quarter'd here ever since the raising the army, should have bin employ'd in that execution; but it was done in ye manner that I relate, whatever private instructions they might have. In the afternoon the [course] was chang'd; and the Bp. of Oxon being consider'd as possess't of the Presidentship, a new question was putt to them, viz. whether they would obey him now he was in by the King's authority? To this the Fellows, Demyes, chaplains, and others of the foundation, answer'd, they would submitt to him as far as was consistent with the statutes of the college; only two refus'd it absolutely, the famous Dr Fairfax,^{a} and the under porter. The D^r moreover, entering his protestation in due forme of law, was depriv'd instantly of his fellow ship, and commanded to depart the college within a fortnight; as the under porter was within three days. In the morning there was putt into the court an answer to that doughty argument that the

---

^{a} Henry Fairfax, afterwards Dean of Norwich.

King's mandate is an inhibition; but they were wheedled off of it by some few sugar words, they then beginning to flinch. I was surpris'd, I must confess, to see it come to this; but I dare not judge them. This is plain, I think, that they have thereby shew'd the King a way to putt into every place; not to say that in it's consequence it affects every man's property in England. They pretend that they have herein follow'd the advice of their most judicious friends; and that there was positive order sent to turn out every man of them that would not submitt. Your Lordship will hear more of it in parliament when it setts. All happiness may attend your noble family.

I am,

My Lord,

Your Lordship's most humble obedient servant,

THOMAS TRAMALLIER.

THE SAME.

MY LORD,   Jesus College, Nov. 17, [16]87.

I presum'd about three weeks agoe to trouble your Lordship with a long tedious account of the proceedings of the Ecclesiastical Commissioners at Magdalen College; and because they are return'd here again, I shall beg leave to continue my relation of what has hapen'd since.

I inform'd your Lordship then, as I apprehended it, and as I think most people did that heard them, that the Fellows had submitted to the Bishop of Oxford, and that they would obey him as their President. But it seems we were mistaken; for on the Thurs-

day following, when the Commissioners would have had them to
subscribe a kind of address of submission, to be presented to his
Ma^{ty}, they putt in this final answer: " May it please your L^{d}ships,
We have endeavour'd in all our actions to express our duty with all
humility to his Ma^{ty}; and being conscious to ourselves that, in the
whole conduct of this business before your L^{d}ships, we have done
nothing but what our oaths and statutes indispensably oblige us to,
we cannot make any declaration, whereby to acknowledge that we
have done amiss, as having acted according to the principles of
loyalty and obedience to his sacred Ma^{ty}, as far as we could without
doing violence to our consciences and prejudice to our rights (of
which we humbly conceive this of electing our President to be one),
from which we are sworn on noe account whatever to depart. We
therefore humbly beg your L^{d}ships to represent," &c. Subscribed
by all but Dr. Thomas Smith and Charnock. Mr. Fulham, one of
the Fellows, had the misfortune then to be suspended from his
fellowship by the Commissioners during the King's pleasure, for
telling them that they had violently enter'd the President's lodgings
without the legal way by the sheriff and the posse comitatûs. But
on Tuesday they came hither again in the afternoon, and lodg'd
that night at the Bp. of Oxon in Magdalen College, where yesterday morning they sate in the college common room; and the Fellows
appear'd before them. The first thing that was done was the
reading of a couple of mandates from the King, out of a bundle
the Bp. of Chester held in his hands, in favour of one Joyner,[a] who
was a Demye there above forty years agoe and sold his place before
the troubles broke out, and one Alibone, a student of St. Omers,

---

[a] William Joyner, or Lyde; a Demy in 1636, and afterwards Fellow. He
renounced his fellowship and went over to Rome in 1644. For some years he was in
the service of Edward, Earl of Glamorgan; and led a retired life. He was now
brought out of his seclusion to be restored to his fellowship, which, however, he held
but one year, and then, as Wood says, he "retired to his former recess, where his
apparel, which was formerly gay, was then very rustical."

but both Papists; and the admitting of them Fellows thereupon by the Commissioners, without taking any other oath but that of Fellow, the rest being dispens'd with by the mandate. Then Chester, being the mouth of the Commissioners, made his speech; where, after a recapitulation of his former charge and their proceedings, he fell a railing most violently against the Fellows, calling them popular, petulent, obstinate, perverse, seditious, libellous, forgetting all this while that he stands register'd at Queen's College for having born arms against the King at Worcester. But amongst other his strange doctrines I must not pass by one, for it is a piece of new divinity, worthy the ambition of the candidate of the Arch-bishoprick of York; and it is this: he told the Fellows, in the exhortative part of his speech, that they must sacrifice their consciences, as a peace-offering to the Father of their Countrey.

After this, there was an instrument produc't, containing the forme of a submission, to which they were all requir'd to subscribe, except Dr Tho. Smith, of whom the Bp. was pleas'd to say that his Mat^y, in consideration of his carriage in that whole affair, did graciously condescend that it should not be putt to him, and Charnock. But they all refus'd it; for which they were presently after sentenc'd by the court, five and twenty in number, to be depriv'd their fellowships and banisht the college. They were denied a copy of the instrument; but it was to this effect: That they should acknowlege themselves to have acted all along disloyally and disobediently, and beg the King's pardon; and that they own'd the Bp. of Oxon as their lawfull President, and would obey him accordingly. There were afterwards three new Fellows putt in by mandates; and two mandates more were offer'd, but not accepted of by the persons for whom they were design'd. The Fellows putt in their several pro testations, and the Commissioners went away in the afternoon; but God only knows where that furious zeal will terminate. The university expects to find in your Lordship a true patriot of your countrey, and does not doubt to see the noble spirit of your ancestors revived in your person, who were the great support of the Church of

England both at the settlement of the Reformation and the late calamities of it, when the same occasions shall return.

*   *   *   *   *

I am,

My L^d,

Your Lordship's most humble obedient ser^{vt},

T. TRAMALLIER.

SIR EDMUND KING.

MY LORD,   March 24, 1687[8].

It was this morning before I could prevail wth Mr Sadlor [a] to see my Lady Hatton's picture, wch is well painted, very fleshey and well colour'd, and is a very fine peice and extreamly like too. But I found a great fault (as I call'd it) in a part of the face; wch I convinc't him of, and he mended it to his owne great satisfaction and his wive's as well as mine, whilst I stood by; and I mended another in my Lady's hand of as great a concern, wch I am sure yor Lord^p will be pleas'd wth too; but yor dear pritty son with his fine diamond eyes I durst not meddle wth, because I have not had him in my sight, in the life, which pray God preserve. We hear the Bishop of Oxford dy'd Tuesday last, not a R[oman] C[atholic]. The Duke of Barwich [b] has the small pox, this the 5th day. My Lord Peterborough is at Drayton since Monday last.

I intreat my humble service to my Lady Hatton, and am

Yo^r Lord^{ps} most affectionte ser^t,

ED. KING.

---

[a] Thomas Sadler, miniature and portrait painter; a pupil of Sir Peter Lely. He was brought up to the law.

[b] James Fitz-James, natural son of James II. by Anne Churchill.

SIR CHARLES LYTTELTON.

My Lord,   Shene,[a] May 15th [16]88.

It's a greate while since I heard from you; and ye longer I think, because, when I did so last, you complaind of ill health. I was all the last weeke and part of that before at Sherenesse and Rochester, to attend his Mat^y, who went to give order ab^t ye navy, making severall new platformes and batteries upon the Medway, and ye putting out some ships to sea and to get others in a readinesse, if there sh^d be occasion for it, as I hope there will not yet awhile. For, tho' the Duch are (they say) out wth a more cousiderable fleet then we yet know w^{ht} they have to doe wth, I can hardly think they will attempt any thing upon us. It will be (tho') to insult us, if they come to brave it on our coast. I left rideing before Sherenesse our R Ad: Strickland[b] wth 3 more men of warr, 4th and 5th rates, and 3 or 4 fireships; and, it may be, these, or ye men of war at least, are designed to carry Q. Dowager to Portugall, who, they say, goes in August. My son Harry has a mind to goe wth her, and from thence into Spain, and then into Italy, if he can get ye K^{gs} leave.

---

[a] Evelyn visited Lyttelton at Shene, and tells us how he came by his house there : " 24, Mar. 1688. I went with Sir Charles Littleton to Sheene, an house and estate given to him by Lord Brouncker ; one who was ever noted for a hard, covetous, vicious man, but for his worldly craft and skill in gaming few exceeded him. Coming to die, he bequeath'd all his land, house, furniture, &c. to Sir Charles, to whom he had no manner of relation, but an ancient friendship contracted at the famous siege of Colchester, 40 yeares before. It is a pretty place, with fine gardens, and well planted, and given to one worthy of them, Sir Charles being an honest gentleman and soldier . . He is married to one Mrs Temple, who was formerly maide of honour to the late Queene, a beautiful lady, and he has many fine children, so that none envy his good fortune."

[b] Sir Roger Strickland.

The same.

June 8 [16]88.

The B^{ps} have bine before ye K^g in Councill and are committed to ye Tower, because they would not enter into a recognizance each of 500^{li} to appeare in ye terme, upon pretence it w^d injure theyr peeriage. I heare they were prest much in it, and severall instances of ye temporall peeres who had done it, as ye Duke of Buck, Ld Lovelace,^{a} and others. As they past through ye courts to ye water side from ye Councill (there being a greate crowd both wthin and wthout doores), the people praid for y^m, and ye AB^p held out his hand and said: " Be dutyfull to ye K^g; hold fast to y^r religion; and God blesse you."

The same.

London, June 11, [16]88.

Yesterday, 5 minutes before 10 in ye morning, ye Queen was delivered of ye Prince of Wales. I come now from seeing him as he was undressing, and he is a delicate fine boy, very well complexioned, and lookes healthy and sprightly. He is to have no wet nurs. Sunday next is appointed for ye thanksgiving in ye churches heere, and ye Sunday following in all the kingdom. I wish my Lady Hatton as much joy as I beleeve the Queene has, for ye same reason. I goe to morrow to Rochester to stay, I know not how long.

^{a} John Lovelace, third Baron.

CHARLES HATTON.

Letcomb, June 18, [16]88.

I must, my Lord, in ye first place return you thanks for y^r present of opobalsamum, from wch I have found more benefit then from any physick I ever tooke; wch 1 experienc'd by accident, for, missing ye regim^t at Aylsbury, I writ to our collonel for leave to be absent from my command for a fortnight or 3 weekes longer, and, ye waters being out, I wase advised to come hither by Oxford, wher, designing to have some pectoral pills and a decoction made up according to a perscription of Dr Fowkes,[a] in wch balsum of Tolu wase to be dissolved, wch wase not to be had (any thing tollerably good) at Oxford, instead thereof I made use of opobalsamum, by wch I have found very great benefit.

I met at Oxford wth Mabillon his Musaeum Italicum,[b] and a peice of Dr Bernards newly out of ye press, de Ponderibus et Mensuris,[c] a subject I know not displeasing to y^r Lo^{ppe}. Therefore I have wth Mabillon sent it to y^r Lo^{ppe}. Thes 2 bookes, wth Ford's Psalms,[d] cost a little above w^t I promis'd for y^r 2 dictionarys. I have like-wise sent some seeds I procured from Mr Bobart.[e] Some of them are very curious plants, and I shou'd advise ye sowing of part of each parcel of ye choicest seeds now, and ye rest next spring. For those plants wch are annual, being sowed soe late, will not I suppose come to perfection this summer, and will therefore continue all winter and flower earlyer and more beautifully next year. I have settled a corispondence wth Mr Bobart, and he hath, in ye season,

[a] Phineas Fowke.

[b] "Museum Italicum ; seu collectio veterum scriptorum ex Bibliothecis Italicis cruta, a Joh. Mabillon et M. Germain." Two vols. Paris, 1687-89, 4to.

[c] "De Mensuris et Ponderibus," by Dr. Edward Bernard, Savilian Professor of Astronomy. The first edition was published in 1685 ; the second in 1688.

[d] "Version of the Psalms of David, together with all the Church Hymns, into Metre." By Simon Ford, D.D. London, 1688, 8vo.

[e] Jacob Bobart, son of a father of the same name, whom he succeeded as keeper of the Botanical Gardens at Oxford.

promis'd me some curious plants wch I design for y^r Lo^{ppe}. Dr Morison 2^d volume is in great forwardness, 120 plates are engraven, and about 40 only wanting to perfect ye worke.[a]

At ye presse at ye Theatre I accidentally met wth Dr Mills,[b] whose Greeke Testament is advanc'd as far as ye 16th of ye Acts. I found I had highly recommended myself to him and many in the University by having been instrumental in prevailing with Mr Dodwell[c] to accept ye history lecture, wch he hath done to ye great satisfaction of ye University. Dr Mills kept me a day longer at Oxford then I designed, treated me all ye time, and brought me into ye acquaintance of soe many persons I had much adoe to get from them. Amonst others he caryed me to Dr Aldrige and Dr Hammond[d] at Christchurch, who both give you their service and testify a great honour and regard for y^r Lo^{ppe}. I went to visit ye 2 black wallnutts trees you soe much admired, but I coud see but one, and y^t a most beautifull tree. Y^e other is cut down, and I doubt y^t I saw will have ye same fate, for it is much slighted and vilified.

The B^p of St Asaph[e] his Chronology did, in ye presse, advance apace; but, as you have heard, ther is an unhappy stop put to it at present. It was printing in Latine and in English, in distinct volumes. If it pleases God he enjoyes his liberty, he will very vigorously pursue ye finishing y^t soe much desired worke.[f]

I am, my L^d,

Y^r Lo^{pps} very humble servant,

C. HATTON.

---

[a] The third volume of Robert Morison's "Plantarum Historia Universalis Oxoniensis" did not appear until 1699. The second volume was published in 1680.

[b] John Mill, D.D., of Queen's College, Principal of St. Edmund's Hall.

[c] Henry Dodwell, of Dublin, Camden Professor of History at Oxford.

[d] Henry Aldrich and John Hammond, Canons of Christ Church.

[e] Dr. William Lloyd.

[f] The work was left imperfect. His son made use of it for his "Series Chronologica Olympiadum," &c., Oxon. 1700 ; and his Chaplain, Benjamin Marshall, composed from it his Chronological Tables, Oxon. 1712-13.

The same.

Letcomb, July 3, [16]88.

I humbly thank y^r Lo^{ppe} for ye accompt of books. If Le Grand hath not got more fame by his animadversions on Burnet Hist. of ye Reformation[a] then by ye Ecclesiasticall History he hath publish'd, he had much better have fixed himself to his study of philosophy.[b] It is more then a fortnight since I sent up to London, by ye Letcomb carier, a parcel directed for y^r Lo^{pp}; but I feare it hath miscaried, for I cannot hear anything from my house of ye receipt thereof. In it wase some seeds I received from Bobart at Oxford, Mabillon his Museum, and Dr. Bernard de Mensuris et Ponderibus antiquis, who wth great earnestness invited me to his chamber at Oxford, received me wth great civility, wou'd have presented me with what he had publish'd on Josephus,[c] but unfortunately ye keeper of ye Theater, where they are layd up, wase not to be found. It wou'd have been a very acceptable present to me, for it is never like to be published; and, tho' it be imperfect, I am assured, not only from his fame but from competent judges who have perused it, that ther are several very excellent discourses in his animadver-

---

[a] " Histoire du Divorce de Henry VIII, et de Catherine d'Arragon ; avec la Défense de Sandérus, la Refutation des deux premiers Livres de l'Histoire de la Réformation de Burnet, et les Preuves," by Joachim Le Grand.　Three vols.　Paris, 1688, 12mo.

[b] He here confounds Joachim with Anthony Le Grand.

[c] " Lectiones variantes et Annotationes in quinque priores libros Antiquitatum Judaicarum."　Oxford, 1686.　Wood adds : " His notes upon those Books were too large and therefore disliked by Dr. John Fell, and the author, being weary of the work, did goe no farther than his Notes on the first five Books, which caused an old Theologist and Pretender to poetry [Clement Barksdale] to sing in his doggrel rhimes—

'　Savilian Bernard's a right learned man ;
　　Josephus he will finish when he can.' "

sions, wch he made soe large, that it wou'd have been soe long
before ye worke had been finish'd, that Dr Fel, B^p of Oxford, chose
to break of ye worke rather then have it soe voluminous [as] it
wou'd have been, had Dr Bernard gonne on in ye like method. The
like fate hath attended what Dr Aldridge had undertaken on y^e
same author.[a] I hope shortly to send you a specimen of ye B^p of
St. Asaph his Chronology, in wch he is soe exact and inserts soe
many things (wch tho in truth seem digressions, yet are very
curious, usefull, and instructive), that it will be long before ye worke
be finish'd. I hope shortly to waite on his Lo^ppe, and shall freely
deliver him my sentiments: That it was highly to be wish'd he
wou'd first finish his Chronol[og]y, and after, by way of appendix
or as addenda, add those discourses; for his Lo^ppe doth only finish
as he prints. Y^e original copy is in short hand, and ye discourses
soe brief, shoud he dy before it wase finish'd, it wou'd be impossible
for any one to proceed according to his designe. But, if his Lo^pp
had finish'd his General Chronology, he might, wou'd health and
oportunity permit, in an appendix enlarge on several discourses.
The actions of Hercules and Theseus take up a whole sheet. Shou'd
he as much enlarge on those of other men of renown, what a
voluminous worke must be expected, and who cou'd hope to live to
see it finish'd? I hope shortly to send you a specimen. In y^e
interim I have sent you ye last cast of Dr Mills his Gr[eek]
Test[ament], that you may see how far it will exceed all others
hitherto printed, and wth what liberty he criticizes; w^ch, tho it may
offend ye bigots, will not I suppose ye Pere Simon. Dr. Bernard,
in his preface in his De Ponderibus, wch I sent you, hints a design
to publish a Chronology,[b] which he shew'd me, and I heartily wish
he wou'd speedily commit it to ye press; for he, having been more

[a] Aldrich's edition of the first and part of the second book of the Bellum Judaicum
was published with Bernard's annotations on the Antiquities in 1687.

[b] This appears to be the "Chronicon omnis Ævi," left in MS., as noticed by
Wood.

conversant in orientall and astronomicall authors, hath inserted many very remarkeable things, of wch ye B^p of St. Asaph coud have no cognisance. But ye D^r designs to publish first a calendarium of all ye oriental and western nations, wch will be a very curious and usefull worke for elucidation, not only of his own, but of all other chronologyes. He hath allsoe in a sheet (wch he designes to be forthwth engraven) compared ye alphabets of all nations,[a] and hath composed a learned discourse of ye original of letters, and shewes how every nation hath borrowed from ye first letters invented, wth several very curious and learned discourses thereon. I am,

My L^d,

Yr truly affect Brother and very humble servant,

C. HATTON.

THE SAME.

Campe, July 4, [16]88.

I know, my L^d, it will not be unwelcome news to you to heare y^t my L^d B^{ppe} of London designes you a visit; and I suppose it may be satisfactory to you to know ye day when, wch is ye occasion of my giving you this trouble.

Next Monday ye B^{ppe} sets forwards for Ashby and designes to be at Kirby, wth Sr Hugh Chomley,[b] y^t day sennight, and from thence to goe to my Ld Gainesboroughs.

I will give y^r Lo^{ppe} an account of some plants wch I know will be very acceptable to you, of wch my L^d hath severall. Oakes from Virginia, wth chessnut leaves. Wallnutts from thenc bearing

[a] " Orbis eruditi Literatura, a charactere Samaritico deducta :" a copperplate engraving.

[b] Sir Hugh Cholmeley, of Whitby, Bart.

flowers. The larix or larch-tree. Breyennius his Leonurus, a most beautifull plant. The Quina-quina, or Jesuits barke. A bastard kind therof from Virginia. I cou'd name severall other plants, but wthout a stove you cannot keepe them, and, if you desire very curious plants, you must have a stove, and I wish you wou'd have a discourse [with] my L$_d$ B^{pp} as to y^e making, ordering, and advantage of one.

This yeare my Ld Mordant's tulip tree flowered. My L^d B^{ppe} justly complained of y^e stupidness of his gardener, who never gave notice to eny curious personns y^t it was in flower. It wase a flower lik a tulippe, but hung down like a Martagon. It is said to be a most beautifull flower.

I have sent you some more seeds of ye large Nasturtium Indicum wth a scarlet flower, said to be vivace, because, if sown now, it will continue all winter, and you may propigate it by slipps. This hath soe disparag'd ye other, ye neglect of it will in a few yeares make it grow scarce. I am

Y^r Lo^{pps}, my sister's, nephew and neice

most humble servant,

C. HATTON.

THE SAME.

London, July 21, [16]88.

I came hither, my Lord, late last Thursday night, by my collonells order, to lay out very unnecessarily 40 or 50^{ll} to buy gaudy cloths, in wch I shall not appeare above 2 or thrice this campe, wch I am assured at ye Office of Warre will not last above a fortnight longer at furthest.

Our collonel [a] is gone by order to the cabinet councell, where it is thought ye speedy proclamation for a parl^t in Novemb^r will be debated, and it is thought will ye next weeke be issued out.

*   *   *   *   *

Y^r Lo^{pps} most truly affect Brother,

C. HATTON.

THE SAME.

July 28, [16]88.

*   *   *   *   *

Last Tuesday ye King and Queen went for Windsor; the Prince of Wales to Richmond yesterday. Ther is a small campe ther form'd of 6 companies of ye Foot Guard, and 2 troops of dragoons.

Last Wednesday his Mat^y came to ye campe, and, after we had march'd and his Mat^y wase seeing ye line fire, one Cob,[b] ye Parson of Wollaston in Northamptonshire, about 60 yeares of age, being a horse back but very drunke, did very disorderly press to have spoke [to the] King, wch his Ma^{ty} perceiving, he asked what he wou'd have. He replyed he wase a minister of ye Ch. of Engl^d; and, hastily endeavouring to light of his horse, he fell and put out his ankle. Ye King sent presently for a chirurgeon, and caus'd it to be set in his presence, and ordered ye parson to be caryed to ye hospital; but he chose to goe to Twitnam. Doth y^r Lo^{ppe} know this parson? And of what reputation is he?

This day ye King and Queen were at ye campe. Y^e army wase drawn out into a hollow square and fired 3 times.

---

[a] Theophilus Hastings, Earl of Huntingdon.
[b] Edward Cobbe, Vicar of Wollaston.

Our collonel is much offended y^t y^r Lo^{ppe} hath not appeared at ye head of y^r grenadiers.

It is confidently reported ye B^p of Chester is soudainly to be Arch^{bp} of Yorke,^{a} ye Deane of Chester^b B^p of Chester, and one Hall,^{c} a London minister, who read ye Declaration, B^p of Oxford.

This day sennight ye Duke of Ormond, finding himself very faint, went out in his coach to take ye aire; but, his faintness continuing, he said y^t day 4 yeares his Duches dyed, and he shou'd dy y^t day, wch he did. Y^e University of Oxford, by ye care of Dr. Hough, who wase with ye Duke when he dyed, had notice ye next day, and on Monday morning, very early, met to choose a chancelor. The Ld Clarendon, Ld Halifax, and Duke of Ormond, were all nominated; but ye Duke of Ormond ^{d} by plurality of votes wase elected, about 8 of ye clocke in ye morning. About eleven an inhibition came from his Ma^{ty}, that they shou'd not soudainly meet to choose a chancelor, and, when they did, to recommend ye Ld Chancelor to be their chancelor; but ye election wase over. What will be ye issue is uncertaine

I am y^r Lo^{pps} and my sisters very humble servant,

C. HATTON.

THE SAME.

London, Augt 9th, [16]88.

Yesterday ye right wing, my Lord, discamp'd, and this day wee in ye left; but tho my collonel obliged me to goe some part of ye way wth our regiment (whose winter quarters are at Plimouth), yet

^{a} Thomas Lamplugh, Bishop of Exeter, who, it will be remembered, hurried up to Court with the news of the Prince of Orange's advance on his city, was then translated to York.

^{b} John Arderne, who died in 1691.

^{c} Timothy Hall, who read the Declaration in St. Matthew's, Friday Street. He was consecrated Bishop of Oxford on the 7th October.

^{d} James Butler, grandson of the old Duke.

he wase soe favourable as to give me leave to be absent for some months. 10 companyes are to be quartered at Plymouth and one at Pendennis; whither it will be y^r Lo^{pps} I cannot tell, for our collonell wase offended to be asked wch it shou'd be.

  *   *   *   *   *

As for Mabillon, truly I turned down noe leaves but sent it just as I bought it. I thinke him ye most ingenious monke I have met wth. He is exspected shortly in England, where among our learned men he will meet wth a favourable reception.

   *   *   *

I am, my L^d,
Y^r truly affect Brother and most humble servant
C. HATTON.

THE SAME.

Augt 24, 1688.

I must and doe, my L^d, returne you my most humble thanks for ye buck I received yesterday, wch wase very well killed and carefully brought up and came very seasonably, for wee are all posting out of town, his Ma^{ty} having given command to all officers to returne to their post; wch is supposed to be a peice of Mr Braithwait's ^{a} pollicy, to get fees for license to be absent, for ye rumour of ye Dutch invasion is generally ridiccul'd.

I am very sorry y^r Lo^{pps} spleene gives you soe just a reason to move for leave to be from y^r command. I have to all virtuosoes of plants shewn y^r leaves you was pleased to send me of y^r broad leaf'd elme, and they are very much surprised. Sr Robert Clayton will bee a petitioner to y^r Lo^{ppe} for some grafts.

  *   *   *   *   *

Y^r Lo^{pps} most truly affect Brother and humble servant,
C. HATTON.

   ^{a} *i.e.*, Secretary Blathwayt.

THE SAME.

Sept[br] 6, 1688.

I am told, my L[d], y[t] frequent councills of warre are now held at Windsor, and y[t] y[e] leave for any governour to be now absent from his command is moved ther to his Ma[ty], and usually y[e] motion seconded by those who are freinds to y[e] person who desires leave. My L[d] Dartmouth hath lately been frequently at Windsor, and it is reported he will command y[e] fleet to be put out, as admirall. Some say S[r] Robt Homes stands in competition wth him.

*   *   *   *   *

I am, y[r] Lo[pps] very humble servant,

C. HATTON.

SIR CHARLES LYTTELTON.

MY LORD,   At Rochester, Thursday, two a clock, Sep[br] 20th, 1688.

I have y[rs] of y[e] 15th, and am glad y[e] tobacco is so well approved and of so much use to y[r] L[p].

The King came hither yesterday, and so down the river of Med way to see y[e] new fortifications and to Shernesse; was pleased to comand me to follow him to Chatham this morning, having not y[e] time to give our orders concerning the placing and remove of some officers in my reg[mt] upon y[e] death of Capt. Plowden;[a] but he was in y[e] same hurry to-day, and s[d] he w[d] send me word. So I have had a very ill journy to no purposse, but to heare all the news, that is, y[e] Duch have most certainly put on board theyr fleet all materialls for landing, as wheelbarros, shovells, &c., sadles and

[a] Edmund Plowden.

bridles; and the King does really expect to heare they are landed upon some part of his dominions the next faire wind. He resolves to draw all his land forces together ab^t London.

To morrow my Ld Feversham tells me will be a declaration out, w^{ch}, 'tis hoped, will give greate sattisfaction as to gov^{m}t and religion. Coll: Hen. Sidney, who asked leave, when he went, to goe to ye Spaw, was forbid to see ye P. of Orange, and promised he w^d not, is now wth him.

The French have besieged Phillipsburgh, and Mr Schombergh is wth 16000 men in Cologne.

The K^g lookes and is very well; so is ye P. of Wales.

WILLIAM LONGUEVILLE.

My L^d 29 Sept^r, 1688.

I wish in so dolefull a case as our countrey now seemes to bee in, that I knew any thing worth writing or of a reviving sort; but so it is (my L^d), the forrein invaders will probably bee landed this next weeke, if not at ye first of it. His Mat^y had 6 Bps. to him yesterday morning, and one of them sayd: omnia benè, as I am told.[a] Too day hath produced a declaracion why ye parliament writts are recalled, and a pardon also as I heare. Ld Lovelace is in England, and was at Wickham election of a mayor a day or two since. Whither Ld Shrewsbury bee wth ye Prince of O. or heere is in uncertain report. And so for other lords. 'Tis s^d the K^g will not delay

------

[a] Clarendon notices this in his *Diary*. The King received the Bishops graciously, but spoke only in general terms. " As the Bishops came from the King, several people in the rooms, as they passed, asked them how things went ? The Bishop of Winton (poor man !) answered ' Omnia bene.' "

when he heares where the landing is. I wish your Lop. much health, and a quiet world to us all in God's good time. My service humbly presented to my Lady and to Mrs Hatton, I subscribe, wth some hast,

My L^d, Your Lops. most obedient

W^M. L.

Sir Charles Lyttelton.

My Lord,   Sheernesse, October 2^d, [16]88.

I hope you are not in Holland, tho' I hant had ye honor to heare from you a greate while, and that there is so much news from thence. The wind is faire to day to bring y^m for England, if they be so resolved, wch it has not bine before a good while. We have abundance of materialls sent hither, and there are at least 40 carpenters to ab^t a hundred laborers at work to put this place in a better defence. All ye platformes allready repaired. Here is come into ye harbor, w^thin 2 days, 7 fireships, where they are to stay for further orders. I had a letter yesterday from a capt^n in ye Downes, that ye fleet was coming to ye Nore; so I hope we are safe here, but I think this countrey or place is suspected to be attempted, because there is lately two regim^ts more come to Rochester. I thank God, I have kept free of ye ague yet, but I have a terrible cold; and every day our people fall down of agues. I have 200 commanded men in constant guarrison of Coll: Hales^a regim^t, and an order to send for ye rest of ye reg^mt upon ye sight of a forraine fleet. They lye at Canterbury and Sittingburn, but there are 100 of y^m commanded away lately, to releeve so many of my regi^mt who were at Landguard Fort; my

---

^a Sir Edward Hales.

reg^mt being commanded to London from Yarmouth. In easterly winds I am ever troubled wth ye hand I write wth a cramp, wch puts me to so much paine I can scarce hold my pen at present.

CHARLES HATTON.

London, October 6, [16]88.

Being, my L^d, by his M^{aties} late proclamation convinced that ye Prince of Orange design'd an invasion, I hastened hither in order to goe to my command and now only stay to attend on my collonell, who, upon ye first change of wind, designes for Plymouth, from whenc wee exspect our regiment will soudainly he commanded to joyn ye rest of ye army. I wase yesterday at Kinginston, wher I found my L^d and Lady Nottingham very well, but wase much sorry to heare ther that y^r old distemper still torments y^r Lo^{ppe}.

*   *   *   *   *

Last Thursday ye Ld Chanchelor went into ye city to cary an instrument under ye great seale, wherby ye city wase restored to their antient charters and priviledges, and Sr Will. Pritchard, in whose maiorallity ye charter wase seized, constituted Maior; but he made some objections to ye instrument and refused to act. This day my Lord Chancelor hath caryed a new instrument, wherby Sr John Chapman is constituted Maior and ye charter restored, wch is accepted, and Sr John sworne Maior; at wch ther is much rejoycing in ye city, and ye greater at ye assured news y^t last night at Councill ye Ecclesiasticall Commission wase superseeded and annull[ed]. I am y^r Lo^{pps}, my sisters, nephews, and neices most faithfull and very humble servant,

C. HATTON.

WILLIAM LONGUEVILLE.

My L^d,   October [9th], 1688.

At such a season as this I hold myself bound to give your Lop.
2 letters for one. Last post I sent your Lop. account where 1000^l
might bee had, and that if you came up I thought the better. The
wind keeping westward, the Dutch fleete is not arrived, as farr as
I can heare. Yesterday our King had the B^{ps} with him againe, and
told them of this invasion again and how little concerned his people
seemed. He declared Magdalen Colledge should bee restored by
the B^p of Winton, the visitor; that a fast should bee held; and
that praiers for ye occasion should bee penned and presently used.
Mr Godwin Wharton is layd in ye Tower, but for what indeed I
have not yet heard.[a] Some report goes as if 16 comissions were
taken with one ——; I forgett the man's name. I heare there
was a disturbance in Lime street last Sonday, and ye mayor was
feigne to quiet the same. The friery by the arch in Lincolns-Inn
Fields also hath been ill treated. L^d lieutenants of ye Romish profession begin to be removed, for that none care to act under them.
I wish your Lop. good health and quiet into your family, being,
My L^d,

Your Lops. most obedient servant,

WM. L.

[a] " Goodwin Wharton, esq., the son to the lord Wharton, is accused for viewing
the fortifications at Dartmouth and sent to the Tower."—Luttrell's *Diary*, 7 Oct.
1688.

CHARLES HATTON.

October 16, [16]88.

—

Here hath been a report that ye Dutch have by ye late storms received great prejudice in their fleet; but y^t report is now quash'd, and they are daily exspected wth a very great force. I trust ye nation in generall will behave themselves wth loyalty to their prince and regard to their country y^t ye Dutch in 1688 will succeed noe better then ye Spaniards did in 1588. As to my own particular, I shall endeavour to act according to those principles of loyalty in wch I have been educated, and to wch I am obliged both by my religion and allegiance, and submit myself to w^tever state Providence de-signes. But, whilst I have breath, I shall ever deport myself to y^r Lo^{ppe}, my sister Hatton, and yours, wth all true affection befitting

Y^r very humble servant

C. HATTON.

THE SAME.

Plymouth, Oct^{br} 30, [16]88.

*   *   *

We are here, as in all other parts of Engl^d, in daily exspectation to heare y^t ye Dutch are landed, ye wind being now S.E. As soon as they are, we exspect to bee commanded from hence.

Some few dayes since a French pickaroon in a small barke wth only 2 gunns lay off here at sea, out of command, sent ashore severall times. At last in ye night time manned out 2 boates wth 15 men each and clapp'd aboard on each side a Duch vessell of 300 tunn,

30 men, 20 gunns; and kill'd all or most of ye men who endeavour'd to make opposition, and cary'd ye vessell clear away out of ye harbour here. She wase bound homewards from Brasill, her lading valewd at 25000^{li}. She had cleered here 2 dayes before, and therefore ye gunners of St Nicolas Island excuse their not attempting to stopp her as she pass'd by y^t island.

I am y^r Lo^{pps}, my sisters, and y^r familyes
most faithfull and very humble servant,

C. HATTON.

THOMAS TRAMALLIER TO JOHN STRETEHAY.[a]

SIR, Jesus College, Nov^{ber} 1st, [16]88.

It is now about a twelvemonth that I writ to my Lord an account of the visitation at Magdalen College, and the ejection of that Society. I suppose his Lordship will not be displeased to hear of their restauration; and therefore, if you thinck it fitt, I shall desire you to read this to him.

On Saturday last was sennight the Bishop of Winchester, as being Visitor of the College, in pursuance of an order from the King forthwith to resettle the Society of Magdalen College, came hither. He was attended into the town by above three hundred persons on horseback, most of them scholars, and six or seven coaches full of noblemen and doctors. The solemnity was to be performed [the day] following; but, to our great amazement, his Lop. was gone on Sunday morning. It seems there came a messenger from Court to summon him to the Council, to be present at the business of the Prince of Wales, as it appeared afterwards. But on the Wednens-

a Lord Hatton's secretary.

day in that week he came again; and the day following, after morning prayer in the chapel and a speech made to him by one of the
doctors of the house, producing the King's letters, he compleated
the resettlement.   Things were put in statu quo, only Mr Charnock
was left out; and thus by the providence of God, and upon a revolution of affairs, that honest and stout society, which was designed
to be the præludium of further attempts, was restaur'd within the
compass of about a year to its full rights and property, having first
seen that illegal anti-Church of England court, by which they had
sufferr'd, fully dissolv'd.

The Bishop went for London, being to attend his Majesty to the
field.   Mr. Walker,[a] it is sayd, is going to resigne up his headship
of University; his disciple, we hope, will follow his steps herein
likewise at Christ Church.[b]   If my Lord goes to the Island this
winter, as Mr Bonamy tells me, and takes Oxford in his way, I
hope I shall have the happiness to see you here.   God preserve his
Lordship and family in these times of great uncertainty and danger.
I am, with great truth,

Sir, your most humble faithfull servant,

THOMAS TRAMALLIER.

SIR CHARLES LYTTELTON.

MY LORD,   Shereness, November 6th, [16]88.

The Duch passed by wth theyr fleet through ye Dover roade westward on Friday even, and, 'tis supposed, went to Portsmouth; of
wch youle heare as soone as we.   My Ld Dart[mouth], as soone as
he c^d get up his anchors, w^{ch}, I beleeve, was not till Sunday, plyd
after y^m.   Yesterday was so dead a calm, he c^d make no way; so is

---

a Obadiah Walker. He was deprived in 1689.
b John Massey, the Dean.

to day, and so thick a fog wthall he cant stirr. One of their fly-boates wth 200 of ye K^{gs} subjects and all theyr officers fell into one of ye K^{gs} frigots way, having lost her rudder in ye storm, and are all prisoners. All the forces in this country are marchd away except that part of Hales regimt. wch are heere, being 200, and 100 more at Landguard Fort; and those are marchd to Rochester. My Lord, I cant tell how to advise myself, if I sh^d presse to be sent for away to march after my regim^t. Loath I am to be out of the ocasion where the King, my friends, and my all are at stake; but this place is a post of greate concern and in my trust; and, if any thing sh^d fall out contrary to expectation, may be imputed to me. I have really no vanity, but w^d doe ^{Wht} I think may he most usefull; and, tho' I doe not think, now they are past by us, this is like to be ye scene of ye war, yet ^{Wht} secret practisses may be I can't foresee. Good my Lord, give mee free advise in this matter, and tell me how you resolve in y^r own station.

WILLIAM LONGUEVILLE.

My Lord, 13 Nov^r, 1688.

*   *   *   *

The Prince of Orange, being at Exeter, hath made much marching hence for Salisbury plaine, whither our King is hastning, and by Monday will bee setting hence they say. The mobile^a has been very turbulent hereabouts, and, after sundry appearances against ye popish chappels of Budg-Row and Lime Streete, they have been last Sunday furiously bent for ye destroying that in ye late house of Earle Berkely, and [with] much adoe were beat off, when they

---

^a The shortened word "mob" did not make its way very readily. Burnet uses it in his History, i. 378, and provokes a sneer from Swift: "A word of dignity for an historian!"

had shewed their discontent; but yesternight, as part of ye goods were removing from thence, the said mobile tooke ye cart and goods and burnt all in Holborne or some other place. Some were hurt and, as 'tis sayd, killed on that commocion. Lieutenant-Gen^{ll} Worden[a] is to bee here wth some 5 or 6000 men, to keepe all quiett if he cann. I have been busyed in my chamber all day, so have no more news.

I am, My L^d,

Your Lops. most obedient servant,

WILLIAM LONGUEVILLE.

SIR CHARLES LYTTELTON.

MY LORD,   Shereness, No^{br} 15, [16]88.

I had a letter this post from Ld Middleton. He tells me his M^{atie} is pleased to make me eldest Brigadeer of Foot, tho' he thinkes it for his service I sh^d continue here. I have y^r L^{ps} of ye 10th, and am heartily sorry you continue to have y^r health so ill, wch I doubt not (too) is ye more trouble at this time you can't be so able to serve the King. Poore Harry[b] is marcht wt^h the army. My regim^t

---

[a] Robert Werden.

[b] Poor Harry went off to the Prince of Orange. Nash in his *History of Worces tershire*, i. 501, prints the following interesting letter from Lyttelton to his wife :—

"I had yours last night. I told the king I could not see his majestie without some confusion that so much of my blood had forfeited his duty in my son's defection, which he was pleased very graciously to return : 'he could not wonder that my son had done so since his own children were so disobedient.' But I should have told you that I said withall as he went without my leave, so he should never have my blessing till he had returned to his duty : and the king was pleased to say, he was satisfied : I was not, he knew, in fault, and told Sir John Talbot to that purpose afterwards. I was with the king last night at his couchee, and he told us my lord Churchill waited four hours after he came to the prince of Orange's quarters before he was admitted to see him, and then had no quarters assigned him, so was faine to go five or six miles off to get any. Indeed they say there is very little regard to those that are gone, and the prince pays nobody a penny but those he brought with him, and those have been stays to keep guard at St James's, and there will be a considerable force left in ye town of ye new raisd men; and I am told ye K^g will be at ye head of 30000 good troopes, ^{Wch} I pray God give him good success wth, and send us a happy meeting. I have some buisness will necessarily require my getting leave, if it may be, to come to London, but for a few days; and, if I thought y^r L^p w^d be there, I w^d contrive not to ask it before.

THE EARL OF NOTTINGHAM.[a]

Nov. 15, [16]88.

I have rec^d y^{rs} by the bearer of this, and should have oftener writt to you had it bin convenient to send letters by ye post, or that I had any thing to impart to you y^t was necessary for you to know, in wch case I would have sent a messenger on purpose, as I shall doe hereafter, in case you do not think fitt to come to town, wch I should

raised by his commission, so that I believe our spark will grow quickly weary of his adventure. Till the trumpet comes back we can tell nothing what to think of the treaty the lords were gone upon : the trumpet went to demand their passe. Here is come an address last night from the fleet, brought by lord Berkley and captain Leighton, signed by lord Dartmouth and every captain, to thank the king for calling a parliament, as the only expedient to preserve his majesty, the peace of the kingdom, and the protestant religion, which they resolve to defend I think with their blood. Sir Roger Strickland's hand is to it. The poor king is mightily broken. A great heart can't so easily bend. I don't know yet if I shall be commanded to stay here or goe back. I hope tomorrow though to come and dine with you. I have not time to say more, and the room is full of officers ; so, dear, good morrow.

"CHARLES LYTTELTON."

[a] Nottingham's letters at this crisis will be read with interest ; and particularly those portions of them which refer to his own action. He is very cautious in the means he takes to prevent identification in case his letters should fall into wrong hands. Besides to some extent disguising his hand and omitting his signature, he uses a common seal and false addresses. The present letter is directed to " Mr. Francis Greene, at Uppingham."

be glad you would resolve to doe; for, tho we doe not yet hear of any disturbances in y[e] North, yet I can't imagine y[t] y[e] P. of O. would not think it very usefull, if not necessary, to his designes to give such a diversion; and, since he did not goe thither himselfe, as was thought he at first intended, tis probable he will not leave those gentlemen destitute of a support to y[m]selves or uselesse to him; and, if there be any creditt to be given to them y[t] saild w[th] his fleet and affirme it consisted of near 800 sail, w[ch] agrees also w[th] y[e] Dutch prints, tis certain there did not goe above 500. to y[e] west, and consequently y[e] rest must be gone northw[d]; and then you will be in y[e] road.   Besides, there daily happen severall things in w[ch] y[r] friends would be glad of y[r] company to consider and advise wth you; and tho I must acknowledge I cant think London a very safe place, because y[e] prentices doe daily comitt disorders in great numbers, and doe threten even y[e] great chappell, for w[ch] reason tis said y[e] King deferrd his journey till after Q. Eliz[abeth's] birthday, yet you have a friends house so near London, where I am sure you will be welcome, y[t] you may have all y[e] opportunities of doing any businesse there, and yet be out of y[e] very noise as well as dangers of any such tumult; and if y[e] King should not goe from London, yet y[r] want of health is not onely a good occasion for you to come hither, but does also answer many other objections ag[t] y[r] coming to town.

This day news is brought to y[e] King that 3 entire regiments are gone over to y[e] P[r] of Orange. S[r] Francis Compton and his regiment of horse, w[ch] was y[e] Earl of Oxford's, Langston's[a] regiment of horse w[ch] was y[e] Earl of Plimouths, and my L[d] Cornbury wth his regiment of dragoons.   Onely one Clifford,[b] a papist officer in my L[d] Cornburys, stays behind; but y[e] men are all gone wth my Lord; and Major Littleton[c] and one officer more in S[r] Fra. Comptons regiment refusd to goe, but are carried away wth y[m] as prisoners.   Thus far is

---

[a] Colonel Thomas Langston.   [b] Major Robert Clifford.
[c] Major Walter Lyttelton.

certain; but tis said also y^t 2 companies of Sr John Laneres regiment are gone also, and tis expected y^t ye foot, when they are advanced far enough to have an opportunity, will follow this example; some, entire regiments, but many, companyes. This news has putt ye King into great disorder, insomuch y^t he did not dine publickly as he usd to doe, and tis uncertain whether he will hold his resolution of going to ye army at Salisbury on Monday; for there are arguments on both sides. If he does not goe, there will want his presence, wch is thought ye best means of restraining ye army from deserting; and yet, if he should goe, his person may be in great danger by mutinies or worse; and tis said also y^t ye Prince of Or. is upon his march wth his whole army towards London, wch is greatly encreasd by a multitude of comon people, tho I do not hear y^t many gentlemen of y^t country are gone in to him.

Y^e news-book tells you of ye taking of my Ld Lovelace,[a] but 50 of his company escapd and are gone to ye Pr. of Or.; and I hear there are about 25 of ye English and Scotch nobility wth him, among wch tis thought my Ld Devonshire[b] is one, and tis said this day y^t my Ld Abingdon[c] is gone to him too, and I am apt to believe y^t both these Lords are wth him.

The B^p of Exeter is come to London, and went this morning to ye King, who has made him Arbhb^p of York, and removd Trelawny from Bristol to Exeter. I fancy Trelawny will not accept it at this time, and, tho ye other did that of York after some importunity, yet I guesse he will repent and refuse it.

You may have heard perhaps of a design of ye Lords about ye town to present a petition to ye King. There was indeed a short petition framd and agreed upon by ye Ld Halifax, E. of Nott., L^d

[a] John, Lord Lovelace; made prisoner at Cirencester in an attempt to force his way to join the Prince of Orange.

[b] William Cavendish, Earl of Devonshire, was engaged in aiding the northern insurrection at Derby.

[c] James Bertie, Earl of Abingdon, the first peer who joined the Prince of Orange's camp.

Weym[outh],[a] B[ps] of S[t] Asaph and Peterb.[b], and, after that, shewd to severall Lords, most whereof did approve it. But my L[d] Clarendon made some objections, not very materiall, much less deserving y[e] weight he laid upon y[m]. Y[e] design of y[e] petition (after a short preamble relating to y[e] present conjunction, w[th]out naming y[e] Pr. of Or., and a recitall of y[e] Kings declarations in w[ch] he said he would call a parl[t]) was to pray y[e] King to call a parl[t] forthw[th], free in all respects, both of coming, sitting, and debate, it being better and easier to prevent a disease then to cure it; and this was intended to have bin signd onely by such L[ds] and B[ps] as had not made y[m]selves obnoxious by any late miscarriages. This excluded, among others, y[e] E. of Rochester, and was apprehended by y[e] E. of Clarendon and some of y[e] B[ps] as a pique of L[d] Halifax to L[d] Roch[r]; and tho I believe there is unkindnesse enough between these 2 Lords, yet y[e] reason of y[e] present distinction at this time is sufficient to justify y[e] L[d] Halifax; for twould have given just cause of suspicion to y[e] Pr. of Or. Y[t] it had bin a trick of y[e] Court, when he saw it to be effect of such men's applications, ag[t] whose actions at least, if not their persons, he had publisht his owne declaration. The countrey also, who were hopd and expected to follow this example, would rather have suspected then imitated such authors; for tis hard to perswade y[e] people they would petition for redresse of their owne acts, and much lesse for y[e] punishment of them. Much more might be added, but the summe of all is that tis quasht; for, tho y[e] B[ps] and E. of Clarendon and Roch[r] are framing another petition, yet I believe the Lords Halifax, Kent, Pembroke, Nottingham, Weymouth, Newport, Faulconbridge, Carlisle, Pagett, &c. will not signe it, and perhaps some of y[m] will not now signe even y[e] first, no, not altho' y[e] L[ds] ag[t] whom exceptions were taken were excluded from signing; for, tho such a petition might have bin of great use to y[e] publick at first, yet now it has taken air and is blown upon, and perhaps in y[e]

---

[a] Thomas Thynne, Viscount Weymouth.
[b] William Lloyd and Thomas White.

present circumstances is wisht for even by ye Court, and tho every man would serve ye King in just and honest things and wayes, yet, since ye news of this revolt of ye army, tis rather a shame then a credit to ye Lords to addresse now, as if they had not dar'd to doe any thing for ye publick as long as ye case was more doubtfull. But to joyn wth ye other Lords might be construed an obstruction to y^t reformation wch is necessary to establish ye peace of ye kingdome; and whether these L^ds and B^ps will proceed w^thout ye rest is uncertain. I should rather think they will not.^a But of this you shall have an acct by ye post, for I doe not foresee any thing y^t will be a sufficient cause to detain the bearer hereof, nor does any thing more occur to me at present.

I àm

Y^r most humble servant.

THE SAME.^b

MY LORD,   Nov. 20, [16]88.

The peticion of ye Lords was deliverd w^thout ye concurrence of the others for reasons y^t I writt in my last. Tis in print and [I] shall therefore say no more of it, only y^t ye King in answer told y^m y^t ye B^ps had better pray and preach for him, and ye temperal Lords appear wth swords in their hands then petition.

Tis said ye Admiral Herbert has met wth 15 French ships of warr; destroyed nine. Three escaped, and 3 more come into Pli-

---

^a Macaulay has taken his account of this petition from Clarendon's Diary, from which it appears that nineteen signatures were procured. The present letter is valuable as giving Halifax's view of the matter, for Nottingham evidently only repeats Halifax's reasoning.

^b Addressed to "Mis Alice Hatton, at Kerby."

mouth shatterd.   This has bin talke of this week, and I should not
write it now, but y^t there is a letter come from Sr John' Jacob, y^e
customer of Plimouth, y^t affirms it; wch makes it probable at least,
tho I confesse I scarcely believe it.

S^r W_m Portman,[a] Lutterell, Palmer,[b] Mallett, Seymour y^e Speaker,[c]
and others are gone to y^e Prince most certainly, and tis said y^t his
army is advanced as far as Wells; but this last is not so certain, tho
most agree y^t his army is come as far as Sherbourne.

The King returnes on Friday.   During his absence he appointed
ye Councill to meet often, and directed 5 to be of the quorum, viz.
Ld Chanc^{lr}, L^d Pr. Seal, Ld Preston, Ld Bellasis, Ld Godolphin,
and nothing to be resolvd on w^{th}out ye concurrence of 3 of y^m, nor
then neither w^{th}out ye approbation of ye Queen.

Bernard Howard[d] caind one of his officers, who drew his sword
and run him thro' ye lungs, and he died in ½ an hour.

Tis variously reported y^t Sr Fra. Compton is, and is not, come
back to Salisbury.   His nephew, Hatton, is gone wth ye troops to y^e
Prince, and I believe there may be come back between 2 and 300
men, officers, and soldiers.

But y^t is s^d is of ye most importance to y^r Lo^p is, that my L^d
Delamere came to Manchester and declard for ye P^r of Or. wth 100
horse, and y^t he was going to Nottingham to meet ye L^{ds} Devonshire,
Manchester, Scarsdale, Lumley, Latimer, &c.   Perhaps you may
have heard this already; but, if not, I think you may depend upon
it as true, at least y^t there will be an insurrection in ye North, if it
be not begun already, wch will make it necessary for y^r Lop. to
remove to ye place I mentioned in my last.

[a] Of Bryanstone, M.P. for Taunton.
[b] Francis Luttrell and Nathaniel Palmer, the Members for Minehead.
[c] He sat for Totnes.
[d] Grandson of Henry, 9th Earl of Norfolk.

SIR EDMUND KING.

MY LORD,   [20 November, 1688.]

Tis true our lot is cast in a dismall time at present; a great storme seemes to be gathering, thunder and lightening threaten'd; God knows who may be struck; every on has cause to feare, especially when we consider wee have (more or less) all too much provokt the patience of God, who has constantly vouchsaf't dayly mercies to us, and we have not made the gratefull returns as we ought to have done. It's now high time we becom seriouslie considerate, and all of us begg of Him to spare us once more, and y^t we may outlive the storm, and see a calme againe before we goe off the stage of this world. But, if God has otherways determin'd, let us retire into our closetts and begg submission to His will and a free pardon for all our neglects of duty and comission of sin, y^t we may be willing to suffer for His sake y^t lay'd downe His life for us, and y^t we may doe it chearfully, if it should be sooner than we at present expect. According to the custome and course of natur, we cannot stay long here; therefore pray God fitt us for Himselfe, and make our passage easie (if it be His will), and at last receive us into His everlasting arms of happiness, wher we shall be out of gun-shott and all manour fears to all eternitie. If ever ther was a time in our days to thinke seriously of things, it's not yet we have encouragm't from God's ' word: " Fear not him y^t can kill the body and can doe noe more, but feare Him that can destroy both soul and body," etc. Perhaps we needed to be put in fear, y^t we may kno we are but men. God's mercie is never so much minded by us as in great danger. Tho our danger is great, wt cannot omnipotence doe? Let us not dispair, but waite His time for our deliverance the way His infinite wisdome has appointed. God knows what will become of us.

Ld Delawar is at the head of a great partie of horse, and many lords are com in to him; they say they meet at Notingham to daye.

Great disturbance is sayd to be in Wales too. I hope these frightful stories will not hinder you from taking things good against the spleen, as you call it. Ld Abbington went wth Ld Cornbury, Sr Will_m Portman, Mr Lutterell, Strangwedg,^a Mallet, and many more a[re] named. The P. of O. has listed they say 6000, and cares for noe more. Moste say Ld Devonshire, Ld Lumley, Lord Chomly, Earl Exeter, Ld Latamore, L^p Exeter.

The King has a brave army, and this day at Salisbury plaine intends to call all the officers together. Bernard Hoard is said to be killed by an officer he beat at Chichester.

Pray excuse him y^t loves his King and country and prays for yor Ld^{ps} body and soul. Pray, my L^d, let us be chearfull and trust God, to whom I desire to resighn my will and intreat you doe so too. Let not the two first parts of this make you mellancholie, nor the last afraide. I tell you only reports. I never write new[s] to any body.

CHARLES HATTON.

Plymouth Cittadel, November 20, 1688.

Since ye Prince of Orange his coming to Exeter, all intercourse by letters betwixt ye officers of this garrison and their friends and relations living beyond y^t place is stop'd, all their letters, my L^d, being intercepted, constantly opened, and rarely sent hither ; and y^t wch makes it ye more vexatious is, yt since y^r last, wch wase long since writ and told mee y^t you wase still tormented wth y^t long and painefull distemper, I have heard noe news of y^r Lo^{ppe} or family, for all whom I have a due concern.

Wee have soe various and uncertaine reports from Exeter, I shall

---

^a Colonel Thomas Strangways, M.P. for Dorsetshire.

not venture to send you any other news but y^t, to our unspeakable joy and happiness, our governor, ye Earle of Bath,^{a} is here; wch having told you, I need not say ^{yt} I thinke myself more happy to be under his command here then under that of any other person on earth, for I am sure y^r Lo^{ppe} (as all worthy men who know him) hath a true honour for him, and his Lo^{ppe} often mentions you wth great kindness. Shou'd ye Dutch thinke fitt to attacque us here, we thinke ourselves very secure under his conduct; and are well assured y^t, by his care and interest in thes parts, wee shall have (whenever there is occasion) soe powerfull assistance as to enable us to make a vigorous defence.

Wee have had some deserters, and I am told it hath been reported ^{yt} I wase one; but I assure myself y^r Lo^{ppe} will never give credit to such a report; for, knowing how firmly I have imbibed ye principles of ye Church of England, you will be secure I can never depart from my allegiance to my Prince; and I hope you will likewise as firmly beleeve y^t, whilst I have breath, I shall ever retaine ye affectionate reguard to y^r Lo^{ppe}, my sister Hatton, nephew, neices, and sister Alice, befitting soe nere a relation and y^r Lo^{ppe} and their very humble servant,

C. HATTON.

WILLIAM LONGUEVILLE.

My L^d,   22 Nov^r, 1688.

*   *   *   *   *

My Ld Grey was mentioned much wthin 2 or 3 daies past to bee among ye uprisers. It is a most miserable condicion of affaires that wee now see and must awaite and feele; and who shall stand, who

---

* John Granville, first Earl of Bath.

fall, who be preserved in part, and who bee utterly ruined time only can discover.   Great estates are in the most immediate danger one would think.   The King, as 'tis writ from Salisbury, was taken a Tuesday with 3 bleedings at nose, so by advice let blood and slept all night after it.   Sarsfield, finding a party of 40 of the enemy commanded by one Cambell, fell on and killed 30 and tooke 6 prisoners.[a]   They say Speaker Scymour, Sir W[m] Portman, and Col. Lutterell are gone into the Prince of Orange.   L[d] Delamer is up in Cheshire; will meet more in Nottingham, as 'tis said.   I am with great respect,

My L[d],

Your Lops. most obedient servant,

W[M]. L.

THE SAME.

My L[d],   24 Nov[r], 1688.

This day wee have certain news that his Mat[y] and his army are upon the return hither; that York has been, by L[d] Fairfax and L[d] Dumblane &c, seized for y[e] Pr. of O.; that many of the nobles and gentlemen goe daily to him.   M[r] Seymour is left govern[r] of Exeter. S[r] Jn. Vowell[b] is newly gone to y[e] Pr. of O., and more then I care to name.   The L[ds] about Nottingham also are said to bee desirous of a free parliam[t].   So your Lop. may judge what is to be by you done, as to your coming up or staying where you are. Many heere do not like y[e] army's returne, but feare as much as any in the country.   Would your Lop. had a good doe to spare and be-

---

[a] The skirmish at Wincanton.   It will be remembered that the result was the other way.

[a] *i. e.* Powell.

stowed it on mee for a little particular purpose; not that I can enjoy at this time of doome. My most humble service to my Lady and Mrs Hatton. I take my leave as

Your Lops obedient servant,

W$_M$ L.

THE EARL OF NOTTINGHAM.

MY LORD, Sunday, Nov. 25, [16]88.

I hope y^r Lop. will pardon me the misinformations I sent you in my letter on Tuesday last; for in such a conjuncture as this, when every man is greedy of newes and talks himselfe as his interest or inclination leads him, tis not to be wonderd at y^t there be many false reports, and tis hard to distinguish y^e true; and therefore I will venture again to write you w$_t$ I hear.

Tis said y^t Plimouth is surrendred to y^e Prince, and y^t Bristol has declard for him, and y^t my L^d of Derby joins wth y^e other Lords in y^e North.

But I think I have better assurance of what follows: That our fleet is much shatterd by the late stormes. S^r Jo. Berry ^{a} is come to ye Spithead wth 3 or 4 ships wch will want considerable repairs, and says he knows not wh^t is become of ye rest; but I hear and believe y^t 7 of y^m are gone to ye Dutch.

The King has bin very ill at Salisbury, and bled much at ye nose, and has bin twice lett blond, and could have no rest but by ye help of opiates. Very few of ye gentlemen of ye country came to him, for indeed most of y^m are gone to ye P^r of Or., who is upon his march wth his whole army; and ye King has orderd his army to come back, and they are now upon their march, and he himselfe is

^{a} The admiral; distinguished himself at La Hogue.

expected on Tuesday; so y^t it looks as if London was to be y^e
stage, especially since it cannot be imagined but y^t ye army wch is
forming by ye Lords in ye North will come to London too. But,
however, I can't think Kirby a safe place for y^r Lo^{ps} family; for,
tho' tis said y^t they were to be at Northampton as last night, yet
no doubt some of y^m, particularly those of Lincolnshire and ye others
in Yorkshire who are not yet gott together, will come by Stanford;
and tho' no injury could be apprehended from a disciplind army, yet
in so great a number of men so suddenly drawn together there will
be stragglers, and y^r Lo^{ps} house is too near ye road (especially if
they goe crosse ye country to Northampton) not to be visited. So
y^t I have this to say yet for Kensington, y^t tis safer then Kirby
from ye violence of disorderly soldiers; and besides, by a speedy
removal from Kirby, you will avoid ye importunities of some whom
you would be unwilling to deny, and yet cannot grant what they
will ask; and in such difficulties tis best to prevent ye necessity of
answering.   I must confesse to y^r Lo^p y^t difficulties must be expected
here too, and I have reason to expect my share in y^m; but I hope
in God to have an honest issue out of y^m, and I shall be ye lesse
concernd whatever it is.

My Ld Danby has certainly possest himselfe of York for ye Pr. of
Orange.

Just now I hear y^t my Lord Churchill and Duke of Grafton are
gone to ye Pr. of Or. wth 6000 horse and foot, and many of ye rest
of ye English and Scotch are going too, particularly Kirk and
Trelawny.[a]

The King is in a very ill condition of health by his bleeding,
insomuch y^t he has writt to ye Queen she must expect no more
letters from him, because he can't hold down his head.

Pray lett me hear y^t you have rec^d this, and ^{wht} your resolutions
are about staying at Kirby or leaving it.

[a] Colonel Charles Trelawney, a brother of the Bishop, who, like Kirke, commanded
one of the Tangier regiments.

THE SAME.

My Lord,   Tuesday, Nov. 27, [1688].

He y^t will write news cant want matter, for he will have enought to contradict one post wt he writt by ye former.

Bristol has not declard for ye Pr. of Or., but are ready for him; for there are not ten men there y^t will oppose him.

The gentlemen of Herefordshire and Gloucestershire are in armes, and Sr Edward Harley at ye head of y^m; and ye Duke of Norfolk is so in Norfolk.

Kirk is not gone to ye Pr. of Or., but is arrested at ye head of his regiment in his march wth ye army back; but he certainly intended it, for he stayd 12 hours at Warminster before he marçhd, after he receivd orders to doe so.

My Ld Churchill and Grafton carried very few men wth y^m, and not 6000 as I writt in my last; tho y^t was ye newes y^t my Ld Middleton sent at first to ye Queen.

Prince George and ye Duke of Ormond and Ld Drumlanerick [a] are gone to ye Pr. of Or.; and yesterday morning ye Princesse of Denmark went away wth my Lady Churchill and Mrs Berkley,[b] but none know whither.

The King came in ye afternoon, and this afternoon summoned all ye L^{ds} Spirit. and Temporall about ye town to Whitehall to consult about calling a parl^t; and he has declard that he resolves to call a parl^t, and thought he should not alter it, but would consider of it, and of ye things necessary in order to it wch had bin mentioned by ye lords, viz: security for ye lords and gent[lemen] now wth ye Prince to come to it, and doing severall acts of grace to ye people.

---

[a] James Douglas, Earl of Drumlanrig, eldest son of William, Duke of Queensberry.

[b] Probably Mrs. Barbara Berkeley, who had been governess to the Princess's children.

And I believe there will some of y[e] lords be sent to y[e] Prince, to treat about it; and I am told y[t] some of y[e] Court lords did declare that y[e] King could not rely upon his army, tho y[e] King seemd yet to have confidence in its fidelity.

Tis said y[e] Pr. of Orange was on Sunday at Salisbury, and last night at Andover, where y[e] L[d] Feversham was to be wth y[e] army; and tis concluded y[t] there has bin action, or else y[t] many of y[m] are gone to y[e] Prince; but just now I hear y[t] the Prince was last night only at Sherborne.

THE COUNTESS OF NOTTINGHAM.

Tuesday, y[e] 27th Nov. [1688].

I hope, being y[r] Losp is so unwilling to remove, you will not be obliged to it, and must confess I am something of y[r] opinion y[t] where you are is a[s] safe from anny y[t] will hurt you as you can be; for, tho there should be rising northward, w[ch] there is reason enough to expect, you wont problably have anny of the Irish neer you, who I find have given every where more terrour then anny forrieng forces. The King returned last night to London. He has been much troubled wth a bleeding of y[e] nose, for w[ch] he has been twice let blood since he went. My L[d] Churchill and the Duke of Grafton and Coll. Berkeley went on Saturday to the Prince of Orange, and on Sunday the Prince of Denmarke and the Duke of Ormond. Yesterday morning the Princess went away, were is not yet knowne, wth her only my Lady Churchill and M[rs] Berkely. Yesterday my L[d] Feversham and my L[d] Dumbarton seised on Coll: Kirk, it being suspected he would goe over to the Prince. I hear to day of a great tumult at Uxbridge, were the soldiers have been a great while very insolent, and yesterday set the twone on fier in three places, w[ch] moved the inhabitants to rise to defend themselves and to quench the fier; whereupon the soldiers fell to blundering,[a] and the inhabitance have killed, they say, 30 soldiers. Y^r Losp. saying nothing how all y^r family does makes me hope they are all well.

I am y^r most obedient daughter and humble servant,

A. NOTTINGHAM.

ROGER JONES.

MY HONOURD LORD,   Nov. 28, [16]88.

My Lord[b] intended to have taken his last leave of your Lordship by a letter; but, in regard he must have communicated something of his designs, which could not be don with safety, he thought it more advisable to deny himself that satisfaction. For this reason he has left his commands with me to give your Lordship this trouble, to assure your Lordship of his unalterable resolution to retain a just and inviolable sence of your Lordship's continued kindness to him. My Lord recommends Mr Yelverton whoely to your Lordships care and direction, and begs your Lordsp. to influence him (as much as may be) in all his actions; but particularly he desires your Lordsp. to have an eye upon him dureing this unhappy warr, least his forwardness may engage him in something that may not be consistent with discretion nor his safety. I found my Lord extreamly tender and fond of him this last time, and is resolv'd (if it pleases God to

---

[a] Although before the age of "boets and bainters," Lady Nottingham occasionally confounds the *b* and *p*.

[b] Lord Grey of Ruthyn.

bless him with life) to make an honourable provision for him; so that he needs not run the hazard of any desperate attempts to make his fortune.

My Lord marcht from hence with two and twenty horses of his own well mounted, besides equipage, ^{Wch} was his coach and car ravan. My Lord Manchester had twenty horsemen well mounted, besides equipage; and Sr Robert Barton, Mr Biggs and Mr Efton in his Lordships company. At my Lord Northampton's Mr Mountague of Horton^a with his two brothers, Christopher and Charles, and other gentlemen mett them. From thence they marcht directly to Northampton, where Captain Atkins and Captain Chapman joynd them with the militia of Buckinghamshire. Sr Justinian Isham joynd them yesterday about nine, by wch time they were three hundred strong and upwards, and expected three hundred more in the afternoon. But at diner they receivd an allarum from Banbury, that on Munday night fifteen hundred of the Kings army from Salsbury were expected to quarter there that night, so that they were forct to march immediately away towards Leicester, and so forwards untill thay joyn my Lord Delameer. In Warwickshire my Lord Northampton is assured of above a thousand horsemen, as they give out privatly.

It is confidently reported Father Peters and Father Warner gave his Majesty the sacrament, and obligd him by vertue thereof to promise neither to call a parliam^t nor to accommodate. His Majesty was forct to take opium severall nights together to give him rest; wch at last so indisposed him that he was obligd to be twice blouded.

Captain Berty summond the militia of Oxfordshire by a pretended order; and accordingly they met on Saturday last with the severall gentlemen in order to joyn this county. Mr Attkins and Chapman pretended to an order from my Lord Chancellor to call the Bucks militia, wch took effect. Mr Palmer of Ecckon is to be

---

^a Edward Montague, of Horton, the father of George, second Earl of Halifax.

interrd to night. That your Lordship and good Lady and all your Lordships hon^ble family may be blessed with all ye blessings of Heaven and earth is the constant prayer of,

My honord Lord,
Your Lordship's most obliged and
humble servant,

ROG. JONES.

THE EARL OF NOTTINGHAM.

MY LORD, [1st December, 1688.]

Pardon me for not writing ye 2 last posts, and for writing so little as I have time to doe now.

The King has appointed ye Lords Halifax, Nottingham, and Godolphin to goe to ye Pr[ince] of O[range], to acquaint him wth his Ma^tys calling of a parl^t, and to adjust ye freedom of it. They are to sett out tomorrow morning.

My Ld Clarendon is gone from hence this morning to ye Prince of Orange, and t'is said w^thout any order from ye King; so that he designes to remaine wth him. He had a great mind to have bin one of ye commissioners, a place wch I doe not hear any of ye 3 Lords desird, but purely obeyd ye King; for, in all probability, this will have no effect, ye affaires of ye Prince being such as will admitt little delay, especially since ye King of France's troops have already advanced to Boisleduc and burnt 12 villages thereabouts.

My Ld Huntingdon is made prisoner at Plimouth by ye E. of Bath, who has declared for ye Prince of Or[ange], and all ye officers of ye Ld Hunt[ingdon]'s regiment except Capt. Hatton.

Mr Griffin^a is made Baron Griffin of Dingley.

---

^a Edward Griffin, created Baron Griffin of Braybroke Castle, co. Northampton.

WILLIAM LONGUEVILLE.

My L[d],   1st of December, 1688.

        *   ⁃   *

Wee are here quiett and have no terrible news at all, save that
such (who are few I doubt) think sadly for his M[aties] sake, and, if
they know not how to doe good, take care to doe no hurt. L[d] Delamere is at Worcester by last night's letters. S[r] Nicholas Butler[a]
is out, or put out, of all. For all that, I was told that Earle of
Salsbury was yesterday made of y[e] bedchamber. 3 or 4 papists
were yesterday dismist by y[e] King out of y[e] London lieutenancy.
Marq[s] Hallyfax, Earl of Nottingham and L[d] Godolphin are going
to treate wth y[e] Prince of Orange. I wish (and that's all a poore
man can doe) that it succeed, which most feare it scarce will, this
endeavour. L[d] Arran is made col[ll] of y[e] regim[t] late y[e] D. of Ber
wick's, and S[r] Fra. Compton but lieut[t] col[ll] still. The parl[t] proclamation is abroad too day, and for a pardon. The Earle of Sand
wich is dead in France. No more now, my L[d], but wth all possible
respect I take leave as,

            My L[d],
                Your Lops. most obedient servant,
                            WM. L.

JOHN HORTON.

My Lord,   Nosely, 2[d] Dec. 1688.

If you have not already an acct, this will acquainte y[r] Lpp. that
the Princesse Anne came privately with y[e] Bpp. of London, my
Lady Churchill, and two woemen more, on Wednesday night, to

---

    a A Commissioner of the Customs and a Privy Councillor.

my Lord Northampton's ; and from thence, in his Lpp.'s coach, to Leicester on Fryday, where she lodged that night, and yesterday went towards Nottingham (in order for Yorke). She did not discover herself till they came to Harbrough, from whence S^r Ch. Shugbrough ^{a}· and about 50 horse attended her to Leicester, where my Ld Cullen ^{b} and diverse Leicestershire gentlemen came to wait upon her and are gone along with her to Nottingham The mayor and aldermen treated both her Highnesse and his Lpp. ye Bpp. with two noble banquetts, and all demonstracions of respect and joy was shewd, with which her Highness was very well pleased, and seemed wonderfull pleasant and cheerful. The Bpp. also thanked y^e gentlemen for their respect, and tould them he was forcd to lay aside y^e Bible at present, but hoped very suddenly to take it into his hands againe. My Lord, this is w$_t$ our country affords, and if you have had it from better hands I hope you will be pleased to pardon y^e bouldness of,

My Lord,
Your Honours most duetyfull serv^t
JOHN HORTON.

It it said all y^e lords and gentlemen at Nottingham will attend her Highnes to Yorke and continue for some tyme there.

WILLIAM LONGUEVILLE.

My L^d,   Thursday, 6 Dec^r [1688].

I am truly troubled for Mrs Hatton and hope shee may soone find amendment. The doe came safe, and is a favour for which my wife and I doe joine in thanking your Lop.

'Tis doubted the 3 Lords gone a treating will scarce succeed to

^{a} Sir Charles Shuckborough, Bart.
^{b} Charles Cockayne, third Viscount Cullen.

compose our difficult matters.   The King wàs in Hyde Park too
day wth some of his army.   Most say heere will bee fighting; but it
is by some thought all will goe wth the invaders side without blowes.
'Tis a very hard and pittiable condition that men of quality are now
in; and another tryal is like to bee added to their many former nice
ones.

I am, wth all respect,
My L^d, your Lops most obedient serv^t,
WILLIAM LONGUEVILLE.

JOHN HORTON.

MY LORD,   Leicester, 10th Dec. [16]88.

Hearing y^r Princesse came to this place last night (in her journey
to Oxford), I came to se how affaires stood.   Here is a greate
appearance of nobillity and gentry (few being left at Nottingham):
15 lords, Dcvonsh: Northton: Chesterfeild, Manchester, Grey,
Carteret, Cullen, Beaumount, Sherard &c.   There are about 14 or
15 troupes of horse.   The Bpp. is captain, Ld Cullen lieutenant, S^r
Justinean Isham cornet, to ye Northamptonshire troupe consisting
all of gentlemen.   Sr Scroupe How,^a Mr Cooke ^b of Derbyshire, and
diverse other gentlemen comand troupes alsoe.   On Satturday came
a letter from diverse of ye principall gentlemen of this county to y^e
severall high constables, desiring ye summons to ye militia, horse
and foote, to meet here at Leicester with a months pay, wch in an
instant was done, and I doe not heare that one failed.   To day I
finde there ¹s an order or warrant signed by Sr Justinean, Mr Montagu, and Mr Andrews, Deputy Lieu^{ts}, for raising ye Northampton-

^a Sir Scrope Howe, Viscount Howe in 1701.
^b ? John Coke, M.P. for Derby.

shire militia, both horse and foot, to morrow to attend ye Princesse
and meete at Daventry on Wednesday, but will march to Coventry
or Warwick with her. She goes from hence to morrow by way of
Coventry.

I know not w^t your Lpp. will please to doe about sending in
horses; therefore I desire not to give any order at Maydwell, but
humbly desire, if your Lpp. send from Kirby, that notice may be
given to Mr Dawson, to whom 1 have sent to provide a man and
horse to goe in upon your Lpp.'s order. I intend to be at Harbrough to morrow, where, if I receive your Lpp.'s comands, they
shall be observed by, my L^d,

Your Honour's most duetyfull serv^t,

J[OHN] H[ORTON].

THE COUNTESS OF NOTTINGHAM.

The 11 of December, [1688].

I heared yesterday, by a servant of my Lord Godolphins yt came
this way, y^t the Lords will be back to day, were they will [find] a
clear coast, for yesterday ye Qeueen and Mr Whales^a went and tooke
watter at Durham Yard, and from thence to Foxhall, were the
coaches were ready for them, for Dover; and wth them, tis sayd,
my Lord Chancellour, my Lord Peterbourough and my Lord Salis-
berry and my Lord Sunderland are gone, but whether wth the
Qeueen or no I cant tell; and tis sayed ye Chief Justice Herbert^b
is gone too. To day the King is gone, as I am told, but I have but
an imperfect account of it from some of my owne servants y^t were
in twone. It has been much talked of, and I think not without a
cause, of the Qeueen Dowagers goeing to Eastwell, my Lord Win-
chelsease; but she has now put y^t of for some time.

^a Poor prince 1

^b Sir Edward Herbert.

There has been a skirmish at Reading, were the Irish were very insolent and threaten us. There manner is to fier the twone, and thereupon the inhabitants being frightnend run out and meet wth some of the Princes forces (they say that regiment that was my Lord Scarsdale, since y^t the Duke of S_t Albaneses), and begged of them to reseu them, as those they looked upon as there delivereres; and so they fell upon the Irish men and killed ten of them and tooke 30 prisoners, for at first they made some resistance, but then betook themselves to their best weapons, there heels, and, because nothing should hinder these last, threw of their bootes and armes and what-ever was cumbersum to them. My Ld Feversham was comeing and meet them in this disorder; so he presently ordered Twyford bridge to be broken downe, y^t they might not be persued. There was in Reading at y^t times my Lord Dunmore regiment, who are Scosh, and some of Sr John Leniers regiment; but they never a man drew a sword, but went of civelly to make roome for the Princeses forces.

They talke much of my Ld Inchaquen [a] being up in Ireland, and my Lord Tryconnel breeding who wold speak to an Englishman wth his hat on. The Duke of Gordon [b] is turn protestant (*sic*) and is up in Scotland wth the Duke of Qeueenbourough. They say y^t one Tuesday last my L^{dy} Marie Fenwick declared herself a papist. I begg the favor of y^r Lops. to present my humble dutty to my Lady and service to my cosen Finch and his lady. I will be sure to let my Lord know, when he comes, what y^r Lordsh. sayes of Mr Pullyn.

I am y^r Losp. most obedient Dau:

ANNE NOTTINGHAM.

[a] William O'Brien, second Earl of Inchiquin.
[b] George Gordon, fourth Marquess of Huntly and first Duke of Gordon.

THE EARL OF NOTTINGHAM.

MY LORD,   Kensington, Dec. 13, 1688.

My wife writt you word by ye last post Y^t ye King was gone away; and he is now seizd at Feversham by the rabble, who will offer him no violence but will not suffer him to goe away w^thout ye consent of ye citty of London. In this conjuncture ye Lords meet every day, and this day they have sent ye L^ds Aylesbury, Middleton, and Yarmouth, to attend ye King; and ye Ld Feversham is gone by their order wth 120 horse and 40 grenadiers to preserve ye King from any violence of ye people, but not to restrain him in ye least from any liberty or resolution y^t he pleases to take; and they have writt to ye Pr. of Or. an account hereof. Tis thought ye Queen and Pr. of W. will be taken too, for some vessels are in pursuit of y^m; and Father Petre is in Kent street, and order is sent to apprehend him.

My L^d, I will not pretend to advize y^r Lop.; but I think it would be very fitt for you to be in town at this time, when every day produces such extraordinary things; and, tho you cant remove y^r family on a sudden, yet you might immediately come y^rselfe, and I should be glad you would come hither Y^t we might consider of ye present circumstances and how to behave ourselves; and London is not yet a safe place, ye rabble committing every night great disorders; and there is another reason for y^r coming, and Y^t is, ye P^r of O^r may be here tomorrow, but there is no doubt but he will be here on Saturday.

I came back on Tuesday night; but I have no time to give you a narrative of Y^t negotiation, most of wch is in print already. My most humble service to my Lady and Mrs Hatton.

I am,

Y^r Lo^ps most obedient humble serv^t,

NOTTINGHAM.

WILLIAM LONGUEVILLE.

MY LORD,   Thursday, 13th of Decr, 1688.

On Tuesday evenning his Maty did leave Whitehall; and, being in Feversham creek retaken, they say heere that hee's come back to Whitehall too night.   Sr Ed. Hales and Mr Sheldon[a] were in his company.   The Earl of Salsbury and Mr Ch. Hales were taken at Ashford, Mr Obad. Walker and others at Sittingborne, Baron Jennor[b] and others at Feversham.

The multitude have done strangely to the Spanish embassadour in burning his books, coach, and spoyling his goods and house and what was there, as in a franchise, layd in.   And so have divers lesser things been spoyled and done.   Last night all the towne were, by false rumours of ye Irish soldiers, kept in feare and upp all night. The Duke of Grafton is come to towne to day.   I wish, my Ld, heere may come good out of all this hurly-burly.   Had I time, your Lop. should heare oftener; but last post I had none, and not much now, being all ye afternoone taken off by Temple businesse, which on this present juncture takes up much of one's time.

I am, with true respect,

My Ld,

Your Lop.'s most humble servant,

WM. L.

SIR EDMUND KING.

Thursday night, Dec. 13, [16]88.

Every day brings new alarms or woonders, nay, allmost every hower.   I intended to send wt papers are out, but I finde 2 or 3 of them in the gazett, wch cam not out till 7 this night.   The mobile have been extreamly insolent and ungovernable, and yet are not supprest.   This day, about 1 a clock, we had news that the King was stopt by fisher boats, and that he is now at Feversham in Kent.

[a] Ralph Sheldon, one of the Equerries.
[b] Sir Thomas Jenner, junior Baron of the Exchequer.

I went to Whitehall and met my Lord Prestons lady,[a] who said it was true, and soe said Lady Peterboro[b] and Lady Clevland and many more; and this night the Duke of Grafton is com to towne. I went to grete him, but he was wth the Lords in counsell to night; and I finde this news has shoakt their measurs for the presant, but I beleeve they must proseed now. The Prince of O. is not com yet. Ld Peterb. is taken too, and his l[ady] beleive[s] it. Sr Edw. Hayles is saide to be wth the K[ing], and the Bis[hop] of Chester (but I doubt y^t). We hear 24 preists taken in one vessell, and all wish it true. I was in Cheapside w^n the Chancellor[c] was brought to my Ld Mayor. Ther never was such joy; not a man sorrie y^t we could see. They longd to have him out of the coach, had he not had a good guard. Dr. Oates, I am told, is drest in all his D^{rs} robes againe, and expects liberty quickly.

We had a terrible alarm last night; at 12 a clock in the night cri'd, "Arm! arm! arm!" 7000 Irish was com from the army, disbanded but in a body, and killing all they met. We was all up in arms till 5 in the morning. It arize from some disorder amongst them in Brainford, and was allayd by telling the Princes van guard of horse pursu'd them and cutt them to peeces. It's a strange thing we have not the truth out yet. We doe not thinke we are safe till the Prince com's; all the Protestants long for him. Ho! you are happie in yor quiet place. God keep it soe. Pray pray for us, as my poore wife desires me to tell you wth her humble service to y^r L^p and to my L[ady] H[atton], and mine too.

Just now I am tolde (just now) that the King is dead 2 bowers after he was taken, if I may use y^t word. I have alsoe word brought me that there is 4 troops of the P. of O. horse come to towne: Coll. Slingsby's regiment.

[a] Anne, daughter of Charles Howard, first Earl of Carlisle, and wife of Richard Graham, Viscount Preston.

[b] Penelope, daughter of Barnabas, Earl of Thomond, and wife of Henry Mordaunt, second Earl of Peterborough.

[c] Jeffreys.

Since I writt this, the news letter came.

I doe not kno which is best: to have the news that belongs to the Bill of Mortalitie true or falce, nor, upon the wholl, I doe not beleive the first, but that he is taken by Admiral Herbert.

WILLIAM LONGUEVILLE.

MY LORD,   Satterday, 15th of Dec^r, 1688.

Now it appeares heere how needfull the Prince of Orange his coming to this populous place is; till which, indeed, heere is nothing but distraction and danger. The King is at Feversham, as 'tis said, and pretty well, at the mayor's house. Desirous hee was of being at liberty to bee gone, but most believe the people there will not, unlesse by the Pr^{ce} of O. his direccion, leave him to himselfe and to bee gone. His Mat^y writt up to Mr Froude to send him a few servants and some linnen and money. Foure lords went unto him, vizt the Earle of Ailesbury, Earles of Yarmouth and Feversham, and Ld Middleton. Most of this day his Mat^y was reported to bee dead; but I heare it was an untruth; altho 'tis by his best friends thought hee cannot but bee heart broken and not long in this life. God looke on him for good; however, his happinesse for this world seemes closed.

Maj^r Wildman and Dr Burnett are in seeming power. Some 50 ladies are now at Windsor wth the Pr. of O. Too day a declaracion is abroad for recalling the disbanded army to their officers or colours, subscribed by the Pr^{ce} of Orange and dated at his Court at Henly.

I am alwaies,
My L^d,
Your Lops most faithfull humble servant,
WM. L.

The Earl of Nottingham.

My Lord,   Dec. 18, [16]88.

I writt to y^r Lo^p last night by ye post, and when I came home I found y^r serv^t here wth a letter, but was unwilling to send him back wthout adding something to my last nights letter; and I was in hopes y^r Lo^p might have bin here if y^r paines had abated, wch I am extremely sorry are very grievous and frequent.

The King came this night to Whitehall, and had sent before my Ld Feversham to Windsor, to invite y^e P^r of Or. to London; and S$_t$ James's House is to be his court. But y^e Prince has made my Ld Feversham prisoner for coming into his quarters wthout a passe, wch seems at present but a pretence, for he is extreamly angry wth him for dismissing y^e army as he did, whereby the countrey has bin exposed to their rapines and outrages, and ye soldiers disperst, w^{ch}, had they bin kept in a body, would have bin more ready for forreigne service; and perhaps it is thought t'was done on purpose.

Besides, the Prince had sent Monsr Zuylesteyn ^{a} to ye King upon ye newes of his being in ye hands of ye rabble (who declard y^t they would not lett him goe wthout an order from ye Prince), that his Ma^{ty} should be at full liberty to doe as he pleased wth himselfe. But, upon ye acc^t he had of ye Kings designe of returning to London, he remanded Zuylesteyn to ye King, to tell him he thought it more expedient for him to stay at Rochester; and I hear y^t ye discourse at Windsor is, y^t ye King's going away is a cession of his right to ye crowne. I shall make no comments, but doe extreamly wish for y^r Lops company here, if y^r health would permitt it.

In ye mean time I shall follow your directions about y^r affair of Guernsey, as well as I can and as I have opportunity; but I hope there can be no need of any sollicitation on y^r behalfe, y^r pattent

---

^{a} William Henry de Nassau, Lord of Zuleistein, created Earl of Rochford in 1695.

being for life, or, if there should be any such need, I am apt to
think I shall not be a very proper advocate. But y^r Lo^p may be
sure y^t I shall alwaies take ye same care of y^r concernes as of my
owne.

I am

Y^r Lo^ps most obedient humble servant,

N.

CHARLES HATTON.

April 9, 1869.

*

This day ye bill for ye coronation oath pass'd, not with opposition
in ye House.   The Commons have voted ye calling a Convocation.
Yesterday they brought in a Comprehension Bill of their owne, if
possible, more favourable to ye fanaticks then y^rs, and more destructive to ye Ch[urch] of E[ngland].   After it wase read, severall
moved for a day to be appointed for a 2d reading.   Some mentioned that day sennight, some y^t day fortnight. Sr Edward Chisnal
said it wase a bill soe destructive to ye Ch. of E. he desired it ly on
ye table till Doomsday, wch occasion[ed] some heats wch quickly
pass'd over; and then Sr Henry Capell, wth a large preamble, attest-
ing his zeale for ye Ch. of E. as ye promoters of y^t bill usually doe,
declared it wase of y^t consequence he must second those who moved
for ye longest day.   Then replyed Mr Speaker: " You move for
Doomsday ?" wch gave noe small diversion to all ye House but
Sr Henry.

And for y^r diversion, if you have not heard it, I shall tell you a
pleasanter story.   The Countess of Dorchester lately went to visit a
certain lady, who received her very cooly; upon wch ye Countess told

her she wase much surpris'd: " For," said shee, " if I have broke one commandement, you have another; and what I did wase more naturall."ª

Here is a reporte 5000 Swedes are landed at North Yarmouth and 10000 more exspected, to remove greivances and defend our liberty and property. All here are yʳ Loᵖᵖˢ, my sister's, nephew, and neices humble servants, but more particularly yʳ truly affectionate brother to serve you,

C. HATTON.

SIR CHARLES LYTTELTON.

London, Apˡˡ 9ᵗʰ, [16]89.

Because I heare nothing of yʳ Lᵖ, I conclude you are yet at Kirby and dare not venture yʳ ill health in yᵉ crowd on Thursday.

I am yet in suspense how my regimᵗ will be disposed, for we are treated so hardly, both in words and deedes, abt it, that, tho' we are not broke, I cant think they care to keep us. They will not allow us, wʰᵗ they doe to others, to make our recruites; and tell us wᵗʰall the King is so dissattisfied wᵗʰ yᵉ officers abᵗ yᵉ deserting of yᵉ soldiers, that, as a mark of his displeasure, this hardship is put upon us. I have plainly told my Lᵈ Churchill, who is now Lᵈ Marlborough, we think we deserve better usage, as being the regimᵗ who's officers have stuck best together in yᵉ service of any in yᵉ army, there being none but Lt Coll. and one capt. who have quitted it; but I doe so despize the opinion I heare is had of me, that I did

___

ª This retort of the witty Catherine Sidley has more point in it when we remember that Mary had shocked observers, and Evelyn among the number, by her levity of conduct on taking possession of her father's palace. Her lightheartedness, whether real or feigned, was no doubt at this moment the talk of the town.

privately contrive the meeting and deserting at Brandford, &c. as ye playing such a 2^{ble} game, when I had taken this Kings com^n, that I am quite wearie of serving any longer and am very willing to resign to those they can be better assured of, and endeavour, as soone as I can, to come to an issue in. Sr George Huet kissd ye K^{gs} hand to day to be a baron;^{a} so is Ad: Herbert.^{b} Mon^{sr} Bentin is Earl of Portland. My Ld Faulkland^c is out, and Mr Russell in his place.

Sr George Lockart, ye Ld Pre: of ye sessions in Scotland, most barbarously murdred, as he lighted from his coach to goe into his own house, by one Cheesly,^{d} who he had given some judgm^t agst in behalf of his own wife and children. He was put to ye torture, had his hand cut of, and hanged up in chaines. I heare the K^g and Queene are proclaimed in y^t kingdom.

The Com^{ns} have voted ye K^g thankes for declaring he will maintaine ye Church of Eng: establishd by law, and that his Mat^y be desired to issue out writts to call a Convocation.

CHARLES HATTON.

April 16, 1689.

*   *   *

This night ye judges are to be sworne. In ye K[ing's] B[ench], Holt, Dolben, Winnington, Aires; C[ommon] P[leas], Pollexfen, Powell, Ward, Rookeby; in ye Exchequer Sr R^t Atkins (if he will accept,

^{a} Sir George Hewett was made Viscount Hewett on the 9th April, and died on the 2nd December, 1689.

^{b} Admiral Arthur Herbert, Earl of Torrington.

^{c} Anthony Cary, fourth Viscount Falkland, was succeeded as Treasurer of the Navy by Admiral Edward Russell, afterwards Earl of Orford.

^{d} Chiesly of Dalry.

but many say he will not), Nevill, Ventris and Turton.ᵃ It is reported Sʳ Rᵗ Atkins is soe disgrrubl'd not to be Ch. J. of yᵉ Com. Pleases yᵗ he sath he will not have his brothers scimm milke. This day Ch. Baron Montagu wase very busy in discoursing severall lords in yᵉ lobby, and many thought he wase turned sollicitor for his old place.ᵇ I have enclosed a printed paper wᶜʰ I borrowed for yᵉ satisfaction of yʳ perusall, wᶜʰ when you have, pray send it backe, for they are not to be bought. When you have read it, you cannot doubt who is concluded to be yᵉ author, who is threaten'd by Sʳ Robt to be excluded out of yᵉ Act of indemnity; and all Sʳ Roberts patrons and partisans are not a little nettled at it.

I am told Sʳ Charles Littleton's regiment is broke, and yᵉ soldiers yᵗ remained put into yᵉ regt of Fusileers.

I am yʳ Loᵖᵖˢ, my sister's, nephew, and neices

very humble servant,

C. HATTON.

THE SAME.

April 20, [16]89.

Last Thursday, my Lᵈ, Captaine Ellis went to Hampton Court by my Lᵈ Nottingham's advise, who presented him. He desired mee to goe wᵗʰ him, wᶜʰ I did out of curiosity to see it, never having before. The outside is very meane. How it is furnish'd within I cannot tell, nor had I curiosity enouf to informe myself. I wase soe

---

ᵃ The appointments weroi in the King's Bench, Sir John Holt, Chief Justice, Sir William Dolben, Sir Giles Eyre, and Sir William Gregory ; in the Common Pleas, Sir Henry Pollexfen, Chief Justice, Sir John Powell, Sir Thomas Rokeby, and Sir Peyton Ventris ; in the Exchequer, Sir Robert Atkins, Chief Baron, Sir Edward Neville, Sir Nicholas Lechmere, and Sir John Turton.

ᵇ Sir William Montagu, Chief Baron, had been removed in April, 1686.

disgusted to see ye front and back side, I admire how anyone can fancy it.   It wase soe late before wee return'd, goeing and coming by water, I cou'd not write y^t night.

I moved y^r Lo^{ppe} for a letter to Mr Temple,^a to expedite Captⁿ Ellis; but, shou'd y^r letter now come, I wou'd not follow him to deliver it, for, last night, about 6 a clocke, he tooke occasion by water to goe into another world.   He went upon ye water about 12 at noone, enquir'd how ye tide wase.   Betwixt five and six in ye evening he tooke boat at Whitehall, went wth ye first oares who plyed him, who wase a stranger to him, refused those who used to carry him, bid ye waterman carry him below bridge, and, just as he wase shooting ye bridge, lay'd down in ye boate a shilling and a peice of paper in wch wase writ ye following words: " My folly in under-taking what I cannot performe hath done ye King great prejudice, wch cannot be stopp'd any other waye but this.   May his under-takings prosper! May he find a blessing!" Then bid ye waterman farewell, and leap'd over.   Afterward, he rise up againe, but ye eddise suck'd him in before ye waterman cou'd bring his boate about, and so wase drown'd.

*   *   *

I am y^r very humble servant,

C. HATTON.

THE SAME.

April 23, 1689.

*   *

The accompt I gave you last Saturday of Mr Temple wase too true.   His body wase found yesterday morning, taken up neere the Tower.

^a John, son of Sir William Temple and Secretary-at-War, the story of whose unhappy death is so well known through Macaulay's History.

The occasion of his writing those words he left in ye boate hath raised much discourse here in town. The discharge of ye office of Secretarie of Warre is not a difficult taske; besides, Mr Blaithwait, knowing how well Mr Temple wase at Court, to gaine his friend- shippe did (I am very well assured) not only give him at present all ye assistance he cou'd to render it easie to him, but promised to continue it as long as he pleased. Therefore ye discharge of y^t office cou'd not bee ye foolish undertaking what he cou'd not performe he soe fatally lamented. But I am inclined to beleeve it wase his undertaking y^t Tyrconnel woud deliver up Ireland upon articles, for I am told by a very intelligent person y^t ye L^d Ch. Justice of Ireland,[a] who came here from Tyrconnel, did, according to his instructions, apply himself to Mr. Temples relations, and Mr Temple negotiated y^t affaire, and being imposed on withth false assurances y^t, if Major Generall Hamilton[b] was sent into Ireland wth advantagious proposall to Tyrconnel, he wou'd deliver up y^t kingdom, and ye expence of sending over men might be saved, Mr Temple, beeing soe imposed on, did wth great earnestness assert his opinion; wch being proved to bee erronious by ye event, some hasty and inconsiderate personns did say some few dayes since to Mr Temple that all ye blood shed in recovering Ireland wou'd call for vengeance from him and his family; the reflection on wch made him, who wase naturally very melancolly, take y^t fatall resolution wch hath disapointed ye delivery of y^r letter, for I have noe intention of following him wth it.

*   *   *

I am y^r Lo^{ppes} very humble servant,

C. HATTON.

[a] Thomas Nugent, Chief Justice of the King's Bench in Ireland ; removed in 1690.

[b] Richard Hamilton, the brother of the author of Grammont's Memoirs.

Sir Edmund King.

MY LORD,   May 23th, [16]89.

Having writt twice to enquire after yr Lordps health and not
hearing, I began to fear I forgot to direct them to the Weldon
bagg, wch might occasion their miscarriage.   Pray give me leave to
send this on the same arrand.   By some I have heard yor Lordp and
familie have continued well, and by others yt yor Lordp had som of
yor olde paines againe, wch I am concern'd at, but hope the Tunbridge waters will prove more successfull than other methods have
done.   'Twill be a kinde of presumption to write yor Lordp any
news, yet, being yesterday wth the Earle of Twedall,a who is come
lately from Scotland on acct of his health (and under my care),
read me his letters from thence; that ye Lord Dundee came to Perth
and tooke away ye Lord Blaire b and two more Conventionors and
part of a troop raising there; that Mackey keeps in those parts, but
Dundee sculks about; that the young men of yt kingdome are very
unanimous and meet in divers places to exercise; that the new
batterie against the Castle at Edenbrough is now finyshd and the
morter peices are planted, and they expect wthin a day or two to
begin to use them.

Yesterday and to day the towne rings wth a report from several
letters that those in Londonderry have made another sally and kill'd
several thousands Irish and a great many great officers; and they
say the Duke of B[erwick] is kill'd, and that the seige is raisd.
Yesterday on told me he heard the K[ing] say ther is now 20 saile
of Dutch men of warr at the Spitthead; but we are informd the
French have taken 7 of the Dutch merchant ships worth 150,000ll
or more.   Many other discourses mak a noise here; but soe few
reports prove true, yt I rather aske your Lordps pardon for wt I

---

a John Hay, 2nd Earl of Tweedale ; created Marquess in 1694.
b The Laird of Blair.

have said than report more, and humbly intreat my humble service
to my Lady, and allways heartilie pray for yoʳ Lordᵖˢ health and of
all yours.

CHARLES HATTON.

July 11, [16]89.

I am very glad, my Lᵈ, to heare yᵉ waters agree soe well wᵗʰ yʳ
Loᵖᵖᵉ, and I am told yʳ presence will be requird here, and by yʳ
freinds exspected, in a short time, ʸᵗ is, when Captⁿ Vaughan, Captⁿ
Mole,ᵃ &c. come to be tryed on their impeachmᵗ; for it is thought
yᵉ day will be appointed to morrow, when their answer is to bee
given in.   The Lords house have sat thes 3 dayes very close and
long on yᵉ bill for reversing yᵉ judgmᵗ agᵗ T[itus] Oates.ᵇ   It hath
been caryed agᵗ generall clauses in yᵉ bill only by 2 votes, yᵉ Lᵈ
Devonshire and Dʳ B[urne]t of Salisbury.   The freinds of T. O. will
have yᵉ judgmᵗ to be erroneous.   Others say yᵉ divesting him of his
ecclesiastic orders wase erroneous, for ʸᵗ lay not in their power to
doe, and ʸᵗ yᵉ rest of judgmᵗ wase not erroneous but too severe.
To morrow yᵉ sages of yᵉ law are to deliver their opinion whither
one branch of a judgmᵗ being erroneous doth not render yᵉ whole
judgmᵗ soe.   It is reported ʸᵗ yᵉ Lᵈ Mountagueᶜ moved for an
address to K[ing] W[illiam] to have yᵉ Lᵈ Hallifax removed from
yᵉ Woolsack and Serᵗ Maynard placed ther; but his freinds wou'd
have had yᵉ question waved.   But my Lᵈ Hallifax put it, and very
few seconded yᵉ Lord Mountague.   This day a bill was brought up

ᵃ Captain Vaughan and Captain Mold, Jacobite agents, who were arrested for
distributing James's declaration.

ᵇ See Macaulay's interesting account of the debates in his 14th chapter.

ᶜ This is a mistake. Charles Mordaunt, Earl of Monmouth, led the attack on
Halifax.

from ye Commons to ye L^{ds} H. by Mr Trenchard, ye Ld Coot,a Coll. Manly, and Sr Tho. Samuel, to attaint severall persons wth K[ing] J[ames] in Ireland, from whence ye papists or some s^d to bee popishly affected say 5000 men are sent into Scotl^d to joyne Dundee.

THE SAME.

Augt 1, [16]89.

*   .   *   *   *

Wee are in great exspectation to see w^t ye designe of ye adjourn- m^t of both Houses wase this day, and w^t will be done to morrow to reconcile both Houses in ye concern of y^t worthy man T[itus] Oates.

It is said at ye Exchange y^t ye French have taken an English shippe coming from Turkey, laden wth silke to ye valew of 50000^{ll}, and y^t 5 shippes laden wth provisions ar taken from within ye barre at Chester, and y^t ye French Toulon fleet hath joyn[ed] their other at Brest, 20 leagues from whenc ye Dutch and English fleet ride and bides defyance to ye French.

Ther is much discourse this day, in coffee-houses, y^t ye notorious rebell Dundee is very potent and victorious and y^t ther is great discord in ye parl^t in Scotland.[b] But many think thes reports are raised by ye papists and not to be credited, for ye Gazette this day doth not mention any such thing.

I am y^r Lo^{pps}, Lady Hattons, Mrs Haslewood, and Sister Alices very humble serv^t,

C. HATTON.

---

[a] Richard Coote, Lord Coote of Coloony, who was created Earl of Bellamont this year ; M.P. for Droitwich, and Treasurer to the Queen.

[b] Dundee was already slain at Killiecrankie, on the 27th July.

SIR CHARLES LYTTELTON.

MY LORD, London, Aug. 8th, [1689].

I am very glad ye fright of ye children is over and y^t you stay to drink ye waters wch seeme to doe you good.

Y^e news to day is: Kirk is in Derry, ye Irish drawn of, and ye prottestants encamped wthout ye town.^a If it be so, as I beleeve, when ye forces that goe hence are landed, I beleeve they will carry all before y^m. Yesterday I discoursed wth a gentleman who was store keeper of ye ordnance in Ireland. He confirmed to mee W^{ht} I had before heard, y^t ye reason ye Irish c^d not take it was want of guns to batter it. He told mee there was but a very few in all ye kingdom of any force, and y^t ye country abt Derry was so rotten they c^d not be drawn thither. He seemed to me a sober intelligent man; but I can't conceive at this time of yeare but ye ground will beare any weight.

He said ye men of Derry and Inniskelling and thereab^{ts} are ever esteemed the best in Ireland, and that there are 20,000. He s^d there is a very good wall ab^t Derry, and well flanqued, a dry ditch, and c^d not be taken wth so many men to defend it, but by scallado, wthout a breach.

News this morning is y^t Dundee is certainly dead.

It's thought ye par: will be adjournd next week. They voted this morn:, I think, y^t, after such a day in 8^{obr}, no body, men nor women, shall come to Court in any thing but wollen, except for linings, and all women, under such a quallity, to weare hatts.

---

^a The siege was raised on the 1st August.

CHARLES HATTON.

Augt 15, [16]89.

Your Lo^{ppe} guessed very right, when you declared ye great offence ye act for wearing woollen wou'd give, for yesterday ye L^{ds} in their House were besett wth soe numerous and mutinous a rabble, that this day, for their security, they were by their order guarded wth 2 companies of y^e trayne bands, y^e constables of Westminster wth their beadles.   My Ld Maior ordred a regim^t of y^e militia to bee on y^e guard in London, and y^e L$_t$ [of y^e] Tower y^e severall companies in y^e Hamlets. And y^e sherif of Middlesex wase ordred to be in a readiness wth a posse comitatus.   Last Tuesday ye Masters of y^e company of silke weavers petitioned y^e H. of C. y^t, before y^e wollen act passed, they might be heard by their counsell; but ye H. of C., to shew their bravour, rejected ye petition and passed ye bill, and ye same day sent it up to L^{ds} House, whither yesterday all ye silke weavers, their wives, and children came.   I beleeve ther were above 20000.   Both ye pallace yards, ye Abby Church, Westminster Hall, ye Court of Request, ye Painted Chamber, wase, from 9 of ye clocke in ye morning till 2 in ye afternoone, soe crouded, it wase scarce possible for any person to pass.   Coll. Birch^a wase ye great promoter of ye Woolen Act, but, forseeing ye storme wase likely to fall on him, he fled into ye country; and it wase well he did, for, had he come to parl^t, I verily beleeve he had been torn to peices.   My Ld North,^{b} ye B^p of Winchester,^{c} and other Lords set up for Publicolas, made severall orations; but their eloquence prevayled very little, the rabble frequently interrupting y^m wth their clamorous shouts, one and all, y^t nothing sho'd satisfy y^m till ye bill wase flung out.   But at last, upon reiterated assurances y^t care sho'd be taken

---

^{a} John Birch, who began life as a carter, became a colonel under Cromwell, and sat many years in Parliament.

^{b} Charles, Lord Grey and North. ^{c} Peter Mew.

of them and nothing should be done as to ye woollen bill till their counsell wase heard, they dispersed. My Ld North boasted how he had preserved ye L^ds House by his prudent managem^t. A clownish fellow by way of reply tooke notice how ye Capitoll of Rome had been preserv'd.

*   *

I am y^r very humble servant,

C. HATTON.

* * * * *

THE SAME.

October 24, [16]89.

*   *   *   *   *

My Lady Essex Griffin^a is sent to ye Tower for a Pewter Pot Plot, much more ridiculous then Mis Sellier[s] Meal Tub. My Ld Griffin's cooke bespoke of a pewterer an oblong square pewter pot, to put brandy in; but it wase to have a false bottom, in wch wase to be put some counterband goods to be sent into France. When the pot wase made, yesterday morning, betwixt one and two of ye clocke in ye morning, ye cooke and a foot boy went to call up ye pewterer, to come to my Ld Griffins house to sodder in ye false bottom. The pewterer told Y^m he cou'd not ther doe it soe conveniently as at his own house, and bid Y^m fetch ye pot and he wou'd get ready his tooles and sodder in ye bottome presently. They went, fetch'd ye pot, and, as soon as ye pewterer had received it, he told Y^m he must know w͏t wase put into ye false bottome. They pretended that ther wase jewells. But ye pewterer, pulling what wase in ye false bottome, found letters to ye King and severall papers, apprehended ye cook and footman, and, sending for a constable, caried Y^m to y^e

---

^a Daughter of James Howard, Earl of Suffolk, and wife of Edward, Lord Griffin.

Secretaries office; but, noe body being ther, he secured y^m in ye porter's lodge, went to Mr Hampden, acquainted him, and early y^t morning they were examined. A messenger wase sent to search ye Ld Griffin's house and secure my L^d; but he wase gone away. My Lady is sent to ye Tower, and my Lady Eliz. Thatcher. Her first husband wase De la Val. The pewter bottle wase to have been sent by one Mon^sr Busy, a Frenchman who maryed my Lady New-burgh; and Mr Thatcher, my Lady Eliz. husband, wase to goe as his man wth him into France, and from thence to carry ye pewter bottle into Ireland. In ye false bottom ther is said to have been found a draught of a patent to create my Ld Griffin an earle, and in his letter he expressed a desire y^t it might beare date before abdication wase voted. What else of any certainty I cannot heare. Some say ther wase lists of "worthy men" and "men worthy." This is for certain, ther never wase a more foolish contrivance, and who ever had any hand in it must be as blind in their understanding as my Lady Essex's eyes are.

It wase thought my Ld Preston, Ld Forbes,[a] Sr John Fenniick, Mr Chomley,[b] and others wou'd by their writs of habeas corpus have been brought up to ye Bench this day; but they not being willing to comply wth my Ld Lucas[c] in paying him ye fees he demanded of y^m, to bee as vexatious to y^m as he can, he will not bring y^m up till to morrow.

I have enclosed yesterdayes votes, and I heare ye H. of C. have voted to-day that they will stand by and assist his Ma^ty in reducing Irel^d, and joyning wth his allies abroad in a vigorous prosecution of ye war ag^t France. And to-morrow sennight is appointed to con-sider of a supply for his Ma^ty. All here give y^r Lo^ppe and all at Kirby their very humble service, and more particularly y^r most humble servant,

C. HATTON.

[a] William, 11th Lord Forbes.
[b] Thomas Cholmondeley, of Vale Royal, co. Chester.
[c] Lieutenant of the Tower.

THE SAME.

Novr 2, [16]89.

*   *   *   *   *

The Parl^{mt} seem as if they resolved to make all incur a premunire, who will not take ye late oathes. This day ye H. of L^{ds} have appointed a private, rather a secret, committee to examine ye murther of my Ld Essex and who were ye occasion of ye death of ye Ld Russel, Coll. Sidney, Cornish, &c, and a committee to examine who were ye promoters of regulating corporations.

The Ld Griffin is come in and layes all ye blame of ye late business on his lady, whose contrivance it wase without his privity; all wch she averres, and y^t a letter writ in his name in a hand very like his wase write by her direction by a very skilfull person in counterfeiting hands, who is since fled into France. You will easily imagine ye intreague of ye Pewter Pot. The managem^t thereof and my Ld Griffins delivering himself up furnishes this town wth various reports. If coffee house tales were to be credited, my Ld Griffin hath impeached at least 20 personns of note.

The H. of C. have appointed a committee to examine by w^{ht} meanes my Ld Grffin had intelligence where ye severall stations of ye winter guard of ye navy were to bee, w^{ch}, it is said, were resolved on on Saterday night and found mentioned in my Ld Griffins paper ye next Monday morning.

The same committee is to examine into ye miscarriages of victualling ye navy and ye transportation of ye army into Irel^d, and all other things relating both to ye war both by sea and land ye last year. All here give their very humble service to y^r Lo^{ppe}, but more particularly your very humble servant,

C. HATTON.

THE SAME.

Nov[r] 12, [16]89.

My L[d] Preston, when he came up to y[e] K[gs] Bench from y[e] Tower by habeas corpus to be bailed, wase frighted (I suppose) by a story ther told him, [yt] my Ld Montague had 80 bailifs ready to seize him when bailed, wth w[ch] he acquainted y[e] court, telling them he wase a peere of England. The court took noe notice of his peerage (nor wase it necessary), but told him y[t], coming and going, he wase under y[e] protection of y[e] court; and y[e] under-Sherif of Middlesex being by, y[e] court charged him at his perill not to arrest my L[d]. Some dayes after, my L[d] Preston gave baile to my L[d] Montague to answer his action. But y[e] L[ds] House, being informed [yt] my L[d] Preston claimed to be a peer of England, ordered him yesterday to produce his patent, w[ch] wase signed at S[t] Germaines, in France, y[e] 1st of January last, and wax put to it, but noe impression, for y[r] Lo[ppe] knowes y[e] great seale wase flung into y[e] Thames and soe cou'd not be affixed to it. This occasioned a great debate what crime it wase to produce such a patent, whither it wase high treason by endeavouring to counterfeit y[e] great seal; and y[e] judges were asked their opinions, w[ch] they were to give in to day, and my L[d] committed to y[e] Black Rod. To day y[e] judges gave their opinions: That y[e] crime wase a high misdemeanor bordering upon treason, for w[ch] my L[d] wase this day committed to y[e] Tower. And yesterday my L[d] Griffin wase brought up to L[ds] House to be examined. He pleaded ignorance to all y[e] designe of y[e] Pewter Plot. But a letter wase produced, said to be under his hand, and one who had been his servant said he knew his hand and thought [yt] to be his hand but could not swear it; upon w[ch] my L[d] wase remanded to y[e] Tower and ordered to be brought up againe to-day. My L[d] Lovelace [a] acquainted y[e] House [yt] my L[d] Griffin wo'd take y[e] oathes, and offered to be his baile. But it seemes bare taking y[e] oathes will not

---

[a] John, 3rd Lord Lovelace.

excuse my Ld Griffin; he must doe something more meritorious, for this day he is committed to ye Tower for high treason.

Yesterday ye new building at Kinginton (*sic*), at y^t wch wase my Ld Nottingham's house, fell down, killed a workman, wounded 7 or 8 more. It is said ye foundation wase lay'd over a vault, and ye weight of ye building broke thro.

THE SAME.

November 21, [16]89.

* * * * *

Yesterday ye Convocation met and ye 2 candidates for ye pro-locutorshippe were Dr Jane[a] and Dr Tillotson, but Dr Jane had so apparently ye majority of votes that his election wase confirmed wth very little dispute. It is reported he wase kick'd into y^t office; for last Sunday he went to preach at Whitehall, according to his turne, y^t afternoone, but wase put by and not permitted to preach, but B^p Burnet did; w^{ch}, it is thought, wase not to Dr Jane[s] disadvantage in his election. Dr Beveridge[b] did yesterday preach ye Latin sermon (wch will be printed). He therein said our liturgy needed noe alteration; and it is now thought y^t ye major part of ye convocation will be of the same opinion, and therfore, as they adjourned themselves till Monday, it is thought that they will then be adjourned till a longer time.

My Ld Arran is gone for Scotland, and Duke Hamilton, it is said, will returne thither as commissioner next weeke. The Popish party discourse much in the coffee houses of great commotions ther, in ye Highlands, and great successes in Ireland; but our gazettes make noe mention therof.

[a] William Jane, Dean of Hereford.
[b] William Beveridge, afterwards Bishop of St. Asaph.

The same.

Novr 26, [16]89.

Yesterday ye Convocation met, and Dr Jane chose Dr Aldridge ^a to present him, who did it in a most eloquent oration. Dr Jane concluded his speech: " Nolumus leges Angliæ immutari." The B^p of London made a speech exactly agreeable to ye expectation of all who are acquainted wth his elocution. It is thought Dr Jane and Dr Aldridges speeches will be printed. As for y^e B^p of Londons, it is much doubted, for, if it shou'd, it wou'd loose y^e graces of eloquent delivery.

Dr Jane was permitted to preach at Whitehall last Sunday morning. The sermon wase ag^t Socinus.

Here is a very pestilentiall pamphlet privately dispersed ag_t y^e Athanasian Creed.^b

Seraphic Horneck ^c preached ther in y^e afternoon. His discourse wase about y^e love and feare of God, and told his auditority (*sic*) y^t one asked his (mystical) countryman Taulerus ^d whither, wase he certain y^t God wou'd damn him, wou'd he yet love Him? He replyed: He had 2 arms, one of humility, ye other of feare. Shou'd God damn him, he wou'd catch hold on Him with both his arms, and pull Him down with him into hell; and, having God ther, he cou'd not feare. I suppose this is a flight beyond y^r country preachers, and I suppose you will not much lament ye misfortune in not having him parson of St Andrews, Holborn.

I and all here are y^r Lo^{pps}, Lady Hattons, and all at Kirby their very humble servant,

C. Hatton.

---

^a Henry Aldrich, Dean of Christ Church.

^b " Brief Notes on the Creed of St. Athanasius." It was answered by Sherlock Dean of St. Paul's.

^c Anthony Horneck, Preacher at the Savoy, famous for his pathetic sermons.

^d Johann Tauler, the mystic.

SIR CHARLES LYTTELTON.

MY LORD, London, No. 28, [1689.]

I am very glad to find you at some ease by y^{rs} I rec^d last night. I have had no letter lately from my son, but I heare he is well; yet can't expect he sh^d long continue so where he is. So many fall down ab$_t$ him, and, by all I can learn of their condition, I think it's liker to be streightned and made more uneasie every day y^n other. At length I heare 'tis confessd on all hands Y^t K^g James has taken Sligo, and, tho' it mayn't be true, yet tis s^d our army deserts and many goes into y^e enemy. I beleeve there has bine a great mortallity in our army, both officers and soldiers,[a] wch has bine such a discouragem^t, I question much whither it will not be very difficult to recruite y^m ^{agst} ye spring; and I heare too there has bine no very good harmony among ye greate officers. I pitty ye old Gen^{ll} [b] extremely, who I take to be a good man as well as a greate captain, to have so much censure for his conduct in this expedition, his greate experience not allowing him to have so much contempt of his enemy as others have, and to overvalue his own untryed troopes. Y^e H. of Com. has fallen heavily on ye Com^{ry} of ye provisions, Capt. Shales [c] voting an adresse to ye K^g to desire his ^{Matie} will enable ye Gen^{ll} to seize and secure his person and all his bookes and papers; and yesterday it was seconded wth another vote to addresse Y^t his M. will be pleased to let ye H[ouse] know who it is advised him to employ Shales.

[a] In the entrenched camp at Dundalk.

[b] Schomberg.

[c] Henry Shales, who had also been Commissary General to the camp at Hounslow, and was continued in his office as the only person of any experience in that department.

CHARLES HATTON.

March 6, 16$\frac{89}{90}$.

Mr Ashmole hath, my L^d, y^e best baking pear I ever saw, both for largeness, firmeness, and good tast. Many eate it raw, but it is then harsh. It keepes y^e year round. It is in his garden grafted on a dwarfe stocke, and an excellent bearer. It is in shape and colour very like y^e Spanish Bon Christien. He calles it ye Ashmole peare. I sent 4 grafts to Mr Knight this morning, desiring him to take care to convey y^m carefully to y^r Lo^{ppe}; wch he promised me he wou'd. I cou'd get noe more grafts, for I knew not of ye goodness of ye peare, till all ye other grafts were cut of.

As for news, I dare venture to send none ; all ye reports here are soe uncertain. Y^e last Gazette contradicts ye precedent. Last Monday's Gazette said Cavan wase burnt, and ye Duke of Berwicke wounded and his army routed. This dayes Gazette sath ye Duke of Berwick is in Cavan still.

I am to y^r Lo^{ppe} and all with you a
very faithfull and humble servant,

C. HATTON.

THE SAME.

MY LORD,   Apr. 8, 1690.

*

The Bill of Recognition is at last past ye L^{ds} H[ouse]. It wase all ye last weeke debated. The Court party wase divided. One great debate wase whither ye acts of ye last parlt (soe called) shou'd be confirmed or recognised. Y^e Duke of Bolton ^{a} brought in ye bill, in wch it wase declared y^t all ye acts of ye last parl^t were lawfull and rightfull. Y^t clause wase opposed by ye Marquis Hallifax, Ld Danby, Pembroke, Nottingham, and others, and, last Saterday, it being put to ye question whither ye acts of ye last parl^t were lawfull and rightfull, the negative carryed it, ther being 36 for ye negative, 31 for ye affirmative. But, presently after, to prevent ye ill consequence such a vote might have, being dispersed over ye nation, my Ld Danby made a tack and movèd y^t ye H[ouse] wou'd declare ther resolution to confirme and recognise those acts, and then, when they had made them lawfull, they were lawfull. And now those acts are recognised and declared that they are and were lawfull. The politick distinctions in parl^t doe far, as to nicenes, exceed ye philosophicall distinctions of ye schollmen; and perhapps ther may be new classes of Aquinas's and Duns's.

*   *   *   *   *

I am y^r Lo^{pps} very humble servant,

C. HATTON.

THE SAME.

April 15, [1690].

I endeavoured, my L^d, to waite on my Ld Nottingham to day, but cou'd not; and shall try againe to morrow, and shall not forget Mr Martin's concern. I have been to day at Chelsey garden, and have made choice of 2 potts of ye passion-flower, and am very confident y^r Lo^{ppe} need not fear but they will thrive very well, they are soe lusty and stronge, and, if y^r garden[er] be carefull to lay y^m well, by this time 12 month you may have 20.

^{a} Charles Paulett, Marquess of Winchester, created Duke of Bolton in 1689.

I have sent y^r Lo^{ppe} y^e protestation of some of y^e L^{ds} ag$_t$ y^e Act of Recognition, about wch ther hath been soe many and hot debates. The reasons of y^e protest are, by order of y^e majority of y^e Lords by five, razed out of y^e journal; but y^e names of y^e protesting lords remaine, and they have with reason entred their protest ag$_t$ y^e razure of y^t reason for their first protest.

Last night a fire begun, about 12 at night, at y^e coffee house over y^e mews gate, wch burnt wth y^t violence y^t it wase thought fit to blow up y^e adjoyning houses on each hand, wch put a stop to it.

C. HATTON.

THE SAME.

My L^d,   April 26, [16]90.

Some of my old botanick acquaintances, having made an appointm^t to goe yesterday to Hampton Court (to see ye famous collection ther of ye rare Indian plantes wch mine Heer Fagel had gathered together), called on me, and I heartily wish'd y^r Lo^{ppe} had been ther, for there is about 400 rare Indian plantes wch were never seen in England; and there is scarce any desirable Indian plant, but a specimen may be seen ther; and some very curious Indian plants are in so great perfection y^t it is very wonderfull and scarce credible. The stoves in wch they are kept are much better contrived and built then any other in England.

Wee went by water and called at a D^{rs} house by ye way, wher I saw a very pretty flowering shrubb in his greenhouse, and I have enclosed 2 or 3 seeds, all I cou'd get; and if carefully sowed on a hotbed, I doubt not but they will come up.

The greatest news I can send you from here is y^t ye Abjuration

Bill is flung out of ye House of Commons, at w^{ch}, it is said, some are soe displeased y^t ther will be another bill brought in much to ye same effect.

My Ld Nottingham's abdication is now contradicted by ye coffee-house newsmongers. Wee are all here both to y^r Lo^{ppe} and all at Kirby most faithfull and very humble servants.

C. HATTON.

THE SAME.

May 15, [16]90.

*   *   *

Wee are likely to have here great bussle betwixt ye Wiggs and modern Tories, for ye Lords have passed ye bill for invalidating ye judgm^t ag^t ye charter of London and restoring ye old charter, by wch all ye old aldermen and magistrates of London, who were displaced when ye charter of London wase judg'd forfeited, are restored, and all vacancies since (by the 26 of this month) are by new elections to be filled up; so y^t by ye 26th a new Ld Mayor, new sheriffs, severall new aldermen, a new common councell, are to be chosen, wch you will easily imagine will occasion warm disputes.

Yesterday S^r Ed. Seymour in ye H. of Commons tooke occasion to fall a little foul upon ye white marquise,^a and wase seconded by Captⁿ Granville,^b my Ld Baths son. In return, some friends to [the] Marquise made some sever reflections on ye Earle of Bath, and, after some wrangling, ye business fell, and ye Marquises and Earle's honour (notwithstanding all reflections) are in statu quo.

C. HATTON.

^a Caermarthen.

^b John Granville, second son of John Earl of Bath, created Lord Granville of Potheridge in 1702.

THE SAME.

June 7, [16]90.

I hope, my L^d, it wase not any increase of y^r indisposition wch wase ye occasion I heard nothing from Kirby ye last post. And, tho' I have not much news to acquaint y^r Lo^{ppe}, yet I will send w^t I heare stirring, and in ye first place tell you w^t will be more surprising then afflicting to you. The famed Ferguson is committed to a messenger's hands on suspition of treason ag^t ye present governm^t.

This day Captn Crone^a wase ye 3^d time tryed and found guilty of high treason; but, before ye jury brought him in guilty, they were shut up from 3 of ye clocke yesterday in ye afternoone till one this afternoone, after wch in arrest of judgm^t he pleaded an errour in ye indictm^t as found by ye grand jury, for they signed it Billa Verra; and the judges have appointed to have it argued by councell before y^m next Thursday.

It is reported y^t ye Queen Dowager is ordered to goe either to Windsor or Audle-End, because ye Papists, on pretence of going to her chappell, doe meet and caball. The truth is, ye popish party are very insolent and impudently give ye ly to all other publick news, and, tho' every publick intelligence tells us how ye Highlanders are run down, y^t ye popish party give out y^t they [are] very strong and have lately received great recruits from Ireland. Wee shall never be happy till all our damnable lyers are confounded, wch God speedily grant.

I and all here are, wth great sincerity, to y^r Lo^{ppe} and all at Kirby most faithfull and humble servants.

C. HATTON.

---

^{a} Matthew Crone, the Jacobite emissary. He saved his life by giving information of the designed invasion.

The same.

June 17, [16]90.

*   *   ⁓   *

Wee have here very little news stirring. These infidells, yᵉ Jacobites, goe about to shamme all yᵉ glorious defeat of yᵉ Thoulon fleet, and wou'd have it pass for a shamme, and they wickedly endeavour to persuade yᵉ people our gazeteer is noe more infallible than yᵉ pope.[a]

*

C. Hatton.

The Countess of Nottingham.

Thursday, yᵉ 26 of June, [1690].

*   ⁓   *   *

I find, when yʳ Losp. writ yʳˢ, you were ignorant of the expectations we are here in of hearing every moment of some engagement at sea between our fleet and the French, for they have layn in sight of one another this 4 days. Wt will the consequence be wee are in great impatience to know.

I thinke from the first yᵗ I heard it till to day I have thought of nothing else; but now indeed wt my uncle Hatton has by his foolishness brought himself into is some concern to me, and I belive will be so to yʳ Losp. when you hear.[b] Upon suspicion and some discovery several people have been secured in the Tower: my Lord

---

[a] The infidels were right.

[b] Luttrell, under date of 22d June, has the entry: " Captain Hatton, brother to the lord Hatton, is committed to the Tower for handing to the presse a treasonable paper against the government."

Clarendon and my Lord Newburgh,[a] S[r] John Fenwick, Charles Turner, and several more;[b] and he, by the foolishness of his talk and the company he kept, together wth the accusation of one Brown, either a bookseller or printer, who is in custody, who sayd he delivered him a booke, w[ch] he published, call[ed] an Answer to a letter to a Bishop (w[ch] was writ by the Bishop of St. Asaph). In y[e] answer to it there are, it is said, very scurolous things on the Governnment; so, upon this, by the messenger of the press he was siezed on this morning and carried before the Councell, were he was soe thorowlly bewitchd as to owne the haveing writ it, w[ch] after all I dont thinke he did, when, if he had not owned it, there was but one witness against him; but now he dexterously adds himself.

Y[r] Losp. speaking of coming up, tho you seem not to be more inclined to it then business oblige you, may not be improper upon this account. I hope it may be no prejudic to y[r] health, because you say nothing of it nor my brother and sisters. I begg my humble dutty to my Lady and service to my Aunt.

I am y[r] Losp. most obedient daughter,

A. NOTTINGHAM.

ELIZABETH HATTON.[c]

June y[e] 28, [1690].

I was not capable, my Lord, y[e] last post of acquainting y[ur] L[dpps] of y[e] ill news of M[r] Hatton being sent to y[e] Tower by y[e] Privy Counsell, for high treason, for writing a book w[ch] he owned. He is

---

[a] Charles Livingston, second Earl of Newburgh.
[b] On the charge of inviting a French invasion.
[c] Wife of Charles Hatton, and daughter of Sir William Scroggs. Her letters are illiterate, even for that age, for one in her position.

now a close prisoner. I resolve to goe to him next week, and I must be confined. I have indeavoured to a got leve to a gon out and in, but it will not be granted. I am in great hopes y^r L^{dpps} will be in town before I goe to ye Tower. He went a Thursday night, wch prevented his writing to y^r L^{dpps}. He sent down 2 books by ye carrier. Y^e dicktionary, wch y^r L^{dpps} sent to know ye price, is seven and twenty shillings. I beg my humble servis to my Lady and my sister Hatton. I hope they will pardon me in not writing, for my sorrows are soe great it makes me not able to pay my duty. My most humble servis to y^r L^{dpps}, my Lady, my sister Hatton.

I am y^r L^{dpps}

Most faithfull,

Humble serv^t,

E. HATTON.

I hope y^r L^{dpps} will pardon me, for I doe not know what I say, I am in such amaise.

THE SAME.

July ye 3, [16]90.

I received y^r Ld^{pps} kind letter, wch at this present time I doe much want. I could wish I wase able to give y^r Ld^{pps} a true account of what Mr Hatton is acused of; but I am very ignorant, for I did not in ye least know of anything tell ye messenger came for him, and then I had not time to inquire of him, and I cannot larne of any person that have seen it what is in it, but most doe say there is nothing in that can tuch his life. I trust in God tis true; but they have pecch him of high treason, wch makes a great sound. He is kept a very close prisoner, for wee cannot get leave that any person should be admited, tho a warder is by. I have don all I can in ye world to get leave to goe into ye Tower, tho I am willing to be a close prisenor; for he hath noebody wth him, and, should he be sick, it may prove of a very ill consequence. As for getting him bailed, it is impossible to have it don, for there is noe hopes of his coming out tell next term, and his clos confinement I much fear will much prejudice his health. I beg of y^r Ld^{pps} to writ to ye President that he may have ye liberty of ye Tower, and that he may be aloud that sumtimes he may see his frends or those persons wch he hath reall business wth concerning his one affairs. And allsoe I humble beg y^r Ld^{pps} will be pleased to writ to som of ye Privi Counsell, that I may have order to goe into ye Tower, for I will asure y^r Ld^{pps} I am under soe much sorrow that tis impossibell to be exprest, or can I support myself, for I can declare I have sleept not one houre in a night sence he hath ben there. I have another favor to desire of y^r Ld^{pps}, that y^u would be pleased to consider his condition, and that ye place is very chargeable, and noe person that he doe owe but sixpence to but is pressing and rude, wch makes me exposed daly to great inconveniencys.

*   *   *   *   *

I am y^r Ld^{pps} most faithfull, humble servent,

E. HATTON.

THE COUNTESS OF NOTTINGHAM.

Thursday, ye 3 of July, [1690.]

My Lord has at this present so little time to himself, he hopes your Lord^{sp} will pardon his not writting to you, but will not be failling to doe what lyes in his power to serve him whom y^r Losp. recommends to him, whoes proceedings as been after his usualle method, and would more have surprised had it been from anny other body but himself.

We are all in twone full of what concerns the fleet,[a] upon w^{ch}

---

[a] The battle of Beachy Head was fought on the 30th June.

account my Lord Torrington is very hardly spoke of, whither diservedly or no, I must have a better insight to sea fight then I have at this distance to, to venter to judge whither he deserves it or no; but wone thing is certaine, y^t, after the engagement was begun, he let all lye upon the Dutch squadron and did not engage at all wth the French fleet, wch squadron had certainly been quite lost, but y^t the Duke of Grafton, who in this expedition has got immortal fame, would fight, and wone ship more came to there assistance. It pleased God to give y^t success to there undertaking y^t wth twenty ships, wch were the number of the Dutch and these two that came to there assistance, they made there party so good wth the French fleet, wch was of eighty two ships, y^t but wone Dutch ship was lost. There is eight disabled, but will in a little while be fitted up againe; of them, a Dutch Vice Admiral and a Rear Admirall and two captaines are killed; and of our, wone Captaine Botham and Captaine Pomeroy. There is a report y^t six ships of the French are disabled, and y^t they are toing them towards some of there owne ports, and y^t the Plimouth squardon is gone after them. My Lord Stweard[a] and my Lord Pembroke[b] have been so brave to offer their service to the Queene, and are gone downe to Dover. I suppose my Lord Pembroke will command his owne Marine regiment, and my Lord Stwart will either be a volontier or have some command.

It is past ten a clock. I am afraid the post will be gone.

I am y^r Losp. most obedient daughter,

A. NOTTINGHAM.

SIR CHARLES LYTTELTON.

MY LORD, Shene, July 5th, [1690].

I was yesterday in town, where I heard such melancholy acct^s of our fleet that I can't see w^{ht} in our time scarce can be hoped will

---

[a] William Cavendish, Earl, afterwards Duke, of Devonshire.
[b] Thomas Herbert, eighth Earl of Pembroke, First Lord of the Admiralty.

redeeme ye honor and the interest we have lost by the late action at sea, nor ye fatall consequence it may be like to be to ye nation and all Xtendom. The best acc^t of it y^t I c^d learn is, that our fleet did not fight, while the Duch were torn to peeces, who have lost severall of theyr best men and ships, and y^t we retreat toward ye Downs as fast as the wind (wch is contrary) and ye tide will bring us, and y^t ye French at great rate pursue us. My L^{ds} Devonshire and Pembroke are sent to ye fleet to examine these matters, but wth w^{ht} powers to mend y^m I know not. Ld Torrington is most miserably reproached by ye mobile, and not y^t I can find excused by any for his conduct; and ye letters he has sent doe but rather increase y^n lessen it.

We are in huge expectation from Ireland, it being ye generall opinion ye armies have fought ere this;[a] but I must confesse I doe not beleeve, for I think, if K^g James can possibly, he will avoid fighting, and you know 'tis not very casie, and in a countrey where there are such strong posts, to force an army to fight. I had allmost forgot to tell you w^{ht} is reported and some suspect to be true, y^t ye French have sent severall gallies full of landmen, wth a fleet of 20 men of war, into St. Georges Channell.

I heard it said that ye parliment is like to be adjourned but for a fortnight, and y^n to meet and sit, there being a necessity for a supply, pour faire roler le monde; yet I phancy, if you doe at this time presse hard for y^r guarrison, you may be more likely to get something for y^m then in a better time. I am very sorry, my Lord, to find that y^r paines have returned so ill on you, but I phancy y^t w^{ht} you say does add to ye uneasiness will abate. My son I hope does mend. He recovers his appetite and strength, but he coughs no blood.

---

[a] It will be remembered that the battle of the Boyne was fought on the 1st July.

The same.

MY LORD, Shene, July 30th, [1690.]

I assure you I had done y^t matter some time since, but y^t I waited for a fit pretence and opportunity to doe it, wch I now took by my neighbour, S^r H[enry] Capell; and I think her Matie was not dissattisfied wth me in it. She was pleased to tell me, as I thought I writt to y^r L^p, that, being my buisnesse wou'd not give me leave to attend it, I did very well to give it up to her hand; so she took it and put it in her pocket, I meane ye commission. I must needes own y^t t'was very inconvenient to my present circumstance to quit or part wth 5 or 600^{li} a yeare; yet I thank God I find so much ease by it, that yet I doe not repent mee and hope I never shall. But, if I had not quitted, truly I found I c^d not keep it but upon such termes as it were not worth ye having, to live, as long as this war last, allmost constantly upon it; for so I found it was expected and y^t I sh^d have bine commanded so to do, w^{ch}, had I neglected, w^d have suspended me, as it did, or turnd me quite out. The suspending I told y^r L^p of was but upon a pretence taken, not given, and, to deale more freely wth y^r L^p, I cou'd not feare ye meane applications I found w^d be required of me from ye noble peer, my Ld Marlboro, to keep myself in, and ye little affronts I rec^d every day from ye officers who commanded there, as to one they thought they might presume to deale with for not being in y^t favour at Court to support me ^{ag}st it. But there is another thing behind wch weighed as much and more wth me yⁿ all this, and that was, I began to find myself pressed to sign an addresse of renouncing my late master, w^{ch}, however, I had sufficiently done in effect, wou'd have bine so odious an ingrattitude I despised any advantage to oblige me to, and, whoever they are that have put that a foot, I am confident have done theyr present Maties no service in.

I dont heare yet who does succeed me in ye gov^{mt}, but, if the

King be returned, who I heare was expected on Tuesday at Chester,[a] we shall soon know.

My Lord, if it ben't past ye season, I beg you will give me a side of venison, baked, in 2 or 3 little pots. I wish your Lord^ps health.

ELIZABETH HATTON.

Augt ye 24, [1690].

Last Tuesday, my Lord, I got an order to have ye freedom of ye Tower. I went immediait thither. I thank God I found him very well in helth, and I did not return to ye Pell Mell tell this day, wch I had not come home soe sune but to meet ye D^trs and sirgent about my son, wch is in a very weak condition. Mr Hatton does asure me there was never anything offerd in ye least to him or proposed sence his confinem^t. He fears he shall not be bailed. He hopes he shall have ye freedom of seeing his frends, wch as yet he hath not. If y^r L^dpps could obtain that favor, it would be to his satisfaction. As for anything elce, he beleives it is to noe purpose for y^r L^dpps to give y^rself ye trouble as yet to endeavor. He gives his most humble servis to y^r Ld^pps, my Lady. Sence I came to ye Tower her hath com to or 3 frends, but I suppose it will be forbid if any more should come, they hereing I had an order, wch maid them conclude he had ye freedom of seeing his frends. If I did in ye least know that anything had been propose to Mr Hatton, I doe asure y^r Ld^pps I would let y^u know. My humble servis to my Lady and y^r Ld^pps.

I am y^r Ld^pps most faithfull, humble serv^t,

E. HATTON.

My servis to my sister Hatton.

---

[a] William remained in Ireland till September.

SIR CHARLES LYTTELTON.

MY LORD,   London, Sep^{br} 6, [1690.]

I have had so much concern ab^t my sons being wounded at a duell wth ye Major of ye Guards, Will Mathews, y^t really I forget if I have told you of it. They fought at Fulham. My son was run through ye thigh, and tis a very great wound, but I hope ye worst is over and he is in a faire way to recover. He came hither, after he was drest upon ye place, in a coach; but bled all ye way. There is no letters from Ireland since Wednesday. One from ye Secretary of War there to Mr Blath[wayt] is much talked of by that post, for it seemes to intimate y^t ye seige w^d be raised[a] and y^t ye weather was so bad they feared they c^d not bring of ye great gunns; but all other letters say they were preparing for another assault, wch we waite wth some doubt of ye successe of, for now we heare of a very strong guarrison, as y^t there are 4000 gentlemen in ye town, whom ye K^g has excepted as to theyr estates, besides 2000 French; and truly so it seemes, by ye defence they make, that they are strong and desperate.

CHARLES HATTON TO HIS WIFE.

Novr 11, [16]90.

I am very sorry, my dearest, y^t y^r son Robin continues soe very ill. God grant he may receive benefit by the advice of ye new surgeon. But, my dearest, I fear my threats will prove more effectual then I designed; for I told thee in jest if thou did pass Sunday thou shou'dst be shut out, wch is likely to prove true in earnest, for ye hungry head jaylor here is soe greedy of his pretended fee h; growes every day more and more barbarous and vexatious. Had he been educated at Ambonia, he cou'd not be more merciless. And finding y^t noe person will take notice of his extravagant usage of me, he is ye more encouraged therto.

[a] The siege of Limerick was already raised on the 29th August.

Worthy Mr Ennis, who being turned out of his living here for not swearing and therfore not capacitated to exercise his ecclesiastick function in his own country, Scotland, is this weeke going to try whither he cannot more quietly live among ye heathens in America, and last Sunday in ye afternoon came to take leave of me, and brought wth him Mr Sawyer, who came to renew y^t 2d time I saw him ye promise he made me ye first time I ever did, wch is to be bayle for me. But on Monday morning came gingle-key, by his masters order, foaming at ye warder for leting any person come to me, and charged him he shou'd let noebody come at me.

Certainly I shall be either tryed or bayled. If tryed, it is a strang outlandish barbarity not practic'd heretofore in England not to have ye advise of counsell to prepare for a defence, and, in order therto, to advise wth y^m. I am certain, in ye Popish plot all ye prisoners had, some considerable time before their tryal, ye freedom of having their freinds and councell come to them.

If I be bayled, it is very reasonable I shou'd endeavour to find out some persons who are willing to doe me y^t kindness, and ag^t whom ther can be noe exception; and y^t I find very difficult; and prithee, my dearest, doe you endeavour w^t you can to find out some, for, tho very probably I shall not have occasion for them, yet it wou'd be very vexatious to want them shou'd ther be occasion.

I am very much concern'd my brother Hatton shou'd for his health be forced out of town. Both for his sake and my own, I wish you cou'd contrive some way to acquaint my brother wth my distress and prevaile wth him to endeavour to get his son in law to stop ye mouth of ye hungry cur here, for I cannot doe it wth a crust, it wou'd be too costly.

My cloak transformed in a coat is too thinn for this cold place. Pray let ye linning of ye cloake be sent to ye taylor to interline ye coat. The buttons are as you ordred, and therfore you may be secure they please me, and I assure you they doe without any compliment; but, if they did not, I durst not find fault, wch I know you will beleeve.

A dieu, my dearest. If you come alone, you are welcome; but more, if wth liberty of my seeing my freinds.

If that honest Scot, Mr. Ennis (whose integrity is a disgrace to most Englishmen of his coate), comes to bid you farewell, pray acknowledge his kindness to me, y^rself, and y^r son.

Elizabeth Hatton.

[12 Nov., 1690.]

I would have waited on y^r Ld^{shpps}, but that I had not ye couveniency of a coach. I am hartily sory to here ye ill news of y^r Ld^{pps} ill helth. I have received a letter from Mr Hatton to send to y^r Ld^{pps}. My Lord Lucus doth ^{yuse} Mr Hatton wth great unkindness. A Sunday last one Mr Ennes came to take his leave, for he was goeing for Barbadoes, and brought wth him Mr Sawyer of Kettering, a barrister of law, who offers himself to be baile. My Lord Lucus, being informed therewith, sent a repremand to ye warder for letting any person goe to him. After he hath petition for a triall, and 5 months close imprisonme^t, to be deprived to advise wth counsell is very hard and never was done before. I beg y^r Ld^{pps}, and soe doe Mr H., that y^u would be pleased to move for more liberty. I suppose y^r Ld^{pps} hath herd how angrey my Ld Lucus was for my Ld Salsbury coming to dine wth Mr Hatton, tho my L^d first went to my L^ı Lucus; he not being at home, sent to ye Deputy. He was not at home. He called Major Hally, and he staid wth them tell my L^d went away. Yet his Ld^{pps} was in a great raig, and then forbid any to come to Mr Hatton. I beg once more of y^r Ld^{pps} that he may not be yoused wth this severity. Y^e inclosed I desire y^r Ld^{pps} to return. Mr H. desires y^r Ld^{pps} to send to sound M^r

Atturn[ey] Gen[eral] and ye Solicitor, to know there intentions how they will proseed. Y^r Ld^pps was pleased to promis y^u would. He shall be in distress of baile. I hope y^r Ld^pps will be pleased to procure him sum, for now in a few days he will have ocation for them, for there names must be sent to Mr Arosmith, to see how he aproves of them. Mr Hatton ordered me to writ to y^r Ld^pps yesterday, and this morning he hath writ to yr Ld^ppa. Perhapps he hath writ this to y^r Ld^pps; but I cannot tell wheather he hath or not makes me give y^r Ld^pps this troubell. My very humble servis to my Lady, my sister Hatton, and prety Miss.

I am y^r Ld^pps most faithfull servant,

E. HATTON.

THE COUNTESS OF NOTTINGHAM.

Y^e 3^d of March, [1691].

I am very glad to heare y^r Losp. and all y^c company gott so well to Maidwell, wch I was so forgetfull not to thinke you were there but sent my letter to Kirby, wch made it longer before it gott to you. My Ld Finch^a has writ a letter to my sister Betty, wch I hope she has recievid. Hear is a most dismal story of my Ld Salisberys two brothers^b who he sent into France. They were at St. Germains, and lay in a room together and quarreld, tis not yet known for what, but rise out of bed and tooke there swords, and fought, tell they both fell dwone, wch was heared in room under them. They that were there run up to there chamber door, wch they found fastend, but, forcing it open, found them weltring in thier blood and craling to ask one another pardon. Tis sayed there was little hopes that either could recover. Some letters say the eldest was already dead, tho

---

^a Her son Daniel.

^b They were William and, probably, George Cecil, younger sons of James, third Earl of Salisbury.

wone cannot say this is certain; there are so manny letters that speake of it y^t there relations are fearfull it is too true.

Sr Edward Villars is to be a Viscount,^{a} but wither English or no I cant tell. I begg the favour of y^r Losp. to give my hum^{ble} dutty to my Lady. I am y^r Losp. most obedient duttyfull daughter,

A. NOTTINGHAM.

CHARLES HATTON.

March 5, [16]9$\frac{9}{8}$.

I have, my Lord, been soe unfortunate y^t I cou'd not possibly dispatch my business this weeke, but I doubt not but y^e next weeke by y^e Oundle coach to waite on y^r Lo^{ppe}.

I wase yesterday at Mr Ashmoles. Both he and Mrs Ashmole are very ill. They give their humble service to y^r Lo^{ppe}, and, had any of ye layers of his arbutus taken root, I had sent you some; for he ordred his gardener to dig y^m up, wch he did in my presence, but noe one layer had any root. He gave me some of ye fruit dryed, wch he sath if sown will grow. I have sent y^m (in a box of toies wch my wife sends to my nephews and neices), and wth y^m some of ye great hawes, and also some of ye Rhodia Radix wch must be planted in a pot. And I have likewise sent 3 little bundles of grafts of peare trees, much commended by Mr Ashmole. They were cut of of standard trees. No. 1, an excellent peare to eat raw. No. 2, a very good baking peare and a great bearer. He calls it ye ladies on [own?] thigh. No. 3, ye Ashmole peare, some of wch have weighed 20 ounces. It is an excellent baking peare. Wth those grafts are 2 bundles of grafts of his famous great haw tree, wch must be grafted on white or blacke thorne and will doe very well to be planted in y^r wilderness.

*   *

C. HATTON.

^{a} Sir Edward Villiers, created Baron Villiers of Hoo and Viscount Villiers of Dartford, 20 March, 1691.

Sir Charles Lyttelton.

MY LORD,   Shene, May y⁰ 30ᵗʰ, [1691].

Yᵉ prorogation lookes like an intention of a new parlimᵗ. The
new ABᵖ ᵃ sent to yᵉ old one to leave Lambeth to him, that he
might be consecrated there; to wᶜʰ yᵉ old answered, he shᵈ make
use of his chappell himself on Sunday, to give yᵉ sacrament; and I
am told for certaine he is resolved not to quitt his house till they
force him out of it; but I am wᵗʰall told he meanes, when they
come to thrust him violently out, to leave it himself, and two
servants in it to keep the possession, and yᵉ doores lockt. The Bᵖ
of London refused to consecrate him too.

The same.

MY LORD,   Shene, June 18ᵗʰ, [1691].

I came home from Chester on Tuesday. I saw yᵉ fleet pass by yᵉ
Wash on Friday and Satturday, and 13 on Munday, wᶜʰ I suppose
were going after yᵐ. I heare yᵉ French lye so in the bay at Belisle
yᵗ, if they will not come out, our fleet will find it very difficult to
goe into them and force them to fight us.

The campagne has opened successfully in Ireland by yᵉ taking of
Ballimore by 'storm.ᵇ There is little from Flanders, as I heare, yet,
but I must tell you of wʰᵗ I heare lately happened. Yᵉ Kᵍ ordred
a great detachment, and a generall officer to command it, to forrage.
Yᵉ officer refused to go, as below his post. Yᵉ Kᵍ brought it to yᵉ
councill of war. Yᵉ councill advised the officer had reason, and that
there was no practisse or president that such a party had bine commanded by more yⁿ Lᵗ Coll: or Coll. The King told yᵐ he wᵈ
make a president himself, and did so, for he commanded yᵉ party in
person.

ᵃ Tillotson, who superseded Sancroft on the 23rd April.
ᵇ On the 7th June.

THE SAME.

MY LORD,   London, Novr 19th, [1691].

  *   *   *   *   *

The spotted feavor has bine in my mother Fairfax's family at Steeton, and carried of my sister Bladen ^{a} and severall of ye servants; and her husband and children had it, but they recovered. He is not like to be so soon quit of my Lord Carmarthens persecution, wch ruine him and his.

The H. of Com^s have passd ye bill for trialls in treason, that ye prisoner be allowd copie of his charges, councell, and wittnesses sworn in his behalf. This was much opposed by ye Attorney Gen^{ll} ^{b} and supported by Mr Finch and most of his robe.

They have voted 1,600,000^{li} for ye navy and passd ye bill of Additionall Excise. However, there seemes to be no great for-wardnesse in the House for ye supplyes. They w^d not consider of y^t for ye army, till they have more sattisfaction how ye K^g intends to dispose of the forces; and I beleeve ye bill they are upon, con-cerning ye musters, will not at all be acceptable to him, because it will highly disgust all ye forces and render ye commands allmost impracticable, if there be not great amendm^{ts} to ye bill. There is great expectation whispered of a project of peace, and in it to allow K^g James a pention for life and ye P. of Wales tittle after King William's. I have told you news enough and more y^n, it may be, is true; yet there is a greate deale more, as y^t the peace with ye Turk is like to be concluded, that ye Emperor is dead or dying, y^t Teckely ^{c} is beaten at ye releife of Warradin. Y^e frigot supposed to be lost got of and come home.

---

^{a} Isabella, daughter of Sir William Fairfax of Steeton, and sister of Lyttelton's first wife. She was married to Nathaniel Bladen, of Hemsworth, barrister.

^{b} Sir George Treby.

^{c} Emeric Tekeli, the Hungarian chief.

There is a pamphlet lately come forth mitily sought after, and ye printer and author; tis stiled Y^e Royall Martyr. 'Tis odds it has bine sent you as well as to others; for I heare it has bin generally dispersd.

SIR EDMUND KING.

MY LORD,   [2nd Jan. 1692.]

My being out of my bed 2 nights together wth Mr Boyle,[a] who's death I foretold the first day he complaind of an alteration, wch was Tuesday; and that day I tolde my Ld Rochester and others of his friends and desir'd an other physician to be sent for, wch was y^t night; and at 10, as I told yor L^p, I was sent for to be in the house all night, but did not let him kno it, for fear of surprizing him (he was up all Tuesday). Wednesday morn was much better, but exceeding low and faint; would rise in the afternoon, and at 5 we met and desir'd him to goe to bed at 7. Dr Stockholm[b] was to sit up; but at 10 or 11 he grew worss, so that my Lord Rana- lough and Lady Thanet Dowager, etc., was sent for, and they sent for me. I was just hot in my bed, after something I had taken for my great colde; and, tho' I had not a graine of hope he would live till I came, yet, considering it was the last attempt I could make to serve won who for many years past had great affection for me and rely'd under God, as he often told me, upon my care, I was resolv'd to goe to him. It was one a clock in the night; but he was dead before I eam. His lamp went out for want of oyle; soe did his sister's too. He was buried last night at St. Martin's, and lyes by his sister.[c] The Bishop of Salisburie preachd his funerall

---

[a] The famous Robert Boyle.　　　　[b] Dr. William Stokeham.

[c] Catherine, daughter of Richard, Earl of Cork, and wife of Arthur, Viscount Ranelagh.

sermon, and gave a large and true character becoming so great a man as he was, and whos 2ᵈ in universall knowledge, etc., 'twill be hard to finde. The Bishop saide he had a conversation wᵗʰ him the better part of 29 years; but mine has been above 30 years, and, the last 10 or 12, not 4 days together from him, if in towne. It would make me look vaine to relate his affectionate expressions to me. He has been kept alive, by God's blessing, upon the dint of care severall years, to a woonder. But I aske yoʳ Lordᵖˢ pardon for being soe long upon this subject. Seeing the subject will bear it, I hope you'l excuse it.

I suppose yoʳ Lordᵖ has heard of the barbarous murder of Dʳ Clinch.ᵃ He liv'd in Browlow street in Holborn. Monday night last about 9 at night, 2 men came in a hacknie coach to call him to won not well; but he was not at home, and they said they'd come againe. About 10 the same night they came to the end of the street, and sent the coachman for him. He, poor man, tooke his cloak and went to them into the coach; they bid the coachman drive to the Py wᵗʰout Algate. But, as soone as they had him, they began their villanies; for his hat was found in the street near Barnards Inn, and we believe he was soon dead. And ther, to blind the coachman, they enquir'd for a man ther near Aldgate noebody knew. By this time the dead man began to be colde and stiffish, yᵗ they was sure he was dead. When they cam back as far as Leaden Hall street, they call'd the coachman and gave him 3ˢ 6ᵈ to buye 2 pulletts for supper. The man gott them quickly, and, when he cam back, ther was only yᵉ Dʳ dead and allmost colde; the murderors gon.

About 14 days since, 2 huffing men cam at night for me in a hack; but I was abroad. They came a 2ᵈ time and was angrie I was not at home. Then my wife sent them word they had best get another Dʳ, (ther's enow,) for she beleivd, if I did com home, I

ᵃ Dr. Andrew Clenche, for whose murder Henry Harrison was tried and hanged.

would not goe wth them, nor should not if she could helpe it; soe they went away much out of humour.

But, before this, I escap'd an eminent danger of ye kinde, I bless God, wch has stuck by me ever since. But this of Dr Clinch is a terrible thing. It was reported in the cittie it was me, to the great concern of many of my friends; but my coach being in ye cittie y^t morning gavc thcm another acct, wch was too true. My [L^d] Falconberge cam to my house himselfe and severall others.

Since I writ this, we are inform'd those taken upon suspition are the very persons y^t murdered him; one Harison especially.

Just now the D^{rs} wife and the Vice-president of the Colledg send to me to com in my gown to assist wth him at the pall this Satterday night. I am not well, yet intend to goe, to pay the last respect to him.

Sir Charles Lyttelton.

London, Jan. 9th, [1692].

*   *   *   *   *

Mr Robt Boyl was buried at St. Martins, on Thursday, in ye same grave wth his sister Ranelagh. He was not sick above 3 houres, but s^d his heart was broke when she died. The B^p of Salisbury preached his funerall sermon, at wch there was a mighty crowd.

There is an odd report goes that, when Lady Ranelagh lay dying, there was a flame broke out of one of ye chimneys, wch being observed by ye neighbours gave notice of it, and, the chimney being looked [into], there was no cause found for it in ye inside, yet appeared to flame for som time to those wthout; and ye same thing happened when Mr Boyl died; but ye B^p, by ye way, mentioned nothing of it in his sermon, but abundance of ye flames of his charrity.

I can say little to w^{ht} you have heard more yⁿ that I had ye report of it concerning Lady Fran: There are many ways proposed to raise ye money, but none yet that will do it, if agreed to, and makes some think will therefore conclude in an excise upon meate &c.

THE SAME.

MY GOOD LORD,   London Jan. ye 28th, [1692].

I acknowledg ye noble kind offer you make me of y^r house at Maidwell wth all the thankes in ye world, tho' I am not like to receive the benefit by it you intended me; for I beleeve I shall have some businesse will oblige me to stay here some time after I leave Shene, wch wont be till ye later end of Ap^{ll}, and Hagley, I think, is much as it was in repaire when you were at it; so y^t, after my rate of living is like to be there, there will need little to do but furnish it, wch I have but too much of. As to my pictures, I have a good many of Sr Peter Lillyes, wch I am told will not yeeld neer w^{ht} they cost; and I doubt those of more esteeme will not be very ready money, unlesse mitily undersold, at this time, because there are so many auctions, as the Duke of Norfolks and others, of ye best collections.

But these are not all he has a mind to part wth, for there is scarce anything talked of but his endeavoring to be divorced from his wife,^a and w^{ht} ye wittnesses have sworn in ye Lords House ab^t her

---

^a Henry, seventh Duke of Norfolk, married Mary, daughter of Henry Mordaunt, Earl of Peterborough. He did not obtain a divorce till the year 1700. She afterwards married Sir John Germain, Bart.

amours wth Mr Germain. To morrow she is there to make her
defence, wch she must have a great deale of assurance to be able in
person to do, as I heare she intends, and has bine once there allready
to give em a pritty good essay. She is not over bashfull where her
honor and innocence are at stake. I don't know if you have heard
that Mr Germain is ye supposed bastard of ye K^g William's father,
as is Monsr de Lawn another, who is ye Queens secretary. The
K^g was all day at ye Lords house a Tuesday to heare ye evidence at
ye Lords House; and 'tis s^d ye K^g and Q. have expressed a great
deale of warmth for ye Duke. But she has a strong party in y^e
House however, and y^t of ye Court faction to support her. My L^d
Nottingham is ^ag^st her.

We have no news from abroad, and I beleeve ye ports are froze
up. Some thing may be expected, when they are open from this
hard frost.

My Ld Churchill's disgrace has yet made no great change but in
ye disposal of his places; nor has it had any consequence to his b^rs,
but that one of y^m who was cornet to ye troop is made 1st L^t

------

THE SAME.

MY LORD,   Feb. ye 9th, [1692].

W^ht you seeme not to heare of ab^t ye reason of Ld Marlboro: disgrace I thought I had given you a good acc^t of, because it all came
from Ld Carmarthen, Ld Nottingham, and Ld Mar: himself; and all
agreed in this, that ye K^g, besides other things of high misdemeanor,
said he had held correspondence wth K^g James. I suppose you
know Ld Twaddale is Chan: of Scotland, who made ye D. Hamilton
ye complim^t to desire he might receive his com^n from his hand, as
Presid^t of ye Councill, and at the same time making him a visit;
this condescention he choosing ye rather to make, as 'tis said,

because he w^d avoid chocquing him, because he affected that honor for himself. He did indeed, the next day, call the Councill together; but did not come himself, nor has he bine there since, and they say has expressd his discontent other[wise] and bin at theyr conventicles, for such they will yet have, tho' the presbittery be settled in all the churches.

Something is the matter. The K^g is ill satisfied wth ye Assembly; and there is an order gon down to breake it up, wch some think will put the rigid party into a flame and beget some disorder in ye kingdom. The Lt Norfolks bill was againe upon the tapis to-day; but I can give you no acct of it, but that I heard y^t 2 of his wittnesses were prooved perjured in ye L^{ds} House at this triall. Last night there was a great ball at Kensington, and, after, ye French made a great supper in ye Kings eating room for as many as c^d sitt at it, and in another room wine and bread for every body ìa mode de Versalles. I do think of sending my pictures to Mr Walton's,^a for, if I dont sell them wth ye house, wch I dont expect, I shant know where to put them.

<hr>

THE SAME.

MY LORD,	Shene, March 7th, [1692].

I have y^{rs} upon y^r return from Maidwell, and am glad you have so good reason still to like y^r purchasse. In a letter I lately had from y^r L^p, you said something by way of caution to my dealing wth Mr Walton, wch pray, my Lord, be a little more plaine wth mee. Have you had any experience of his not dealing fairly wth you? For I have bine advised and know not who to trust better in y^e

^a Parry Walton, keeper of the pictures to James II.

disposal of my pictures. Y^e method I use wth him: I send y^m to a house closs by him, for he has not room in his own, it is allready so full, and there he cleanes them and mends w^ht is worn or torn; and, after, I am to get a couple of painters who, together wth himself, appraise y^m; wch appraisem^t the 2 painters set theyr hands to ye list of; and then they will be exposed in an auction, but such as will be privately bought. And onc I sold so here a Satturday, wch was a half length of Antonio Mores drawing, for 30^li. My ink is so bad I can scarce make it doe. Y^t picture was crackt quite through and on ye side of ye face, wch made it 10^li ye wors.

I have a very good copy, wch you may remember to have seen upon my staires, of Ch: ye 1st upon ye white hors. Y^e originall is Vandike and ye copy Remee. If I had y^r hall or a good staire case to put it, I sh^d not be tempted to sell it. If you know anybody it will fit, pray tell em of it; 50^li will be ye lowest price of it.

THE SAME.

MY LORD,   Shene, March 13, [1692].

*   *   *

One writt me word last night y^t my Fort Major was sent up by my Lt Govr wth a gentleman he arrested at Sherenesse, who brought him a message from K^g James and Q. Mary and a key, w^ch, being unscrewed, had a letter in it to him, as ye man told him. But he did not unscrew ye key, so saw not ye letter, but sent it up to my Ld Shrewsbury wth ye gentleman prisoner; and this is all I know of it as yet.

The same.

My Lord,   Shene, March 15, [1692].

Since Thursday I rec^d a letter from C[apt?] Crawford, giving me a more particular acc^t of ye bringing him ye message and letter in ye key, wch was pretended to be from Q. Mary in France. The man, wth ye greatest seeming secrecy in ye world, told him privately he had a letter from her to him, wch he imediately so rated him he was mitily surprized, and just as he was going to committ him he urged him to take ye letter, ^{Wch} he s^d he need not scruple, it was so privately done up in ye pipe of a key. But y^n he calld in out of ye next room to see and heare w^{ht} was offred him and w^{ht} he had done to resent it, and, when he saw he w^d commit him, y^n he pulld out a passe or gen^{ll} protection from my L^d Sh[rewsbury], wch Crawford s^d sh^d serve him from being used like a rogue, as he deserved, but not from being a prisoner; and so he sent up ye key and letter in it unscrewd to my L^d Sh., begging y^t, when his ^{Matie} had inquired into it and was sattisfied, he might be righted. Y^e man told him soon after that, as he had resented ye thing, it might doe him ye greatest right imaginable, for ye King, he said, saw ye key and letter and sent him down to try him &c.

Crawford ^{a} is chose a member of parlim^t.

---

^{a} Robert Crawford, M.P. for Queenborough.

CHARLES HATTON.

Pell-Mell, April 10, [16]92.

      *   *   *

The only news 'we have yet heard is y^t great preparations are making to send forces to Guernsey and Jersey, and y^t engineers are going thither to fortify those islands, whereof some of ye cheifest officers are to be made governors, as ye common report is; wch I thought fit to hint to y^r Lo^{pp}, who will, I assure myself, receive a more perfect and fuller account then I can give.

Harrison is condemned for ye murder of Dr Clinch. All provisions here are very dear. A loaf of bread, wch used to cost but 9 pence, costs now 12^d. Mutton ye best is 5^d ye pound. Beef 3^d. This is news more welcome to those who live in ye country then to them who are forced to be in town.

      *   *   *

C. HATTON.

SIR CHARLES LYTTELTON.

Ap^{ll} 18th, [1692].

It may be, you have not heard y^t my Ld Monmth layd a wager in a coffee house before he went away (wch was but yesterday), as they say, for Guernesey, 40^{li} to 10 that ye French w^d make a descent here before we made any in France. Whither this have given more ground for this allarum, or ye coming over of severall persons lately from K^g James, who have spread abroad y^t report, nay, that he is actually embarqued wth an army of 30000, whereof 8000 are hors, and Mareshall Belfond[a] to command y^m under him, I cannot tell; but 'tis in every ones thought and mouth, there is like to be an attempt of landing an army, and y^t very soon. And to make it more practicall, all ye forrain gazetts speake of a great army upon ye coast of Normandy, and that the French fleet is allready joynd and out. Ours is, in ye meane time, very sickly, and wanting many thousands of their complim^t to man them. Y^e K^g is expected too here very suddenly. The exchecquor shut up yet. There went away to-day 12 collonells for Flanders. L^d colchester,[b] it's said to-day, is taken coming over from thence in y^e Crown frigot wth others. I heare y^r L$_p$ has a letter sent you from y^e Councill to hasten to y^r command, wch I wish y^r L^{ps} health were such you c^d readily obey.

I have made but a poor market at y^e auction and not sold above 5 or 6 pictures.

S^r Ch: Hairo y^t commands the regim^t of Guards is killd by Collonell Hodges in Flanders.

THE SAME.

London, May 3^d, [1692].

I had y^r L^{ps} and give you many thanks for ye acct you are. pleasd to give mee of ye fayres, wch is little encouragem^t to send to y^m; besides we are so allarumd ab^t ye French that I have no mind to lay out my mony till y^t be over, for they tell us K^g James has bin twice abord ye French fleet and put out to sea and driven back by ill weather, not wthout great damage to his transport ships and losse of men. We have now 80 sayle, ye Duch quota being come wth Ld Portland, who came last night, ready, and orders to go to ye westward; and tis my poor. opinion ye French won't think it advizeable to try theyr fortune a 3^d time, when there is such a fleet to trouble y^m. Here is every night such breakeing of houses, and in y^t bold

---

[a] Bernardin Gigault, Marquis de Bellefonds.

[b] Thomas Savage, Viscount Colchester, son of Thomas, Earl Rivers.

manner, as if wee lived in a state of war. My Ld Dovers, ye last
night; and severall of his servants bound and wounded.

I wish y^r L^p better health.

THE SAME.

May 5th, [16]92.

Yesterday my L^{ds} Huntington and Malborough were both seized,
and, after being examined at Councill, sent to ye Tower. Ferguson
was seized to night and sent, too, to ye Tower. There are warrants
out for a great many: L^{ds} Scarsdeale,[a] Lichfield,[b] Griffith[c] and his
son, who all absent themselves. The guards are doubled and hors
centinells set at all ye avenues to Whitehall. Y^e Traind Bands, 2
companies every night in armes. The allarum is very hot of y^e
French coming; but I am not of opinion they can land, if ye fleet
we have out do theyr parts, as I think cant be doubted.

It's said ye Princess will be confined.

THE SAME.

Shene, May 10th, [1692].

I have y^r L^{ps} of ye 7th. I went to town yesterday ab^t some
buisnesse, els I had not gon out of my cell; for I am, my L^d, of y^r
advise in such times. 'Tis best to keepe closse, yet not lye hid, as I
allmost think some do that they may be looked after, and who els
w^d not. However it is, 'tis a very jealous time, but tis w^{ht} I wonder
at I confesse y^t people of such different principles, and one w^d think
interests, should be jumbled together under ye same prejudice as
papists, Ferguson, and they say Oates too; and y^t those noblemen
and great officers in ye army as stuck by K^g James sh^d now joyu
to consult and ingage theyr lives and fortunes wth ye Ld Malborough

----

[a] Robert Leke, third Earl of Scarsdale.   [b] Edward Henry Lee, Earl of Lichfield.
[c] A slip of the pen for Griffin.

and other officers of ye army, who once so traiterously deserted him, of wch there are s^d to be a great many of them who are allready secured, and warrants out for others; ye B^{ps} of Rochester ^{a} who is confined to his house wth a messenger, Bath and Wells ^{b} sent for.

My Ld Feversham was sent for and told y^t, by reason of ye great obligations he had rec^d from K^g James, ye gov^{m}t c^d not be sattisfied wth his conduct, unlesse he w^d retire into Holland till ye storme was over. I heare his answer was y^t he had given no ground to give ye gov^{m}t any reall ombrage; y^t he had much buisnesse here, both of ye Queenes his M^{rs} and his own; and y^t he resolved not to banish himself, but claimd his right of a peer and subject. My Ld Fanshaw brought his habeas corpus yesterday and had it; but, when he came to ye Hall, the judg told him he was charged wth high treason and he c^d not be bailed, so went back to ye Tower. I heard yesterday my Ld Exeter is sent for in custody.

I have but one little hors, but if I had 2, and I dare not buy one for feare of being thought to do so for w^{ht} I little think of, I w^d go neer to be wth you for a few days at Kirby, and so slip down to Hagley, to put matters a little to rights there before I remove wth my little family, wch I design to do as soon as we can dispose of w^{ht} we have yet left here. But I have some doubt, if I were there now, I might be more unquiet y^n I am here. Our fleetes and ye Duch are joynd, and a great fleet it is; and probably, if the French will venture it, there may be a battle in few days. 'Tis a strong east wind to keep y^m back and to carry us on theyr coast. I heard ye K^g will be here in a few days. I wish y^r L^p health and ye nation peace and ye prottestant religion.

I heard L^{ds} Macklesfield and Mountague refused to sign Ld Mallbo: warrant for his committment. He is s^d to be kept closs prisoner, but his lady has got leave to be lock'd up wth him, tho it's s^d he sent to her not to ask it, but to stay wth the P^{sse} and take her fortune. Her Hig^{ss} has but a melancholy court at Sion.

---

^{a} Thomas Sprat. ^{b} Thomas Kenn, the deprived Bishop.

CHARLES HATTON.

May 17, [16]92.

This day, my L^d, a proclamation is come forth signifying y^t, ye fleet being out and all things soe well prepared ag^t ye publick enemy, it is thought fit to prorogue ye parliament to ye 14th of June.   The rencounter I told y^r Loppe of in my last betwixt ye Ld Thanet and Ld Clare ^{a} wase very true; but ye Ld Thanet wase not hurt in ye thigh but shoulder, and wth parrying wth their left hands ye thrusts ye hands of both ye lords were cut.   But it is said my Ld Thanet, before company came in and parted y^m, had his sword ag^t ye Ld Clare breast, but very generously wou'd not thrust home. Ld Yarmouth is sent to ye Tower and his lady is wth him.   The Ld Middleton, Ld Dunmore, and Sr Andrew Forrester (all 3 in ye proclamation) were seized yesterday.   My wife and self are to y^r Loppe, Lady Hatton, and all at Kirby most faithfull and very humble servants.

C. HATTON.

It will be time to watch the ripening of ye seeds of ye broad leaf elme.

SIR CHARLES LYTTELTON.

Shene, May 21th, [1692].

MY LORD,

It was everybodys talk yesterday, when I came out of town, ye fleetes were ingaged or w^d be so before they parted, being in sight one of other at·ye Isle of Wight; and my Ld Monmouth, who is arrived from Jersey wthout leave, brought that acct; and y^t the French, wth ye transport ships wth 24000 foot and 3000 hors, w^d be readie to put to sea and endeavor to land, when ye fleets were ingaged; but I can't think how that can be practicable y^t they sh^d be readie to time it so.

^{a} Thomas Tufton, sixth Earl of Thanet ; and John Holles, Earl of Clare, afterwards Duke of Newcastle.

CHARLES HATTON.

May 31, [16]92.

*   *

We have yet noe certaine particulars of ye great victory obtained at sea over ye French.[a] Mr Trenchard, who wase at Kirby, says his brother, who is wth Capt^ne Clousely Shovel, sath the capt^ne hath had one of his buttocks shot of and is dangerously sick of a feavour.

The forreign letters say Great Wurradin is taken. Everybody is full of exspectation w^t success ye seige of Namurs will have. The letters from Flanders say ye French are lodgd on ye counterscarp; but ye confederat army are hastening to releive it, and ye greatest business on ye Exchange is wagering y^t by this time ye releif hath been attempted.[b]

The bells here have of late rung changes. Last Sunday we had a great ringing for ye happy restauration, wch wase observed wth a most surprising solemnity; and it is much disputed whither ther wase most jangling in ye steeples or pulpitts.

Here are severall new bookes come over. A most noble edition of Diogenes Laertius in 2 voll., 4to.[c] The lesser paper, wch is very good, is 30 shillings; ye imperial paper, 3^ll. Madam D'Acier hath translated Aristophanes,[d] and it is much admired; it is 3^sh price. The first part of ye 22nd tome of ye Bibliotheque Universelle[a] is come over, and ye Histoire des Ouvrages des Sçavans[b] to February last.

I am

Y^r Lo^pps very humble servant,

C. HATTON.

[a] In the battle of La Hogue, on the 19th and 23rd of May.

[b] The town surrendered after an eight days' siege; but the citadel held out for three weeks longer.

[c] The Amsterdam edition.

[d] Madame Dacier translated the Plutus and the Clouds in 1684, but nothing else of Aristophanes.

[e] "Bibliothèque Universelle et Historique," in 25 vols. Amsterdam, 1686-1693.

[f] The Journal des Sçavans.

SIR CHARLES LYTTELTON.

London, June 16th, [1692].

Yesterday morning y[e] prisoners in y[e] Tower were brought upon thcyr habeas corpus to y[e] K[gs] Bench, and gave baile for each 4 severall men.   My L[d] Marlborow had L[d] Hallifax, Carbery,[a] Shrewsbury, and M[r] Boyle; but it was but for 6000[li].   The Lords who were not prisoners and others who removed themselves gave baile at y[e] Ch. Justice chamber.   My Lord Lich: gave in 15000[li] baile; and there were some Lords, as L[d] Midleton, Huntington, Dunmore,[b] S[r] And: Forrester, sent back to y[e] Tower, Aron Smith having given oath he had evidence ag[st] them, w[ch] he s[d] he was not readie to produce; but, tho' he were asked by y[e] court and y[e] councill for y[e] prisoners why they were not readie and if they were sick or beyond sea, no answer was made; and how many wittnesses there were, and whither they were evidence ag[st] all, to w[ch] there was no answer made.   But y[e] court, after consulting the act, thought fit to send y[m] back, w[ch] some talk much of, especially for my L[d] Huntington being a peer, and y[e] parlim[t], as it were, sitting.   The officers of y[e] army y[t] were baild were, after, sent for by my L[d] Lemster[c] and confined wth a guard upon them; and so continue, it's said, till they have bine tried by a court marshall and cashiered.

There was a talk to night that there has bine some men landed lately in Scotland, and that Marquis de Crequy is wth y[m].   They expect to heare of a battle in Flanders; tho' I heard one y[t] has, I think, pritty good intelligence say that both armyes are unwilling to ingage.   God direct all for y[e] best.

Tuesday come sennight I hope to be gone.

---

[a] John Vaughan, thrd Earl of Carberry.
[b] John Murray, first Earl of Dunmore.
[c] Sir William Fermor, created Lord Lempster in April of this year.

CHARLES HATTON.

This is an account sent from a considerable officer who wase in y^e action, and is confirmed by severall letters, in wch are y^e names of more officers kill'd then are herein mentioned.

" Lembech nere Nostredame de Hall, 3 leagues from Brussells, July 25, 1692. O. S.

" Yesterday, ab^t 4 of y^e clocke, his M$_a$^{tie} ordred y^e march of o^r army to y^e left towards Enguien, 3 leagues from hence, in order to attacque y^e French in their camp, where it happened y^t Monsr Luxemburg had ordered y^e greatest part of his infantry to advance and line y^e hedges of many enclosures nere y^e way we were to march; and it wase betwixt 8 and 9 of ye clocke in ye morning when o^r vanguard charg'd y^m. Ther wase briske work on both sides, o^r pass being very narrow, so y^t, as o^r men advanced, ye gen^{ll} ^{a} drew y^m to ye r^t and left, to gain w^t ground he cou'd to make head ag^t ye French. We were upon ye offensive part, and were forc'd to gain o^r ground by inches, and ye engagem^{mt} held very furious till ab^t 7 in ye evening, when ye King, seeing y^t o^r horse cou'd not advance to charge, ordered o^r retreat, wch wase in pretty good order and without very great loss during o^r retreat. This day's worke fell hard on ye English and Scotch.^{b} The second battalion of ye English Guards lost 4 parts in 5 of their men. Both ye Warcupps, Coll. Hamilton (ye son of James Hamilton), Coll. Colthrop, Coll. Eden, Coll. Bristow, Capt Sherlock, Kendler Stroud, wth half ye subalternes, are killed. Coll. Stanley (brother to ye Earle of Derby) is wounded. Coll. Mackay killed. The Ld Montjoy and ye Earle of Angus killed or taken. Sr Rob. Douglass, Coll. Lauther, Coll. Hodges, Coll. Francis Hawley of ye dragoons, Lt Coll. Harleston, Maj^r Keith, are all kill'd, with about 200 captains and subalterns and ab^t 6000 men, besides officers of note whose names

^{a} Count Solmes commanded the British troops.
^{b} Five regiments were cut to pieces.

are not herein mentioned, most English and Scotch; ye Dutch suffering very little, haveing but little share in this honorable action.

" The French galled us mightily wth their cannon, we having but few cannon come up by reason of ye ill wayes. In this action we lost some few peices of cannon, ye horses being kill'd wch shou'd have drawn y^m of. We hope ye French have lost much more then we.^{a} The ground wase soe bad ye gen^{ll} cou'd not ride to and fro to give orders, wch made severall battalions suffer much for want of timely relief. At ten at night we came back to o^r camp, where it is beleeved we shall stay some time.

" One battalion of Douglasses wth ye greatest part of English and Scotch were detach'd under ye command of ye Duke of Wirtemberg to make the onset."

THE SAME.

Augt 4 [16]92.

I have my L^d received y^{rs} of ye 1st inst., and shall send ye enclosed as you directed.

The gazet to-day for o^r comfort tells us y^t in ye engagem^t at Enquien ye French lost as many as ye confederat, wch ye Dutch gazetts likewise reports wth this addition, y^t it needs a confirmation and y^t tho ye confederate army outnumbered ye French by 15000, for ye French were but 58000 and ye confederates 73000, yet ye French were soe advantageously posted y^t ye confederates were forced to retreat wth ye loss of many considerable officers and 2000 men slain and 1000 wounded, as is reported; but ye certain loss cannot be yet known.

Tho this is but melancholly news, ye return of o^r fleet to Spithead is much more, because it is attributed to be occasioned by a

---

^{a} The loss on each side at Steinkirk was about 7,000 men.

dispute betwixt ye admirall and general who is to command in cheif; and ye enterprise is thought to bee more hazardous y^n y^t of Enquien.^{a} But severall lords, Nottingham, Devonshire, Dorset, and others, are gone to Portsmouth to accommodat ye business. And, w^n y^t is done, ye success of ye discent and ye conquest of France is not to be doubted of by any but some silly Jacobites, who are soe incredulous they have noe faith in ye modern Merlin's prophesies.

I am

Y^r Lo^{pps}

very humble servant,

C. HATTON.

THE SAME.

My L^d,   Aug. 10, [16]92.

We have had noe intelligence this fortnight w^t wase become of o^r great fleet and all our transport shipps, but ye Gazett this day tells us y^t, God be praised, they [are] all safe in ye Downs; and I doe not hear y^t in this glorious expedition we have lost many men. But there is very terrible news from Jamaica, where an earthquake and hurrican hath been and in less than 2 minuits destroy'd and sunke ye greatest part of Port Royall with all ye factories, store-houses, and magazins. It is said ye church is sunk 6 fathom under water; that ther and in other places of ye island above 5000 people are destroyed; and y^t ye whole island wase under a dreadfull con. sternation when ye last letters came away, fearing ye return of ye earthquake and least ye Moores and slaves shou'd, according to ye example of others, rebell. The Swan frigot and severall vessels in port in Jamaica are destroyed. I and my wife are to y^r Loppe and all at Kirby most faithfull and humble servants.

C. HATTON.

^{a} The expedition was fitted out for a descent on the Freneh coast and actually put to sea; but the project was given up at a final council of war.

184 HATTON CORRESPONDENCE.

SIR EDMUND KING.

MY LORD, Sept. 8, [16]92.

I cannot be satisfied but to send this to enquire how yor Lord$_p$ and yor familie does, and how Mr Hatton is since my laste to yor Lord$_p$ y^t I writ in answere to yor Lord^{ps} concerning his illness, and to enquire if you have felt anything of a frightfull earthquake we have had here this Thursday, about 2 a clock. I had been out of towne, just come home; and, as I was at dinour in my dineing roome (one paire of stairs), on a suddaine the table and room shakt, put us all into a strange confusion. My wife said: "Mr King, w^{ts} this?" Her woman y^t was at diner wth us started from the table, as pale as death, and cri'd: " Oh! an earthquake!" I rise from the table too in the universall motion I saw and felt; it lasted about a minute and halfe. Whilst we was talking of it, a neighbour cam in and ask't if we perceivd anything of an earthquake, for a great many gentlemen came running into the coffee house, pale and frighted, out of their houses, and the women and children in great numbers cam runing out of theire houses too into the street in great amazment; and it's the wholl talke now all the towne over; much more frightfull than w^{ht} we felt. Some say the Exchange in Cornhill was heard to crack; and the people cam runing downe from thence, for fear it should fall. I have been since at Westminster wher was the same alarm; and a message from Kensington about the same thing ther. You'l here more of w^t is past. I pray God we may have no 2^d part of it. But all pray God to keep off the judgments we have deserv'd. This is a serious thing, and so thought of by yor Lord^{ps} faithfull humble servant, EDM. KING.

CHARLES HATTON.

September 10, [16]92

We had here, my L^d, last Thursday, at 55 minutes past 2 of ye clock in ye afternoone, an earth-quake, ye effects of wch were more or less felt, not only over all London and Westminster but, it is reported, as far as Canterbury and Cambridge. I hope y^r Lo^{PPe} wase free from it at Kirby. I wase at home; but none in my little house were sensible of it, wch occasioned my not mentioning it to your L^{ppe}. In all places those who were highest were most sensible of it. A person of very great truth and sincerity assured me his bookes, wch were on shelves in his chamber, were flung down. Mr Lownds in ye Pell-Mell, a watch maker and very honest man, did averr to me y^t all his clocks did soe shake he thought they wou'd have fallen down. In severall places all ye people ran into ye street s out of their houses in great distraction, and in many places ye corn e houses in ye streets were seperated from ye adjacent houses.

Last Thursday Admirall Russell came to town, but very privately, to avoyde ye triumphall reception he much feared wou'd have been made for him, and for ye like reason chose to come by Hampton rather then Portsmouth. But I doe not heare of any triumphant arches wch were making for him, neither for routing 44 French shipps wth 90 saile, nor for saving ye fleet by disobeying his orders by refusing to comply wth y^m, wch his friends ye commonwealth men say wase ye most meritorious and deserved better to have a marble statue erected for him then his first, tho upon y^t account his relations had agreed for one. But it's thought his humility will not let him comply wth their desires; for he is soe humble he declares he will resign up all his publick employments, and not yeild, as he did this last summer, to any pressing importunity to take any publick imployment upon him, till he can better doe service for ye good of ye commons of England then he finds in this juncture of afaires he can.[a]

The next week ye Ld Brudnells daughter[b] is to be married to my Ld Newborough.

The act of parl^t for staving French wines is expired, and severall privateers are gone out in hopes of meeting with some nere y^e

[a] Russell was dismissed early in the following year.
[b] Frances, daughter of Francis, Lord Brudenell, son of Robert, Earl of Cardigan.

coastes of Bourdeaux.   Capt^ne Cotton writes to me very pressingly
to move y^r Lopþe to endeavour to obtaine for him a shippe to cruise
in this winter, wch if he can obtaine he engages to furnish y^r Lo^ppe
wth some tunns of French wines.   Those are his words, and I
verily beleeve he doth not doubt but to be enabled to performe his
promise.   I am

Y^r Lo^pps very humble servant,

C. HATTON.

THE SAME.

November 12, [16]92.

I have, my L^d, enclosed ye votes of Thursday and yesterday, for
this day's votes you must not exspect till Tuesday's post.   Yesterday
it wase moved in ye H. of C. y^t it shou'd be voted y^t this day the
non pursuing ye famed victory at sea shou'd be enquired into.   But
Mr Montague told ye house he was surprised y^t motion shou'd be
made, for it seemed to reflect upon ye victorious admiral who he
thought had merited ye thankes of ye House; to wch ye House agreed,
and voted him thankes, wch accordingly he had.   After wch it wase
declared y^t, ye House haveing therby manifested their satisfaction in
his conduct, it cou'd not reflect upon him to enquire into ye non
pursuit of ye victory; and accordingly they did this day, and have
made some progress therein, and have, for their farther satisfaction,
voted S^r Jo. Asby^a to be sent for.

The Lords are still upon ye first business they entred upou, and
have treated soe roughly ye worthy Aaron Smith, y^t ye modest man
takes it soe much to heart y^t an affidavit wase this day made in y^e
H. of L^ds that he wase not in a condition to appeare as he wase
required.

I and my wife are to y^r Lo^ppe, Lady Hatton, and all at Kirby,
most faithful servants.   C. HATTON.

---

^a Admiral Sir John Ashby, who was present at La Hogue.

The Countess of Nottingham.

The 13 of December, [1692].

I am very glad to heare that y^r Losp. and all are well at Kirby. I thinke I shall never meet wth Mrs Portman, for I have been several times to waitt on her, and she done me the favor to come to me, but wee have both always been gon out.

We have but little news here except of killing. That wretched creature my Lord Mohun,[a] who is not sixteen years old tell April next, about a fortnight agoe was in a drunken quarrel wth my Lord Kennedy;[b] on Friday night, wth one Hill[c] about his one age, killed poore Monfort[d] the player, and, as tis related, very barbarously.

I wont this post trouble my Lady, nor this time y^r Losp. more wth

Y^r most obedient duttyful daughter,

A. Nottingham.

Charles Hatton.

Jan 24, [16]9$\frac{2}{3}$.

I suppose, my L^d, y^e votes herein enclosed will much surprise, for therby it is ordered that K[ing] W[illiam] and Q[ueen] M[ary] Conquerours and Dr. Burnett's Pastorall Letter are to morrow to be burnt by y^e hangman.[e] God's Way of Disposing of Kingdomes, by y^e B^p of St Asaph,[f] very narrowly escaped ye like destiny. Amonst those who signalized their favour to Dr. B. in speaking in his behalf

[a] Charles, fifth, and fortunately last, Lord Mohun.

[b] John, son of John Kennedy, seventh Earl of Cassilis. He died before his father.

[c] Captain Richard Hill, who absconded.

[d] William Mountford.

[e] The tract entitled "King William and Queen Mary Conquerors" was written by Charles Blount. Burnet's Pastoral Letter contained a paragraph, the language of which bore some resemblance to that of the pamphlet. See Macaulay's account of the affair.

[f] "A Discourse of God's Ways of disposing of Kingdoms." London, 1691. Sm. 4to.

yᵉ late Lᵈ Justice Conisby ᵃ appeared very zealously, and said yᵗ, tho their were some expressions wᶜʰ might give offence, yet ther were many excellent things in yᵗ booke, and, therfore he hoped that they wou'd only censure yᵉ passages wᶜʰ gave offence and not burne yᵉ booke.   Coll. Titus reply'd to him and said : " In yᵉ year 1639, in an edition of yᵉ Bible, ' not' wase left out in yᵉ 7ᵗʰ commandemᵗ, and then it wasc : Thou shalt commit adultery, wheras it ought to have been : Thou shalt not commit adultery; and yet yᵉ Bible, in wᶜʰ were very excellent things, wase ordred to be burnt." The Lᵈ Ren[elagh]ᵇ said this day yᵉ House had taken away a letter out of Bᵖ Burnet's name, for hereafter he wou'd only be called Bᵖ Burnt.

Killigrew, Delaval,ᶜ and Shovel are all 3 declared admiralls for this summers expedition, and all to goe in yᵉ Britania.   The Lᵈ Cornwallis ᵈ hath layd down his commission to be First Com. of yᵉ Admiralty.   I shall send yᵉ paper you desired, of wᶜʰ I heard nothing till you mention'd it.

I am to yʳ Lₒₚₚₑ and all at Kirby a very humble servant,

C. HATTON.

THE SAME.

MY LORD,   Jan. 31, [16]9¾.
    This day my Lord Mohun wase tryed.   My Lᵈ Danby sat as Lᵈ High Steward.   He had yᵉ largest and finest coach and yᵉ richest liveryes I have seen.   Yᵉ tryall held from twelve a clocke till after five; then yᵉ Lords went to yᵉ Lords House to debate, and severall of yᵉ Lords slipt away, wᶜʰ occasioned a long debate whither or noe yᵉ Lords who slipt away shou'd not he sent for by yᵉ Black Rod and

---

ᵃ Thomas Coningsby, late Lord Justice of Ireland, afterwards Earl of Coningsby.
ᵇ Richard Jones, third Viscount Ranelagh.
ᶜ Admirals Henry Killegrew and Sir Ralph Delaval.
ᵈ Charles, third Lord Cornwallis.

committed prisoners. But ye great debate was whither or noe in murder all persons accessory, assisting, and present are to be accounted principalls. This debate held 3 houres, and the Lords have adjourned till to morrow morning to give their judgment; and ye generall opinion is my Ld Mohun will be acquitted.^a I wase not at ye tryal. My Ld Litchfield sent me a ticket, but I gave it Mr Gylby.

To morrow Whitney,^b ye famous highwayman who wase reprieved last Fryday (upon a pretence y^t he would discover a plot to take away ye life of my Ld Danby), is to be hang'd at ye Maypole in ye Strand.

C. HATTON.

THE SAME.

Feb. 9, ⌈16⌉9¾.

*   *   *   *   *

Ther is sent 2^ll of juniper seed and halfe a pound of very fresh and good bay seed, and I will take w^t care I can to get very good barberries and w^t you order further, as also ye pen-knife and canarie birds. Y^e right canarie birds are very scarce; German birds very common. I lately saw some very pretty birds wch were called Indian sirens, but were bastard birds bred out of a hen canary bird and a cocke goldfinch. They sing very well. The price 12 shillings a peice.

As soon as my Lord Mohun tryall is publish'd I will take care to send it you. Yesterday Young^c wase tryed, and by impudence

<hr />

^a He was acquitted by sixty-nine votes to fourteen.

^b James Whitney, who had tried to obtain a reprieve by undertaking to raise a troop of highwaymen-cavalry to serve in Flanders.

^c Robert Young, who tried to follow Oates's steps as false accuser, and whose career has been sketched by Macaulay. He was tried for perjury, subornation of perjury, and forgery. He came to his end at Tyburn in 1700.

far outbid even Dr Oates.   He had not a ranting impudence, but a
most unparalleled sedate composed impudence, and pretends to be
as great a martyr for his zeale for ye preservation of ye present
governm^t as Oates did for his for ye protestant religion.   The jury
without stirring from ye barre found him guilty; but he will not
be sentenc'd till ye last day of ye terme.   Doe you desire his tryal
when it comes out?

   Dr. Burnt hath a new mortification befallen him.   Very smart
and ingenious reflexions are come out upon his History of ye Reformation;[a] ye price 2^s 6^d, tho but a thinne 8° booke.

   A knavish wagge writ a lemma on his Pastoral Letter and sent it
him:

> Parve, nec invideo ; sine me, liber, ibis in ignem ;
> Hei mihi, quod domino non licet ire tuo !

Here is set forth a very curious draught of a first rate frigate done
by Philipps, but soe well y^t it is said he wase not of his owne
invention able to doe it, but stole it from a designe done by one
Dammer who is said to be a great artist.

I am

Y^r Lo^{pps} very humble servant,

C. HATTON.

THE SAME.

Feb. 23, [16]9⅔.

I have, my L^d, this day sent by ye caryer Capt^{ne} Philipps shippe
wth ye specimen of ye errours in ye History of ye Reformation by

---

[a] " A Specimen of some Errors and Defects in the History of the Reformation of
the Church of England wrote by Gilbert Burnet D.D., now Lord Bishop of Sarum."
By Anthony Harmer [*i. e.* Henry Wharton].   London, 1693.   Small 8vo.

Dr Burnt, and Sr William Temple's reply to Le Cross,^{a} by wch he hath much more injur'd his fame then ye coxcomb Le Cross cou'd ever have done. And tho he sath Dr Freeman publish'd his memoires wthout his consent or privity, yet in his gibberish and fanfaron stile he is pleased to complement him wth ye title of Reverend Prelate, and some thinke he had much better have passed over ye misfortunes and disorders of his family then to have proclaimed y^m by mentioning y^m, nor doe ye friends of ye noble Marquisse,^{b} ye Ld Rochester, and others on whom he hath reflected, thinke he hath lessened, but rather encreased, ye offence he gave by ye slight apology he hath made. Y^e Dutch gazettes say y^t ye pope hath granted to ye French king ye tenths of all ye ecclesiastical revenues in France for his assistance to King James.

I am

Y^r Lo^{pps} very humble servant,

C. HATTON.

THE SAME.

March 11, [16]9⅘.

I received, my L^d, yesterday 2 letters from y^r Lo^{ppe}. Anthony Harmer^a is Henry Wharton, chaplain to my Ld Archb^{ppe} of Canterbury, who hath publish'd severall very learned workes, and amongst others a collection of English writers of ye lives of B^{pps}, wch you

---

^{a} This was : " An Answer to a Scurrilous Pamphlet lately printed, intituled a Letter from Monsieur de Cros to the Lord ——." London, 1693. 8vo. The scurrilous pamphlet was : " Lettre de Monsieur Du Cros à Mylord ——, afin de servir de réponse aux impostures de Monsieur le Chevalier Temple, cy-devant Ambassadeur de l'Angleterre à la Haye et à Nimegue," printed at Cologne this year, an English version of which appeared at the same time in London. S. Du Cros was envoy from the Duke of Holstein-Glottorp.

^{b} Caermarthen. ^{c} See above, p. 190, note ^{a}.

mention. This day Dr Burnt hath set out a reply[a] in a papal haughty stile, in generall magnifying his former performances and expressing a great disgust not to have been treated wth y[e] great respect he claimes due to himself, but not vindicating himself from any particular falshood he is charged w[th].

*   *   *

I am

Y[r] Lo[pps] very humble servant,

C. HATTON.

THE SAME.

March 28, [16]93.

This evening, my L[d], about 7 of y[e] clocke, his sacred Majesty returned backe thro y[e] city wth as great silence as y[e] Grand Seignior marches thro any city in his territories. As soon as y[e] windes are more obedient then of late they have been, he returnes to Harwich. The Lord Lansdowne,[b] when y[e] parl[t] wase sitting, moved K[ing] W[illiam] for 6000[ll], due to him on account of his salary unpay'd whilst Envoye Extraordinare in Spain from King James. He wase answered y[t] noe monies had been, or cou'd be, exspected to be pay'd on y[t] account; to w[ch] his Lo[ppe] replyed y[t] severall personns had since y[e] Revolution received monies on y[e] like account, and amonst others instanc'd in y[e] Marquiss d'Albeville.[c] But he wase told y[t] wase to enable him to pay y[e] debts he owed to y[e] poore people in Holland. But in conclusion he was promised he shou'd be pay'd y[e] monies he claimed. Yet nothing having been ordred therin, last

---

[a] "A Letter writ by the Lord Bishop of Salisbury to the Lord Bishop of Cov. and Litchfield concerning a Book lately published, called A Specimen," etc. London, 1693. Sm. 4to.

[b] Charles Granville, eldest son of the Earl of Bath.

[c] White, Marquis d'Albeville.

Thursday, in ye great crowd then at Kensington, his Lo_{ppe} claimed ye performance of ye promise made to him, saying he did not desire favour but demanded justice; and did it wth that importunity, he wase told he wase very troublesome and impertinent; at wch reproof his Lo_{ppe} wase soe much offended y^t ye same night, in ye bed-chamber, he told his most sacred Majesty that, having received such language, he wase unfit to serve longer, and therfore surrendred up all his commissions. And last Saturday my Ld Bath applying himself to ye Lords of ye Treasury for his pension, he wase told that ther wase a stop to y^e payment of all pensions; at wch his Lo_{ppe} is soe disgusted, my Lady Neville sath she hears he hath resigned up all his commands.

C. HATTON.

SIR EDMUND KING.

MY LORD,   June 27, [16]93.

I never write news, because I kno yor Lord_p allways has it from better hands. But we are all in great paine about the Turkey fleet still, and the more because the Tholoon fleet is joyn'd Destre. But I shall not forget a storie my Ld Cuttes tolde me, 3 days agoe, of the Duke of Brandenburg just goeing to fight against 60 thousand wth 50 thousand, and all just readie, a great officer comes in mightie haste, tolde him he fear'd it impossible to succeed in such a place, and askt w^t he should doe. His answer was, in as great haste: " Goe on, go on; you must allways leave something for God Allmightie to doe." Soe they went on, and kill'd 10 thousand upon the place and routed the whole army. I am sure we have a great deale for God Allmightie to doe for us. At this rate I wish yor Lord^{sp} will not feare letters from,

My Lord,
Your Lord^{ps} moste humble and faithfull servant,

EDM. KING.

CHARLES HATTON.

July 27, [16]93.

Here is come very terrible news, my L^d, from Flanders. Yesterday wase sennight, ye Duke of Luxembourg fell on ye confederate camp, and after 5 hours dispute they entred ye camp and have entirely defeated ye confederate army.[a] It is reported K. William received a slight contusion on his side with a musquet bullet, Count Solms had his leg shot of wth a cannon ball, and y^t mine Heer Benting is desperately wounded. The Duke of Ormond is missing.[b] Further particulars you may exspect by ye next, for ye letters were not all deliverd out this night. It is said ther wase 20000 killed on ye place of battle, and on ye pursuit ye French tooke all ye artillery and tents; but it is said ye heavy cariage wase sent away ye day before. Mecklin is appointed ye place of rendezvous.

It is reported y^t Monsr Tourville, having effected his design on ye English Streights fleet, is returned to Brest. The French privateers have taken severall colliers and severall of ye English Virginia shipps.

C. HATTON.

THE SAME.

Aug. 3, [16]93.

I heare nothing as yet, my L^d, of ye orange tree you mentioned. As soone as I receive it I will take all care to convey it safe to ye caryer.

This dayes gazette confirmes ye report of ye totall defeate of ye confederate army; but for our comfort tells us y^t such another

---

[a] The battle of Landen or Neerwinden was fought on the 19th July.
[b] He was taken prisoner, and exchanged for the Duke of Berwick.

victory wou'd ruine ye French king by. ye destruction of all his officers and soldiers; but it is to be feared this last victory will not bee made much more prejudiciall to him then y^t of Fleury and Steinkirke wase.

The English horse have learnt of ye Dutch to run away; and it is said were much too nimble for them and far outrun ye Dutch. Mr Blaithwaite, ye secretary of warre, wase soe carefull of his papers y^t, for feare of loosing them, he never stopt till he came to Breda.

I am,

Y^r Lo^{pps} very humble servant,

C. HATTON.

THE SAME.

MY LORD,   Aug. 5, [16]93.

* * * * *

Here is publisht this day a collect, only to be read in ye precincts of ye Bill of Mortallity, in wch is a passage wch clashes wth all ye relations here printed of ye battle of Landen, for ye preservation of his Maty, in wch this collect is a forme of thanksgiving, and ther are thes words:

Blessed be God of our salvation who hath given this great and marvelous delivrance to ye King from his strongest enemy, and from them that hated him and were too many and too mighty for him.

* * * * *

C. HATTON.

THE SAME.

Aug 24, [16]93.

* * * * *

The great news is ye 2 great sisters are reconciled, and my Lord Churchill hath (as report sath) effected it, and y^t for his reward

he is to be declared Generall of ye forces here.   The Princess of
Denmarke this day made her visit to her sister.   For joy of y^e
reconciliation ye bells (wch have all this summer been very silent)
ring very merrily.   Wirtenburg is declared Generall of ye foot in
ye place of Solms killed at ye first battle of Landen.

I am

Y^r Lo^{pps} very humble servant,

C. HATTON.

THE SAME.

October 21, [16]93.

*   *   *   *   *

We are in a house^a from whence we have soe great a prospect
into ye country y^t out of our parlour window, whilst I am now
writing, we can plainly and distinctly see ye hounds as they are
hunting in ye adjacent fields, and heare ye sound of ye horns and cry
of ye doggs.   My wife is much pleased, but it will occasion me many
a long walk, and ye stones are much harder then they were 20
yeares agoe and every day grow harder and harder, and ye last yard
of ye way coming home seems much longer then ye first furlong
going out.   *   *

C. HATTON.

THE SAME.

November 7, [16]93.

Here is very great news, my L^d, at wch many here, who either
cou'd not see or wink'd, are much surpris'd at.   The signet is taken
from my Ld Nottingham.   The most credible report is y^t yesterday
morning, about 9 of ye clocke, Mr Sec. Trenchard came to my L^t
Nottingham and signify'd to him his master's pleasure y^t he should

---

^{a} In Stratton-street, in Piccadilly.

resign up his office as Secretary; wch my L^d declared he wou'd not doe, for he had serv'd ye King faithfully and done nothing but what he cou'd justify. Sr J. Trenchard then told him y^t ye King had sent by him his commands to his Lo_{ppe} to deliver to him ye signet. My L^d reply'd ye King might require him to deliver up ye signet and he wou'd doe it, but wou'd not send it by anybody, but deliver it to his Ma_{ty} wth his own hand; and accordingly he carryed it to Kensington, and ther delivered it up himself.^a It is reported y^t ye signet wase offred to my Ld Shrewsbery, but he declined it, as did Sr John Lowther, tho what ground ther is for any such report I cannot assert.^b But Mr Russel is declared sole admirall to command ye fleet ye next summer; and Rook, Killigrew, Delaval, and Shovel turned out. I cou'd wish my despised information, for wch I wase soe knabb'd, had been groundless.

The members of parl^t met this day, and after ye speech ye House of Commons adjourn'd till next Monday, and then are to consider ye speech, the substance of wch wase to express a regret for ye disadvantages ye armies received this yeare at land and ye great miscarriages befell ye navies at sea; that ye defeat at land wase solely occasioned by ye French far outnumbering ye confederates in all places; and, for ye miscariages at sea, his Ma_{ty} declared, as he highly resented it, soe he wou'd take care to punish all persons who had not done their duty, and that ye sea affaires shou'd be better managed for ye time to come. And, as ye confederates had resolved to encrease their forces both by land and sea ye next yeare, he recommended the members of ye House of Commons to take care speedily to supply him wth effectual supplies. This I heare is ye substance of ye speech, wch by ye next I shall send you printed.

I am

Y^r Lo^{pps} very humble servant

C. HATTON.

^a Macaulay's account is misleading, as he makes Nottingham's resignation to follow, instead of precede, the early debates in parliament.

^b Shrewsbury at length accepted the seals in April, 1694.

Sir Charles Lyttelton.

No^{br} 9th, [16]93.

I heare y^t, when Mr Secre: Trencher came to Ld N. for y^e seales, he told him, wth y^e usuall complim^t, that he was sorry to come of y^e message, wch was, that his M$_a$^{tie}, understanding he was willing and desireous to deliver y^e seales, had sent him for y^m. My L^d replied: " Not I, before God; [I] am not willing;" and he beleeved he was mistaken in his message, that he had told y^e King y^e contrary, yet, if y^e K^g commanded them, he w^d wate on him wth em, for he rec^d em from his hands and so w^d render em. The Secretary told him y^t he did indeed mistake his message, and y^t y^e King commanded em. So my L^d went wth em.

Y^e K^g, after, tis s^d, sent for Ld Shrewsbury and told him that now he had opportunity to offer him w^{ht} he hoped w^d make y^m live together as they had done, by making him cheife Secretary again. My L$_d$ acknowledged y^e honor, but said there was something for him to offer before he c^d accept, wch was, y^t y^e Trienniall Bill, wch his Ma^{ty} had refused and y^t he had appeared so in, when it w^d be brought ag^n into y^e House, he beleeved so good for his service and y^e nation, he must be for it; and, if his M$_a$^{tie} did not like it, he sh^d not serve him agreeably. The K^g said he did not think fit to purchasse any ones friendsp and service so dear as at the expence of passing that bill, and so they parted. Sec. Trencher is declared Chiefe Secretary; and not known yet or declared who is to be y^e other. I heare Ld Dursly ^{a} and Ld Lexington ^{b} named.

Ld Keeper,^{c} Admirall Russell, and ye Secretary are ye governing men. I wish they may do it so y^t we may have peace and ease of our taxes. wch tis thought will be yet greater y^n they have bine.

---

^{a} Charles Berkeley, Viscount-Dursley, eldest son of George, Earl of Berkeley.
^{b} Richard Sutton, second Lord Lexinton.
^{c} Somers.

THE SAME.

Tuesday, No. 15, [1693].

I heare my Ld Nott. comes yet to Court, into the drawing roome. Y^e H. of L^{ds} were very hot this morning of sending for all theyr members up; and there was some offence taken of some Lords y^t wont take ye oathes, that they were walking in ye Court of Requests, wch they had notice of and made hast away. If y^r L^p comes, as I imagine you may, I shall be ye more sorry to leave ye town before you come.

The H. of Com^s were very hot yesterday. Paul Foley layd open ye greevances very naked; was seconded by Sr Tho: Clergies and Titus, and there were very severe reflections; but, at length, they voted to support ye gov^mt and to examine ye miscarriages at sea on Wednesday, and have ordred ye Com^{rs} of Adm^{ty} to bring in all theyr orders to ye Admiralls and ye Admiralls to attend. A^d Russell, I heard, moved that a present creditt might be given to supply ye Navey, and it was said that (by Sr Phillip Musgrave) there was a sufficient summe given to pay ye fleet to Jan:, and that there was a proclamation that ye fleet sh^d not be p^d of till March; so he supposed there was money for it in bank. This morning the House made an order to bring in ye Trienniall Bill agⁿ, and I heard y^t it will be brought in againe into ye Lords House; but I think it was moved or ordred in ye Com^s House to be a Bienniall Bill. I cant tell if I expresse it well, but that there be a new parlim^t chosen every 2 yeare.

I heare they are very sharp to discover ye pensioners, w^{ch}, for a jest, they say that Har: Guy is made capt. of, tho some say 'tis in reallity Ld Oxford, and Ld Essex to have his regim^t. It was s^d yesterday y^t Archb^p Sandcroft died on Tuesday [a] and y^t AB. Tillotson has had an apoplectic [fit] lately.

---

[a] He died on the 23rd November.

CHARLES HATTON.

MY LORD,   Feb. 6, [16]9¾.

We have little news, only y^t last Sunday morning ye Lord Mor
daunt^a had intimation by mine Here Benting that he wase dismissed from all his commandes and publick employments. The
common discourse is y^t his disgrace proceeded from his bringing in
ye bill for a triennial parliament.

This day is observed in our quarters wth illuminations and other
rejoycings, suitable to ye solemnity thereof.^b The Princess Anne
her son^c came to Berkeley House wth a guard of young youths
about 10 or 12 yeares of age, all armed and clothed alike, marching
rank and file wth their captain, l^t, and ensign, and ye insignia
belli, wch how nere it approaches to high treason, not being com-
missionated by ye King, ye judges (if they please) may determine.^d

                    I am
              Y^r Lo^pps very humble servant,
                                          C. HATTON.

THE SAME.

MY LORD,   Feb. 13, [16]9¾.

We are a very ungratefull, rebellious generation. The ominous
13th of Feb.,^e to ye worke of wch day we owe ye present felicity,
prosperity, wealth, glory, and renown of ye nation, wch I doubt not

----

^a Charles Mordaunt, Earl of Monmouth.
^b Princess Anne's birthday.
^c William, Duke of Gloucester.
^d Luttrell has the following : " This day being the princesse of Denmark's birthday,
the Duke of Glocester will head his company in Hide park; the officers have batts
and feathers and the soldiers all red caps, and four little drakes for cannon."
^e The date of William and Mary's accession.

but will be recorded to all posterity, and wch day but five years agoe wase thought soe auspitious that upon y^t account Ash Wednesday wase made a festival, yet now it hath had noe observancy paid to it but what ye noble and loyall Lt Lucas hath done by ye discharge of ye gunns at ye Tower. I doe not heare it nor have seen this evening ye expence of one farthing candle to make an illumination, nor have we one poure squibb or cracker.

C. HATTON.

THE SAME.

March 27, [16]9¾.

We had yesterday, my L^d, very joyfull news of ye safe arrival of ye Virginian fleet. But this day a most dreadfull account is come of ye Turkey fleet.

The Sussex, a new 3rd rate shippe, in wch Sr Francis Wheeler went admiral, wth all ye men except 2 moores were lost. Sr Francis his body wase afterwards found cast ashore.

The Cambridge and Lumly castle, both men of war, the Fortune fire shippe, the Serpent a bomb shippe, the Mary and William, both tender ketchs; 4 merchant shipps bound for Turkey, ye Great George, ye Aleppo Factor, the Italian Merchant, ye Berkshire, all bound for Scanderoon; the Golden frigat bound for Legorn; the William for Venice; 2 Dutch merchant men bound for Turkey, and one for Legorn, were all cast away at Gibraltar by a hurrican wch happened ther, Feb. 19, 9¾; and all ye rest of ye fleet most terribly shattered and disabled. Besides ye shipps and goods wch perish'd, 15000 sailors were drownded. God make us so truly penitent for our sins as may induce Him to avert His judgments.

This day ye Commons I heare have voted a quarterly poll bill.

I am y^r Lo^{pps} very humble servant,

C. HATTON.

THE SAME.

MY LORD,   April 10, [16]94.

All our neighbourhood hereabouts are in great lamentation for ye death of Wilson, by some called Beau Wilson, by others Wonder Wilson, who wase yesterday morning killed in a duel by one Laws, a Scotchman.   Mr Wilson, when he came last out of ye country, brought up his sister wth him and tooke lodgings for her in Berkley street, where lodged a gentlewoman who pretended to great devotion and much frequented ye churches, and therby recommended herself to Mis Wilson, who tooke notice to her brother how happy she was to be lodged in ye same house wth soe religious a person; of wch Mr Wilson making mention to some of his acquaintance, they informed him y^t ye pretended devot wase a wench kept by one Laws, wch as soon as Mr Wilson knew, he presently removed his sister to her aunts house, ye Lady Ash at Twitnam; and publickly taking notice of ye occasion, Laws, instigated by his wench, came last Saterday night and challenged Wilson, who, having long lay'n under ye imputation of being a coward, desired one of his acquaintance to be his second, declaring y^t, to save his reputation, he must and wou'd fight. And, accordingly, yesterday morning he took a hackney coach and met about 11 of ye clocke in ye morning wth Laws in Southampton Square.   And it is generally reported y^t Laws gave Wilson his mortal wound before he had drawn his sword; and ye wound wch wase in his breast had so large an orifice y^t many thinke it wase made wth a bayonett.   Wilson instantly dropt down dead, and Laws, who was making his escape in a hackney coach, was pursued by ye boys who were playing in ye Square and seized, and is now in Newgate.   It is reported y^t ye morning before he fought he made his will, and just as he was going to fight he tooke out of his pocket about 50 guineas and gave y^m to his friend wth him; and if he was killed he told him he should keep y^m as a legacy withall, giving him ye key of his escritoire; and engaged him to promis him, if he then dyed, to take out all ye papers he shou'd find, in ye presence of his brother, in a drawer he described to him, and without looking into y^m burn y^m. Mr Wilson lived very generously and payed very punctually all personns he had any dealing wth, and is generally very well spoken of and much lamented. But how he was enabled to live at such a rate as he did is as great a mystery as ever.[a]

The Lord Newbury·is dead and left his lady wth child, and hath given all his estate to her.[b] His brother who killed Hayward dyed in Newgat.

The enclosed will give you all ye publick news I heare. My wife and self give our most humble service to Lady Hatton and all at Kirby; and we both are y^r Lo^{ppes} very humble servants.

C. Hatton,

THE SAME.

Augt 2, [16]94.

Ther happened, my L^d, lately a difference betwixt my wifes son at Oxford and his tutor, to accommodate wch I was obliged to goe to Oxford, wher ye Vice Chancelor^c and y^e Master of University Colledge^d did wth all due respect mention y^r Lo^{ppe}. They are printing catalogues of all y^e manuscripts in all y^e publick and all y^e private libraries in England, and if you please to send them a catalogue of y^r mss^{ts} they will owne it as a favour.$_e$ They are prose-

---

[a] Luttrell has this account under the 10th April : " A duel was yesterday fought between one Mr. Lawes and Mr. Wilson in Bloomsbury Square ; the latter was killed upon the spott, and the other is sent to Newgate ; 'tis that Mr. Wilson who for some years past hath made a great figure, living at rate of 4000*l.* per ann., without any visible estate ; and the several gentlemen who kept him company and endeavoured to find out his way of living could never effect it."

[b] See above, p. 185, note [b].

[c] Dean Aldrich.

[d] Dr. Arthur Charlet, sometime Fellow of Trinity College.

[e] The Hatton MSS. are described in the " Catalogi Librorum Manuscriptorum Angliæ et Hiberniæ in unum collecti," which was published at Oxford in 1697.

cuting very earnestly ye finishing and publication of Dr Morisons Herball,[a] and beautifying their physick garden.

Here is at Vesprit's garden an-aloes in flower, wch is much admired. I am glad y^r Loppe likes ye Heleborus Albus Flore-atrorubeate. You laughed at me when I wase at Kirby for liking it.

We have little news stirring, only that ye French privateers have in St George's channel taken ye Scarborough frigat, ye Irish paquet boat, and 12 shipps comming from Virginia, Barbadoes and Jamaica full laden. 　　　　　　I am

Y^r Lo^pps very humble servant,

C. HATTON.

THE SAME.

Augt 21, [16]94.

We have here, my Lord, terrible rainy weather, and I hope it may be news to y^r Loppe to heare of such, otherwise I fear y^r harvest will receive great prejudice. And, upon pretence y^t ye harvest is much damaged in ye northern parts, our knavish bakers here in town raise ye prise of bread.

We are in great exspectation to heare w^t feats o^r two admiralls Berkeley and Russel have done. It is beleeved there will be little done in Flanders. Y^e Dauphin is going back for Paris.

Here is a little booke come out wch makes a great noise, said to be writ by Sr Robt Howard, entitled The History of Religion; and, agreable to the piety of thes times, pretends to proove that in all ages religion wase (and still is) nothing but priest craft.

I am very glad your Loppe soe well approves of Sr Philip War-wick's booke.[b] The preface was writ by Doctor Smith, who pre-

---

[a] The third volume of Morison's "Plantarum Historia Universalis Oxoniensis" appeared in 1699.

[b] "A Discourse of Government," &c., published this year with a preface by Dr. Thomas Smith.

sented ye booke to y^r Lo^{pp e}, and will in a little time another, and
wch I beleeve will be a valuable one: the Life of Sr Robert Cotton
illustrated wth severall sculptures of ye greatest curiosities of ye Cot-
tonian library, and an exact catalogue of all ye manuscripts therein.^a
This day ye Doctor intimated to me his intention, when publish'd,
to present it to y^r Lo^{pp e}, as he had all ye bookes he hath set forth
since he had ye honour to be known to you; and at ye same time
repeated his thankes for ye venison you had formerly sent him, w^{ch}
he said wase ever very acceptable to him, and he had received none
this year from anybody.

*   *

C. HATTON.

THE SAME.

MY LORD,   September 15, [16]94.

  We have here very little news stirring, only y^t Huy was invested
by ye confederates ye 2^d inst., and in great exspectancy to hear of
ye success of bombarding Dunkirk, to cover wch by land, as also
Furnes and Ipres, ye French have sent into those parts a flying army
of 6000 men.

  I was this day in ye Kings garden, and saw ye finest collection
of amaranths and hollyoke I beleeve were ever seen in England,
and, besides severall very curious plantes, a very rare and beautifull
one, a tuberous hyacinth wth a blew flower, but it hath noe smell.

I am
Y^r Lo^{pp s} very humble servant
C. HATTON.

---

^a Smith's "Catalogus Librorum Manuscriptorum Bibliothecæ Cottonianæ," to
which was prefixed a Life of Sir Robert Cotton, was published at Oxford in 1696.

THE SAME.

September 29, [16]94.

Y^r L$_{oppe}$ commends Mr Dolbins walkes in his garden, but, my L^d, Mr Gylby tells me you have set up y^e gate (you removed) at y^e end of y^e middle walke in y^r upper garden, repaired ye walls and coping, and are gravelling y^e walkes; and he tells me he thinks you have made it y^e finest garden in England. I am very glad you have had such fine weather to bring y^r gravel, for I suppose you must fetch it far. I lately saw at Hackny a holly-hedge round a garden about ten foot high, and all soe close a mouse cou'd scarce creep thro' in any place. I never saw in my life soe fine a hedge. I told you of a blew hyacinth without smell, soe they called it at ye Kings garden, wher I saw one single flower; but, since, I have seen y^e whole plant. It is not a hyacinth, but a Lilio-Narcissus. Y^e stemme is about 4 foot high, and at y^e top beares a tuft of about 40 blew flowers, in y^e manner of y^e Narcissus of Japan. It is truly a very stately, beautiful flower. I am promis'd some amaranth and fine hollyoake seeds for y^r L$_{oppe}$. I heare George Loudon hath been at Burley on y^e Hill, and drawn a design for a very spatious garden ther. Here is great talke of vast gardens at Boughton; but I heare my Ld Mountague^a is very much concerned that y^e water wth wch he hoped to have made soe fine fountaines hath failed his exspectation.

*   *   *   *   *

I am

Y^r Lop^{ps} very humble servant,

C. HATTON.

THE SAME.

My Lord,   October 13, [16]94.

Here are some narcissus of Japan come, but ye flowers are all quite whithred, and therefore I desire y^r orders whither I shall send them down to Kirby. They came but yesterday morning. We

---

^{a} Ralph Montagu, now Earl of Montagu.

have little news stirring. Ther is much discourse about y[e] tryalls of y[e] prisoners of state, who were lately brought up out of Lancashire and Cheshire and returned back again ther to be tryed. They were sent down in great parade, the gentleman porter and gentle-[man] gaoler of y[e] Tower attending them, and two wardours on each prisoner. The old decrepid Lord Mollineux,[a] who [is] 86 yeares of age and very infirme, is, wth y[e] rest of y[e] Roman Catholicks, to be tryed at Manchester, in Lancashire. S[r] Thomas Stanley[b] and M[r] Legh of Lime,[c] our kinsman, are to be tryed at Chester. The chief evidence ag[t] them is one Lunt, who was coachman to my L[d] Carington, and, y[e] last session a bill of felony for having two wives being found ag[t] him, he was not long since by a warrant from y[e] Lord Mayor taken up, but bailed out, Aron Smith and one Culli-ford entring into a recognisance of a hundred pounds each for his appearance at y[e] Old Baily y[e] first day of this present session. But he never appeared. His recognisance is forfeited, and a bench warrant granted to seize him wherever found. But, he being now on their Ma[ties] service, it is to be presumed noe person will be soe audacious as to execute y[e] warrant on him, either in Cheshire or Lancashire, whither he is gone to give evidence ag[t] y[e] state prisoners, especially when it is known y[t] very lately nere twenty personns, who talking of his having two wives and mentioning some other such like transgressions of his, were taken up by messengers upon warrants for conspiring ag[t] y[e] lives and reputation of their Ma[ties] evidencers. A most wicked and horrid conspiracy ag[t] y[e] personns of such note and deserved fame. God Almighty defend us ag[t] all traytors. I am

Y[r] Lo[pps] very humble servant,

C. HATTON.

---

[a] Caryll, third Viscount Molyneux.

[b] Sir Rowland, not Sir Thomas, Stanley. Sir Thomas was one of the commissioners at the trial. See " The Trials at Manchester in 1694," edited by Dr. Goss, for the Chetham Society, in 1864.

[c] Peter Legh, of Lyme, co. Chester.

THE SAME.

December 8, [16]94.

Archb[p] Lauds vindication of himself is come out, to y[e] great confusion of his enemies and satisfaction of his freinds.[a] Dr. Tenison is declared Archb[p] of Canterbury, but it is said he will not be translated thither till Easter. It is generally reported y[r] acquaintance Dr. Hall[b] of Pembrook Colledge will be advanced to Lincoln from Bristol.[c]

The letters from France say y[e] Prince of Wales hath had y[e] small pox, but is perfectly well recovred and not marked.

D[r] Smith hath finished his catalogue of y[e] Cotton library, and when he hath y[e] life of S[r] Robt Cotton he will send it to press. He gives his most humble service to y[r] Loppe and sath venison will be very acceptable whenever y[r] Loppe pleases. I am

Y[r] Lo[pps] very humble servant,

C. HATTON.

THE SAME.

6 at night. December 27, [16]94.

I have just now, my Lord, met wth an officer who is newly come from Kingsinton, who tells me y[e] Queen is alive but past all hopes of recovery. She fell ill this day sennight. Last Saterday, by y[e] advise of S[r] Thomas Millington, she was let blood. On Sunday D[r] Ratclif was called in. He declared it wou'd be y[e] small-pox, and y[t] in his opinion she ought to have been let blood sooner, or else

[a] "The History of the Troubles and Tryal of the Most Reverend Father in God, and Blessed Martyr, William Laud, Lord Arch-Bishop of Canterbury, wrote by himself during his imprisonment in the Tower." With a preface by Henry Wharton. The entire volume was published in 1695, but portions of it appeared previously.

[b] Dr. John Hall.

[c] This promotion did not take place. James Gardiner succeeded Tenison at Lincoln.

her bleeding shou'd have been deferr'd till ye small-pox was come out. Monday and Tuesday it was generally reported it was only ye measles; but y^t night ye physitians concluded it was ye small-pox, wch after they were come out they fell and turned black, and severall purple spottes appeared. She spit blood . and wthall had an erysipelas. The publick concern may be better guess'd at then expressed. I am Y^r Lo^{pps} very humble servant,

C. HATTON.

THE COUNTESS OF NOTTINGHAM.

My Lord, Y^e 31 of De., [1694].

The sad confirmation last nights letters brought me of the death of my most deare mistress, the Queen,[a] gives me so just an affliction that I am but little thoughtfull of my neerest concerns. The want of coach horses has, since my Lords going, hinderd me from waitting of y^r Losp., and the news this last week of her illness from sending to know how you did. God has been pleased to shorten her days as a reward of her sufferings, wch in this world were not slight, w^{ch}, wth the goodness of her owne nature, had formed in her so great a degree of vertu, it might truely be sayd the world was not worthy of her. A poore lamentation is all the gratitude that can be payd her now for that favor so undeservedly she bestowed on me, is all that now can be returned by, my Lord,

Y^r most obedient, duttyfull daughter,

A. NOTTINGHAM.

THE SAME.

My Lord, Twelfth Day, [1695.]

My Lord Nottingham has so great a share in this loss himself, that his owne affliction makes him apprehend mine. I must be

[a] Mary died on the 28th December.

excesively ungratefull to that incompareable Princess, to be unconcerned that she is gone; and yet more ungratefull to God, to be insensible of those many blessings he still continues to me. I cannot express myself better upon this sad occasion then as the Dean of Pauls has already done: We must be dumb and not open our mouths, because God did it. I have obeyed y^r Losp. commands to the two Lady Marys, who give you their humble service and hope I shall return from London so soon, they may wth me waitt of you. I should have been very glad to have waitted of you as I went up, but my coachman tells tis much the worse way, and, I confess, upon this occasion I am desirous to have as few delays as I can in that performance of my poore remaining dutty to my deare mistress. Essex[a] I thinke to take wth me, and the others have not yet got there mourning. At my return I hope they may waitt of you, wth y^r Losp. most obedient, duttyfull daughter,

A. NOTTINGHAM.

CHARLES HATTON.

Jan. 10, [16]9⅘.

I am much concerned, my Lord, to heare ye paine in y^r arme continues. I hope, when ye sharpe weather alters, y^r paine will abate. I cannot fully enforme you of w^t sort ye papers are wch will be publish'd in ye 2^d vol of Ab. Lauds vindication;[b] but I will endeavour by my next to doe it, and then send you ye prices of ye bookes you enquire after. The just detestation of ye barbarous proceedings ag^t y^t great and good man must occasion an abhorrence of all paralell procedures. It was to have been wished ye Ab^{ps} caracter of K. Char. ye 1st, p. 178, had not been too true,[c] but it must be

----

[a] Her eldest daughter.

[b] The second volume of Laud's "Troubles and Tryall" did not follow until 1700.

[c] The words which are referred to are : "a mild and gracious Prince, who knew not how to be, or to be made, great."

confessed he was good even to a vice in a prince. What may be a virtue in a private person may be a vice in a publick magistrate. Meekness in some personns is a desirable and admirable quality; but old Eli's meekness brought down a heavy judgment from Heaven upon him. The sylogisme, p. 35, is not true in form, but ye sence in wch alone it can be understood is very rationall. The religion of ye papists is rebellion. But ye religion of ye papists is a branch of ye Christian religion. Therefore a branch of ye Christian is rebellion. W^{ch} I think is very false doctrine; for, tho both papists and protestants have turned religion into rebellion, they have therby departed from Christian principles, wch can never favour rebellion. It cannot be supposed ye Ab^p cou'd say and meane ye religion of ye papists to be more then a branch of ye Christian religion.

This day ye Princess Anne of Denmarke had a guard sent to doe duty, as formerly, at her doore; and it is exspected y^t ye Ld Churchill and his lady will be advanced, as in favour, soe to a higher degree. He was very zealous for passing ye Treason Bill; but last Tuesday he absented himself from ye committy, wher it was caryed by 7 votes that ye Treason Bill shou'd not commence till 1698. My Lord Nottingam hath made himself very popular by arguing soe zealously for Treason Bill. I am

Y^r Lo^{pps} very humble servant,

C. HATTON.

THE COUNTESS OE NOTTINGHAM.

Y^e 5th of Feb., [1695].

The post served me just as it did y^r Losp., for last night I received both y^{rs} of the 30 of Jan: and that of the second of this moneth. Heneage^a is so well, he plays about his room, and to morrow is to take phisick. I have endeavoured all I can that Essex should have

---

^{a} One of her children who died young.

them; and she herself has tryed if the small pox is to be catched, for the second day they were come out of her brother she gott into his room and kissed him, yet hitherto she keeps well.

I do not yet know when I shall leave this twone. Whenever I do, twill be wth less relucktancy then ever I did in my life. There is so slow a progress made in ordering the dismal ceremony of the Queens funeral, that I cant ges when it will be finishd. I was told this day that the heralds had yet a quarter of their work to do; and I fear, when there work is over, there will come severall things betwixts that and the Abby. The King sent yesterday for all the Queens chief officers, and, upon seeing of them, fell into a great passion. He told them the Queen had recommended all her family to his care, wthout wch tho he should not have been forgetfull of them, yet he had now another tye upon him to take care of them. I belive this was part of what he found written in the Queens desk. I do not yet hear of anny other thing mentioned, but I suppose this was not all.

I find it begins to be doubted wether the Princess be wth child. A little time will resolve it. The Parliment setts very late every day, but what they do is so much above my understanding, I cant pretend to give an account of it; so this time will trouble y^r Losp no more wth y^r most obedient, duttyful daughter,

A. NOTTINGHAM.

THE SAME.

MY LORD,   Y^e 9 of Feb., [1695].

The slow preparations for the Queens funeral, and the uncertainty when it will be finished, not only keps me in twone but makes me unable to gues when I shall come out. The Queens great bed-chamber is furnishing, and at last bed and all to be black velvet, w^{ch}

is not I belive the first time some of it has been used; and the top
of the bed is a painted escutcheone, wch we are told for cost is
painted upon silver tapy. I confess I see no difference, but in the
arms, from those that hang upon houses. The King went one
Thursday to Richmond, and comes againe this evening. It is sayed
the Duke of Shrewsbery is to be Master of the Horse, and Sr William Trumball Secretary. To day was like to be a busy day in the
House of Commons upon the Leather. How it has gone I doe not
know.

Y^r Losp. most obed. Dau:,
A. Nottingham.

Charles Hatton.

March 3, [16]9⅘.

Yesterday ther wase delivered at ye doore of both Houses of
Parl^t, to all ye members except ye bishops, a book wch makes a great
noise: Julian Johnson's answer to ye Phoenix Edition of ye Pastorall
Letter, meaning Dr Burnets edition of his Pastoral Letter ^a after it
was burnt by ye common hangman. Instead of a license for printing
ye answer, ye vote for burning ye letter is printed, and it is dedi-
cated to ye Barons and Commons assembled in Parliament. I will
give you a specimen how he treates ye Doctor. He sath ye author
of such opinions as he assertes is not to be respected, whither he
appears in his fiocco or his top-knotts. Johnson is noe wayes
modish in changing his opinion, but firmly adheres to his darling
doctrine of ye power of ye people over kings.

I am
Y^r Lo^{pps} very humble servant,
C. Hatton.

---

^a " Notes on the Phœnix edition of the Pastoral Letter of Bishop Gilbert Burnet,"
by Samuel Johnson, who got his nickname from his book " Julian the Apostate."

The Countess of Nottingham.

MY LORD   Y^e 21 of March, [1695].

I fear my Lady found it a wearisome day when she went to Exton, and they very much unprovided for her. I left them no cooke but a little boy, wch I doubt could perform but ill to entertain company. Mr Isaac, the dancing master, tells me he hears y^r Losp. had a mind to have a master to teach my sisters. Their is a German who he recommends for a sober man and very capable of teaching. His price will be three pound a moneth for each child, and for my little brother Will he will into the bargain teach him to walk and make a legg, and expects to have his charges born downe and up againe. Wither y^r Losp. has any such intention I know not; but, if you approve of this, if you please to lett me know y^r pleasure, I will tell it Mr Isaac.

Sr John Walter is going to be marryed to my Lady Stoel,^a wch will be very happy for him. With my humble deutty and thankes to my Lady, I will end from y^r most obedient, duttyfull daughter,^b

                                                    A. NOTTINGHAM.

Charles Hatton.

                                          April 6, [16]95.

In my last I told y^r Loppe y^t my Ld Hallifax was so ill, it was apprehended y^t he coud not live till my letter came to you; w^ch

---

^a Margaret, daughter of James, Earl of Salisbury, and widow of John, Lord Stawel, took for her second husband Richard, Earl of Ranelagh.

^b It is worth noticing, as an instance of what in the present day would be thought restraint between parent and child, that Lady Nottingham first began the subscription to this letter with the word " affectionate," which, however, she erased in favour of the formal " obedient, duttyfull."

apprehension proved very ominous, for he dyed yesterday at six of ye clock in ye evening. And I shall now give you a very true account of ye manner of his illness and ye occasion of death.

He had had, for severall yeares last past, a rupture; but wou'd never be prevailed on to weare a truss. This day sen-night he was soe well in health and last Sunday that he declared he had not been better for severall years. At supper on Sunday night he eat very plentifully of a roasted pullet, wch his lady thought not to be roasted enouf, and desired him not to eat of it, but cou'd not prevail, he declaring he lik'd it very well, and having a good appetite and digestion it wou'd not hurt him. But in ye night he was taken very ill and vomitted much, and ye next morning tooke a vomit wch, when it worked, forced the cut [*i. e.* gut] out through his rupture. For 2 or 3 dayes before he had had noe stoole, and the gut being filled with hard excrement, all his physitians and chirurgions cou'd doe cou'd not reduce it, but it gangreend; wch occasiond his death. The present Lord Hallifax a came to him but a houre before he dyed, at what time he was speechless and, it was thought, knew noe body. But as soon as my Lord Elan come to ye bedside, tho he cou'd not speake, he reach'd out his arms and embrac'd him. Dr Birch b attended on him as a divine in his sickness, and last Thursday gave him ye sacrament, wch he received very devoutly, and wth great Christian piety expressed his resignation to ye will of Heaven. He hath given order to be buryed privately at Westminster.

C. HATTON.

---

a William Savile, Lord Eland. He was summoned to his father's deathbed from his own wedding. He married Lady Mary Finch, Nottingham's daughter ; and died in 1700.

b Dr. Peter Birch, Prebendary of Westminster, and, this year, Vicar of St. Bride's.

SIR CHARLES LYTTELTON.

London, Ap[ll] 6th, 1695.

    ＊   ＊   ＊   ＊

I came now from my L[d] Weymouth who was going to my young L[d] Hallifax. His father died last night about six a clock. He says his gut was gangrened where he had the rupture, w[ch] wth y[e] violence of his vomits swelld exceedingly. He died with great humility and submission, and desired to receive y[e] sacram[t], which D[r] Birch gave him and was sent for by him. He was speechlesse when my L[d] Elan came to him, but he knew and embraced him.

D[r] Busby of Westminster died last night too; and I heard an od story, that y[e] people in y[e] street, when he was expiring, saw flashes and sparks of fire come out of his window, w[ch] made them run into y[e] house to put it out, but when they were there saw none, nor did they of y[e] house.

CHARLES HATTON.

April 11, [16]95.

For thes 2 last nights a great mob have been up in Holborn and Drury Lane, and let out betwixt 2 and 300 prisoners out of two marshalls' houses, where criminall solldiers and press-men were kept; and they gutted y[e] houses (as they call it) and burnt all y[e] furniture they found in them, nay, even y[e] doores and window frames. The souldiers who came to disperse them fired amonst them, kill'd 5 or six personns and wounded severall others.

The same.

Apr. 20, [16]95.

We have had of late, my Lord, soe warme and seasonable weather y^t I hope by ye next to hear y^r Lo^{ppe} is quite freed from ye rheumatisme.

Of late severall very eminent clergymen have here departed this life, as Dr Busby, Dr Scot,^{a} Dr Dove,^{b} Mr Kettlewell,^{c} and Mr Wharton.^{d} The last, who had been very long sicke of a consumption, ye night before he dyed, had compiled together as many miscellaneous originall papers of Archb^p Laud as are sufficient to make a second volume, and they are now in the press; and, as soon as they are printed, Achb^p Parkers Antiquitates Ecclesiæ Britannicæ wth severall additions therto, made by Arehb^p Parker himself and his secretary Joseline who compiled them, and many very considerable things added by y^e late most pious and learned Archb^p Sancroft, will be put to y^e press; for wch intent Archb^p Sancroft on his death bed gave them to Mr Wharton.e

Your Lo$_{ppe}$ enquired after a booke, put forth by one Trevor, of Heresies, but I cou'd never hear of any such author. But I suppose it is a tract put forth by one Turner, at y^e end of a very trifling frivolous booke wch he stiles y^e History of all y^e Religions in y^e World.f

I am

Y^r Lo^{pps} very humble servant,

C. Hatton.

^{a} John Scott, Rector of St. Giles-in-the-Fields and Canon of Windsor.
^{b} Henry Dove, Vicar of St. Bride's.
^{c} John Kettlewell, Vicar of Coleshill, co. Warwick.
^{d} Henry Wharton, Rector of Chartham, co. Kent.
^{e} No new edition of the " De Antiquitate Britannicæ Ecclesiæ" appeared before 1729.
^{f} By William Turner, Vicar of Walberton.

JOHN VERNEY.[a]

MY LORD,   Apr 26, [16]95.

Our thoughts are all so full of the transactions of this day that I cannot forbear letting your Lordship have part of them. The Committees of both Houses have sate very close in examining those that were concerned in distributing the money of the East India Comp[y]. Great art has been used to baffle their enquiry, and very great sums of money are yet not accounted for; but, so far as they have gon, the accusation has fallen upon the D[uke] of Leeds, the late Speaker,[b] M[r] Harry Guy, M[r] Attorney Gen:[c], and some others. The Duke, by his own desire, was heard today in the House of Commons; but, as soon as he was withdrawn, an impeachment against him was voted, no body speaking in his behalfe. M[r] Wharton carried it upp to the Lords. The sum was 5000 guineas which was received by M[r] Bates,[d] by whom this matter, after great examination, was discovered. The D[uke] did upon his honour declare in the House last weeke, when he spoke against the bill, that he was not at all concerned in this matter, and does still today assert his innocency; but yet the circumstances of the story are hard uppon him. The money was payd back to the goldsmith, last Tuesday, from whom it was received.

My Lord Nottingham has great right don to his honour by everybody, that his vertue set him out of the reach of these temptations, hee being the only person yet named where their applications were unsuccessful. I have not heard what more is don in this matter, the two houses being yet sitting.

Your Lordship will easily imagine what distraction this matter causes, and theirfore I need not give you any farther trouble to

---

[a] M.P. for Leicestershire.   [b] Sir John Trevor.   [c] Sir Edward Ward.
[d] Charles Bates, an agent.   See Macaulay's account of the affair.

repeat it; but beg your Lordship's pardon for the trouble I have given you, who am your Lordship's

Most obedient servant,

J. VERNEY.

SIR EDMUND KING.

MY LORD, Feb. 25th, 169⅘.

Tho it's impossible but you must have heard of the great mercie of God in discovering a barbourous and villainous plott lay'd to assasinate King William, yet, we being hear full of it and in the midst of search and enquirie after those y^t were to act it, I cannot but acquaint yor Lordp w^t is generally known by the confession of some of those 15 y^t are taken. It's to long to tel all we hear. It was intended to be done on Tuesday last at Richmond, wher the King had appointed to be, but had some intimation of it (he kept it close); and ther was 40 batalions readie at and near Callice with tr[ans]port ships and [men of] warr to cruyse [about] and land as [many a]s they had . . . . But [he] disappo[inted them] . . . .
. . . . ^a as he cam[e fr]om St James chapp[el] to return to Kensington between the gate y^t com's out of St. James Park and Hyde Parke Gate. But he, haveing 3 or 4 letters successivlie sent him y^t did agree in the matter intended, and a particular won from Holland, from the Duke of Wirtimburg, he was convinct, and took care to send and seiz 9 or 10 of them in theire bedds, at 2 or 3 a clock in the morning, Sunday last, and double all the guards, by 4 or 5 at a time, without beating any drumms or making any doe; and forbore coming to St James, as was expected. But imediatly early calld a counsell, and at night a

^a The letter is injured.

counsell of war and the Admiraltie, and sent away Admiral Russell
in the night and my Lord Barkley another way (and my Ld Rumney^a
to Dover etc.), wth necessarie orders to the fleet, and went Monday
morning to the Parliament house. The rest I leav to the inclos'd
prints to inform yor Lord^p as you will see. The Dutch were informd
of it, and have sent us 19 men of war into the Downes, and we have
25 redy to joine em, and the D. of Wirt[imburg] is sending 10000
men. Besid's I hear ye K. has sent for 12000 [men] from Flanders
and ordered   .   .   .   .
.   .   .   . to the present
government, will now   kno, if they can, w^t was their
expe[die]nt y^t we should not have been ten times worss, if they had
succeeded. However, Ile say: " Blessed, blessed be God! they did
not." You cannot imagine how this has renewd the affections of
the generallite of the people to this King. The D. of Barwick is
said to be in towne, as youl see by the proclamation. I finde some
names I am sorrie for amongst em.

The votes of yesterday are not yet out.

JOHN VERNEY.

MY LORD,   March 5 : [16]9⅘.

I believe you are very much alarumed in the country at the noise
of this plot. The conspirators against the King's life will be tried
the next weeke. 'Tis sayd by every body that the evidence against
them is full and unquestionable. Mr. George Porter ^b is one of those
that confesses the King owes the discovery of the French preparations to invade us chiefly to the Duke of Wirtemberg. 20000 foot

---

^a Henry Sidney, Earl of Romney.
^b One of the conspirators, who turned evidence.

and 6000 horse were the forces designed, and about 26 men of war
to cover the descent. Admirall Russell is now endeavouring to burn
those small ships which ly at Calais. Our fleet is now so great that
it is impossible for them to proceed in their attempt, and they will
have great difficulty to secure those ships that ly out of Dunkirk;
so that we look uppon their design as intirly disapointed, and have
reason to rejoice at it, because it would have made England the seat
of the war, and what confusion and ruine would have attended that
is easy to guess.

This matter has produced two Associations little differing from
one another. I was present at the debates in both Houses. In ours
it was passed and opposed with more heat and fier I ever saw there
before, and the next day refused to be signed by 95, who, each of
them, generally declard that they did not refuse it for what was
contained in it, but for the manner it was obtruded uppon them,
which they sayd was unparliamentary; and, when they expressd
themselfes without doors, they termed it a trick.

In your Lordship's House the debates were regular and very fine,
and as those who stumbled at the word Rightfull gained their point
in having it explained to be According to law, so they admitted the
words added by my Lord Rivers [a] concerning the pretended Prince
of Wales. When they came to the division, it was very particular;
for my L[d] Nottingham, my Lord Thanet and others, who have since
refused to sign, divided with my L[ds] Monmouth, Tankervile, &c.
who pressed it. They were Not Content; but the Contents carried
it by a great majority. It has been refused their I think by 16.

Our Association I find will be sent and recommended in all
countys and boroughs; and I find the world here inclined to judge
of affection, or disaffection, to this government by its reception.

I beg your Lordship's pardon for this long letter.

I am your Lordship's obedient servant,

JOHN VERNEY.

[a] Richard Savage, fourth Earl.

SIR CHARLES LYTTELTON.

MY LORD,   Monday, March 16th, 169⅜.

I had 2 messengers came hither on Satturday, and they brought the constable with em to search for me by a warrant from ye Council, upon suspicion of high treason, and to bring me before them to be examined. They are just at ye hall doore. After he had shewd me his warrant, he told me he had order to be civill to me, and so, if I w^d give him my word and honour to meet him at London, he w^d take his leave on me; for y^t he must return to Hereford, where he left a prisoner that he had committed there to goale and who he must take more charge of and go wth himself to London. But, after, he resolved to come back hither, or his deputy y^t was wth him, and go wth me to London, for feare I might be stopt on ye roade, there being such strict enquiry of all y^t passe. He was doubtfull if I might not be taken into [fresh] custody, and so, after they d[ined], he left me, and I am not to expect y^m or one of em again till ye later end of this weeke; and I find they are in no hast of my going to town, it may be that I may continue ye longer in his hand to encrease his fees. I wish y^r L^p may continue y^r retirement wth more quiet in these evill times, wch God amend.

CHARLES HATTON.

May 12, [16]96.

*   *   *   *   *

Dr Smith his life of Sr Robt Cotton wth ye catalogue of ye library is now finish'd and printed at Oxford, but severall lines are struck out by ye inquisitors ther in a compliment to a bold Scot,^a to whose fioccoes they thought he had not pay'd sufficient respect by discovering some of his prevarications in not transcribing faithfully

---

^a Burnet.

severall things he hath published out of ye Cotton Library. Dr Smith will very soudainly send y^r Lo^pp^e one of his bookes in quires; want of money not permitting him to present them any otherwise to any person.

C. HATTON.

SIR CHARLES LYTTELTON.

Hagley, March 9th [16]9⅘.

I told you but yesterday y^t I w^d let you know how ye commissioners dealt w^t us in our taxes, and last night the assessors came to let me know they had made severall exceptions, but most particularly in my concerns ; for they wou'd not be sattisfied but that they sh^d charg me 2^ble as a reputed papist, tho' they assured them I went constantly to church, and that I had bid em say, if they were asked, I had taken ye oath and Test, as I really did and must, or I could not have bin so long Govr of Sherenesse in ye present Gov^mt. Yet this it seemes was not sufficient, and I must be charged 2^ble, wch I suppose they have no power to impose on me; for ye Act says all papists or reputed, not having taken ye oaths, is to pay 2^ble, unlesse they shall &c. So I have this day writt to them myself, to assure y^m I have taken ye oath, and, if they require it for theyr further sattisfaction, I will send for a certificate from ye record in ye Court of Chancery, where I was sworn and signed the role; but, if this will not do, I shall advise if I may not insist on it, and, if they do destraine, whether I may stand the triall. For I know 'tis done to affront me and to pick a thank by a pragmatick shopkeeper, and a broken one as they say among em. I suppose, having really taken ye oath allready, my insisting on it now will not be construed in law for refusing it, and so consequently bring me under a conviction.

*   *   *   *   *

CHARLES HATTON.

May 22, [16]97.

* * *

Notwithstanding ye dearness of paper, ye paper warre goes on betwixt Dr Stillingfleet and Mr Lock. Y^e D^r, in his excellent book ag^t ye Socinians, had attak'd Mr Lock, who wth great acuteness and seemingly very complimentall did very sharply reply to ye Doctor, who hath very seveerly retorted againe upon Mr Lock.^{a} And Dr Sherlock in a late printed sermon hath made warre wth ye philosophers, in wch he pretends philosophy is very prejudiciall to faith. I cou'd wish Mr Lock and Dr Stillingfleet were reconciled, of wch I feare ther is noe probability; and y^t Mr Lock wou'd undertake Sherlock, wch if he did he wou'd handle him as sharply, tho not soe roughly, as Dr South did ;^{b} for Lock is a very ingenious, acute, and gentle writer.

Here is a new history of China writ by ye Pere le Conte,^{c} translated out of French and very well approved of. Dampier's Voyage takes so wonderfully, 2 editions are already sold of, and he tells me he is fitting ye second part for ye press.

I have of late been very much troubled wth y^r Lord^{pps} distemper, gravell and gripes, wch have for thes 10 dayes confined me to my chamber, but I am now much better and alwayes

Y^r Lo^{pps} very humble servant,

C. HATTON.

---

^{a} Stillingfleet's " Discourse in Vindication of the Trinity" was answered by Locke's "Letter to Bishop Stillingfleet concerning some passages relating to his Essay," &c. ; and the war was carried on for some time.

^{b} In his "Animadversions" upon Sherlock's " Vindication of the Doctrine of the Trinity ;" and in his " Tritheism charged upon Dr. Sherlock's new notion of the Trinity."

^{c} " Nouveaux Mémoires sur l'Etat présente de la Chine," by Louis Le Comte. Two vols. Amst. 1687, 12mo.

THE SAME.

May 27, [16]97.

*   *   *   *   *

The History of China in ye originall French is much preferable to ye English translation. I have discoursed wth Dampier. He is a blunt fellow, but of better understanding then wou'd be exspected from one of his education. He is a very good navigator, kept his journall exactly, and set down every day what he thought remarkable; but, you must imagine, had assistance in dressing up his history,[a] in wch are many mistakes in naming of places. Y^e Isle of Vash, as ye French call it, and ye Spaniards Vacca, from ye great encrease of cows ther, he calls it Ash; and he mistakes ye names of many other places and ye descriptions of plants. He is wonderfuly out in ye account he gives of cochinel and achiot or roucon, wch he sath is made of ye leaves of ye flower; wheras it is made of ye seed.

THE SAME.

May 29, [16]97.

As I was writing, my Lord, to you last Thursday, I was soe taken wth my griping paines I was forsed to give of very abruptly, for wch I beg y^r pardon and shall now give you ye accompt I then intended about Ringrose his relation of Sharps voyage into ye South Sea, wch is called ye 2^d part of ye History of ye Buccaneers. About ye yeare 1680 ther came out a history of ye Buccaneers, printed in Flanders, in Spanish, pretended to be a translation from Dutch writ by one Esquemeling, a Dutch buccaneer, wch Crooke a bookseller got translated into English and printed, in wch Sr Henry Morgan was represented as a very barbarous pyrate. Sr Harry

[a] "A New Voyage round the World," by William Dampier. London, 1697, 8vo. Two additional volumes followed later.

brought his action ag^t Crooke, proved all he did was by virtue of a commission of ye Governor of Jamaica and ye Kings authority, and recovred 300^{ll} or 400^{ll} damage from Crooke, about y^t some I am sure Crook himself told me.   After w^{ch}, his History of ye Bucca-neers wase looked upon as fabulous and sold for noe more then wast paper.   But Sr Harry Morgan being return'd to Jamaica, and Sharp and his comrades their voyage into ye South Sea making a great noise, and Sharps journal being printed and selling very well, Crooke agrees wth Ringrose, who had been a buccaneer wth Sharp, for a relation he had of ye exploits done in ye South Sea by Sharp and other pyrats; and, to make some recompense to Sr Henry Morgan, he was mentioned very honorably, and Ringrose his booke stiled ye 2^d part of ye History of Buccaneers, and is generally sold wth ye first, they being both printed in 4to.[a]

The first part of ye History of ye Buccaneers wase put forth in French wth some variations and aditions, pretended to have been writ in Dutch by one Oxemelin.[b]

Sr John Narborough's Voyage was about five yeares agoe, as I thinke, printed for Smith and Watford, in an 8° volume,[c] together wth Martins voyage to Spitsbergen[d] and other voyages, wch have sold very well, as also another booke of voyages by Ran Wolfius and others.

---

[a] " Bucaniers of America : or a True Account of the most Remarkable Assaults committed of late years upon the Coasts of the West Indies by the Bucaniers of Jamaica and Tortuga, both English and French.   Wherein are contained more espe-cially the unparallel'd exploits of Sir Henry Morgan, our Jamaica Hero. . . . Printed for William Crooke." London, 1684, 4to.   The second volume contains " The Dangerous Voyage and Bold Attempts of Captain Bartholomew Sharp and others" from the journal of Basil Ringrose ; 1685.

[b] Alexander Olivier Exquemelin. " Histoire des Avanturiers qui se sont signalez dans les Indes," &c. Paris, 1686, 8vo.

[c] " An Account of several late Voyages and Discoveries to the South and North." London, 1694, 8vo.

[d] Frederick Marten. Observations on his voyage to Spitzbergen and Greenland were printed with Narborough's Voyages.

Dampier is sensible of many mistakes he hath made, and in his next volume he will correct them; wch he very honestly wou'd not doe in ye 2^d ed. of his first volume, for y^t wou'd have been to ye prejudice of all who had bought his first volume.

Dr Wakes^a character of ye temper and discretion of many of ye present clergy is suitable to their and his desserts. He wou'd make a rare vice-president for an inquisition; and what bookes and authors his pen cannot answer, fire and faggot shou'd.

Unless it be some disputations of our fiery zealots, playes, news-pamphlets, and pulpit pamphlets, ye parliam^t tax on paper and printing and all forreign bookes will prevent ye sale of all others. Severall foreign bookes are come over, but most, if not all, will be returned back.

Tho I am now much better then I was last Thursday, I cannot brag, for I am still much griped but ever y^r Lo^pps

very humble servant,

C. HATTON.

My wife did design to have given her most humble service herself, but her collick in her stomach will not let her; but she joynes ye presentm^t of hers to mine both to y^r Lo^ppe, Lady Hatton, and all at Kirby.

This day hath been kept wth great solemnity in all places but ye churches. Most of ye parsons had a burr in their throats; they cou'd not preach.

THE SAME.

Aug. 7, [16]97.

I am very glad, my Lord, to heare y^r eyes are better, and y^t my Lady Hatton and all at Kirby are well. I have been very much indisposed, either continually tormented wth gripes or, when y^t

---

^a William Wake, Dean of Exeter; afterwards Bishop of Lincoln, and Archbishop of Canterbury.

humour is stopp'd, wth an intollerable headach. I was this after-noon to see ye few best plants yet remaining of ye noble collection of plants at Hampton very well painted by one Bugdan, a Hungarian and excellent painter of fruits and flowers. I saw a cereus or sort of prickly Indian figg wth a most wonderfull flower, differing from all ye flowers I ever saw; the lilium superbum in flower, as also ye corall tree, and one of ye small sorts of aloes wth a scarlet flower, and severall very fine tulipps, painted from tulipps growing in my Lord Dovers^a garden at his house in ye country, for whom Bugdan hath painted severall very large and curious pictures of flowers for my Lords house here in town. But having lately, wth old Mr Evelyn, seen Montague House, I doe not think my Lord of Dovers pictures of flowers comparable to ye flower pictures in Montague House.

Having given you an account of some pictures I have seen, I shall tell you of a very large rattle-snake I saw alive, lately brought over from Virginia. It is very curiously couloured and strip'd. We look'd on him till, by rattling his tayle much louder then I cou'd have imagined he cou'd, he gave notice y^t he was angry and ready to fly at us; to prevent w^{ch}, ye lid of ye chest he was in was clap'd down.

Mr Evelyn is putting forth a book in fol^o of English medallions,^{b} in imitatation of ye Histoire Metallique du Holland. But he can heare of soe few y^t, instead of medailles wth ye inscriptions and reverses, he is forced to make up his booke wth severall discourses relating to y^t subject. His book hath been long in ye press and is not yet ready to come out, ye medailles being not yet all engraven. If y^r Lop^{pe} hath any or cou'd procure any relating to any eminent English person or any action done in England, if y^r Loppe wou'd please either to send a design of ye meddail or lend ye meddail to be here designed, it shou'd carefully be restored wth thankes. Mr Evelyn desired me and all his acquaintances here in town to try w^t medailes they can procure to illustrate his worke.

---

^{a} Henry Jermyn, Earl of Dover.
^{b} "Numisma ; a Discourse of Medals, ancient and modern." London, 1697, folio.

I choose rather to entertaine y^r Lo$^{pp e}$ wth these things then publick news wch is very fabulous. I remember Johannes della Casa in his book De Officiis sath: Impudence in courtisanns is noe fault, for it is absolutly necessary for their carying on their trade, wch he justly condemns. The like apology is y^e best can be made for our publick newsmongers. I am

Y^r Lo^{pps} very humble servant,

C. HATTON.

THE SAME.

September 2, [16]97.

I have this day, my Lord, been at Hampton Court, wth Dr Udall, to see all ye fine plants ther, but, tho I saw severall very curious ones, yet ye pleasure was much abated by ye regret for ye loss of a great many very choice plantes, wch I saw when I was formerly ther. But y^e sight best pleased me was y^e cartoons by Raphael, wch are far beyond all y^e paintings I ever saw. They are brought from y^e Tower and hung up ther, and are copying for my Lord Sunderland. I am invited to goe, this day senight, to Dr Udalls at Enfeild, and, if y^r Lo$^{pp e}$ wou'd be pleased to favour me wth a pcice of venison to present him wth, it wou'd be a very great favour, and I shou'd not doubt to procure you, next spring, some choice plants from him. Of all y^e hardy plants I saw at Hampton Court, I saw none I liked better then y^e Swedish juniper they had from Dr Udall. I hope y^r Lo^{pps} thrive wth you. I am &c.

C. HATTON.

THE SAME.

December 4, [16]97.

My wife, my Lord, did last Thursday return her most humble thankes to y^r Lo^{pp} and my Lady Hatton for y^r obliging present of excellent venison, and gave an account how she had dispos'd of it.

To hers I now, my Lord, add mine, being prevented writing then by going to see ye fireworkes, for wch ther had been soe long and costly preparations.^{a} I was very desirous to see y^m, but, not knowing whither conveniently to goe, I had given over all thoughts of seeing them, and my curiosity was quite abated; but ye day they were to be I had 3 or 4 tickets sent me, and by my wifes earnest persuasion I went; but my curiosity was as little satisfyed as any person's ther. It is generally reported ye expence for them amounted to 12000^{ll}. Ther was in St James's Square a sort of triumphall arch built, but very ill design'd, on ye topp of wch were 4 figures made of wood and painted, one at each corner, and, had ther not been ye names of w^t they were design'd for, noe person cou'd have guess'd what they were meant for. Peace out of a cornucopeia flung out rockets of wild fire. Conduct had a death's head in one of her hands. Concord held in a dish a flaming heart; and Valour had by it a ravenous lyon. The whole was an emblem. Ther was a great unnecessary expence of treasure; severall killed; a vast number of crackers; and all ended in smoake and stinke. Sr Martin Beckman hath got ye curses of a great many, ye praises of noebody. Ther was only a vast number of chambers shot of, and a prodigious number of serpents and large rockets, the cases and sticks of wch were soe large that, when they fell down, killed assuredly 3 or 4 persons, hurted many more. One falling upon ye Lord Hallifaxes his house broke quite thro ye roofe, but hurt noebody. Mr Portman and his lady were ther. My Lord denyed noe person who asked leave to come into his house.

Mr Secretary Trumball hath resigned ye seales, and is succeeded by Mr James Vernon. The House of Commons are adjourn'd till Tuesday. Upon a motion of ye Lord Mulgrave, ye lords have voted an address to his Sacred Majesty.

I am y^r Lo^{pps} very humble servant,

C. Hatton.

---

^{a} To celebrate the peace secured by the Treaty of Ryswick.

THE SAME.

Jan. 4, [16]9⅞.

I must, my Lord, write much breifer than I intended, for I have been hindred by a dreadfull sight, seeing all Whitehall reduced by fire to ashes. About five of yᵉ [clocke] this evening, we saw from my house a great fire towards Westminster. Upon enquiry I heard it was in yᵉ Lᵈ Portlands lodgings, in Whitehall. I went immediatly to endeavour to speake wᵗʰ .my Lady Denbigh, to know if I cou'd doe her any service. I cou'd not be let into Whitehall nor Scotland Yard, but I sent to my Lady. She sent me word she was not afraid and gave me thankes; but, as I return'd, I call'd in at one of yᵉ houses where my house stood in yᵉ Pell Mell, and from thence, before ten of yᵉ clocke, I saw all yᵉ maine body of yᵉ house consumed; all yᵉ buildings on yᵉ water side, from yᵉ further end southward of yᵉ stone gallery to yᵉ kitchens inclusive. I wish yᵉ Banqueting House and any part of Scotland Yard may be saved, for it now burns more feirce than ever, and yᵉ blowing up of houses is done soe unskilfully and violently, it doth great hurt but noe good. God divert his judgments!

THE SAME.

My Lord,

Jan. 6, 169⅞.

Last Tuesday I acquainted you yᵗ Whitehall was then in flames, wᶜʰ burnt till six of yᵉ clocke next morning, and by yᵗ time had consumed or ruined all yᵉ buildings except yᵉ Banqueting House; yᵉ row of buildings from thence eastward towards yᵉ street; the Jewell House and Scotland Yards; the Signet Office, and all yᵉ buildings from thence in a direct line towards yᵉ water; the butteryes, sellers, kitchings, ye Comptrolers lodgings, yᵉ chappel, guard chamber, yᵉ King and Queens lodgings; all yᵉ whole pile of buildings towards ye water side, from y^t wch was Mr Clement his lodgings to ye end of ye stone gallery; and from thence, all ye long gallery, ye Secretary's office, ye Treasury office, ye Councill chamber, ye Queens chappel, are all burnt downe. Only some few lodgings nere ye stone gallery, y^t wch was Bab Mayes lodgings towards ye water side, and ye next lodgings to y^t, and some part of lodgings wch I was told was ye Lord Portlands, are left standing, but terribly schattered. The house in Scotland yard built by Sr Alexander Fraisier, and Mr Windham's next to it, are standing but much schattered. All ye rest of ye buildings in both Scotland Yards are not at all prejudiced. Next ye water side ther are noe buildings standing, except from Sr Stephen Fox his house to ye Ld Godolphins lodgings, inclusive, wch are not prejudiced. The Ld Montague lodgings are burnt down, but his fine pictures and furniture saved. The fire broke out betwixt 3 and 4 of ye clocke in a garret in ye lodgings, as some say, of Collonel Stanley, next to ye Lord Portland, occasioned by a Dutch serving maide laying a sack of charcoale soe nere ye fire it all tooke fire, and ye servants hoped to quench it without any help from others, but it increas'd soe violently it occasion'd ye ruine of ye whole pallace. All persons were intent to save their goods, and all ye gates were lock'd up to prevent ye mob coming in; and, when ye houses were blown up, most of wch were blown up very high, ye timber and rafters lay bare, and ther wanted hands to remove y^m, soe y^t, instead of stopping ye fire, it help'd to increase it. All ye buildings westward, joyning to ye Banqueting House, by being blown up about six of y^e clocke on Wedensday morning, saved that wch remaines, as monument wher the Blessed Martyr, K^g Charles y^e First, was murdered by his rebellious subjects. God divert his just judgments!

I am y^r Lo^{pps} very humble servant,

C. HATTON.

THE SAME.

MY LORD, Feb. 12, 169$\frac{7}{8}$.

The great discourse in town is about y^e L^d Ch. Justice Holt.^{a} The Lords summoned him to appear before y^e committee of Lords, who were to enquire why y^e judges refused to try y^e Lord Banbury soe called. When y^e Ch. Justice appear'd, he told y^e Lords upon their enquiry y^t what he had done was in open court, acting as Ch. J[ustice] of England, and therefore was not responsible to any but ye King. The Lords then asked him whither he might not answer what they asked of him. He told them: " Yes, if he pleased, but he did not thinke fit then to doe it." This did soe incense ye Lords, that they talked of nothing but sending him to ye Tower, but at last they cooled upon it and summoned him to appeare againe last Thursday; and then he told them that he never desired ye office of Ch. J[ustice], but it was forced upon him, and, whenever ye K^g required him to surrender his place, he wou'd willingly doe it, but whilst he kept his place he wou'd support ye dignity of it; and y^t he was not responsible to any but ye K^g for what he did as Ch. J[ustice]; if ye Lords thought he had given a wrong judgm^t, they might order a writ of errour to be brought, and, if they thought fit, reverse ye judgment. The Lords have not as yet made any determination, but ye beginning of next weeke are to declare againe this concern.

I am

Y^r Lo^{pps} very humble servant,

C. HATTON.

---

^{a} Sir John Holt, Chief Justice of the King's Bench. Charles Knollys, self-styled Earl of Banbury, had pleaded his peerage to an indictment charging him with the murder of his brother-in-law, which the judges had allowed.

THE SAME.

June 30, [16]98.

*   *

I am afraid y^r Lo^{ppe} doth not soe much value ye horn'd cattle I sent down. I assure y^r Loppe tho ye horn'd family be of great antiquity; few can shew soe ancient and authentic a pedigree. For by ye records in ye archives of Thomas, Earle of Arundel, Earle Marshall of England, it doth appeare they were descended from those of Illyricum, wch Pliny sath Fulvius Hirpinus kept in his snayle parke. I had but 10 of y^m given me; and a virtuoso of Oxford beg'd 4 of them, y^t noe species of curious horns might be wanting ther. And I doe seriously assure y^r Lo^{ppe} y^t, for snayle water or anything els for wch snayles are to be used, this sort of snayle (wch ye writers of Naturall History call Pomatia) are much preferable; ye flesh is much whiter and tenderer than y^t of any other snayles. And shou'd they prejudice y^r forrest trees, I will (for feare Mr Horton shou'd forget to tell y^r Lo^{ppe} w^t I desired him,) acquaint you wth a very curious and usefull secret a gentleman of my acquaintance hath practis'd to raise oake trees, wch grow very fast, and he transplants y^m as frequently and wth as little prejudice as any other trees are removed. He sowes acorns, and the 2^d spring of their growth he cutts of ye tappe-root, wch making but a small wound, it quickly heales up, and ye remayning root shootes out a great many fibres wch bush out; and after 2 or 3 years ye trees may be, in ye season, transplanted wthout any prejudice. I have seen severall soe ordered, wch far outgrew those wch had never been removed, nay few other species of trees grew faster in y^t ground.

Here is a new translation of Tacitus his workes[a] done by severall persons, as Mr Dryden, Mr Bromley, Sr Hen. Savil, Sr Roger

---

[a] " The Annals and History of Cornelius Tacitus, by several hands ; with Political Reflections and Historical Notes by Mons. Amelot and Sir Henry Savile."

l'Estrange, and others, in 3 vol. 8°. How far y⁰ translators have perform'd their parts I know not, for I but just cast my eye on y⁰ bookes; but they have added a great many publick notes of Amelot la Houssay,ᵃ who is an author for whom I have not half y⁰ veneration he hath for himself, and his notes seem to me very triviall and trifling.

*

C. HATTON.

THE SAME.

Nov^{br} 1, 1698.

*   *   *   *   *

I was told this afternoon that y⁰ Duke of Bolton, as he is stiled, dyed last Fryday. But, tho one be gone, it is to be hoped y⁰ number of y⁰ people in England will quickly be made up, for y⁰ Dutchess of Grafton, who never was thought to be barren, is lately marryed to a young handsome gentleman, one Mr Hanmer,ᵇ y⁰ nephew to Sr John. His mother was Sr Henry North's sister, and inherits all his estate; and it is said he hath a very considerable paternall estate.

Last Saterday night my Lord Warwick, Lord Mohun, Captaine Coote, one Docwray, with one Tully and French, were all six at Lockett's drinking till late at night, and then quarelling they called for six chaires, went into Leicester Square, ther fought; and Captain Coot was mortally wounded, being stabb'd in at y⁰ neck on y⁰ left side into y⁰ body, and, before he cou'd be carryed to a surgeons, he dyed in y⁰ chair.

I am

Y^r Lo^{pps} very humble servant,

C. HATTON.

ᵃ Nicholas Amelot de la Houssaye.

ᵇ Isabella, daughter of Henry Bennet, Earl of Arlington, and widow of Henry Fitz-Roy, Duke of Grafton, married Thomas Hanmer, afterwards Bart., of Mildenhall, co. Suffolk.

THE SAME.

My Lord,   Dec^{br} 1, 1698.

I herein enclose for y^r perusall a letter from Benhaddn.   He was ye Morocco embassador here.   I must confess I was much pleased to see ye orientall people still retain ye same style they ever had, since we had any account of them.   I borrow'd it, promising not to make it common; and therfore I must desire your Lo^{ppe} not to suffer any copy to be taken of it, unless you desire one for your own use.   It was brought over by one who was cast away on ye coast of Barbary, being bound for Teneriff, about 8 years since.   He sath ther are about 250 English, Scotch, and Irish slaves in Barbary.   The Emperor of Morocco was forced to buy his peace wth ye Algerians at a deare rate; and I verily beleeve Ben Haddn, who, as Isaac Voscius called him, is versutus nebulo, writ this letter, not so much out of a desire of pad-naggs and deep-mouthed hounds, and which he by mistake calls mastiffs, as out of a desire y^t an ambassador might be sent thither to [treat for] ye redemption of slaves.   The Arabic word wch is translated, mightily, mightily, mightily, when spoke in praise, signifies mighty well, when in dispraise, mighty ill, and in this letter shou'd have been translated mighty well.   I only borrowed ye letter, and therfore must desire it to be return'd me.

I am intirely of y^r Lo^{pps} opinion it is no matter to us wch of ye candidates prevails.   Their very standing seems to me to be as it was a declaration, Quantum dabitis; and I thinke we need not be at ye expence to make new purchases.   We have pay'd deare enouf those of ye same set we have allready.   I am

Y^r Lo^{pps} very humble servant,

C. HATTON.

THE SAME.

December 17, [16]98.

I sent you by ye carier last Thursday ye History of Quietisme,[a]

---

[a] " Dialogues Posthumes du Sieur de la Bruyere sur le Quietisme."

but it is only borrowed of a French gentleman. I cou'd not buy it at any of ye booksellers. When you have done wth it, pray return it. I didnt heare, nor cannot be enform'd, y^t Madam Dacier translated Florus. I am very well acquainted wth her brother Tanaquil le Fevre, who hath been severall times at my house; and he told me he lodg'd in Suffolk Street, " vis à vis le Livrre Rouge," but his Red Book proved to be ye Roe Buck.

    *   *   *

C. Hatton.

THE SAME.

My Lord,   Dec^br 24, [16]98.

  *   *   *   *

Madam Dacier never translated Florus, but she put his History out in Latin in usum Delphini.[a] If you desire it, I will endeavour to procure it. I am very much pleased to heare y^t not only my nephews but my neices are so good Latin schollars; and it must needs bee a very pleasant entertainment to y^r Lo^ppe to heare y^m cappe verses, of wch I doubt not but y^t an excellent choice is made before they charge their memory wth them, and capping them will fix in their minds several usefull instructions.

I cou'd not this day, being Christmas Eve, and not being very well, goe to Arlington Garden to enquire after ye fruit trees you mention. I hear a nectarin called ye Elrage much commended. As for peaches, the Ramboullet, Violet Muske, Belle Chevreuse, Alberge, Maudlin, Sion, and Newington, are ye most esteemed. Ther are white and red nutmegg peaches. Your Lo^ppe must please to declare wch kinds you will have and how many of each.

I am
Y^r Lo^pps very humble servant,
C. Hatton.

<hr>

[a] " L. A. Flori rerum Romanarum Epitome. Interpretatione et notis illustravit Anna Tanaquilli Fabri filia." Paris, 1674, 4to.

THE SAME.

Jan. 19, [16]9⅘.

*   *   *   *   *

Yesterday yᵉ Disbanding Bill pass'd yᵉ House of Commons.
About 11 of yᵉ clock in yᵉ morning, Sʳ Christopher Musgrave
moved yᵗ yᵉ Bill being then engross'd and lying on yᵉ table might
be pass'd. Sʳ Richard Onslow seconded him; after wᶜʰ severall of
yᵉ great officers of yᵉ Court opposed yᵉ Bill, and were not by any
personns replyd to, till three country gentlemen, Sʳ Will. Blacket of
Newcastle, Sʳ John Phillips, and Norton ᵃ of Hampshire, speaking
in opposition to yᵉ Bill, they were replyed to by Sʳ Christopher
Musgrave, Mʳ Hartcourt,ᵇ Mʳ Harley, and severall others of yᵗ party.
Sʳ John Packington made yᵉ House very merry by his speaking;
for all who spoke agᵗ yᵉ Bill brought arguments from yᵉ dangers
were to be apprehended from Kᵍ James and yᵉ King of France. To
whom Sʳ John Packington replyed: that, if His Majestys title was
precarious, some danger might be apprehended; but, his Majesty
being declared to be yᵉ lawfull and rightfull King, he cou'd not
apprehend any danger, and he did not know any person but yᵉ
Bishoppe of Salisbury who had ever question'd his tittle, but yᵉ booke
in wᶜʰ he did it had been burnt by order of yᵉ House of Commons;
but, for his part, he must declare he thought it below yᵉ dignity of
yᵉ House only to burn yᵉ pamphlett, but, if they had voted yᵉ author
to be hanged, he beleeved yᵉ whole nation wou'd have been pleased
at it. At last yᵉ House came to a division. Ther were 154 agᵗ yᵉ
Bill, 221 for it; so it pass'd by a great majority. Sʳ Edwᵈ Seymor
spoke nothing, but voted for passing yᵉ Bill.

The House of Lords have voted letters to be sent to summon up
all yᵉ absent Lords, so yᵗ, if yʳ Loᵖᵖˢ health will permit it, we shall
have yᵉ happiness of seeing yʳ Loᵖᵖᵉ soudainly in town.

ᵃ Richard Newton.   ᵇ Simon Harcourt, M.P. for Abingdon.

Orders, I heare, are issued out to disband, in England, the Earle of Macclesfield's reg^t of horse, as also Duke Shombergh's, 3 troopes out of ye Ld Oxford's regiment, 3 out of ye Ld Scharborough's troop of guards. Foot to be disbanded: Mordants, Brudenells, and Colts, regiments. Earles regim^t is to be made marines. Ld Portland's reg^t of horse are to be sent for Holland; Ld Arrans for Ireland.

In Ireland, Cunningham's Dragoons are to be disbandad; and ye following regiments of foot: Gustavus Hamilton's, Pizars, Bridges, Bellasis, and Tiffanys'

I am

Y^r Lo^pps very humble servant,

C. HATTON.

THE SAME.

Feb. 9, [16]9⅘.

We have had here a very terrible storme, wch hath done damage to most houses in and about London, killed severall personns, tore up by ye rootes very many great trees in St. James's Park, Moorfields, and Gray's Inn Walkes. My Lord Cardigan had a wonderfull escape. Last Tuesday morning, when ye storme was most furious, my Lord being just got out of his bed, as he was dressing himself by ye fireside, a great turret on ye top of ye house, being blown down, broke thro ye house and crush'd ye bed my Lord lay'd on all to pieces. God be praised, we had only the topps of our chimneys blown down and severall tiles broke; but my wife was in so terrible a fright, she almost forgot her cough, wch of late hath been soe violent I thought she wou'd have dyed.

C. HATTON.

THE SAME.

Apr 18, [16]99.

I this day saw at Dr Sloan's house a sort of orange wch came originally from ye East Indies to Barbadoes, and from thence to Jamaica. It was esteem'd but a little one of ye kind; but I weyed it, and it was by weight three pound seven ounces and a halfe, and in girth 19 inches and a half. The Doctor hath sent the fruit to ye Dutchess of Beaufort; but he hath promised me to procure for me some of ye seeds, wch I will send to y^r Lo^ppe. My Lady Hatton shew'd me some walking sticks your Lo^ppe sent up to be fitted up and varnish'd, as they were before I saw them; but ye lightness of y^m made me suppose them to be arbor vitæ. Pray, were they not?

I am

Y^r Lo^pps very humble servant,

C. HATTON.

ALICE HATTON.[a]

MY LORD,   [Sept. 1699.]

I return my most humble thankes for ye honour of y^r Lord^ps letter. I have not yet bin any were, but at shopes and a veseting; but I believe shall be on Munday at a ball at St. Jeames, where, as they tell me, ther is a famose new danser to apere, which is to charme us all, but not make amends for ye loss of Mrs Ibbings who danced at Lincolns Inn Feild and is lately dead. But as ye quallity of ye Ladys that dance at Court is not to be compared wth so mean a person as a player, so I am shure most of there indiferent danceing is not to be mentioned wth her good. There is one Mr Colson I am shure my Lady has seen at diner wth my Unckle is going to

---

[a] Daughter of Lord Hatton by his second marriage.

be married, wch one would wonder at, there being nothing to be liked in him but his fin diamond ring. I beg humble duty to my Lady. I will write to her next post.

I am, my Lord,

Y^r obedient daughter

A. E. H.

THE SAME.

MY LORD,   [Sept. 1699.]

I am so overjoy'd when I hear from y^r Lord^sp, its not to be express'd. I desire you will beg pardon for me to my Lady for writting such a short letter to her, and tell her I was last night at St Jeames, and y^t ther was but a few dancers. Y^e best were Lady Hartington,^a Lady Betty Candish,^b Mrs Lutteril, Mrs Godfery, and Laay Essex,^c and Mrs Roper who was ye new dancer. Indeed she did it very well, but had too much indeavour'd to imitat Lady Hartingtons noding her head, wch is only becomeing to herself. Y^e best of ye men was Lord Antrim,^d Lord Anglese,^e and Lord Essex. But my Lord Antrim has cut of his hear, and got one of ye new fassioned perewks, wch have so much hear in them y^t a good one cant cost les then 60 pound, and y^t monstros bignes wth his lettle face did not look so well. I hear Lady Banbery is dead,^f and y^e

---

^a Rachel, daughter of Lord William Russell, married to William Cavendish, Lord Hartington, afterwards second Duke of Devonshire.

^b Daughter of the first Duke of Devonshire.

^o Mary, daughter of William, Earl of Portland, married to Algernon, second Earl of Essex.

^d Randal MacDonnell, fourth Earl of Antrim.

^e James Annesley, third Earl of Anglesey.

^f Margaret, daughter of Edward Lister, of Barwell, co. Leicester, married to Charles Knollys, self-styled Earl of Banbury.

Wardon of All Souls.[a]   Next week Lady Ann Churchil is to be married to Lord Spenser.[b]   My Aunt Portman[c] desires you to write to my Aunt Mary, to bie her a set of y[e] French baskets they use for a desert, and y[e] couler are to be white and gold and grean, and, when you get hers, Nevil desires a set too, and if you will take care to bay[d] my Aunt Mary for them, and they'l bay you again. My Aunt sayes y[t], if you will give me leave to learn to draw, M[rs] Tollett shall teach me.   I desire my duty to my Lady and service to all my friends at Kirby.

I am, my Lord,

Y[r] dutyfull daughter,

A. E. H.

CHARLES HATTON.

September 28, [16]99.

I shall endeavour to procure you from Paris some acorns of y[e] Ilexs you desire.   M[r] Evelyn hath been wth me, and tells me he hath a new booke of sallating just finish'd at y[e] press, and will be publish'd y[e] next week.[e]   He setts up for a great virtuoso in sallating.   In his booke he takes notice y[t] juice of oranges in salats is preferable to vinegar.   But y[e] oranges must be cut wth a silver knife, for a steele blade will give a tincture of steel to y[e] juice.

---

[a] This is in anticipation.   Leopold William Finch, D.D., fifth son of Heneage, Earl of Winchelsea, died 14 Nov. 1702.

[b] Anne, second daughter of the Duke of Marlborough, married Charles Spencer, afterwards 3rd Earl of Sunderland, on the 14th September, 1699.

[c] Penelope, daughter of Sir William Haslewood, of Maidwell, and wife of Sir Henry Seymour Portman.   She was sister of Lord Hatton's third wife.

[d] The confusion of b and p seems to have been a family failing.

[e] "Acetaria ; or a discourse of Sallets."   London, 1699, 8vo.

Last Saterday ye Ld Ferrers came to town wth his new lady,[a] wth a very great equipage. Mr Cooke and his lady caryed her mother in their coach to Barnet to meet them, and they came directly to her mothers house in Dover Street, wher they had a supper wch is said to have cost 50 pound. The discourse thereof ever since serves to entertaine ye gosseping neighbours, for at present we are here very barren of news.

I am

Y^r Lo^{pps} very humble servant,

C. HATTON.

THE SAME.

December 12, 1699.

I am very glad beech, wch is my favorit tree, thrives so well wth you. My Lord Pembroke[b] hath heen pleased to make me a very noble present of a most extraordinary fine herball. It is ye Hortus Amstelodamensis,[c] most nobly printed, wth rare cutts of choice and Indian plants, wch are so incomparably painted with water colours, noe painted plants exceed them. Truly I did not beleeve it possible any printes cou'd be so well painted, nor cou'd they have been but that they are painted after originall paintings, and touched over after ye original plantes. It is a very costly booke. I had all ye printes of Dominicus Custos given me some yeares since, wch Mr Evelyn borrow'd of me and cites it in his Book of Medalls, where my Lord Pembroke finding it mentioned, and being informed y^t it

---

[a] Robert Shirley, Lord Ferrers of Chartley, married secondly Selina, daughter of George Finch.

[b] Thomas Herbert, the eight Earl.

[c] The "Hortus Indicus Malabaricus," published at Amsterdam, in twelve volumes, folio, 1678-1703.

was my booke, he employed severall personns, after he had had y^e
perusall of it, to [ask] me to set a prise on it, wch truly I knew not
how to do, for it was a rarity scarce to be met wth againe.   After a
long and frequent sollicitation, Mr Evelyn told me my Lord Pre-
sident^a was so very desirous of my booke he wou'd give me what
rate I wou'd aske for it.   I told him I did not know how to put a
just price on it, and I wou'd not an extravagant, but, since my Lord
did so importunatly desire it, I wou'd present it to him; and did so
by Mr Evelyn, who ye next day brought me from my Ld Pembroke
my fine herball, wch hath drawn all ye virtuosos in town to see it.
And, presently after, my Lord, having taken out of Dominicus
Custos his workes what printes he wanted, ye remaining part wth
like generosity he sent me back.

*   *   *

C. HATTON.

THE SAME.

December 30, [16]99.

Yesterday an acquaintance of mine came to see me and did much
divert me wth some stories he told of Sr Francis Compton, y^r old
acquaintance, his fondness of his new virtuous and pious lady.^b The
day before, Sr Francis came into company wher my friend was; he
told them his lady was so very devout, she was every day severall
hours in her closet at her prayers.   And he having then seen her
take up her bible and prayer booke and go into her closet, he was
assur'd she wou'd be ther shut up for severall honres.   In ye meane
time he came abroad to divert himself wth taking a glasse of wine.
Presently after w^{ch}, my friend going to ye playhouse, he was fully
convinc'd my Lady Compton did not make so long prayers as S^r
Francis reported, for he found her in a vizard and maske in ye 18^d
gallery.   C. HATTON.

---

^a Lord Pembroke was made President of the Council this year.
^b Sir Francis Compton had several wives, all of whose names are not recorded.

ALICE HATTON.

[20 Jan^y, 1700 ?]

I take it, my L^d, as very great honour y^t you will trouble y^rself to write to me, but when I consider how weak y^r eyes are I had rather be w^thout ye happynys of y^r Ld^sps letters then have you in ye lest hurt y^r eyes. I was last night (wth Lady Longuevil^a and Lady Arundel^b) at ye Princess's, and Lady Long: was so kind to offer to carry me to ye Oppera to day wth her and Lady Portland ;^c but I was so unfortunate as to be engaged to go to Lady Denbighs^d to see ye famous Mrs Binges dance, or els I should have bin glad to have waited on Lady Long:, tho I had seen it before and think it very silly. Mr Abel is to have a fine musicke meeting to morrow, and ye tickets are guineas a ·piece, wch is a little to much for me to throw away; so I shall not be there, and l find so many y^t can afford it better of my mind, y^t I fancy, if he had had lower rates, he would have got more. They say here y^t Mrs Reves is to have my Lord Leicesters second son,^e whom Ld Romney f designes to make his heir. Tis to be hoped he will use her better then his B^ro did her sister; for, as the town sayes, he beat her w^thin a week after she was married, which I think should make this young lady afraid. I have so much buisness here y^t I hope my Lady will excuse me till next post. I beg my duty to her, and I am, my L^d, Y^r Ld^sp   most obedient and dutyfull daughter,

A. E. H.

^a Barbara, daughter of John Talbot, of Lacock, co. Wilts, and wife of Henry Yelverton, Viscount Longueville.

^b Margaret, daughter of Thomas Spencer, of Upton, co. Warwick, and wife of Thomas, fourth Lord Arundell of Wardour.

^c Jane, Dowager Lady Berkeley, daughter of Sir John Temple, Bart., married secondly William Earl of Portland.

^d Hester, daughter of Sir Basil Firebrace, and wife of Basil, fourth Earl of Denbigh.

^e Thomas Sydney, fourth son of Robert, fourth Earl of Leicester, married Mary, daughter of Sir Robert Reeve, of Thwaite, Bart. ; his eldest brother Philip, Viscount L'Isle, married Anne Reeve.

^f Henry Sydney, son of Robert, second Earl of Leicester ; created Earl of Romney in 1694.

Charles Hatton.

Jan. 20, 1$\frac{699}{700}$.

Tho I know, my Lord, you have every post a much better infor-mation of all proceedings in parl^t than I can then send you, yet ther having lately been by accident so wonderfull a turn here, perhapps I may have heard some passages not unworthy of y^r knowledg, wch you have not, and therefore I shall adventure to relate them to you.

Some time since, ye E. of Pet^{b} ^{a} brought into ye L^{ds} House a very libellous booke, publish'd in defence of ye Scotts settlement at Darien, and pretended to be printed at Glasco;^{b} and, at ye same time, moved y^t ther might be a union betwixt Engl^d and Scotland, for ye Scotts were under great hardshipps, were a warelik bold nation, and there was a young prince abroad who perhapps in this age, when it is so fashionable for princes to change their religion for a crown, might follow y^t mode, and, if he turn'd Presbiterian, might not only be acceptable to ye Scotts but to ye English too, as annother prince, tho educated by a bishop but a Scott. When ye aforementioned booke, wch I doubt not but you may have seen, was taken notice of in ye H. of C., during ye debate Mr M.^{c} said ther was a lord who, in another place, had moved for an union betwixt ye two nations; but certainly he did it only in jest, for in truth it was only a jest. At wch it is said ye Ld Peterb. was so incens'd y^t he sent a challenge to Mr M. And, during ye debate in ye H. of C., Sr Edwd Sey[mour] said it was not now a proper time, he thought, to debate ye union betwixt Engl^d and Scotl^d, but, if ever it shou'd be debated, he shou'd oppose it for this reason: that a woman being proposed to a neighbour of his in ye country for a wife, he said he wou'd never marry her, for she was a beggar, and whoever marryed a beggar cou'd only exspect a louse for her portion; wch hath most wonderfully exasperated all ye Scotchmen here in town, who daily

---

^{a} Charles Mordaunt, who became Earl of Peterborough in 1697.

^{b} "An Enquiry into the Causes of the Miscarriage of the Scots Colony at Darien." Glasgow, 1700, 12mo.

^{c} Charles Montagu.

cast aspersions on y^t knight, telling old storyes how roughly y^e present Duke Hamilton did formerly affront and abuse him. Before I have done speaking of Scottishmen, I must acquaint you y^t y^e aforementioned bishoppe, differing in opinion wth B$_p$ Floyd of Worcester, in y^e heat of y^e debate told him he was an old dotard, intoxicated wth tobacco and Revelations, as B$_p$ Floyd did himself lately declare.

_____

THE SAME.

Feb. 6, 1$\frac{688}{99}$.

No body doth more detest than I doe printing bookes wth fictitious cutts, such as are in Knocks his History of y^e Island of Ceylon^a and many such other bookes. But yet I shou'd be very well pleased to see Caesars Commentaries, illustrated (as they designe at Oxford) wth cutts well designed of all ye Roman millitary instruments, their habitts, their manner of encamping, their warlike engines, their manner of sacrifising, and things of this nature, wch may be much better described by cutts design'd from Antiquies than is possible to be done by wordes.^{b} And was it possible to have true designes rightly adapted to Vitruvius his architecture, I verily beleeve your Lo$^{pp e}$ wou'd prefer an edition of Vitruvius adorned wth such cutts before y^e commentaries of Philander, Leo Albertus, Perrault, or Huzout.

Propose to any of our English booksellers proper and usefull cutts to illustrate any author they are printing, they cannot be prevailed wth to have them engraven. But, on ye contrary, give them any fictitious or fabulous design, they will be very ready to have th^m printed. They printed Wafers voyage^c wth fictitious cutts very readily; but Dampier wou'd have given them a true draught of Guam prows, ^{wch} arc ye swiftcst vcsscll9 in ye world, but they wou'd

^{a} "An Historical Relation of the Island of Ceylon in the East Indies," by R. Knox. London, 1681, fol.

^{b} An edition of Cæsar with engravings was published by Tonson in 1712.

^{c} "A New Voyage and Description of the Isthmus of America," by Lionel Wafer. London, 1699, 8vo.

not engrave y^m nor severall other curious draughts wch might have been usefull. But they wou'd not be prevayled upon to cause them to be engraven.

If y^r Lo_pp desires any more mellonn seeds from Italy, I can furnish you wth some wch I have lately received.

I saw a letter this day wch came from Rome, wch sath my Lady Salisbury[a] is recovered, but my Lord of Exeter indispos'd, but making a very fine equipage to appear wth as soon as he is recovred. I am　　　　　　　　　　　Y^r Lo_pp^s very humble servant,

C. HATTON.

THE SAME.

May 21, 1700.

*　　　*　　　*　　　*　　　*

It is reported y^t y^e B_p of Durham[b] is maryed to one Mis Offley. Her uncle was groome-porter, her father a parson, and her brother is a parson. She had 2 sisters marryed to parsonns; one of y^m (who is dead) to y^e Deane of Carlisle.[c] Whilst his wife was alive and at Durham, where he is Prebendary, she and her mother (it is thought), by their interest wth y^e B_p, prevai'd wth him to marry his last lady, and, ever sinc, y^e mother hath improv'd her interest so as to pervayle wth y^e B_p to marry her daughter, who is about 40 yeares of age, not handsome, and hath been long known by y^e name of Duck-leggs. The match is assuredly concluded betwixt Dr Burnet and y^e widow Berkley, of Worcestershire,[d] who was Sr Ric^d Blages daughter. I am　　　　　　　　　　Y^r Lo_pp^s very humble servant,

C. HATTON.

[a] Frances, daughter of Simon Bennet, of Beechampton, co. Bucks, and widow of James, fourth Earl of Salisbury.

[b] Nathaniel, third Lord Crew. He did not marry the lady mentioned so discourteously above.

[c] William Grahme, Dean of Carlisle from 1686 to 1704.

[d] Elizabeth, daughter of Sir Richard Blake, and widow of Robert Berkley, of Spetchley. She was the author of "A Method of Devotion," which was published after her death.

THE EARL OF MARLBOROUGH.

MY LORD,   Hague, Oct. $\frac{8}{19}$, 1701.

The enclosed treatys[a] being all that are as yett concluded, I take the liberty to send them as to a friend whose judgment I much depend upon. I desire you will take noe notice of the having seen them, and when I have the honour of seeing you, which I hope may be before the parl. meets, I shall let you know my reasons for what is done as well as acquaint you with all that shall be done. For I call God to witnesse that I have had noe thoughts but what might be for the good of England. If the wind proves fair, the King will embarke in 4 or 5 days. I shall continue here till the end of this month. I am with much truth and respect,

My Lord,

Your most obedient

humble servant,

MARLBOROUGH.

SIR CHARLES LYTTELTON.

Hagley, 21 Sep. 1702.

I think I have since seen what you tell me of Mr Metwin's[b] letter. I think ye Portugall interest not much to be depended on either way, being obliged to follow ye successe of the Sp^d and confederates; and y^t of Cales will most concern them, except when it comes neerer em. I had a letter last post from Sr J. Tal[mache] at Bath, of ye 12th, and, having made his court, he says he would return y^t night to Laycock. He says he went to Bath from thence in ye stage coach, wherein were 3 women, 2 of which were set down

[a] The Grand Alliance between England, the Emperor, and Holland, against France.

[b] John Methuen, Ambassador at Lisbon.

at an inne in Cosham, wch was but 2 miles from Laycock.   One of em was, as much as she could, disguised, as w^d not let him alight to help her out of ye coach.   He suspected something extraordinary, and by her books of devotion, wch she left in ye coach and sent her footman for with other things, wch he looked in and perceived her religion and confirmed him in his guesse, it was my Lady Tircon-nell^a in her way to Ireland; and he says Lady Malborogh went y^t same day to see her and returned that night.

CHARLES HATTON.

June 5, 1703.

*   *   *   *   *

Mr. Pepys, who was a very valuable person and my particular friend, to whom dying he left mourning,^b is dead, and was yester-day buryed: severall persons of quality and note being at his funerall.

C. HATTON.

THE SAME.

March 9, 170¾.

*   *   *   *

Some time since I gave to Mademoiselle Verron some garden seeds to be sent to y^r Lo^{ppe}; but she told me she cou'd not send them down till this day, when I doubt not but she hath.   The like care I tooke to supply y^r Lo_{ppe} wth perry sugar and manna I have now taken to furnish you wth soape, for I have sent some seeds of ye soape tree from China.   The seeds are newly come over, and some of ye trees

^a Frances Jennings, sister of the Duchess of Marlborough.
^b Hatton appears in the list printed at the end of Pepys's Diary as recipient of a twenty-shilling ring and mourning.

have been rais'd and thrive here. Ther are wth them some tee
seed, but only for a curiosity to see them. They are not worth
sowing, for they will not be rais'd here. But ye licer sativum will
thrive well here, and ye mallowes in China. They prefer ye liches
before any peases, and they eat ye mallowes for sallads. But I am
inclinable to thinke our pease and sallads exceed them in goodness.
The carob seeds are very fresh; I wish they can be rais'd in a pot
set in a hot bed. It is a beautifull tree. Some say ye fruit is y^e
locust wch St John eat in ye wilderness, and therefore called St Johns
Bread; some say they were ye huskes which were given to y^e
swine, and wch ye prodigal son desired.

Yesterday was generally observed here as a day of mourning, not
of thanksgiving.^a Severall sermons for K^g William were preach'd
in most churches; and, in our market, ye butchers shopps were
generally shut up, and few wou'd sell any meat, tho it was market
day, they postponing their gaine to faction; from ye effects of w^{ch},
good Lord, deliver us!

I am

Y^r Lo^{pps} very humble servant,

C. HATTON.

---

^a The anniversary of the death of King William.

INDEX.

2 L

Borosky, George, condemned and executed for murder of T. Thynne, ii. 14, 16
Botham, Captain, ii. 155
Bouillon, Duchesse de. *See* Mancini, Marie Anne
Boyle, Charlotte, natural daughter of Charles II., her marriage, i. 115
Boyle, Jane, Lady Clifford, her death, i. 207
Boyle, Robert, his death, ii. 166, 168
Boyne,The, rumours of the battle at, ii. 156
Bradford, Earls of. *See* Newport, Francis; Newport, Richard
Brandenburg, Duke of, his victory over the Swedes, i. 173 ; anecdote of, ii. 193
Brandon, ——, ii. 35
Bremen, Major, ii. 35
Bridgewater, Earl of. *See* Egerton, John
Bridgman, Sir Orlando, Lord Keeper, removed, i. 101, 102
Brisbain, John, i. 214
Bristol, Bishops of. *See* Carleton Guy ; Hall, John; Trelawney, Sir Jonathan
Bromley, Thomas, i. 86, 92
Bromley, William, joins in a translation of Tacitus, ii. 234
Broughton, Captain, i. 78
Brouncker, Henry, i. 58, 67, 72
Brown, Captain Ambrose, closeted, ii. 66
Browne, John, Clerk of the House of Lords, his death, ii. 50
Browne, Sir Richard, Clerk of the Council, i. 75
Bruce, Ensign, i. 62, 66
Brudenell, Frances, married to Lord Newburgh, ii. 185
Brudenell, Lord Francis, i. 171; ii. 47
Brudenell, Robert, Earl of Cardigan, his miraculous escape, ii. 239
Bruges, garrisoned by the English, i 161
Buccaneers, History of the, ii. 225, 226
Buckingham, Duchess of. *See* Villiers, Mary
Buckingham, Duke of. *See* Villiers, George
Buckly, ——, duel with Lord Ossory, i. 119
Buda, operations of the Turks at, ii. 70
Burnet, Gilbert, afterwards Bishop of Salisbury, i. 129 ; with Lord Russell at his execution, ii. 32 ; his letters on his travels, ii. 67 ; preaches R. Boyle's funeral sermon, ii. 167, 168 ; his Pastoral Letter burnt, ii. 187 ; Wharton's reflections on his History of the Reformation, ii. 190 ; his reply, ii. 192;

his remarks on the Bishop of Worcester, ii. 247 ; marries Elizabeth Berkley, ii. 248
Busby, Dr. Richard, his death, ii. 216, 217
Butler, ——, i. 83
Butler, James, Duke of Ormond, Lord Lieutenant of Ireland, i. 27, 35, 38, 42, 107, 233, 237 ; his death, ii. 89
Butler, James, 2nd Duke of Ormond, elected Chancellor of Oxford, ii. 89 ; deserts to the Prince of Orange, ii. 113, 114 ; taken prisoner at Landen, ii. 194
Butler, Sir Nicholas, ii. 118
Butler, Richard, Earl of Arran, i. 42
Butler, Thomas, Earl of Ossory, i. 57 ; in the attack on the Dutch Smyrna fleet, i. 81 ; volunteers in the fleet, i. 105 ; his duel with Buckly, i. 119 ; last illness, i. 231; his loss felt, i. 233
Byron, Sir Robert, i. 76

Cæsar, C. Julius, projected illustrated edition of his Commentaries, ii. 247
Cagua Point (Port Royal), Jamaica, i. 31
Cambridge, Duke of. *See* Stuart, Charles
Campbell, Archibald, Earl of Argyll, ii. 13; suppression of his rebellion in Scotland, ii. 56
Campden, Viscount. *See* Noel, Baptist.
Canterbury, Archbishops of. *See* Laud, William; Sancroft, William; Sheldon, Gilbert; Tenison, Thomas ; Tillotson, John
Canterbury, Archbishopric of, candidates for, i. 156
Capel, Algernon, Earl of Essex, ii. 241
Capel, Arthur, Earl of Essex, i. 182, 183, 203; ii. 2; Lord Lieutenant of Ireland, i. 76 ; his speech in Council on the prorogation, i. 212; opposes a parliament in Ireland, i. 237; sent to the Tower, ii 27 ; commits suicide, ii. 29 ; his goods at Cassiobury claimed by Lord Salisbury, ii. 31 ; division of opinion on his death, ii. 35 ; pamphlet on the same, ii. 50; parliamentary enquiry on his death, ii. 141
Capel, Sir Henry, i. 221 ; ii. 128
Capel, Mary, Countess of Essex, ii. 241
Carbery, Earl of. *See* Vaughan, Richard
Cardigan, Earl of. *See* Brudenell, Robert
Carew, Sir Nicholas, i. 174
Carleton, Guy, Bishop of Bristol, i. 81

262

INDEX.

Westminster: Printed by Nichols and Sons, 25, Parliament Street.

Lightning Source UK Ltd.
Milton Keynes UK
UKOW01f0940180717
305535UK00002B/75/P